A Sephardi Life in Southeastern Europe

The Autobiography and Journal
of Gabriel Arié, 1863–1939

A Sephardi Life in Southeastern Europe

The Autobiography and Journal of Gabriel Arié, 1863–1939

Edited by

Esther Benbassa *and* Aron Rodrigue

Translated by Jane Marie Todd

A SAMUEL AND ALTHEA STROUM BOOK

University of Washington Press

Seattle and London

To the memory of the Jewish communities of Bulgaria

This book is published
with the assistance of a grant
from the Stroum Book Fund,
established through the generosity
of Samuel and Althea Stroum.

Copyright © 1998 by the University of Washington Press
Printed in the United States of America

Library of Congress Cataloging-in-Publication Data
Arié, Gabriel, 1863–1939.
    [Vie judéo-espagnole à l'Est. English]
    A Sephardi life in Southeastern Europe : the autobiography and
journal of Gabriel Arié, 1863–1939 / edited by Esther Benbassa and
Aron Rodrigue; translated by Jane Marie Todd.
      p. cm.
    "A Samuel and Althea Stroum book."
    Includes bibliographical references and index.
    ISBN 0-295-97674-8 (alk. paper)
    1. Arié, Gabriel, 1863–1939. 2. Jews—Bulgaria—Sofia—Biography.
3. Sephardim—Bulgaria—Sofia—Biography. 4. Sofia (Bulgaria)—
Biography. I. Benbassa, Esther. II. Rodrigue, Aron. III. Title.
DS135.B85A75313 1998   97-33415
949.9′004924′0092—dc21   CIP
[B]   r97

Contents

Contents

Illustrations

Illustrations

Preface to the English Edition

This is a slightly revised version, in translation, of a book that appeared in Paris in 1992 under the title *Un vie judéo-espagnole à l'Est: Gabriel Arié (1863–1939)*. It contains the autobiography, journal, and selections from the correspondence of Gabriel Arié. Arié was born in Bulgaria in the last years of Ottoman rule, was educated by and became a teacher and major actor in the Alliance Israélite Universelle, the foremost Jewish organization of the time, and created and directed important Jewish schools and institutions in Ottoman Turkey. Upon his return to Bulgaria after ending his teaching career because of tuberculosis, Arié went on to become a successful businessman and an important notable and participant in Jewish politics. He also wrote most of the two volumes of the official history of the Alliance, *Cinquante ans d'histoire,* which appeared in print under the authorship of the organization's president, Narcisse Leven, and which was until recently the definitive history of the diplomatic and educational work of the institution. He also published a history of the Jews, *Histoire juive depuis les origines jusqu'à nos jours* (1923), which was adopted as a textbook for Jewish schools in France until World War II.

The public work and activities of this Sephardi figure became familiar to us as we conducted research in the archives of the Alliance for a variety of projects over the years. It was by chance that Aron Rodrigue's *De l'instruction à l'émancipation* caught the eye of Gabriel Arié's grandson Dr. Elie Arié of Paris, who contacted him to reveal that he was in possession of his grandfather's autobiographical manuscripts. Writings of this kind are quite rare in the Judeo-Spanish world, and this provided us with a unique opportunity to publish and to analyze both the public and the private lives of one of its important personalities. Together with selections from his letters to the Alliance Central Committee about a variety of political and educational matters, Arié's writings provide a special perspective on the political, economic, and cultural changes undergone by the eastern Sephardi community, in the decades before its dissolution, in regions where it had been constituted since the expulsion from Spain in 1492. They also offer insight into these changes from the unique vantage point of an individual life and throw light on representations of the self by one of the members of the first generation of Westernizing Sephardim.

Arié's writings are organized into two parts in this book. Part I contains the autobiography that he wrote in 1906, when he thought that he would not survive tuberculosis, and a selection from his correspondence to the Alliance up till that year. Part II presents the yearly journal entries that he made to the manuscript after this period until his death, again accompanied by a selection of his letters.

The publication of this book would not have been possible without Gabriel Arié's son Narcisse Arié and his grandson Dr. Elie Arié, who provided us with the manuscripts of the autobiography and the journal, with the photographs and the genealogical data, and with all the information that could be of use to us. We also extend our thanks to Lisette Blottière (née Arié), Mathilde Arié, and Nancen Arié of Bulgaria, and to Eli Arieh of Israel, who were kind enough to help us in this work by providing us with information and documents.

We thank Bernard Lory, lecturer at the Institut National des Langues et Civilisations Orientales and specialist on Bulgaria, whose erudition was of immense help in our project.

We are grateful to the entire staff of the library and archives of the Alliance Israélite Universelle, from which we have taken excerpts from the correspondence of Gabriel Arié.

We thank the Maurice Amado Foundation (United States) and the Ministère de la Recherche et de l'Espace (Délégation à l'Information Scientifique et Technique, France) for subsidizing the cost of the translation.

We are also grateful for the ever-welcome input by Jean-Christophe Attias.

A Note on the Documents

This edition remains faithful to Gabriel Arié's text. We have conserved his spelling of the names of individuals. We have also replicated his transliteration of Hebrew, giving a more precise one in a note when that seemed necessary. We have corrected a few spelling errors here and there. Gabriel Arié often gives two dates for a single event, that of the Julian calendar and that of the Gregorian calendar, which are thirteen days apart; we have maintained them. We have systematically compared the information in the narrative with that in the genealogical tree provided by the family and have noted any possible discrepancies. We were unable to identify certain names of cities cited by Arié. We have changed the place names to reflect the English usage of the time to facilitate the reader's comprehension, giving modern equivalents in brackets or in the notes upon first mention. The principal cities of Bulgaria appear on the map; we give information in a note only on the smaller towns. Generally, we have been careful in our notes to give an accurate idea of the itineraries followed by Arié and his family throughout Bulgaria and Europe in the principal vacation spots and health centers. Finally, a few pages were missing from the manuscript that came to us; we have signaled them in a note.

The reader will find a map of Bulgaria and its neighboring regions and the immediate genealogy of Gabriel Arié at the beginning of the book.

Map of Bulgaria and neighboring regions

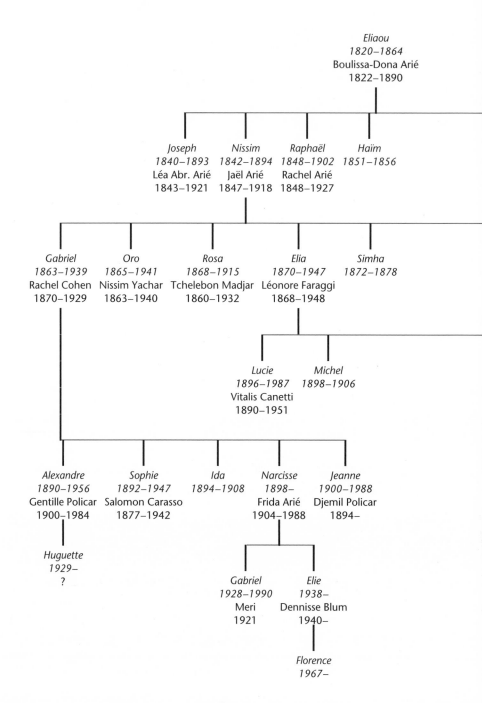

Eliaou
1820–1864
Boulissa-Dona Arié
1822–1890

Joseph
1840–1893
Léa Abr. Arié
1843–1921

Nissim
1842–1894
Jaël Arié
1847–1918

Raphaël
1848–1902
Rachel Arié
1848–1927

Haïm
1851–1856

Gabriel
1863–1939
Rachel Cohen
1870–1929

Oro
1865–1941
Nissim Yachar
1863–1940

Rosa
1868–1915
Tchelebon Madjar
1860–1932

Elia
1870–1947
Léonore Faraggi
1868–1948

Simha
1872–1878

Lucie
1896–1987
Vitalis Canetti
1890–1951

Michel
1898–1906

Alexandre
1890–1956
Gentille Policar
1900–1984

Sophie
1892–1947
Salomon Carasso
1877–1942

Ida
1894–1908

Narcisse
1898–
Frida Arié
1904–1988

Jeanne
1900–1988
Djemil Policar
1894–

Huguette
1929–
?

Gabriel
1928–1990
Meri
1921

Elie
1938–
Dennisse Blum
1940–

Florence
1967–

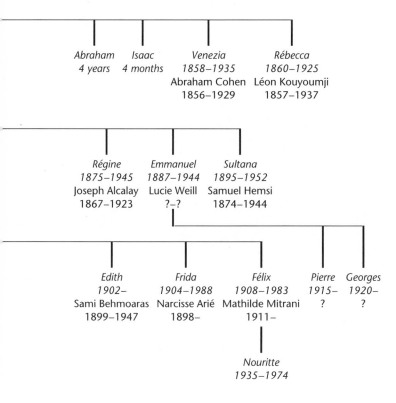

Abraham   Isaac   Venezia   Rébecca
4 years   4 months   1858–1935   1860–1925
                        Abraham Cohen   Léon Kouyoumji
                        1856–1929   1857–1937

Régine   Emmanuel   Sultana
1875–1945   1887–1944   1895–1952
Joseph Alcalay   Lucie Weill   Samuel Hemsi
1867–1923   ?–?   1874–1944

Edith   Frida   Félix   Pierre   Georges
1902–   1904–1988   1908–1983   1915–   1920–
Sami Behmoaras   Narcisse Arié Mathilde Mitrani ?   ?
1899–1947   1898–   1911–

Nouritte
1935–1974

Genealogy of Gabriel Arié
based on the manuscripts and documents of the Arié family

A Sephardi Life in Southeastern Europe

The Autobiography and Journal
of Gabriel Arié, 1863–1939

Introduction

PUBLIC LIFE

For his entire life, Gabriel Arié—instructor, pedagogue, community leader, notable, businessman, and historian—found himself caught between the East and the West. Born in the Balkans in 1863, in a remote province of the Ottoman Empire, he witnessed the disappearance of an old order that had lasted for centuries and its replacement by a new political organization, new ideas, and new ways of life, which would irreversibly change the shape of Jewish existence in the East.

As a child, Arié received a traditional Jewish education, soon to be followed by a Westernized education at the schools of the Alliance Israélite Universelle in Bulgaria and later in Istanbul (Constantinople) and finally at the organization's institute for training its teachers, the Ecole Normale Israélite Orientale in Paris. He moved without difficulty from the traditional Jewish world, which had been the natural environment of his family for generations, to a completely new universe, marked for him by the Western education he had received. His life was shaped by the use he made of the passport that had been granted him by the new culture he had acquired. In the end, it opened the possibility of a remarkable social ascension not only in his native Bulgaria but also in the Jewish world in general, where he became a trusted partner in the educational work undertaken by the primary Jewish organization of his time, the Alliance Israélite Universelle, which propelled him to the rank of a Jewish notable.

The Jewish community into which Gabriel Arié was born was an integral part of the Judeo-Spanish culture area that had been constituted in the Ottoman Empire after the arrival en masse of exiles from the Iberian Peninsula, on their way to the eastern Mediterranean, at the end of the fifteenth century and throughout the sixteenth. Most Jews from Bulgaria were the descendants of those exiles, who had emigrated north along the trade routes linking the great commercial axis of the Danube to the port of Salonika on the Aegean Sea and, further to the east, to

3

44 *Introduction*

Istanbul, the Ottoman capital. The Jews had formed flourishing communities under the Ottomans and had been very active in the empire's international commerce in the sixteenth century. Many of these communities also participated in regional commerce and acted as intermediaries between rural and urban markets.[1]

Nonetheless, at the end of the sixteenth century and the beginning of the seventeenth, the power of the Ottomans began to decline, and when the insecurity resulting from a weakening of the central authority began to have disastrous effects on commerce and the economy, the prosperity of Jewish communities in the Balkans experienced a considerable decline too. One of the aggravating circumstances was the rise of the Greek and Armenian bourgeoisie, who soon established close ties with the West and replaced the Jews in numerous sectors of the country's economic life.[2] A few Jews did continue to play an important role in certain areas of the economy, however. A case in point is the maternal side of Gabriel Arié's family; throughout the eighteenth century and during the first part of the nineteenth, it was one of the most important Jewish families in the Balkan economy.[3] But the exceptions cannot hide the fact that the community, taken as a whole, had declined considerably in relation to its apogee in the sixteenth century and that, at the time of Arié's birth, it needed outside help to get back on its feet.

With the exception of a few families of notables commanding enormous fortunes, the majority of Sephardi Jews in the East lived in poverty, and the endemic social frictions generated by that situation had created deep chasms in all the Jewish communities. These chasms

1. For the latest overview of the history of the Jews of the Ottoman Empire, see Esther Benbassa and Aron Rodrigue, *The Jews of the Balkans: The Judeo-Spanish Community, 15th to 20th Centuries* (Oxford, 1995). See also Stanford J. Shaw, *The Jews of the Ottoman Empire and the Turkish Republic* (New York, 1991); Walter Weiker, *Ottomans, Turks, and the Jewish Polity: A History of the Jews of Turkey* (Lanham, 1992); Avigdor Levy, ed., *The Jews of the Ottoman Empire* (Princeton, 1994). For a general history of the Jews of Bulgaria, see Haim Keshales, *History of the Jews of Bulgaria* (in Hebrew), 5 vols. (Tel Aviv, 1969–73); and Vicki Tamir, *Bulgaria and Her Jews: The History of a Dubious Symbiosis* (New York, 1979).

2. The economic role of the Jews in the fifteenth and sixteenth centuries is analyzed by Halil Inalcik, "Jews in the Ottoman Economy and Finances," in C. E. Bosworth, Charles Issawi, et al., eds., *Essays in Honor of Bernard Lewis: The Islamic World* (Princeton, 1989), 531–50. For an analysis of the situation in the Balkans, see Traian Stoianovich, "The Conquering Balkan Orthodox Merchant," *Journal of Economic History* 20 (1960): 234–313. See also the discussion in Benbassa and Rodrigue, *The Jews of the Balkans,* 36–49.

3. See Tamir, *Bulgaria and Her Jews,* 64.

proved to be particularly important during the era of Westernization and especially later, with the arrival of Zionism. Schools became the stakes in a conflict between rich and poor, modernizers and conservatives. But these schools also offered possibilities of social ascension to a certain number of poor children, who were able to use education to improve their condition. Such was the case for Gabriel Arié.

The weakness of the Ottoman government, with ensuing insecurity and turbulence in the provinces, played a role in the continuing poverty of the Jewish communities in the Balkans. At the end of the nineteenth century, the attitude of the state toward the Jews could be characterized as benign indifference. The Jews had never been a threat to the Ottomans, and though they had lost the utility they had had at the beginning of their residence in the area, they still constituted an important group. The principal preoccupation of the Ottoman governments toward most of their non-Muslim subjects concerned the collection of taxes. Aside from that, each non-Muslim community enjoyed relatively great internal autonomy in the management of its affairs. As far as the Jews were concerned, that translated into autonomous community leadership, with rabbinical authorities having the first word in Jewish public life.[4] The Ottoman Empire was a mosaic of religious and ethnic groups brought together under a central authority that was dependent on the army; these groups maintained relations with the state that were essentially tributary. Of course, Muslims were privileged as the dominant group, and Islam was the official religion of the country. From every point of view, non-Muslims were legally and socially inferior to Muslims.[5] Nonetheless, except in periods of trouble or in regions that were less subjugated to the control of the central power, this did not translate into oppression. Jews and Christians occupied firmly established positions in the Ottoman regime and generally coexisted in relative harmony with their masters, though in a clearly hierarchized context where they had to know their place. It was only when Christian groups began to pursue nationalist and separatist objectives that the situation deteriorated and the system as a whole collapsed, under the effect of the corro-

4. For an analysis of community structures and leadership, see the studies published in Aron Rodrigue, ed., *Ottoman and Turkish Jewry: Community and Leadership* (Bloomington, 1992).

5. For a study of the legal status of Jews in the land of Islam, see Bernard Lewis, *The Jews of Islam* (Princeton, 1984). See also the discussion in Aron Rodrigue, " 'Difference' and Tolerance in the Ottoman Empire: Interview by Nancy Reynolds," *Stanford Humanities Review* 5/1 (1995): 81–90.

sive influence of a triumphant West and the arrival of the most Western of ideologies: nationalism.

Before the appearance of the modern nation-state in the region, community, religious, and ethnic identities were under no pressure to assimilate. In this context, the Judeo-Spanish language, culture, and identity remained intact and evolved according to their own internal dynamics—hence the survival of Judeo-Spanish (Ladino), Gabriel Arié's native tongue, and of the traditional way of life that marked his childhood. Later, in the new nation-states introduced into the formerly Ottoman regions, the influence of the old Ottoman paradigm of religious and ethnic hierarchies persisted under the Christian regimes, blocking successful integration, even though the equality of all citizens was stipulated in the constitutions. In the nineteenth-century Ottoman Empire too, this paradigm remained at the foundation of relations between Muslims and non-Muslims, despite reforms guaranteeing the equality of all citizens and the half-hearted intentions to bring all groups together under the Ottoman banner in order to check nationalist movements. There emerged no real will to integrate on either side.

Gabriel Arié was born in Samakov, a small provincial town in Ottoman Bulgaria, not very far from Sofia; it was the site of a regional market and had large iron mines nearby. The maternal branch of his family owned and operated some of these mines. They were a Jewish family originating in the Léon region of Spain who had been expelled in 1492 and, after many tribulations, had arrived in Vienna by the eighteenth century.[6] Expelled once more in 1775, this time from Vienna by Maria Theresa, the family settled in Vidin on the banks of the Danube, with later branches in Sofia and Samakov. One of Gabriel Arié's ancestors, Abraham Arié, established a business when he arrived in Vidin that experienced considerable expansion until the Russo-Turkish War of 1877–78. That branch of the family distinguished itself in the trade of grains and manufactured goods, the operation of iron mines, and banking, with bank branches in Europe and the East. The family also included patrons of the arts and displayed a certain artistic refinement. The Russo-Turkish War, which, along with Bulgaria's independence, marked the beginning of a new era, put an end to that prosperity. Arié's

---

6. See the manuscript in our possession tracing the history of the family between 1768 and 1914: [Nahim J. Arié and] Tchelebi Moshé Abraham Arié II, "Biography of the Arié Family" (in Judeo-Spanish), 4 vols., completed in 1914. This information is also contained in biographical notes provided by Gabriel Arié's son Narcisse, which accompanied his father's manuscript and are dated 8 November 1989.

mother stemmed from this line. His father, in contrast, belonged to the poor side of the family, never succeeded in attaining a social position comparable to that of his in-laws, and struggled for subsistence his entire life, for the most part without great success.

Initially, Gabriel Arié received a traditional Jewish education in the local *meldar,* the equivalent of the Ashkenazi *heder* in eastern Europe. The *meldar* was a religious school where children learned to read Jewish prayers. The aim of this essentially religious education was not so much to diffuse knowledge as to pass on eternal truths and socialize the child, as a means of ensuring behavior in keeping with the precepts of Judaism and perpetuation of the community. At the apogee of that educational system in the Ottoman Empire, in the sixteenth and seventeenth centuries, many young people pursued their studies after the *meldar* in the *talmudei-torah,* where they could acquire a number of the more advanced Jewish disciplines. Although that continued to be the case in quite weakened form in certain of the large Jewish centers of the empire in the nineteenth century, a small provincial town such as Samakov offered few possibilities of the kind, and the experience Arié had in the traditional educational system lasted only a few years.[7]

Even though it cannot be said that the education Arié received at the *meldar* marked him profoundly, it seems to have left him with a certain knowledge and a certain tendency to mark all events in the cycle of Jewish life, to observe the rites associated with them, and to commemorate Jewish holidays. As we shall see, as a teacher for the Alliance, Arié was a vehement critic and adversary of the traditional system of education. His sense of sacred time and ritual, however, had been shaped by the traditional world in which he had lived his first years, and he was involved in certain important areas of public Jewish observance until his death. It is nonetheless true that the most important formative episode of his life was not his experience at the *meldar* but his attendance at the Alliance school opened in Samakov in 1874.

The arrival of the organization and its network of schools was a watershed event in the life of Sephardi Jews in modern times. The Alliance Israélite Universelle was founded in Paris in 1860 by a group of French Jewish intellectuals and militants. Its purpose was to struggle for the rights of Jews throughout the world, defend persecuted Jews, and bring

7. For a presentation of the traditional educational system in the Ottoman Empire on the eve of Westernization, see A. Rodrigue, *French Jews, Turkish Jews: The Alliance Israélite Universelle and the Politics of Jewish Schooling in Turkey, 1860–1925* (Bloomington, 1990), 35–38.

about the legal emancipation of those who were still being treated as second-class citizens. Depending on transnational solidarity among Jews, the organization brought together through its programs a large number of members throughout the world. It was particularly effective as a mouthpiece for the Jewish world in international events such as the Congress of Berlin in 1878, where it contributed toward the granting of equal rights to the Jews of Romania. It continually struggled for the rights of Jews and often succeeded in obtaining reparation for injustices.[8]

Its principal work, however, was in the field of education. Civil and legal emancipation was not enough. The society incarnated all the impulses that had contributed toward the formation of a modern form of French Judaism after the French Revolution; it was the very crystallization of this new republican Franco-Judaism, which had emerged with such force by the second half of the nineteenth century. The Alliance and its leaders were deeply permeated by the message of the French Revolution and its implications for Jews. Jews were to be emancipated and become full citizens. The entire progress of history was perceived teleologically as leading to the act of emancipation. At the same time, having internalized the Enlightenment discourse on the Jews, which found one of its best expressions in the Abbé Grégoire, who defined the emancipatory model for the French Revolution, the Alliance also believed that Jews had to reform and civilize themselves, or "regenerate" themselves, to show they were worthy of becoming citizens. In practice, that meant abandoning as much as possible all forms of particularism— Jewish languages, for example—and "fusing" into modern civilization, of which French culture was considered the fulfillment. World Jewry as a whole was to reform itself, and all its members were to become modern emancipated citizens. In regions where the cultural level of Jews was considered to have fallen too low, the administration of a healthy dose of French culture was deemed to be an important factor in "regeneration." The agent of that transformation, of course, would be the modern school.[9]

The Alliance embarked upon its self-imposed mission of reforming and "regenerating" the Jewish world. For various reasons, but in particu-

8. For a general history of the Alliance, see André Chouraqui, *Cent ans d'histoire: L'Alliance Israélite Universelle et la renaissance juive contemporaine (1860–1960)* (Paris, 1965); and Aron Rodrigue, *Images of Sephardi and Eastern Jewries in Transition: The Teachers of the Alliance Israélite Universelle, 1860–1939* (Seattle, 1993).

9. For an analysis of the ideology of emancipation and regeneration, see Jay Berkovitz, *The Shaping of Jewish Identity in Nineteenth Century France* (Detroit, 1989); Rodrigue, *French Jews, Turkish Jews*, 1–24; Rodrigue, *Images*.

lar because the Russian government did not allow foreign organizations to influence any part of its population, the Alliance made no headway in the Ashkenazi world. That was not the case in Sephardi regions. By the second half of the nineteenth century, the time of triumphant imperialism, the Ottoman Empire and other Muslim states were greatly weakened, and none of them provided any resistance to the Alliance. Thus, the activities of the organization would be particularly important around the Mediterranean basin.

The first Alliance school was opened in Tetuan, Morocco, in 1862 and was soon followed by others elsewhere in North Africa and in the Middle East. By 1914, the Alliance had established a network of schools extending from Morocco in the west to Iran in the east and including 183 institutions, nearly 1,200 teachers, and 43,700 students. It had succeeded in eclipsing the traditional Jewish educational system and had even supplanted it in numerous places.[10]

In general, the Alliance intervened at the invitation of Jewish notables from the area, who felt that a diffusion of European education among local Jews would contribute to improving the economic situation of the community as a whole. In a context where the West had become a major partner in public life and in the economy, it was very clear that a knowledge of European methods and languages was a necessity. And it was the French language above all that served as lingua franca.

The institutions opened by the society were primary schools, where French was the language of instruction. Although greatly inspired by the curriculum in use in the French system of elementary education, in time these institutions developed their own programs, making a place for the study of local languages and Hebrew and for instruction in Jewish religion and history.[11] In a context where secular and European disciplines began to take on ever greater importance, the Jewish disciplines were quickly relegated to the background, losing the central place they had occupied in the traditional system of education. Although it was never the intention of the Alliance to minimize the importance of Jewish education, it is obvious that for many of its students, what counted above all was learning French.

The love affair that many Sephardim had with French is perfectly illustrated in Arié's writings. He indicates that, for him, learning French in the Alliance school was a marvelous "game," a real pleasure. Arié soon

---

10. See Rodrigue, *Images,* 15–21.
11. Ibid., 25–30.

demonstrated his intellectual abilities and become the favorite of his teachers, a situation that was repeated when he pursued his studies in Paris. He had free access to the school library and became a voracious reader during his adolescence, consuming most of the French and foreign classics. His imagination was shaped by his readings, and he himself draws our attention to the fact that it was Fénelon's *Télémaque* that marked him most profoundly, particularly its style. Through the French language, he entered the fabulous world of the West and began to live there vicariously, even though he was still in the Levant. The Gallomania that was increasingly to characterize Westernized Sephardim often had its roots in Alliance schools and in the initiation into the French language and its literature they had undergone there.

Arié arranged to pursue his studies at the Alliance school in Balat (a Jewish quarter of Istanbul) after the upheavals in Samakov at the time of the Russo-Turkish War of 1877–78 and the Bulgarian declaration of independence. Along with thousands of Jews who fled the battles and became refugees, he reached the Ottoman capital, along with several members of his family, and entered the Alliance school at the first opportunity. In Istanbul, as in Samakov, Arié was the student of Nissim Béhar, one of the most important of the teachers of the organization and destined to have a remarkable career in the Alliance schools in Jerusalem, where he was particularly active in the rebirth of Hebrew.[12] Arié does not often mention Nissim Béhar and seems to have been more impressed by his wife, who was also an Alliance teacher and died very young in Balat. But there is no doubt that the Alliance schools in Samakov and Balat shaped the early years of the precocious child.

It was, therefore, very natural for Arié to choose the career that seemed the most promising to him, by becoming an Alliance teacher in his turn. His father was barely able to provide for his needs and was not in a position to offer his son an appealing way of earning a living. In addition, it is very clear that the attraction of the Alliance was irresistible to a young man such as Gabriel, who decided to join the organization that had liberated and emancipated him intellectually and that had opened entirely new worlds to his curious mind. The Ecole Normale Israélite Orientale (ENIO) was the logical next stop in his itinerary.

Although, in the beginning, the Alliance sent French Jews to teach in its schools, it soon became quite clear that the society could not recruit an adequate number of instructors in France. The Central Committee de-

---

12. On the activities of Nissim Béhar, see Shlomo Haramati, *Three Who Preceded Ben Yehudah* (in Hebrew) (Jerusalem, 1978), 83–125.

cided to sign up the best of the schools' alumni from the Middle East and North Africa, bring them to Paris to undergo intensive training for four years, and then send them back to teach in the schools. The ENIO opened its doors in 1867. The institution was first located in a Jewish trade school on rue des Rosiers in Paris and, after several moves, finally established its own campus in Auteuil in 1889. For many decades, the ENIO trained hundreds of young Sephardim destined to become the backbone of the society's educational infrastructure.[13]

Like Arié, many had come from relatively humble backgrounds. The career of instructor was an excellent means for social ascension. At the ENIO, these Sephardim did not merely acquire pedagogical tools, however. They were also permeated with the ideological message of the Alliance, which they internalized; with the zeal of neophytes, they became in turn the missionaries of the ideology of emancipation and regeneration, the mark of the Alliance and of Franco-Judaism in the second half of the nineteenth century. They spread that ideology and that message throughout the Middle East and North Africa, establishing ties between the Jews of Europe and their Sephardi coreligionists and transforming themselves into effective agents of Westernization.

Arié not only was deeply influenced by the education he received at the ENIO but also established a broad network of contacts there who would prove very useful during his career in Alliance schools. His fellow students Loria, Loupo, Niégo, Fresco, Nabon, Benveniste, and Navon belonged to the first generation of Alliance teachers and went on to form the elite of its faculty. Owing to the work of such young and enthusiastic followers, the organization was able to establish its network of schools and realize a number of the objectives it had set for itself. The esprit de corps that marked that generation was very strong, and Arié was to remain in contact with his colleagues throughout his life, exchanging letters with them and following developments in their lives and in the activities of the Alliance in the various regions where they were pursued.

Arié was very different from his fellow students in one respect, however. He was one of the rare alumni of the ENIO to enjoy the absolute trust of the leaders of the Alliance. In fact, in the annals of the society, the level of intimacy in the friendships he developed with members of the Central Committee is unequaled. Even at the ENIO, he proved his value to Maurice Marx, the severe and authoritarian director of the institution, and was chosen by him to direct the school in his absence. In his first post, at the Alliance school of Ortaköy (Ortakeuy; a Jewish quarter

13. See Rodrigue, *Images*, 34–67.

of Istanbul), he earned the friendship of Félix Bloch, secretary of the Regional Committee of the Alliance in Istanbul, soon becoming his right arm on inspection tours of the schools in the capital, which elicited the jealousy of his colleagues. The close relations he had established with members of the Central Committee proved to be very important when, having resigned from the Alliance for financial reasons in 1885, he managed to be reinstated in 1887 as director of the Alliance school in Sofia. The Alliance never looked kindly on the resignation of its instructors for whatever reason, and it was altogether exceptional on its part to rehire them. Not only did his career with the Alliance not end with his resignation, but in finding himself in the right place at the right time, when a good school director was needed in Sofia, Arié showed how indispensable he was to the organization. The secretary general, the scholar Isidore Loeb, helped him obtain funds for constructing a new school building during his trip to Paris in 1891. It was also during that stay that Arié met Jacques Bigart, who was to occupy the post of secretary general following Isidore Loeb's death. The relations between the two men were very close. Not only did they meet frequently during vacations and Arié's visits to Switzerland, but Arié also regularly frequented the home of Bigart's sister, who lived in Geneva. Bigart also visited Arié during his stay at the Montana sanatorium in 1903. This seems at the very least remarkable, given the widespread image of Bigart as cold, reserved, distant, and authoritarian, which we find in the correspondence of the Alliance teachers.

His status as "favorite son" of the Alliance opened many doors. He was greatly appreciated by the president of the organization, Narcisse Leven, whom he often introduced as a close friend. At the Alliance, his closest friend seems to have been Sylvain Bénédict, inspector of schools, on whom he exerted a great influence. Owing to these ties, Arié also met Zadoc Kahn, chief rabbi of France, Baron Edmond de Rothschild, the famous philanthropist, and Rabbi Moses Gaster and Frederic David Mocatta, two influential personalities among English Jews at the time. This network of relations allowed Arié to influence a number of decisions made by the Alliance and by other Jewish leaders in matters concerning the Sephardi Jews of the East. His perspicacious and incisive analysis of events and problems made him an important source of information for the leaders of Western Jewry.

Of course, the whirlwind of activities Arié became involved in to advance the work of the Alliance made him all the more appreciated by that body. Like his colleagues, he was not merely a teacher or school director, occupied exclusively with questions of a pedagogical nature. To a degree that went far beyond the extracurricular activities of most of the organization's instructors, Arié was also remarkably active in constituting a complete associational structure around the school. From the beginning of his career in Ortaköy (1881–85), he actively organized regular meetings between Alliance teachers throughout the city to debate pedagogical problems. He also participated in the apprenticeship program of the schools; the placement of students with artisans to learn a trade was one of the means used by the society to modify the socioeconomic profile of Eastern Jewry.[14]

Arié showed the same energy while director of the Alliance school in Sofia, between 1887 and 1893. During his trip to Paris in 1891, he succeeded in obtaining the support of the Central Committee for the construction of a new school and considerably increased the number of students recruited for it. But it was during the years when he was director of the boys school in Izmir, particularly between 1893 and 1902 (the date when tuberculosis obliged him to cut back his activities considerably), that Arié showed what he was capable of accomplishing. At that time, he worked to found the Alliance school in Karataş (Karatash), a suburb of Izmir. He also visited various Jewish communities of Asia Minor and established schools in the cities of Turgutlu (Cassaba), Tire (Tireh), and Aydin in Turkey. In Izmir, he formed a Jewish workers association to encourage the development of institutions of mutual aid within the Jewish community. He created the alumni association for the Alliance in Izmir, which brought together all the former students of the town's schools, and the Cercle Israélite, a Jewish reading club, hoping to help calm the discords that divided the community. Even though many of these institutions survived for only a few years, Arié remained indefatigable and continued to believe firmly in the modern principles of associational life as a way of strengthening the community and extending the "regenerative" work of the Alliance.

Arié was also behind the establishment of a school farm for the Alliance in Asia Minor. One of the society's articles of faith was that the transformation and "regeneration" of world Jewry could not be fully realized without the creation of a substantial group of Jews living from agriculture. The work carried out by the schools and by the apprenticeship program would be fully effective only if a portion of Jewish young people were directed toward cultivating the land. Only in that way

14. See Esther Benbassa and A. Rodrigue, "L'artisanat juif en Turquie à la fin du XIXe siècle: L'Alliance Israélite Universelle et ses oeuvres d'apprentissage," *Turcica* 17 (1985): 113–26.

would the destructive influence of centuries of commercial activities and peddling be effaced and thousands of people who had been living from hand to mouth on odd jobs engage in healthy manual work. The Alliance took this productivization program very seriously; beginning with the Enlightenment, it had been a constant in the modern social thinking of European Jews.[15] The society founded the first agricultural school in Palestine, Mikveh Yisrael, with the goal of teaching the latest agricultural techniques to students recruited from its institutions who were destined to become farmers. This was the first school of its kind in Palestine, and the leadership of the Alliance attached a great deal of importance to it.

In 1891, the founding of the Jewish Colonisation Association (it was known as the ICA), in response to needs related to the settlement of the growing number of migrants fleeing the pogroms in Russia, further highlighted the necessity of developing new skills among the Jewish masses. The Alliance and the ICA were closely linked, sharing the same president, Narcisse Leven. The Alliance created another school farm in Djedeida, Tunisia, in 1895 to advance its plans for the agricultural training of Jews in North Africa.[16]

Gabriel Arié was fully convinced of the need to spread a knowledge of agriculture among the Jews of Asia Minor, one of the most fertile regions of the Middle East. His predecessor in Izmir, Shemtob Pariente, had already bought a farm for the Alliance. After numerous inspections, Arié decided the soil of that farm would not ensure good results, and with the authorization of the Alliance, he sold the property in 1895. During the next few years, he moved throughout the region, sending long reports to the ICA on the possibilities for establishing a future school farm. On his recommendation, a farm close to the Turkish town of Akhisar (Axar) was bought and in 1900 became the school farm Or Yehudah, placed under the authority of the ICA. Arié's zeal in this matter was a determining factor.

Arié's value for the Alliance and the ties of friendship he had established with its leading personalities did not disappear when he was forced to stop working because of illness. Rather remarkably from an institution little known for its financial generosity toward its staff, the Central Committee allowed him to settle in Switzerland and live in a climate more favorable to his health, which had been ruined by tubercu-

15. Georges Weill, "Charles Netter ou les oranges de Jaffa," *Nouveaux Cahiers* 21 (summer 1970): 2–36; Rodrigue, *Images*, 94–104.
16. See Rodrigue, *French Jews, Turkish Jews*, 110–11.

losis. It did not suspend his salary for four full years. When it finally had Arié take his retirement because it seemed unlikely he would ever be able to return to full-time employment, it still extended a supplemental income to him, adding to his retirement pension a salary remunerating his work for the official book being prepared on the history of the Alliance. This work finally appeared in two volumes in 1911 and 1920, under the title *Cinquante ans d'histoire: L'Alliance Israélite Universelle, 1860–1910*, bearing Narcisse Leven's name. The second volume, relating to the history of the Alliance schools, was written entirely by Arié. He had maintained a voluminous correspondence with his colleagues in various institutions of the organization, asking them to compile histories of their schools based on the documentation conserved in their archives. Once he had received these minihistories of the schools, he edited them, inserting them into the framework of a unified narration. He was also the author of a large part of the first volume: he completed the hundred pages already written by Narcisse Leven, who, given his advanced age, was not in a position to finish the book. Nothing better expresses the Alliance leaders' confidence in Arié than the way they turned to him to write their official history. When he finished that work, Arié became, on his own initiative, the editor of a new periodical, the *Bulletin des Ecoles de l'Alliance Israélite Universelle,* designed to provide the staff of the Alliance with a glimpse of pedagogical literature. Another publication, the *Revue des Ecoles de l'Alliance Israélite Universelle,* had already appeared between 1901 and 1904 but had been suspended by the organization because of the independent and often negative criticisms the instructors had increasingly come to express. Arié's *Bulletin des Ecoles* clearly followed the party line of the Central Committee and did not allow for the expression of any dissent.

The favor in which the Central Committee held Arié was not only due to the esteem he elicited by his zeal in pursuing his activities in the service of the organization. There existed as well a more extensive affinity of style between the leaders of the Alliance and Arié. Although the society began as a relatively radical organization, by the turn of the century it had become an integral part of the French Jewish establishment and, as a result, more and more conservative. The leaders of the Alliance were comfortable in a world where the notables led and the masses followed. When, for example, their leadership was called into question by the bulk of their membership, as it was in Germany in 1911 (members wanted a greater voice in the management of the society), the Alliance suspended the system of direct elections to the Central Committee and replaced it with appointments by committee members. This politics of notables was a style of leadership that conformed to Arié's temperament. He was not a democrat. He hated local committees whose function was to represent the community in the management of the schools, and he was delighted to discover there was no such local committee in Izmir. He denounced the "absurd" Bulgarian law stipulating the election of school committees and saw it as the root of all the Alliance's problems in that country (see his letter of 22 May 1913).

Arié's conservatism was also apparent in his approach to the internal functioning of the organization. When, in the first decade of the twentieth century, the instructors began collective bargaining with the Alliance leadership for certain retirement benefits, Arié immediately broke ranks with his colleagues (see letter of 5 November 1905). Although he complained bitterly about the meager retirement pay provided by the Alliance and had a keen sense of his rights (he even toyed with the idea of suing the society), he greatly preferred solving this kind of problem individually with the Central Committee. His politics were founded on respect, and finding himself closely associated with the Alliance leadership, he adopted the behavior of *primus inter pares* in his relations with the leading personalities of the organization and expected that those who did not occupy as high a position as himself would show him consideration. The intense feeling of insecurity underlying this attitude was in part appeased by an identification with "important" personalities, with whom he was henceforth linked.

Arié was also infatuated with discipline. While a growing number of instructors were demanding more and more from the Central Committee, he forthrightly blamed the growing "laxity" of the ENIO (in his letters of 29 September and 13 October 1905). He criticized the education given by the school as too liberal and even libertarian. He was also a critic of the large number of outings allowed students in Paris; he feared these would expose students to negative influences and the spirit of revolt, which he considered part of the *mal du siècle*. His ideal was the missionary institution, in which future teacher-missionaries would be strictly kept from too close a contact with the external world. He also criticized the disappearance of direct relationships between the students and the leaders of the Alliance, which had been caused by moving the ENIO to Auteuil. He evoked as the good old days the time of his own studies, when students were in daily contact with the leading personalities of the Alliance, were invited to their homes, and could thus learn to follow their example. His perception of the Alliance as an organization was that of a large family, and his vision of the world in general was largely marked by his paternalism. That fit perfectly with the paternalism of the Alliance leadership and with the relation of guardianship it maintained with its teachers and with the Jewish communities in the East generally.

This paternalist attitude and its predilection for the politics of notables characterized all his relations as a community leader, especially in Bulgaria. This was the case not only during the years when he was the director of the school in Sofia, between 1887 and 1893, but also when he returned there definitively after his recovery in 1913, having officially retired as an instructor but continuing as the official representative of the Alliance in that country.

Arié's writings about Bulgaria reveal an interesting perception of the developments experienced by that country and their impact on the Jews. Bulgarian Jewry is particularly important in that it was the first Eastern Sephardi community of some size to encounter the modern nation-state. That community, most of whose members lived in Sofia, Plovdiv (Philippopolis), Ruse (Ruschuk), and Vidin, had until that time been a satellite of larger centers of Ottoman Jewry such as Salonika, Edirne (Adrianople), and Istanbul. It now found itself cut off from the traditional multiethnic and multireligious organization of the Ottoman Empire and developed in the ever more nationalist context of a new unitary state.

Whereas the beginning of Bulgarian domination had been difficult, with thousands fleeing the hostilities and advances of the Russian armies in 1878, the new state was quick to grant complete equality to Jews, with the Constitution of Tirnovo in 1879. The local synagogue was recognized by the state as the fundamental Jewish structure, and the chief rabbi was elected by the communities. Very often, Ashkenazim from abroad were chosen, and that is how Shimeon Dankovitz, Moritz Grünwald, and Marcus Ehrenpreis were elected to represent Bulgarian Jewry.[17]

Arié was not favorably impressed by these rabbis and, having made his opinion known, attracted their hostility. His directness and elitism earned him many enemies, even among the members of the school committees responsible for organizing contacts between the communities and the Alliance. The resulting frictions were aggravated when, in 1891, a new law augmented the hours devoted to Bulgarian, eliciting doubts in the minds of many regarding the very survival of an autonomous Jewish system of education in that country.[18] In the conflicts that

17. See Keshales, *History*, 2:195–210.
18. Ibid., 173.

followed, Arié's position became untenable, to the point that he left the country in 1893 to occupy the post of Alliance school director in Izmir and returned to Bulgaria only twenty years later.

His years of absence, however, were those that saw the most important evolutions in the history of Jews in modern Bulgaria, with the emergence of Zionism as the majority ideology. The development of that movement was accompanied by violent conflicts between the Zionists and the Alliance Israélite Universelle.

The anti-Zionism of the organization was deep. It emerged in the first place from profound ideological differences regarding the meaning of the Jewish historical experience. The Alliance ardently believed in the benefits of emancipation and assimilation: Jews were to become equal citizens in every country they lived in, and Judaism would be reformulated on a strictly denominational basis. Zionism, in contrast, was the belief that emancipation was a chimera and that antisemitism was a constant of history that would not disappear with Jews' assimilation. Whereas the ideology of emancipation had its source in the liberal model of western Europe, Zionism came about in reaction to the persecutions the Jews had undergone in eastern Europe and to the obstacles in the way of emancipation in those regions.

The rift between the Alliance and the Zionists became particularly serious at the local level with respect to the schools, as was the case in Bulgaria. The educational philosophy of the Zionists and that of the Alliance diverged considerably. The Alliance wanted to "civilize" the Jews by teaching them French and modernizing their daily existence. Their "regeneration" would prepare them to benefit one day from the advantages of citizenship in the East. The Zionists maintained that teaching in French would lead to de-Judaization and to the loss of the national Jewish spirit, and they emphasized the rebirth of Hebrew, the Jews' national language, and its adoption as the language used in the schools. When community conflicts, class divisions, and rivalries between notables were added in, the differences between the Alliance and the Zionists created an explosive situation. Beginning in the last years of the nineteenth century, the Alliance schools were the object of attacks in numerous locations. But nowhere was the struggle so intense as in Bulgaria.

From the beginning, Zionism made serious inroads within Bulgarian Jewry, and the community as a whole was largely Zionist by the end of the first decade of the twentieth century. The Alliance schools were taken over by Zionist school committees, which, in conformity with Bulgarian law, were elected by the communities. Practically all the Alliance schools were closed during the years that preceded the Balkan Wars of 1912–13. The conflict ended with a complete rout of the organization.[19]

Even during his absence, Arié remained abreast of the developments taking place in his native land, and he regretted the turn taken by the events. There was little doubt that, given his ideological options— shaped by the ideology of the Alliance and the course of his own career—and the intimacy of his relations with the leaders of the society, Arié would be anti-Zionist. In his letters to the Alliance, he gave an immediate account of any activity that smelled of Zionism, even when it took the form of societies working for the rebirth of Hebrew, such as Dorshei Leshon Ever (Friends of the Hebrew language), which was founded in Izmir in 1895 (see letter of 20 May 1895). He was full of consternation when an emigration movement to Palestine manifested itself within Bulgarian Jewry the same year, and he wrote frankly that the Jews of Bulgaria already had a nation and had no reason to leave (see letter of 28 November 1895).

His return to Bulgaria coincided with the outbreak of the Balkan Wars and the fall of large Ottoman Jewish communities such as Salonika into the hands of new masters. The reports between Arié and the Alliance at that time expressed a faith in maintaining these communities under Bulgarian domination, a hope that vanished with the Bulgarian defeats of the Second Balkan War in 1913. It is nevertheless interesting to note that Arié was overflowing with plans regarding the policies the Alliance ought to pursue in the face of these new developments. His conservatism and his alliance with the notables are particularly obvious in this correspondence. In his eyes, it was the Jewish bourgeoisie that counted. According to his analysis, although the majority of Bulgarian Jews were Zionists, the notables remained close to the Alliance and sent their children to foreign schools rather than the community institutions managed by the Zionists. He suggested the Alliance return and create strictly private schools beyond community control, in order to attract this bourgeois clientele (see letter of 22 May 1913).

All these plans came to nothing when World War I broke out. Arié lived through the war in Bulgaria. The defeat of that country began a

19. On Zionism, see Esther Benbassa, "Zionism in the Ottoman Empire at the End of the Nineteenth and the Beginning of the Twentieth Century," *Studies in Zionism* 11/ 2 (fall 1990): 127–40; Esther Benbassa, "Associational Strategies in Ottoman Jewish Society in the Nineteenth and Twentieth Centuries," in Levy, ed., *Jews of the Ottoman Empire*, 457–84. See also Benbassa and Rodrigue, *The Jews of the Balkans*, 116–54.

period of great instability, particularly with the exacerbation of antisemitism, which was linked to Bulgaria's irredentist claims on Macedonia. As usual, Arié was careful to give an account of all antisemitic incidents (see letters of 7 August 1919 and 2 February 1924). This unrest decreased quickly, however, and only began again in the 1930s.[20]

In the meantime, Arié's social position as a notable—a position he had acquired through the Alliance, by virtue not only of his education but also of his status as representative of the organization in Bulgaria—was confirmed and reinforced by the growing prosperity he enjoyed in his business affairs. To a great extent, however, he was an outsider in the Jewish political life of Bulgaria, given the preponderant place of the Zionists in all community life (see letters of 17 September 1920 and 3 May 1924). His accounts affect the lofty attitude of an Olympian, and his interpretation of the Zionist activism of his fellow Jews adopts the paternalist language of an adult recounting the foolishness of spoiled children.

Nevertheless, despite the criticism addressed to Zionists and the exhortations directed at his coreligionists, whom he called upon to become good Bulgarians, we find no fire in Arié's writings on Bulgaria, no patriotic passion, no expression of regret when children or members of the family increasingly sought their livelihoods elsewhere. Although sensitive to Bulgarian antisemitism, he could not claim the situation in that regard was worse there than elsewhere. On the contrary, the Bulgarian balance sheet on this point was relatively positive, and Bulgarian Jewry did not have to suffer major persecutions until the Holocaust. And yet, in direct continuity with the Ottoman period, nothing indicates that the Jews were ever considered true Bulgarians or that they considered themselves as such.

Notwithstanding his official attitude and his ideological assumptions, Arié's true identity remained that of a Levantine Sephardi Jew, considerably Westernized, born in Bulgaria, from Bulgaria perhaps, but nevertheless not a Bulgarian. In fact, in keeping with the tradition whereby Jews of the Middle East became foreign subjects, Arié acquired Spanish nationality in his old age,[21] most likely without renouncing his Bulgarian nationality. This acquisition of a new passport was the effect of a policy adopted by Spain in the interwar period attempting to redraw Sephardim into the Spanish orbit. Arié also became a chevalier in the

20. See Tamir, *Bulgaria and Her Jews*, 126–31; Benbassa and Rodrigue, *The Jews of the Balkans*, 163.
21. Biographical information compiled by his son and dated 8 November 1989.

order of Isabella the Catholic,[22] a distinction that was at the very least ironic and paradoxical for someone whose ancestors had been expelled from Spain in 1492! In Arié, this rather dissonant configuration of identities, nationalities, and allegiances, characteristic of the Jews of the Levant in the modern period, coexisted with ideological views that were difficult to reconcile with it.

Like the Alliance, Arié was fundamentally convinced of the need to reform and "regenerate" the "fallen" Jewish communities of the East. And help could only come from the West, which was showing the path to the future, leading the progress of civilization on a global scale. Arié's attitude toward the West and the East exhibits signs characteristic of the first generation of Westernization. Europe represented progress and absolute good. The East was the quintessence of negativity and backwardness. Orientalist discourse, so common in the correspondence of Alliance teachers, also recurs in Arié's account. His descriptions of the various communities he visited were largely influenced by a binary perception of the opposition between East and West. In fact, he often expressed himself explicitly in these terms, as in his letter of 23 April 1894, where he recounted his visit to Asia Minor and compared that region and the Jewish communities it sheltered to the zones of Africa where the rays of European civilization had not yet penetrated. He had only scorn for many aspects of the Eastern world, which he accused of being exclusively concerned with appearances (see letter of 25 March 1898). And when he was disappointed by the ICA's refusal of his request to oversee the affairs of the school farm of Or Yehudah, which he had worked so hard to create, the best method he found to express his discontent was to once more apply the binary opposition he was in the habit of using. He expected hypocritical behavior from the Middle East, where it was "natural," but he was disappointed to see it manifested in the West.

As it has done on so many Westernized non-Westerners, the idealized West never ceased to exert a seductive influence on Arié. It was identified with the enlightenment of civilization; and of course, in his case, it later represented a hope for a cure for his tuberculosis. Thus, for Arié, the Westernization of Eastern Judaism was an ultimate good. Salvation had come in the form of the Alliance. As he notes in a letter to Isidore Loeb in 1890, in which he asks for recommendations of books that would allow him to learn more about the history of Jews in Spain, the Alliance had "repair[ed] the effects of 1492," which, in the long term, had led to

22. Ibid.

the decay of Sephardi Jewry. Emancipation was of capital importance. The Jews had to be transformed into good citizens. That is why he continually recommended that the Jews of the Ottoman Empire be encouraged to learn Turkish and to attend government schools (see letter of 24 July 1894). He launched a similar appeal in Bulgaria, forcefully criticizing the Jewish community for not having become better integrated and for not yet speaking Bulgarian after thirty-two years of Bulgarian independence. It was important that the Jews be represented at all levels of public life in the country, that they even become deputies in the Bulgarian Chamber (see letter of 11 June 1911).

Like the Alliance, Arié was vigilant when faced with any manifestation of antisemitism. In the famous affair involving an accusation of ritual murder in Vratsa,[23] the accused Jews were acquitted owing to his efforts and to the financial aid for their defense that he succeeded in obtaining from the Alliance. Like other Alliance instructors, Arié gave a meticulous account of any antisemitic incident to the Central Committee.

Always in the spirit of Alliance ideology, which echoed Enlightenment discourse on the Jews, Arié was also firmly convinced of the need for Jews to show they "deserved" emancipation and to earn the "esteem" of their compatriots. Although antisemitism was an absolute evil, Arié was persuaded it was often exacerbated by the behavior of Eastern Jewry itself, which was not yet sufficiently "regenerated." It was important that the behavior of Jews themselves give no excuse for antisemites to launch an attack. That eminently conservative position, which Arié shared with most of the Jewish establishment in western Europe throughout the nineteenth century and at the beginning of the twentieth, was indissociable from a criticism of traditional Judaism. Arié was irritated by the noise and disorder he observed in the synagogues of Izmir (see letter of 28 March 1900) and attributed the decline in the attendance of worship services to the absence of solemnity that characterized the traditional synagogue, going so far as to attempt to open an "oratory" at the Alliance school where services would be conducted with a certain amount of decorum.

Nevertheless, he was very concerned with the need to maintain and perpetuate Judaism and Jewish identity. At the end of the nineteenth century, the Alliance itself had become alarmed at the drop in religious observance in the Jewish communities of the Levant and had sent circulars to its teachers in which it insisted on the teaching of Jewish history and religion as the remedy to that situation. Arié fully shared that position. Taking stock of the situation prevailing in the Alliance schools, he

---

23. See Tamir, *Bulgaria and Her Jews*, 116.

criticized the fact that the school curriculum was very strong in nonabstract subject matter but much weaker in the area of "moral" education (see letter of 17 July 1896). Moralizing was the remedy, and the Alliance schools had to recognize they were "denominational" institutions and thus obliged to reach that objective by accurately and effectively transmitting the ethical message of Judaism. Arié greatly disapproved of the fact that local rabbis had the responsibility for religious instruction in the Alliance schools. He did not have a very high opinion of the Sephardi rabbinate. He had been scandalized by the hostility toward modern schools manifested by the rabbis of Ortaköy and wrote a sarcastic letter describing the funeral of one of the principal opponents of the Alliance, where his feelings on this subject were clear (see letter of 11 January 1884). He did not appreciate the "obscurantism" of the rabbis and their ignorance of the ethical specificity and essence of Judaism. It was imperative that the Alliance place the responsibility for the religious education of children with teachers capable of stressing this core aspect of the religion.

It is striking that Arié was systematically critical of each of the rabbis he met in the Levant, including those originally from the West, such as Dankovitz, Grünwald, and Ehrenpreis, chief rabbis of Bulgaria. He expressed admiration only for certain French rabbis such as Zadoc Kahn and Israël Lévy. Arié's ideals were in keeping with a certain form of Enlightenment Judaism, namely, Franco-Judaism in its Third Republican form; any other manifestation of Jewish religiosity, any other style of Jewish leadership, left him cold. He had absorbed too much of the Alliance's message to accept anything else.

That vision of Judaism and of the history of the Jews found its best expression in his *Histoire juive depuis les origines jusqu'à nos jours,* published in Paris in 1923 and reissued in 1926. This book was a great success and was immediately adopted as a manual in the Jewish elementary schools in France (see letter from Israël Lévy, chief rabbi of France, dated 17 October 1923, reproduced in the second edition of the book, p. 5). It was to remain the standard textbook used in classrooms until World War II. The fact that Arié's book could become the authorized narrative of the history of Jews, that it could be used to train the youth in his adopted culture, is excellent evidence of the extraordinary trajectory of this Sephardi Jew from an "obscure" region of the Levant, and of his capacity to assimilate the main principles of Franco-Judaism.

Arié's interest in the history of the Jews was long-standing. His history-writing project began to take shape with the approach of the four hundredth anniversary of the expulsion of the Jews from Spain;

Arié regretted the fact that the classic work of the time, Théodore Reinach's *L'histoire des Israélites depuis la ruine de leur indépendance nationale jusqu'à nos jours,* which appeared in 1884, did not deal with the history of the Sephardim. Thus, in February 1890, he began to consider working on the subject and to collect the necessary material: "So much the better if, in 1892, I can give my compatriots a sketch of our history that would help them reflect upon themselves."[24]

The awakening of an interest in Jewish history was an integral part of the process of Westernization within the Sephardi intelligentsia in the second half of the nineteenth century. More generally, the opening toward the West relegated the production of writings in Hebrew to the background. Hebrew texts were now reserved for scholarly and religious milieus. A literature in Judeo-Spanish, the vernacular of Sephardi culture, began to flourish. That language was to constitute an important vehicle for Westernization among the masses, through the translation of works originally written in foreign languages and through the press, which also experienced considerable expansion at that time. French, Russian, Italian, and Hebrew history books and novels were translated, adapted to the tastes of the public, and published in shortened form in serials in the newspapers. Historical works, biographies, poetry collections, plays, books on morality, and pedagogical books in various areas were published. There was a desire to rapidly embrace what was happening in the West, to learn and adapt to the new context. And yet, despite the Westernization under way among the Sephardim, local publications were not in European languages. Moreover, the abundance of translations suffocated local literature, and we find few works that show signs of a specifically Sephardi originality.

The same drive also focused on the history of the Jews and tried to introduce the locals to it—a way of eliminating the isolation in the East, a region that had remained somewhat apart from the great upheavals experienced by the Jewish people in the West. The rapprochement that resulted between the two branches of Judaism also entailed a knowledge of history, the shared history that could justify that rapprochement. The Jewish Enlightenment movement (Haskalah), in full flower in the Ashkenazi East in the nineteenth century, and the contacts between educated men and scholars from the two spheres of the East—the Sephardi and the Ashkenazi—were at the origin of these intellectual currents that developed in Sephardi culture. Gabriel Arié's attraction to history is part of this context contemporary to him. Other intellectuals, all autodi-

24. Archives de l'Alliance Israélite Universelle, Bulgarie XII.E.153a.

dacts, began to take an interest in Jewish history. Thus Abraham Danon, Moïse Franco, Salomon Rozanès, and Abraham Galanté wrote books on the history of Jews in the Ottoman Empire, laying the foundations for scholarly study to come on the history of the Sephardim of the East. Arié was in contact with certain of these historians, including Abraham Danon and Salomon Rozanès (see letter of 3 February 1908) and wanted them to participate in the history project on the Alliance schools.

Nevertheless, though representative of that generation of historians, Arié was also different in that he did not conduct any original research on the history of Ottoman Jewry, being content to compile a synthesis of the history of the Jews as a whole. His declared goal in his *Histoire juive* was limited: summarize the major nineteenth-century text of Jewish history, that of Heinrich Graetz, and bring it up to date by summarizing Narcisse Leven's *Cinquante ans d'histoire*.[25] Long chapters in *Cinquante ans d'histoire* had in fact been written by him. Furthermore, that book ended with World War I. Arié continued the narrative to include the peace treaties signed after the war and discussed the principal developments occurring in the Jewish world, such as Zionism and the Balfour Declaration. In the end, the *Histoire juive* reflected his own views; in the chapters dealing with the modern period in particular, the book was much more than a paraphrase of the works of Graetz or Leven.

In a general way, Arié's history is the consummate expression of the liberal emancipatory ideology of western European Jewry, particularly the French, an ideology that was to remain dominant in the western European Jewish world for a good part of the first half of the twentieth century. Echoing a number of themes of the Jewish Enlightenment and certain aspects of Reform Judaism, it systematically emphasized the "message" of Judaism, namely, the monotheism and justice propounded by the prophets, and its "mission," the diffusion of these ideas and concepts among nations. Arié was explicit on this point from the very beginning: "We took it as a rule . . . to focus primarily on what makes up the intellectual and moral past of the Jewish people." The sentences that follow announce the recurrent theme of the book:

> The political role of Israel was always minor, but its literature and its religious conceptions exerted such a profound and decisive influence on a large part of the human race that we must know them in some detail if we wish to understand the considerable place that the small Jewish population occupies in the annals of humanity. That is why, without neglecting

25. Gabriel Arié, *Histoire juive depuis les origines jusqu'à nos jours* (Paris, 1923), 1.

any important event, we have particularly sought to shed light on the history of ideas that constitute the essence of Judaism. We have thus dedicated some discussion to the Prophets, to the organization of the faith, to religious sects, to the Mishnah, to the Talmud, to the origins and foundation of Christianity and Islam, and to all the Jewish thinkers and writers, whose principal works we have analyzed.[26]

This insistence on the essence of Judaism implicitly disputed the validity of the formalism that traditional Judaism in decline was accused of perpetuating. The distinction between essence and form was at the center of debates on modern Judaism, in which most nineteenth-century Jewish reformers were engaged, and it is not surprising to rediscover it in a writer such as Arié.

In fact, the "mission" of Judaism, which purportedly consisted in ensuring the triumph of monotheism in the world, appears at the beginning of *Histoire juive,* with the evocation of Abraham. All biblical history is placed in that light, to the point of making the Greek translation of the Bible, the Septuagint, a crucial turning point in the history of the Jews. For Arié, that translation was the first Jewish apostle sent out into the world to begin to exert a profound influence on the history of civilization.[27]

Arié's narrative presents itself as the evolution and development of the principles of monotheism and of justice through the Bible, the Mishnah, and the rationalist Jewish thought of the Middle Ages. The Jews and their ideas resisted constant persecutions and flourished under the most difficult conditions. Following Graetz, Arié has the age of obscurantism begin within Judaism itself, with the triumph of Jewish mysticism, the Kabbala, in the sixteenth and seventeenth centuries. Like his role model and like most historians of the *Wissenschaft des Judentums* (science of Judaism), Arié could not tolerate the irrationalism of the Kabbala and called that period "an age of shadows and superstitions, which constitutes a kind of Jewish Middle Ages."[28] It had led to the deadly messianic excesses of the false messiah Shabbatai Zvi and to a growing mediocrity among rabbis. The emergence of Hasidism (a religious movement that was mystical in inspiration and appeared in eastern Europe in the eighteenth century), which Arié perceived negatively, was associated with these developments and with the "aridity of Talmudic education in

26. Ibid., 2.
27. Ibid., 65.
28. Ibid., 236.

Poland."[29] Having arrived at this point in his analysis, Arié judged tradi-tional Judaism at the dawn of the modern age in these terms: "The decadence of Judaism ran deep."[30]

Renaissance and renewal came with the Haskalah and the French Revolution. Moïse Mendelssohn redeemed Judaism from the inside, making its authentic meaning appear, while the revolution emancipated the Jews and began a new era in Jewish history. Echoing the Alliance's discourse, Arié was quick to indicate that "regeneration" followed rap-idly: "French Jews knew how to make themselves worthy of the act of justice and generosity that had been granted them and became sincerely attached to their nation. . . . Under the regime of liberty that was hence-forth their own, they quickly lost the humble and fearful ways that had so often exposed them to ridicule."[31]

Arié felt sympathy for Reform Judaism in Germany and saw it as a remedy for some of the problems of extreme assimilation, such as the conversions occurring in Germany during the age of emancipation, and for the excesses of traditional Judaism: "Those who clung to the past did not want to tolerate any change in religion and instruction; they even refused to modify the loud and disgraceful way the faith was celebrated in the synagogues."[32]

As might be expected, the founding of the Alliance and its subse-quent activities occupied a privileged place in Arié's history, and the organization was presented as the principal defender of the cause of world Jewry in all situations. Two entire chapters are devoted to the history of the Alliance, depicted as the catalyst for the best and most noble impulses of modern Judaism. It is interesting to note that it was only through these activities that the history of the Sephardim in the contemporary period succeeded in making a brief appearance in the book. Like most modern European historiography dedicated to the Jews—even up to our own time—Arié's narrative did not allow the post-1492 Sephardim to speak, nor did it consider them actors after the expul-sion from Spain and the wrong turn taken with Sabbateanism (the move-ment composed of followers of the false messiah Shabbatai Zvi). They came into existence only with the West as reference point and when they were the object of the activities of Western Jewry, in particular, those of the Alliance Israélite Universelle. This vision was shared by

29. Ibid., 262.
30. Ibid.
31. Ibid., 278.
32. Ibid., 279.

most Alliance teachers, who were, of course, themselves Sephardim. As neophytes of Western civilization, they could interpret their own history only through the prism of their adopted culture.

In clear contrast on this point to Leven's *Cinquante ans d'histoire*, Arié's text adopted a more somber and less optimistic tone when he discussed modern antisemitism. He focused on the birth of modern antisemitism and racism and on the ravages caused by the pogroms in Russia, and he established a direct parallel between the situation prevailing in Europe at the end of the nineteenth century and the beginning of the twentieth and the darkest days of the Middle Ages. Even his beloved France was not free from such symptoms, and Arié reported the vicissitudes of the Dreyfus affair in the greatest detail. His own evaluation of the importance of the affair, worthy of the perspicacious observer that he was, hit the mark: "The republicans have understood it is the very principles of the Revolution that the clericals are combating behind the cover of the Jews. From now on, the cause of the Jews can no longer be separated from the cause of the Republic, and that is the most fortunate consequence of the Dreyfus affair for the Jews of France."[33] The voice of Franco-Judaism finds expression here. A remarkable premonition also echoes in these words, illuminated by the subsequent developments under Vichy.

It was in discussing Zionism that Arié began the most delicate part of his *Histoire juive*. Given the conflicts between the Alliance and the Zionists and the situation in Bulgaria, he had to proceed with caution in his presentation. He could not allow himself to alienate either the Alliance or the broader public to which he addressed his book. His presentation of Zionism is in fact rather positive and laudatory. The growing importance of the movement in the Jewish world and the persistence of antisemitism led him to clarify his position in his preface to the second edition of the book in 1926:

> Our preference for the political conceptions of the Alliance has not prevented us from setting out with impartiality and sympathy the efforts by Zionism to find a solution to the Jewish question that many good minds judge contrary to the true interests of Judaism. The aspirations of sincere Zionists proceed from such respectable convictions and are the echo of voices that have reverberated in Jewish consciousness for so many centuries that criticism of them would have been at the very least out of place in a book such as ours, especially at a time when the decline we are witnessing

33. Ibid., 337.

in liberal ideas is accompanied by such a sharp outbreak of antisemitism throughout the world.[34]

Arié also added to this second edition an entirely new chapter on the birth of modern Hebrew and modern Hebrew literature, which immediately preceded his presentation of Zionism. He saw the emergence of that literature as a powerful civilizing force for the Jews, and he was not afraid to give an account of the literary activities of Hebrew authors who were linked to Zionism. The fact that the chapter devoted to this movement immediately followed the chapter on Hebrew showed that in Arié's view the two things were inextricably associated.

Arié presented the birth of Zionism as linked to the persistence of antisemitism in eastern Europe and to the absence of emancipation for Russian Jewry. Nevertheless, he did not fail to credit Western Jews, especially the famous philanthropist Moses Montefiore and the Alliance Israélite Universelle, with the redemption of the Holy Land. Returning to a theme dear to his heart, Arié focused on the school farm Mikveh Yisrael and the role it played in the creation of modern agriculture in Palestine. The Alliance was thus considered one of the protagonists in reestablishing a Jewish presence in Palestine, even though Arié did not forget to indicate explicitly that many Jews from western Europe were hostile to Zionism and that as late as 1923 the society had professed its "neutrality" toward the movement.[35]

Arié underscored what the Zionists had been able to achieve in Palestine: the progress in agriculture and the creation of Jewish colonies and cities. He nonetheless pointed out the problems that remained, from the persistence of Arab hostility toward the movement to the ambiguous attitude adopted by the English mandatory government. In conclusion, his verdict was mixed:

> It appears today that Zionism can only be a partial solution to the Jewish question; it must not therefore exclude the other solution, the emancipation of Jews and their civil assimilation into their respective countries. But even if it cannot satisfy all the hopes it has awakened, Zionism will have the indisputable merit of having intensified, among oppressed and persecuted Jews, the feeling of their value and the awareness of their dignity.[36]

34. Gabriel Arié, *Histoire juive depuis les origines jusqu'à nos jours,* 2d ed. (Paris, 1926), 3.
35. Ibid., 348.
36. Ibid., 349.

Even as he recognized the importance of Zionism, Arié maintained his faith in the ideology of emancipation.

This faith, however, was now tempered by a strong dose of realism. In his analysis of the persistence of antisemitism and in his interpretation of the situation in the East, Arié proved to be much more perspicacious than the leaders of the Alliance, who until Vichy were to cling tenaciously to the emancipatory vision of the nineteenth century. In the conclusion of his book, he recognized that the era of emancipation had not solved all the problems. Whereas in the West, the Jews could continue to "live as a religious denomination with the same status as Christianity," that could not be the case in the East, where they had to "constitute themselves as a national minority."[37] Arié again paid tribute to the Alliance by concluding that unity would come if all the forces of Jewry rallied around the principles of fraternity and solidarity incarnated by the organization.[38] Nonetheless, he had clearly broken with the linear vision of the Alliance, which considered emancipation and assimilation the only path to follow among Jews throughout the world. For Arié, the "national" path taken by many was a fact and had come to constitute a second option.

It is important to note that that divergence from the Alliance went back a long time, having first been expressed in a letter to Bigart in 1909 (see letter of 15 January 1909). Bringing up the question of whether to write *Juif* and *Israélite* with initial capital letters, Arié made a distinction between the West, where Judaism had become simply a denomination and where lowercasing was therefore called for, and the East, in particular the Ottoman Empire, where Jews were legally treated as a "nation" and continued to exist as such, that is, as a clearly defined ethnic group for whom an initial capital letter was necessary. This suggestion was angrily rejected by Bigart, who insisted that no concession be made to the nationalist use of the term.[39] It is therefore probably no coincidence that Arié, though he was not absolutely systematic on this point, wrote *Juif* with a capital letter throughout almost the entire book. But it is undoubtedly more significant that he chose to conclude his study by putting the spotlight on the two different paths of modern Jewish existence, without deciding absolutely which one was or ought to prevail.

Arié's approach was in fact symptomatic of his position midway be-

37. Ibid., 366.
38. Ibid.
39. Archives de l'Alliance Israélite Universelle, Suisse A, response by Bigart to a letter from Arié dated 15 January 1909.

tween the East and the West. This man whose intellectual life was a pure product of western European emancipationist Judaism, who had devoted most of his public career to spreading this message, nevertheless remained in the East, and a man of the East. Unquestionably, Arié never became a Zionist and remained anti-Zionist his whole life. And yet, as a perceptive observer of the world around him, he could not be unaware that the western European path of Jewish emancipation seemed unable to succeed in the East, where ethnic and religious ties appeared to attach people most profoundly and lastingly to their particular and particularist identities. In the East, the nation-state whose birth Arié had witnessed, though it used the vocabulary and the language of Western liberal nationalism, had remained anchored in the hierarchical power relationships specific to the multiplicity of groups that constituted the Levant. With group identities remaining of capital importance, the Western path of emancipation could not suit the majority of Jews in the region. Jewish individuals such as Arié could effectively opt for radical Westernization, but none of them succeeded in carrying out that program at the collective level.

To a certain extent, Arié's life and career illustrate both the realization and the contradiction of the Westernization of a portion of Jews in the Levant. That movement, progressively carrying with it entire generations of Sephardim, opened many new prospects for progress and individual freedom. But at the same time, that vision of the world in general and of the Jew in particular was peculiarly ill-adapted to Levantine realities. In the end, many experienced Westernization vicariously, and the ideal world remained separate from the real world in which they lived. Arié's life, his career, and his writings are the expression of that double, divided, and in the end dissonant existence. At another level of course, that existence represents the very essence of modernity, which bears within it a corrosive shattering of accepted truths in all areas. Paradoxically, in living the very contradictions of the process of Westernization, the Judeo-Spanish intelligentsia, of which Arié was a major representative, had finally become truly modern. The autobiography and journal he wrote are a remarkable expression of this development.

PRIVATE LIFE

Autobiography and the journal did not constitute common literary genres in the Sephardi world of the nineteenth century, or even later on. "Like the intimate journal, which appeared at the same period, autobiography is one of the signs of a transformation in the notion of *person* and is intimately tied to the beginning of industrial civilization and the coming to power of the bourgeoisie."[40] Two questions arise: Are the two main documents by Gabriel Arié published here an autobiography or a journal? And was there truly a transformation in the notion of *person* in the Sephardi cultural environment from which the author originated?

We have purposely presented the text in two parts, which we have titled, respectively, "Autobiography" and "Journal." If we consider autobiography to be a life narrative centered on the personality, this first part qualifies as an example of that genre.[41] Like any other, Arié's autobiography is a retrospective and global narrative tending toward synthesis, but it covers his life only from 1863, the date of his birth, until 1906, the year that saw the aggravation of his illness and the beginning of his long stay in Davos, Switzerland. It was also in 1906 that the author definitively abandoned his post as director of the boys school in Izmir and, in doing so, his duties as an instructor in the service of the Alliance. His stays in Switzerland for his health began in 1902. Beginning in February 1905, he settled in Davos, leaving that city only in 1913. The autobiography was probably drafted between February 1905 and October 1906.

In this autobiography, which is divided into sections, past and present intersect, thus opening the way for the yearly journal entries that follow. Arié was not yet a professional writer, but he did nourish some ambition of writing, which led to the drafting of historical works and to contributions to pedagogical magazines. From his education and profession, models of the genre of autobiography were not unfamiliar to him. Nevertheless, although his concern for an agreeable, and especially a correct, writing style was constant, he did not intend to produce the work of a literary writer. His autobiography is closer to a chronicle, a collection of memories. At the beginning of the second part of his text, which we have called a "journal" and which comes after a break he himself introduced, the author indicates that until that time he had recorded a series of events from his life and that he intends to do the same in what follows. In fact, he titled the second part simply "Notes constituting the rest of my memories." Arié wrote his text in French, his intellectual language, perhaps in the secret hope of seeing it published in France, his adopted environ-

---

40. Philippe Lejeune, *L'autobiographie en France* (Paris, 1971), 10.
41. Ibid.

ment. His work resembles many others written by unknowns, at least those works that escaped the oblivion that lies in wait for this kind of enterprise when it is practiced by unknowns.[42]

Apparently, the concern that guided Arié in the beginning was to leave to his children a positive balance sheet of his existence, at a time when he believed he did not have very long to live. A victim of tuberculosis, Arié saw his condition worsening from one day to the next. That was the reason for seeking salvation in Davos, following a custom that originated in Switzerland and that recommended a stay in the mountains, which were considered beneficial for tuberculosis patients. This practice was later exalted in the novel—most famously in Thomas Mann's *The Magic Mountain*.[43]

The retrospective of Arié's childhood and youth is combined with the evocation of a very recent past, continuing right up to the day before the manuscript as a whole ends. Thus a continuity is established between the author's past and his present, without any break in temporal linearity. The laws of the genre are somewhat bent in the process, allowing for the inclusion of the journal, where the "present" is recounted from a year's distance. This in turn goes against the laws of the genre of the journal, whose temporal unity usually pertains to a single day. Arié's journal is an annual chronicle, a log book, and an account book all in one; in it, the author calculates the balance sheet, judging the positive and the negative. Thus, in the case of Gabriel Arié, "journal" does not mean a work written day by day.[44] But in his autobiography as in his journal, Arié's "self"—that of a sick man who fears he will die at any moment—dominates.

"The act of writing [of autobiography] presents itself to each of its addressees as a demand for recognition or love, or as a defense plea, destined to depict and impose an image of oneself as lovable. It is a plea able to disarm the other's gaze."[45] That is exactly what Gabriel Arié did when he offered his history as an example to the family. At that time, the audience of autobiography was above all the family.[46] For the author, his life was a lesson in morality for his children. At the end of his autobiography, Arié wrote:

42. Ibid., 70.
43. Pierre Guillaume, "Tuberculose et montagne: Naissance d'un mythe," *Vingtième Siècle: Revue d'Histoire* 30 (April–June 1991): 36–37.
44. Béatrice Didier, *Le journal intime* (Paris, 1976), 18.
45. Lejeune, *L'autobiographie en France*, 210.
46. Ibid., 216.

> In a sense, I can consider myself a happy man, since, having come to the end of the day, I can rest a little and can depart with the awareness that I leave my children, in the absence of a fortune, the example of a life of work, probity, and devotion. I would be happy with them if, in their own lives, they found inspiration in these principles, even while avoiding the faults and excess of zeal to which I may have succumbed. It is to help them avoid the latter and to acquire the former that I thought it useful to recount to them in all sincerity what my life was.

In the end, he erected himself as a model for his descendants, a paterfamilias who had nothing to hide and whose life was exemplary, founded on the values of work and honesty. As a result, sincerity became the raison d'être of the act of writing, an act that would memorialize the history of a man in order to pass it on to his descendants, as a legacy capable of guiding the life of those who perpetuate his line. This legacy would stand in for an inheritance that could be converted into cash; at the time of the writing, Arié had not yet amassed the fortune that was to come to him after World War I.

Arié's text casts a somewhat nostalgic gaze on the past, a traditional world in the process of disappearing; the author evokes it with tenderness, even though he remains merciless in regard to a number of its aspects. It is no accident that this man, initiated into Western values but not entirely cut off from his origins, wrote an autobiography and spent so much time on his family's past. "Autobiography appears at the point where traditional civilization becomes fissured, but appears in the most diverse forms. It is first of all linked to social mobility."[47] Gabriel Arié measured the distance traveled, not without some pride. His autobiography was not only the narrative of social ascension but also the written record of the "lost paradise" he would never find again. And throughout the narrative, the history of a family, anchored for centuries in the region after its expulsion from Spain, also emerged in writing.

The chronicle, a relatively rare genre in the Sephardi world, was already familiar within that family; we can thus cite the chronicle by Nahim J. Arié (1849–1907) and Tchelebi Moshé Abraham Arié II (1849–1919), written in Judeo-Spanish and never published in its entirety in any Western language.[48] A relatively complete genealogical tree[49] of the

47. Ibid., 210.
48. See n. 6 above.
49. Mme Mathilde Arié of Israel, wife of Félix, nephew of G. Arié, sent us three genealogical trees: the first goes from 1780, the date the ancestor of the line, Abraham

Arié family was established in 1963 by one of its members, Joseph Abraham Arié, an equally rare undertaking on the part of those from the Sephardi culture area. It was constructed from the chronicle already mentioned, from documents belonging to the family line, from data gathered and systematized by Gabriel Arié himself for the period 1766–1929, and from a genealogical tree elaborated in 1901 and transmitted to the compiler by his father, Abraham Joseph Arié, in 1944. That tree goes back to the arrival of the Ariés in Bulgaria in the eighteenth century, during the Ottoman era. Its last architect, Joseph Abraham Arié, who in fact continued Gabriel Arié's work for the period 1923–63, belongs to the branch of the family that emigrated to Israel; we thus better understand the wish to preserve the memory of a name that was illustrious in its time in Bulgaria.

The tradition of transmitting the family memory to future generations, out of a kind of pride nourished by the awareness of belonging to an elite group, an aristocracy, was thus persistent in the Arié clan, and also in Gabriel, who was involved in the different stages of this transmission. Like aristocrats, the Ariés made up and passed on genealogical trees. Gabriel did not just follow this tradition in turn but went beyond it, writing a book on the history of the Jewish people and thus moving from personal to general history. Once we know that this was a pedagogical work for use in Jewish primary schools, we understand even better his search for transmission on a more general level. Hence, Gabriel Arié combined the preservation of his own experience with the preservation of that of his people, a sign both of openness and of modernity, if only by virtue of the form he adopted to transmit to others the history of a people without land at that time, a history that was also his own. His history writing developed in concentric circles, growing ever larger: from the fragile self, liable to disappear at any moment because of an incurable illness; to his family; his cultural group; his professional group, the Alliance, whose history he wrote in part; and finally, to the ethnic or denominational group to which he belonged, the Jewish people, whose history he also retraced. These circles interpenetrate at different moments of his own history and are an integral part of the protagonist. The same self expresses itself through these detours, which all come together to form a totality. Of course, Arié was backed into writing the history of

---

Arié, arrived in Samakov, until 1890, and was no doubt compiled by the father of G. Arié; the second was compiled by G. Arié himself; and the third is a later, supplementary copy. Different members of the family, who are dispersed in various countries and who sometimes do not know one another, possess copies of these trees.

the Alliance, acting as ghostwriter for the president of the organization, a man he admired so much that he named his younger son, Narcisse, after him. This undertaking once more reflects Arié's dependence on the Alliance, a financial and moral dependence, where the very selfhood of the author was effaced behind an institution and an ideology. (That ideology influenced him so much that, by his own free will, he was led to denigrate a large part of his own Sephardi culture.) We know that the name "Arié" does not figure on the book's cover, which bore the signature of Narcisse Leven. Later, in contrast, the book on the history of the Jewish people was written on his own initiative. He drafted it at the beginning of World War I, after the Balkan Wars, at a time when everything was beginning to collapse in Europe. It was when humanity, and therefore his own people, were in danger that Arié felt the need to consign his people's history to paper. Disappearance and death always occupied a central place in his existence, and it was by writing his own history, and history in general, that he brought them under control, transforming them into "memory," into a kind of symbolic immortality.

At the same time, the move from autobiography to the journal constitutes the move from the definitive to the provisional. Until that time, the author had reported a past that he controlled and looked upon with the distance implied in the notion of retrospection, though he made the leap into the present at the end, preparing the way for the journal. This immediate present links the journal, recounted at a year's distance (a distance that, conversely, introduces distanciation and longer-term perspective), to the autobiography that precedes it. It is on this level that the interrelation between the two genres intervenes. We are now in the register of a present time relegated to the past—a kind of hoarding of time, hence of life, because the future is unforeseeable. We might even wonder whether Gabriel succeeded in living in the present, given the place occupied in his everyday life by his illness and its inexorable ritual. The year was quantified according to the number of times he spit blood, the days of fever, and the days spent in bed. A drop in that number was transformed into a sign of improvement, hence a triumph over the illness. The rhythm followed was that of the illness; that triumph was tangible only in the overall accounting of the year, since another year of life amounted to postponing death for a year. It was not the day that marked the journal but the year, and especially the year gone by, since the past was reassuring to the gravely ill Arié. The journal thus became a chronicle of the past year; the day would have been a present too close to the future, a future Arié could not even imagine. He begins his journal this way: "In a first notebook, I noted the important events in my life until 1906. I now propose to continue the account and to note each year, as long as Providence will allow me, the important facts concerning my family and myself."

Why did Gabriel Arié keep a journal? We are no longer dealing with the issue of exemplarity, the moral scope of autobiography, a monument erected to his glory and given as an offering to his descendants. "Prisoner of his illness and traveler into his own abyss, the ill man will have a tendency to keep a journal, which sometimes helps him get well and, in any case, can have medical value."[50] Arié's journal, begun when he was extremely sick in Davos, was continued until the author's death in 1939. Did he write it for himself? We know that the journal both is and is not addressed to the Other.[51] It would be very risky to question the sincerity of this journal. Why must a journal be sincere, even when, fundamentally, its author aspires toward sincerity? In what way is sincerity an asset in this kind of writing? We might presume that everything can be said in a journal, but we know that, in fact, all kinds of prohibitions and taboos intervene and form obstacles.

Arié's journal is permeated by the theme of illness, which, once the illness stabilizes, is transformed into the theme of professional success and money. Illness and money are often linked and interchangeable. Illness is a factor that takes away one's security, while the lack of money does the same. Throughout the pages of this journal the fear of being without money and the satisfaction of possessing it recur; the benefits money procures are given less importance than the security it provides. We know that money problems generally have an important place in journals.[52] Year after year, Arié tallies up the money amassed and looks with satisfaction on the distance traveled. From being a mere teacher, obliged to take odd jobs to make ends meet, then an invalid supported by his brother or living on the pension granted by the Alliance, he slowly made his way later on. Between 1885 and 1887, he tried his luck at business, resigning for the first time from the Alliance, his protective mother. He returned to the fold after his failure. It was only after he left Davos that he began to make a name for himself in insurance and banking. By the 1920s he was a rich man, free from want. Even though he never tallied up his fortune, he noted that he was wealthy. In any case, his many trips abroad and his photographs attest to his bourgeois way of life. His relative recovery also delivered him from his lack of self-

50. Didier, *Le journal intime,* 63.
51. Ibid.
52. Ibid., 47.

confidence. For him, becoming an instructor in the Alliance schools had represented the beginning of financial security, as opposed to what he had known at his parents' home, since his father's economic situation had always been mediocre. For a long time, he lived haunted by the idea that what had happened to his father—a series of humiliations endured from his employers, his mother's brothers—would be replicated in his own life. His first business failure confirmed him in his fears. The departure from Davos in 1913 was thus accompanied by a new social and economic departure. The parenthesis had lasted eight years.

Family also occupies a preponderant place, but it is not always spared, which is common in journals in general.[53] Individualism is subordinated to family life, a trait of bourgeois civilization.[54] The Other occupies an important place and situates the author in relation to those who surround him, even though the primary protagonist remains the omnipresent self. The author also dwells on misfortunes and good fortune, more on the first than on the second; there is nothing astonishing in this either. And although in the journal it is common to record everything relating to one's love life,[55] Gabriel Arié does so with a great deal of circumspection, thus conforming to local mores, which obliged him to say little and to resort to subterfuges when doing so. We nevertheless find, next to certain explicit confessions, others that are barely outlined but easily discernible.

"The journal allows for a certain leveling of events. A war or revolution often holds no more place than a headache or the purchase of a pair of shoes."[56] Arié does not completely escape that constant, even though he remains relatively sensitive to what is going on around him in society. In fact, it was as much to complete the public aspect of the individual, of this self with which one becomes familiar throughout the text, as to situate him in the social and political context of his age that we added a selection of letters written to the Alliance. We have thus been led to mark the text and establish the exchange between the private and the public man, even while respecting the text's original continuity and linearity. Of course, the letters are administrative in nature, of a kind one finds by the thousand in the Alliance archives. The Alliance teachers had a style particular to them, which corresponded above all to the imperatives of the leadership, who were very keen on spelling and syn-

---

53. Ibid., 79.
54. Lejeune, *L'autobiographie en France*, 217.
55. Didier, *Le journal intime*, 79.
56. Ibid., 64.

tax. In addition, there was the ideological mold into which instructors poured everything, so as not to cross the leadership and thus bring trouble upon themselves. Gabriel Arié was no exception, but for most of his life he had the privilege of addressing the leadership as an equal. It is through this relationship that we discover certain of the traits of the man Arié, who adopted a way of expressing himself proper to himself even though he shared the ideas in force within the organization. Arié expected nothing from the Alliance except a certain respectability, which he no longer needed after Davos once his fortune had bestowed it upon him. It was within this space of freedom created by his independence that we begin, by seeking the public man, to find the private man, once the masks have been removed. The correspondence itself, read at a second level, links up with the autobiography and the journal, completes and enriches them; at certain times, the public and the private combine regardless of the lines separating them, as they do in life. The man in his completeness offers himself, flees, and reemerges beyond the conventions imposed by the institutional correspondence. Nonetheless, we would have liked to have his private correspondence, which would have allowed us to encounter him somewhere else, once more, and perhaps differently.

Properly speaking, Arié's journal is not an examination of his conscience, as is often the case in this genre of writing; even less is it an act of contrition for sins committed.[57] The confession aspect, with its secret side, does not truly appear. There again the character's circumspection is manifest; we no longer know if he was writing his journal for himself or for others. The dialogue with himself does not leap out from the page. In a society turned toward the outside, could the individualist act par excellence—the writing of a journal—also be turned entirely toward the outside, in this case toward his immediate family? The author provides a balance sheet of the facts marking the year, with the event taking precedence over analysis, except on a few occasions. Accumulation, a prominent trait of Arié's conduct, returns at different stages in both the autobiography and the journal. As a young man, he accumulated readings, livelihoods, women, businesses, moves, and, to a certain extent, children, if he is compared to other members of his immediate family, who belonged to that generation where adopting the Western bourgeois values led, for the wealthy strata, to a progressive drop in the birthrate. Was it by class reflex that he accumulated personal property and real estate

57. Ibid., 56–57.

the way the bourgeoisie stores up money, or was it first of all a manifestation of his insecurity?

The author judges others more than he judges himself, and there sometimes emanates from the text the satisfaction he feels in contemplating himself, especially when he succeeds at his new departure in life. Does he contemplate himself in relation to others or in relation to what he once was? In any case, the distance traveled is not negligible. Once again the exemplarity of the man leaps out, the example of a life worthy of being recounted, one that could serve as a model for his descendants. The author does what he must to be equal to his ambition. This trait links the journal to the autobiography, which also aimed for exemplarity. The circle is completed. Less than two years before his death he wrote: "In sum, I have reason to be satisfied with my health, which causes me worry but not torment, and with my excellent material situation, which causes me no concern, and with my children, who are following the path of honor and work. Can one ask for more out of life? No, and that is why I am ready to leave them when it pleases God, praising Providence for having all in all given me the good life in this world." Arié passed on not only his business and his fortune to his children but also his example. The nineteenth-century bourgeois family was also, as we know, the vehicle of patrimony,[58] ensuring continuity and reproduction.

Gabriel Arié created a history for himself in writing it down,[59] his history and that of his family. That history is also a true memoir of the incipient Sephardi and Levantine bourgeoisie of the time, in the Balkans in evolution, though it is a bourgeoisie seen through the eyes of Gabriel Arié, restored as a function of what he wanted to transmit, or was able to transmit, to us. That history has been conserved almost intact despite the vulnerability of this type of writing, which is very often reworked by members of the family, sometimes obfuscated through the allusions of the author—or simply destroyed.[60] Other than a few insignificant cuts made by the family, Gabriel Arié's autobiography and journal have been faithfully handed down to us.

Autobiography and individualism are closely linked,[61] and "the inti-

---

58. Michelle Perrot, "Drames et conflits familiaux," in Philippe Ariès and Georges Duby, eds., *Histoire de la vie privée* (Paris, 1987), 4:264; Adeline Daumard, *Les bourgeois et la bourgeoisie en France depuis 1815* (Paris, 1991), 153.

59. Anne Martin-Fugier, "Les rites de la vie privée bourgeoise," in Ariès and Duby, eds., *Vie privée*, 4:195.

60. Didier, *Le journal intime*, 21.

61. Lejeune, *L'autobiographie en France*, 181–82.

mate journal rests entirely on the belief in a 'self,' the desire to know it, to cultivate it, to have a relationship with it, to record it on paper."[62] It was in fact during the nineteenth century that the sense of individual identity and its representation increasingly crystallized.[63] Hence it is no accident that autobiography and the intimate journal experienced a real expansion in the nineteenth century and that they were closely linked to the bourgeois context of the West. At that time, however, the East had not yet produced a bourgeois class in the Western sense of the term, because it had not experienced the same political, economic, and social evolution. The Eastern bourgeoisie, for the most part non-Muslim groups in the Ottoman Empire who were at the forefront of commerce and trade, had neither the same status in society nor the same values as their Western counterpart. In the new nation-states, it would be a long time before a national bourgeoisie would come into being; in the meantime, the old multiethnic bourgeoisie continued to hold ground despite the upheavals provoked by the change of masters. This Levantine bourgeoisie, characteristic of the entire Middle East, mimicked that of the West, and the petty bourgeoisie, composed of salesmen and shop owners, imitated it in turn. These were the wealthy classes, who, owing to their fortunes, distinguished themselves from the autochthonous peoples through their style of life; yet they still conserved some of their specificities. The non-Muslim bourgeoisie in the Ottoman East had neither its own ideology nor the possibility of producing one. Since there was no local model to follow, it turned toward the Western model— which reaffirmed its specific Levantine character, a specific mix of East and West.

Westernization, the result of the impact of a particular type of civilization from Europe, marked the local scene increasingly as the nineteenth century wore on.[64] In Gabriel Arié's time, the Westernization of Levantine Jewry was in its infancy. Western values were reaching that part of the East, which was opening up to the West, but were mediated through various levels.[65] The Jewish elite, in keeping with their counterparts in western Europe, imported Westernization and attempted to im-

62. Ibid., 59.

63. Alain Corbin, "Coulisses: Le secret de l'individu," in Ariès and Duby, eds., *Vie privée*, 4:419.

64. S. N. Eisenstadt, ed., *Patterns of Modernity* (London, 1987), 1:5; Jacques Le Goff, *Histoire et mémoire* (Paris, 1988), 61.

65. For Westernization in Sephardi regions, see Esther Benbassa, "La modernisation en terre sépharde," in Shmuel Trigano, ed., *La société juive à travers l'histoire* (Paris, 1992), 1:565–605.

pose it through the modern networks of communication, associations, the press, literature translated from foreign languages, and—the most effective tool of all—European-type schools. Westernization did not run deep, however. A selection took place locally, as is generally the case, with the local peoples opting for the aspects that suited them best. For a long time, these local Jewish populations, like the non-Jewish environment, experienced a fragile Westernization. It was the middle strata who extracted the greatest benefits. The process followed a progressive vertical movement, from the top down. Those at the bottom took a long time to be permeated by it and remained the closest to Jewish traditional values and to those borrowed from the Muslim environment. Arié had grown up there. In his childhood, he was awash in that atmosphere, a mixture of the traditional Jewish school, family life, and the synagogue and of the influences of the Turkish environment (such as the Turkish music sung and played in his home). In the beginning, nothing predestined this young man for the life he would know. Nonetheless, by his own choices, his frequent travels to the West, and his extended stays there for his health, he lived in osmosis with Europe. Yet he never entirely lost certain cultural particularities of his original environment.

Westernization occurred first at the level of the signifier. Western dress was introduced into wealthy families, to the detriment of the traditional costume worn by the older people. This evolution is clearly visible in the photographs from the end of the nineteenth century and the beginning of the twentieth: in front of scenery depicting pleasure gardens, decorative fabrics, columns, drapery, and landscapes, old people in traditional costumes and the young in European dress, seated in European-style armchairs or standing, serious, often rigid, or barely cracking a smile, pose for eternity in the studio.[66] This was the golden age of photography. The wealthier the client, the more often he went to renowned photographers, not only to fix the great events of life with the requisite props—modern hats and dresses, city clothes for the men—but also to indulge a taste for souvenirs. At the beginning of the century, traditional costumes progressively disappeared from the photographs, and nothing distinguished these Jews, at least in their appearance, from Westerners, except for a few decorative touches in the background of the photographs that betray their Eastern origin: a pointing minaret or a floral pattern on the fabrics, for example. These Eastern signifiers are more numerous in the photographs taken by less renowned photographers, frequented in general by

66. For photographs, see various private collections and also Esther Yuhas, ed., *The Sephardi Jews in the Ottoman Empire* (in Hebrew) (Jerusalem, 1989).

the middle class because of their lower prices. In fact, those who went to these photographers were often not yet Westernized to the point of wishing at all cost to efface any reminder of the East. Sometimes in very Europeanized photographs, a fez, the traditional male head covering, recalls the origin of the photographed subjects, which is otherwise lost in the accumulation of Western signifiers, especially in wedding photographs. These photographs are X-rays of the Levantine bourgeoisie and of its composite identity.

These same wealthy strata also adopted Western ways in diet, behavior, interior decoration, and leisure activities. They went to the country every summer, as much for medical reasons ("fresh air") as for the pleasure of escaping the heat of the city. With the progress in Western education among the middle and wealthy strata came a penchant, especially among the daughters, for certain European bourgeois principles of childrearing and education. Owing to the Alliance schools, a certain number of poor girls also had access to that education.[67] There was a tendency to focus on the question of manners, on the signifier, which is the most easily detectable. As Gallicization took hold, even in homes of the middle strata, families began to speak French, which would long remain the distinctive sign of social ascension. This language began to replace Judeo-Spanish, without supplanting it altogether. And with the formation of nation-states in the former Ottoman territories, the languages of the country also began to be introduced very slowly into Jewish homes, depending on the degree of integration. Women were an important vehicle from the base for Westernization and Gallicization.

Everything coming from the West was appreciated and thus sought out: fabric, knickknacks, decorative objects, etc. The foreign-language press spread the latest novelties in dress. The West became the referent. But the traditions and customs that had come with the family and with the social heritage of the bourgeois environment[68] were not those of the West; they stemmed from Levantine specificity, itself heterogeneous, from the denominational and ethnic diversity of this Greek, Armenian, European, and Jewish bourgeoisies. Each group had a particular identity as well as elements of convergence. The signifiers borrowed from the West were added to these already heterogeneous identities.

Arié's Westernization was not limited to these signifiers but went beyond with the act of writing an autobiography and a journal, which

67. Esther Benbassa, "Education for Jewish Girls in the East: A Portrait of the Galata School in Istanbul, 1872–1912," *Studies in Contemporary Jewry* 9 (1993): 163–73.

68. Daumard, *Les bourgeois et la bourgeoisie,* 152.

was linked intimately to his type of trajectory; it expressed the uniqueness of his approach, his originality.

Contrary to what happened in the second half of the nineteenth century, when literature and history written in the West were imported and presented to the local public in the vernacular, Gabriel Arié wrote his history books in a Western language, that of the Alliance. That organization had given him access to the West, with which he then felt familiar. But he also wrote the history of the Jewish people, a manual intended for French Jewish children. This reverse approach deserves mention, if only because of its rarity. Not only did Arié submit to Western influence, but he also transformed himself into a protagonist of the culture he so admired. In contrast, though he had planned to write the history of his cultural environment, the history of Sephardim, he did not have the means at his disposal to do so (or did not really want to do so?). Was he still too close to a kind of Sephardism that prevented him from taking the necessary distance, or was he, in contrast, sufficiently Westernized to believe his own history minor next to that of a Jewish people more easily accessible to the French public he intended to address? His failure to complete this undertaking reveals the complexity of the man Arié. But by a happy chance, his intimate writings were published a hundred years later, at the commemoration of the five hundredth anniversary of the expulsion of his ancestors from Spain.

It is undeniable that Gabriel Arié's personality also played a primary role in the choice of that mode of writing. He describes himself as rather withdrawn as a child, with a pronounced taste for reading. He began very early to retreat from the daily life of the family to indulge in that solitary pleasure. He also alludes to melancholy, which he calls a family malady. In that environment, isolating himself was already a modern act, a way of asserting himself as an individual in the collectivity. Family still meant extended family, and living arrangements meant that the neighborhood was omnipresent in everyday life, further enlarging the family circle. The Jews, because of their status, were part of a community, circumscribed as such and defined as a denomination; this reinforced the community identity, of which the family was the nucleus, and did not favor the development of individual identity. There were, in addition, the imperatives of Jewish traditional life and its social control. Autobiography and the journal require a certain withdrawal, an entrenchment, and a certain intimacy; at the same time, they are the proper site of that entrenchment. "To write one's journal is thus to

rediscover a sanctuary of peace and interiority, to reintegrate that lost
paradise 'inside.' "[69]

At the beginning of Westernization, did anyone really have the notion that a world was disappearing? Autobiographies and journals are
written to be repositories of recollections and may constitute true memoirs.[70] It was only at the beginning of the twentieth century that an
awareness of the passing of an era emerged and that people began to
write history, as amateurs of course, but in a way that revealed the
necessary distancing taking hold, as Sephardi Jews in the Levant experienced change and as irreversible losses occurred. There was a turn toward history, a concrete tool for fixing time.

Gabriel Arié was a man whose past was gone and who made the leap
toward modernity; the terrain was favorable for such an undertaking;
the tendency toward interiority aided him; and his illness was the ultimate trigger. Tuberculosis distanced Arié from his profession, cut him
off from his habitual social environment, and forced him to uproot
himself temporarily to a foreign region. His writing was situated in that
rift, in that break from his place of origin, his profession, his health, and
his past. In fact, he began his autobiography in the no-man's-land of
Switzerland, a neutral place propitious for the distancing necessary for
retrospection. It was in Europe, the site of his culture of adoption, that
he began to write. Hence, the act of writing his autobiography came
about in the very place of the genre's origin. The journal began in the
same context and was continued in, hence transplanted to, Gabriel
Arié's native environment, thus making the transition between these
two universes to which the author himself belonged. The journal that
followed ensured continuity: Gabriel Arié returned to his native country
and lived there until the end of his life. His autobiography and journal
were the culmination of his Westernization and his social ascension,
and above all of the distance taken from his own environment, which
was both familiar and strange.

Family and illness were the two poles of the life of this man and were
closely linked. Arié believed that the family transmitted illness. He
blamed his grandparents and parents for having passed illnesses on to
him. He attributed his physical defects to them. He also evoked his
father under the sign of illness. The focus of his ills was thus the family.
But he did not succeed in doing without family and established relations

69. Didier, *Le journal intime,* 91.
70. Martin-Fugier, "Vie privée," 195; Didier, *Le journal intime,* 18.

of a familial kind with the Other. The relations he had with the teacher Mme Béhar, with the Alliance, with his future in-laws in Ortaköy, and with his uncle in Galata were all of a kind. He created a large family, lived for a time with his mother and wife in the same house, brought mother, brother, and sister to Izmir after the death of his father and provided for their needs, married off brothers and sisters, took care of them when their material situation was not as good as it might have been, worried about their material future, brought his family to Davos during his illness, brought his children into his business, and maintained long-term relationships with the different members of his family throughout his life. As a newlywed, Gabriel Arié lived with his parents; later, his mother, younger brother, and sister moved in with him. He shared the same building with his brother, and then his son came to live with him. We thus have a portrait of the typical Sephardi family, where young and old lived together. Arié tried to break with this practice numerous times, but in the end was obliged to go along with it. There was a gap between his own aspirations and local contingencies. This was not yet the framework of the contemporary urban family of the nineteenth century, where intergenerational solidarity dissolved.[71]

To a great extent, Gabriel Arié also conducted his business with members of his family, and later with his descendants. His sense of family was very developed and his penchant toward egocentrism did not prevent him from managing his family relationships as a powerful and omnipresent—but attentive—paterfamilias, preoccupied with the material future of those close to him. Like any bourgeois, he made it a duty to place his children on a firm financial footing and made sure they did not lose their class standing by the choice of an occupation or spouse whose status was unworthy of them.[72] In fact, his male children, like himself, made careers in insurance. Arié's solicitude extended to his less immediate family as well. First Davos, then summer stays in vacation spots abroad and in Bulgaria, became occasions for family reunions. Everyone moved through these places in a continual coming and going, which pointed to both the wealth of the family and the affection that linked its members together. Summer tourism in the mountains and spas or in the country became a habit, as in the European bourgeois family of the nineteenth century.[73]

Gabriel Arié welcomed his niece, whose health was fragile, to Davos,

---

71. Michelle Perrot, "Figures et rôles," in Ariès and Duby, eds., *Vie privée,* 172.
72. Daumard, *Les bourgeois et la bourgeoisie,* 152.
73. Martin-Fugier, "Vie privée," 228–32.

oversaw her education, and reproduced in exile the family atmosphere he was accustomed to. As in any family, in this case a large one, frictions were not lacking. Certain conflicts persisted and caused the author sorrow, most of them due to the touchiness of the protagonists. Questions of money were also a subject of conflicts, such as the one that broke out between him and his brother Elia. But Elia provided for his needs during his stay in Davos, testimony to the family solidarity that existed among the Ariés. And Gabriel did not at any moment reproduce the conflictual atmosphere that reigned between his impoverished father and the wealthy family of his mother, voluntarily coming to the aid of those in his family who needed him.

The genealogical tree of the family, beginning in the eighteenth century, clearly testifies to the practice of endogamy, which was current at the time. It persisted even in the twentieth century, since the last son of Arié, Narcisse, married his cousin. Gabriel Arié himself tried to marry off his daughter to a cousin. Although long turned in upon itself, the Jewish family of the Balkans, progressively influenced by Westernization, began increasingly to look toward the outside. Marriages outside the clan became more and more frequent; leaving one's birthplace and settling abroad began to occur; and travel was common. A number of family members of Gabriel Arié's generation and that of his descendants established their homes outside Bulgaria, either in bordering countries or in Europe. Mobility—both vertical and horizontal—characterized this type of family, which was still in the minority. The geographical situation of Bulgaria, a gateway to the West, also facilitated that opening.

Gabriel Arié had an "arranged" marriage.[74] He married the young Rachel Cohen, whom he knew in Ortaköy and whose family he visited frequently. The family was eager to bring about the marriage. The wedding was traditional and Arié received a dowry, following the local custom, which, in fact, was not particular to Sephardi culture. He himself attempted to arrange the marriage of his eldest daughter and of his brother; progressively, his other children chose their own spouses. Nonetheless, Gabriel Arié had very fixed ideas on the subject of marriage. He first had an amorous relationship with his colleague Rachel Lévy, whom he met when she was working in Ortaköy; he did not marry her, because her ways were too free. Later, in love with an Alliance teacher whom he met in Sofia only shortly before his marriage to Rachel Cohen, he sacrificed love to reason. Sara Ungar was an emancipated woman practicing a

74. Michelle Perrot, "La famille triomphante," in Ariès and Duby, eds., *Vie privée,* 4:94.

profession, was much older than Gabriel Arié, and had ways very different from those of the Eastern women around him in his family environment. She did not possess the necessary assets to become his wife; moreover, she was Ashkenazi. He did not dismiss the possibility of living with her as his mistress, but he did not envision marriage. In the end, he preferred the security of a domestic woman, the future mother of his children, which was a type familiar to him. Arié also probably wanted to keep his promise by marrying his fiancée. The sense of honor so valorized in that culture had to play a role in that decision. He preferred order. Is not the family "the cell of living order"?[75] After the birth of the Arié couple's first child, Mlle Ungar, offended and without hope, left the girls school in Sofia for another position.

In marriage, Gabriel Arié behaved like any Western bourgeois. Marriage was the decisive element in advancement and a serious matter;[76] Gabriel was well aware of this. In the first place, he took a wife from a wealthy milieu. And given his position, the affair with Mlle Ungar would have meant trouble at the beginning of his career. That did not prevent him from having relationships with other women later on, including Mlle Julie Naar, another teacher, whom he imposed on his wife, establishing a kind of ménage à trois.

Gabriel Arié criticized Eastern women, did not always appreciate the mores of emancipated women, married an Eastern woman to follow tradition, and yet was attracted by women teachers, symbols for the age of female emancipation in the environment he had grown up in. He was haunted by the image of Mme Béhar, née Melanie Rosenstrauss, whom he loved with an innocent and lasting love. Barely a year after the death of his wife in 1929, he married one of her friends, a Sephardi woman who had also led a public life and directed an orphanage. This contradiction between respect for the practices of his cultural environment and attraction for the Western universe he had conquered was inherent in the life of the man Arié, even though it was not verbalized. Gabriel Arié's associations with women were limited to the Jewish circle. We find no indication of any relationship whatsoever in the non-Jewish world.

As a privileged space of privacy, the family remained riveted to the Jewish sphere. Despite its Western ways, Arié's family does not seem to have maintained relations with non-Jews, or if they did, these relations were exceptional and circumscribed, such as visits by doctors or the presence of a domestic staff during his stay in Europe and in Bulgaria itself.

75. Perrot, introduction to "La famille triomphante," 91.
76. Ibid., 136.

Nor does Gabriel Arié indicate the existence in his family of marriages with non-Jews. If, on the outside, there was some contact with non-Jews, with rare exceptions they were not introduced inside. Despite the openness toward the Western exterior that was occurring, the inside symbolized by the extended family remained Jewish, though this Judaism was not manifested in any consistent observance of religious precepts. This was an ethnic Judaism based on habit. Thus Gabriel Arié adopted a compartmentalized way of life common in that cultural environment, where the community lived relatively closed in upon itself as a result of denominational borders imposed from above, which penetrated everyday life and persisted even when the borders were officially abolished. The outside, the public arena, was the place for these interrelations—Gabriel Arié even joined a non-Jewish Masonic lodge—but they usually stopped at the threshold of the house. The family thus remained the place of memory, where the rites of the life cycle and the celebrations that mark time were respected.

The Jewishness of the Arié family does not seem to have been affected by external influences, which it was able to integrate without losing its identity. That, in fact, is what made all the difference between him and the Jews of western Europe, who experienced a different process of emancipation and, as a result, of modernization, under the impulse of a strong state that imposed its values on the Jews. In the Levant, however, modernization was a choice for the elites. Since they had borrowed their new values from the outside, they did not have the force or means of a state at their disposal to impose them on the rest of the Jewish population, as they would have liked to do. The actions of the elites also did not have as much at stake as those of a state. That also contributed in great part to safeguarding Jewish identity and its routines among the wealthy Jewish strata and those most oriented toward the West, even when respect for the everyday precepts of Judaism had been eroded.

Arié himself observed a similar kind of Judaism, and his intimate writings do not reveal a great religious sensibility. His bitter meditations, following the death of his father, on the vanity of all human efforts and all faith, are an expression of his sadness and grief, but they also convey a lack of the kind of assurance he might have drawn from a more solid Jewish faith and observance. In some sense, in a manner that points ironically to his criticism of Easterners, Arié acted out of concern for appearances, conserving certain external, and therefore social, signs of Jewish observance all his life. He observed the Jewish liturgical rite in mourning the death of his father, made sure that his sons were bar mitzvah (even teaching them the sections of the biblical text they were

to recite for the occasion), was a member of a synagogue, and commemo-
rated Jewish holidays. Nothing indicates, however, that he kept kosher,
since this issue was never evoked in his writings, even in the context of
his stay in Davos, where it probably would have been impossible to find
kosher food. Yet all this did not prevent Arié from returning to Hebrew
studies at the end of his life.

The new nation-states that had formed in the region were still weak
and could not take decisive action to enforce "assimilation." When they
did manifest the will to do so, the Jews were already confronting the
new option that presented itself to them, Jewish nationalism and Zionism, which contributed toward reinforcing Jewish identity among a
large part of the population in countries such as Bulgaria, for example.
Of course, the members of the elite long remained hesitant about that
option, which placed their positions as notables within the community
at risk, since those positions were progressively taken over by nationalist
militants.[77] This time, the base imposed its will on the elites, who, in
spite of themselves, bowed to the new context in the nation-states,
including Bulgaria and even, in part, Greece.

At first glance, at least at the level of signifier, the Arié family was
indistinguishable from the petit bourgeois family and, later, from the
urban bourgeois family of the West at the end of the nineteenth and the
beginning of the twentieth century. Family photographs are testimony
to this. The prolonged stay by Gabriel Arié in the West made him feel
more at ease in the role of the bourgeois. While still in Davos, he began
to have a house rebuilt in Sofia, a city that had undergone great transformations. Homes, the material foundation of the family and pillar of the
social order, are also property, investments.[78] That is what Gabriel Arié's
behavior manifested: he intended to draw on the revenues from the
rental of the stores and apartments in the building, while his brother
lived in another part of the house. Upon his return, he also lived there.
Toward the end of his stay in Davos, he slowly introduced himself into
business and later made his fortune. Thus, he made the transition from
illness to a new enterprise in life. The mere fact of having a house built
signified the hope that he would get well.

---

77. See on this subject Esther Benbassa, "Haim Nahum Efendi, dernier grand rabbin
de l'Empire ottoman (1908–1920): Son rôle politique et diplomatique," 2 vols. (thèse
de doctorat d'état, Université de Paris III, 1987); Esther Benbassa, *Haim Nahum: A
Sephardic Chief Rabbi* (Tuscaloosa, 1995).

78. Michelle Perrot, "Manières d'habiter," in Ariès and Duby, eds., *Vie privée*, 4:307
and 309.

Even during his long years of being somewhat cut off socially and economically, he was free from want, owing to the Alliance, his brother, and his own ingenuity. Money was very attractive to Arié. Knowing well the material difficulties that confronted instructors, he directed his children toward more lucrative careers. They and other members of the family made their careers in insurance, a modern profession in the tertiary sector. They founded and directed local representations of foreign insurance companies or merely sought employement there—which linked them even professionally to the West.

Distrustful by nature and sure of his own abilities as an instructor, Arié intermittently took on the education of his children and his niece, not trusting the school. In that, he conformed with fathers who, in bourgeois families, act as teachers, at least for their sons.[79] Arié attached a particular importance to the instruction and upbringing of his younger son, Narcisse. In addition, he earned part of his living in Davos from tutoring. In Sofia, he continued to concern himself with the education of his daughters by giving them French lessons. His ambition for them was that of a bourgeois of his time: his daughter Jeanne enrolled in the Weill and Kahn Institute, where Alliance teachers were trained, but Arié also requested piano, dance, and needlework lessons for her—an ambivalent attitude characteristic of the man.

Above all, Gabriel Arié's autobiography and journal are the testimony of a self-made man who carries within himself the stigmata of those who force the hand of "destiny." Life struggle was the credo of this man, who, by his own will, climbed the rungs of the social ladder and succeeded in conquering illness. Beneath this voluntarist lay a fragile, insecure self who needed to be loved, needed to be the center of attention. Anxious by nature, he hid behind order, which protected him from anything unforeseen that might have generated anxiety. He bore no illusions. Both intellectual and pragmatic, he knew men through their actions and did not always see them in their best light. The bitterness he sometimes expressed bore witness to this. And knowing human beings, he also seems to have known how to get around them, to manage them (in the best cases), which permitted him to constitute an entire network of relations. He rarely used them for himself personally, since he was not really an opportunist and was better at giving than at taking, with a kind of pride characteristic of his cultural universe. In contrast, he called on their services when advancing a public, rather than a personal, cause. At the same time, this was a man with direct ways, who said what he thought, which did not

79. Perrot, "Figures et rôles," 154.

fail to attract enemies very early. It was always with the community—institutions and their representatives—that he, as a man of the Alliance nonetheless, entered into conflict, as was the case in Sofia and Izmir. In fact, Arié remained a free agent before anything else.

Although he had character, he was also hypersensitive, in part because of his illness. He experienced the death of his father, his daughter, and his wife as tragedies, but he succeeded in overcoming them. A man of action, he knew he had to continue living in spite of everything. He remarried quickly to avoid the loneliness that pursues men of his age, and him more than others, since at that stage most of his children and the members of his extended family were dispersed. In his advanced age, he continued to look on women as nurses, angels of the house, whom it was difficult to do without. Death was disorder; remarriage, a remedy.

His pessimism—or, rather, a fatalism of the Eastern type—and his superstitious side broke with the apparent rigidity that seems to have marked his character. For him, the love of order, the remedy for his anxiety, was continually shadowed by the disorder that was at the very foundation of his trajectory and his being. Instead of continuing on his family's path, he changed course and led a different life; his carefully planned career as a teacher was interrupted by his illness, generating disorder. And yet illness was already part of the family history. He opted for a conventional marriage but found himself involved in love affairs that went against that conjugal order. He sought financial security in a post as a teacher, but at the end of the road found himself once more in business, an area known for the unforeseen, for risk. In the beginning, he sought treatment in a sanatorium, a regimented environment, a disciplinary universe,[80] but he rapidly lost confidence in doctors and medication and definitively abandoned them. Gabriel Arié also chose the school, the regimented place par excellence, as his professional environment, but he abandoned it, not appreciating it overly much, since he chose not to send his children to school whenever he could manage it. He lived in that duality between order and disorder, and he provoked that disorder by revolt, by breaking with the established order at the very foundation of his social class of adoption.

Conservative in his ideas on education, politics (fear of Bolshevism), family, marriage, and many other points, by the life he led he also incarnated revolt. One of the most important revolts was illness. Through enclosures—institutions—in this case the Alliance, the school, the fam-

---

80. Pierre Guillaume, *Du désespoir au salut: Les tuberculeux aux XIXe et XXe siècles* (Paris, 1986), 233.

ily, and the sanatorium, Gabriel Arié sought desperately the security he lacked. He went so far as to specialize in insurance, also setting up his children in a career that, as its name indicates, insures beings and goods. The sanatorium, with its rhythms and rituals, claims to be a reassuring universe, where the patient is taken in hand by the medical corps, but it is at the same time a place of anxiety.[81] As soon as that security was guaranteed, he found it suffocating and attempted to break through these enclosures and go elsewhere, to breathe, as he did in the mountains associated with his treatment. He fled his family of origin to conquer new intellectual and social horizons, because it was suffocating him—like the coughing episodes that prevented him from breathing.

School, the sanatorium, illness, and even Judaism are major sites of rituals, which are reassuring because of their repetition. In his tuberculosis, there was also that duality of order and disorder, the first ensured by incessant observation of the development of his illness, typical of tuberculosis patients, the second by the break and, as a result, the upheaval at every level that it provoked his life. Although he created new barriers for himself, he liberated himself from others, but without knocking them down altogether, as in his relations with the Alliance, for example.

The link between Gabriel Arié and illness resembles that between himself and his family. It was a tie of attraction and repulsion. Influenced by the fashionable theories of heredity, or rather by the "mythologies of heredity" developed by doctors and novelists of the time,[82] he did not dissociate illness from family: "The terror of 'defects' transmitted and of 'damaged' blood places the family into a link in a chain, a link whose fragility requires vigilance."[83] Illness sometimes emerged as a mode of expression within the family. Arié himself alluded to the fact that his mother resorted to it to get attention and that she stopped doing so when her son or daughter-in-law became ill. As a result, illness became commonplace and no longer had the same meaning. This extended family, living within the same house, was suffocating, and manifested its discomfort in illness. Illness was also a distinctive sign of the family, whose members were affected by the century's malady, tuberculosis. Gabriel Arié's own son Sandro suffered from it and had to stay in Berck, France, for a long time. The son was at the seaside while the father was in the mountains. Diabetes was the second illness that affected the direct family: both his daughter Ida and his wife Rachel died of it. Arié especially associated

81. Ibid., 261.
82. Perrot, "Fonctions de la famille," in Ariès and Duby, eds., *Vie privée,* 4:115.
83. Ibid.

defective lungs, the organ of breathing, with the family. It was to have the air he was lacking that he sought out heights, mountains, the symbolic place of healing. "The ill are people of the plains, who rise above their places and environments of origin, having to overcome anxiety, sometimes physical in nature, as a general rule."[84] Gabriel Arié was destined to experience that anxiety inherent in his existence, which he tried to stifle in the enclosed worlds he chose for himself, but which in their turn suffocated him and from which he attempted to escape. He continually moved back and forth between these places and the outside, the symbol of deliverance. His illness, which in itself represents a break, linked Arié to the West, his universe of adoption, just as the family illnesses he bore within himself and the career he chose late in life linked him to his lineage and his cultural environment.

The practice of a career associated with the intellectual domain had only been a parenthesis. And yet his wish to exercise a career other than commerce, the traditional career path for Jews, particularly in the East, manifested a desire to leave his environment. In business, Gabriel Arié continued to write and to find a place for himself in the intellectual realm. Always regretting what he was leaving behind, he was one of those beings whose choices exile them from the universe for which they were destined, and who are condemned to live in the duality and tensions exile produces.

He attributed the causes of his illness not only to family heredity, which he experienced as fate, but also to external factors. These also stemmed from the environment he had wanted to reject: worries caused by the people of the Izmir community, who did not seem to appreciate him, and by the evil eye, a superstition anchored in the popular realm. Arié thus found himself once more prisoner to the same interpenetrating circles: family, community (the official family to which every Jew in traditional milieus belonged), and the cultural group in general, the Sephardim, the great ethnocultural family.

From the beginning of his illness in 1898, he undertook a tour of spas and mountain villages. He was seeking purification, which would come about through water and air. The conquest of a new physical universe also signified the conquest of the new identity he was seeking. Arié moved a great deal. He hid his anxiety in each change of location—escape, combined with hyperactivity. As a teacher, he changed countries and cities several times; he traveled a great deal within and outside the Balkans; then, with his illness, he once more took to the road in pursuit of recov-

84. Guillaume, "Tuberculose et montagne," 37.

ery, in all senses of the word. Gabriel Arié's itinerary allows us to reconstitute the path of tuberculosis, where Switzerland was the locale of choice. From one sanatorium to another, he tried to kill off his death anxiety, to regulate it, to enclose it in these enclosed places, in order to familiarize himself with it and thus get around it. Death at an early age was also hereditary in his family. Would he inherit nothing from that family but illness and death? They hung about him continually. They made their mark on his relations with the family.

Of course, Gabriel Arié was in the first stages of his illness, since sanatoria were open only to patients whom medicine considered curable. At one point, he thought about ending his life, but he continued to struggle to conquer obstacles, as he would throughout his life. During his stay in Switzerland, he looked within himself for the will to get well, putting an end to the regimentation of the sanatoria and the closed universe of illness and healing. There again, it was in activity that he found salvation. This was one way for him to reconnect with life and escape the exclusion that threatened anyone who transgressed. At no moment in his stay did he entirely set aside his profession or his family. He adapted to the new conditions and thus adapted his familiar universe to his new status. It is that adaptability that makes Gabriel Arié an interesting figure and a rich character. Like all those who took the path he did, adaptability was the condition sine qua non of success in the unknown.

It was also in illness that Gabriel Arié crystallized his individual sense of self, his profound being, whose tribulations he narrated in his autobiography and journal. These works are the testimony of a long internal journey, written by an engaging and courageous man seeking the irreconcilable—a fate reserved at a certain moment for those Jews who had gone in search of modernity and had witnessed the slow crumbling of a world that had been theirs for centuries. A proud man, he wanted to show himself in his best light; yet the weaknesses of a tortured being also show through. These weaknesses contribute to his strength. His was the order and disorder of a full life, which began in the second half of the nineteenth century and underwent the transformations and upheavals affecting the Sephardi world in the East up to the eve of World War II. Arié did not have the misfortune of experiencing the horrors of that war. Instead of an exemplary life—which is not truly life—the memory of which he would have liked to pass on to his children, Arié leaves us a life example, the memory of a man and of an age-old Sephardi culture that he saw slowly disintegrate and disappear.

ESTHER BENBASSA AND ARON RODRIGUE

PART I

Autobiography
and
Correspondence

(1863–October 1906)

Preface

I dedicate these memories to my beloved children

I wish to record here the most important events of my existence. My life, which, it seems, will not be of long duration, has been filled with difficulties, struggles, a few joys, and much disillusionment. It is fitting that a trace should remain of it so that my children, when they have reached the age of reason, may read these pages and benefit from the experience I have had of men. Warned of some of the dangers and traps along the way, perhaps they will pursue their careers without sustaining too many wounds or damage. It is with that goal in mind that I recount my life in all sincerity, dissimulating nothing about my good actions and my faults, my successes and my disappointments, my ideals and what reality offered me. The moral of my story will emerge from the facts themselves. My children will endeavor to benefit from it and to extract from it principles of moral and practical conduct.

That is why I dedicate these memories to them.

GABRIEL ARIÉ
Davos, October 1906

1/ My Parents, Childhood Memories
(1863–1873)

I was born in Samakov on 10 Iyar 5623, which corresponds to 29 April 1863. At that time, Samakov was part of the Ottoman Empire. It was a small town of ten thousand, an industrial town with little trade: the iron found in great quantity in the alluvium was extracted from the ore in the primitive blast furnaces called *viggnas* and *madens*. My family on my mother's side possessed several of these. The weaving of wool, from which fabric called *chaïak* was made, and the production of cheese and butter were sufficient to maintain a bit of activity and commerce in the city.

My father, Moïse, who received the second name Nissim after a grave illness in his childhood,[1] was born in 5602 (1842) of Elia Arié, called Ham[2] Liatchouno, and his wife, Dona. My grandfather, who lived in almost constant poverty, died prematurely of typhoid fever at age forty-four, in 1864, leaving behind three sons, Joseph, Nissim, and Raphaël, and two daughters, Venezia and Rébecca.

My mother, Jaël, the fifth child of Juda Arié, called Tchelebi[3] Juda, was born in 1847. She had three sisters, Boulissa Arié,[4] Reyna Tagger, and Tamar Arié, and four brothers, Moïse, David, Nahim, and Samuel.

My mother's family was the richest in Samakov and perhaps in Bulgaria. Their style of living and the abundance in which they lived contrasted markedly with what my mother was to find with her in-laws. But

1. Nissim is a Hebrew given name that can be translated as "miracles." It was the custom to change the name of a sick child to hasten recovery. See Michael Molho, *Usos y costumbres de los Sefardies de Salonica* (Madrid and Barcelona, 1950), 68.
2. Ham (probably from Hebrew *hakham*, "wise," "rabbi") is a title placed before the name of aged persons who deserve special respect. Here, the given name that follows is a popular form of Elia.
3. *Tchelebi* (*çelebi*, Turkish) is a title given to a man with a good education and a lucrative position who is from a good family.
4. On the genealogical tree in possession of the family, the name Simha appears instead of Boulissa, but this is probably the same person.

the change did not weigh heavily upon her, for the attachment she had for her husband led her to accept with joy the modesty of her new condition.

Until the age of twenty, my father received quite an intense Hebrew education, the only kind of education available at that time, and from it his religious principles, from which he never strayed. I attribute the mediocrity of his commercial aptitudes in part to his long training in the *midrasch*.[5] He was married at twenty (my mother was fifteen at the time) and found himself the head of a family, without the slightest resources and with no occupation. His father-in-law took him into his service at the office, not to handle accounts but to run errands, and my father thus found himself the servant of his brothers-in-law, who in fact treated him with indifference and often hostility.

The family life of my parents, then, began under rather sad conditions: lacking means, they were obliged to accept the hospitality of my grandfather Juda for two years. It was in my grandfather's home that I came into the world, and he was my godfather. They say he was very fond of me, just as he particularly loved my father and mother. But his goodness could not prevent the constant humiliations to which my parents were subjected by their brothers- and sisters-in-law.

In 1866, my grandfather arranged a partnership between my father and Mr. Moïse Lévy, a salesman of manufactured goods, and obtained a small house for him, consisting of a single bedroom and a kitchen. My oldest childhood memories go back to that time, for I remember having seen my sister Oro at the breast. She was born in 1865. Although now settled into their own home, my parents spent almost every Saturday at my grandfather's. Without my mother, there were no holidays or excursions to the country. It was during that time, which continued for about ten years, that my very keen taste for country life began. Even today I like to recall those delicious days spent under the trees, those evenings, each one a holiday, accompanied by the noise of the *viggnas* whistles and the grunts of workers as they hammered the iron, or those summer weeks spent at the farm in Bania,[6] where we watched the lighthearted, lively fieldwork. My grandfather oversaw everything, not neglecting the pleasures, quiet pleasures that consisted in watching the men and

5. *Midrasch* (Hebrew, *midrash;* plural, *midrashim*) is the name given to the elementary classes in traditional Jewish education, the equivalent of the *heder* in eastern Europe or of the *meldar,* the word more commonly used among the Sephardim in the East. *Midrash* also designated the place of prayer.
6. The hot springs of Gornia-Bania south of Sofia.

women who harvested the land dancing in the evening around great fires, to the sound of flutes and bagpipes.

After my grandfather's death, these excursions, these holidays, continued until 1877, the eve of the Russo-Turkish War, but it seems to me they no longer had the mark of cordiality, of good humor, that had earlier characterized them. The quarrels that accompanied the division of my grandfather's effects projected a shadow of mistrust, of ill-humor, on the entire family, which got worse and worse, leading to the almost total dispersal of the shared inheritance, of which there now remains only odds and ends.

On this subject, I cannot understand why, at the death of my grandfather, my parents did not ask for part of the inheritance due my mother. At the time, it was an accepted principle that daughters had no right to the paternal inheritance, but lawyers supposedly offered to claim part of the fortune left by Tchelebi Juda. My father refused them.

My childhood was thus spent in a mediocre financial condition close to poverty. Nevertheless, my father was still the wealthiest of his three brothers and, because of this, he had to supply a dowry and marry off his two sisters, Venezia and Rébecca. He faced up to all these burdens, even though his own family was gradually growing: Rosa was born in 1868, Elia in 1870, soon after a sister, Esmeralda, who died, and Régine in 1875. We lived in succession with Samuel Avdala (where Rosa and Elia were born), then with Mochon de Ham Aron, and finally in our own house, acquired in about 1875, situated on what is now 1 Moïseova Street.

This progress in our way of life reflected a certain prosperity in business. This business developed little by little: in addition to a shop of manufactured goods we had in the marketplace, my father established a branch in the Turkish quarter; in addition, he established relations with Salonika, from whence he imported copper, colonial foodstuffs, etc. It seemed that fate would shine on us. You will see what happened, and how that modest position was mercilessly destroyed by my Uncles Moïse and David.

Even at my grandfather's death in 1870, my uncles, fearing my father would demand part of the inheritance, incited him to abandon his trade in manufactured goods, promising him the moon if he would become their agent. The store was liquidated and my father was sent to Kyustendil in the middle of winter, to recover something or other. All I remember of that adventure was that my father almost froze to death on his horse during the journey, that upon his return he developed a grave illness, and that, as soon as he had recovered, he hastened to reestablish his shop and to take up his trade as in the past. That is all my grandfather's inheritance ever gave us.

A few years later, my father, before heading for the fair in Uzundje[7] as was his habit, bought iron from my uncles to be resold at the fair; the proceeds of the sale were to be used to make the necessary purchases for the store. That was in 1876: business was bad, given the troubles in Herzegovina and the war between the Serbs and the Turks. The bonds for 60 Turkish pounds that my father had subscribed to with my uncles could not be paid. My uncles, furious, obtained authorization from the pasha of Sofia to have my father thrown in prison. I no longer remember how many days he was incarcerated, but I remember every detail of my father's stay in prison, the food I brought him from the house, the anguish and tears of my mother, the curses she heaped on her brothers, the scene with her mother, and, above all, my father's attitude of resignation. Such a scandal would not be possible today; but under the Turkish regime that was ending, my all-powerful uncles could easily crush a poor defenseless man. And they did so without scruples.

My father returned to his business soon afterward; he reopened his store. Since there had not been a bankruptcy properly speaking, all his bonds in circulation were paid in full, except the 60 Ltq.[8] to my uncles, which I redeemed in 1886 for 25 Ltq. I was wrong in this, for my uncles were in debt to us—because of our weakness in fact—for at least a hundred times the 60 Turkish pounds. In any case, the trade in manufactured goods was reopened and continued until the Russian invasion in 1877.

I have gone into some detail regarding our means of existence during my early childhood because it explains some of the traits of my father's character and of mine as well.

My father had a frail constitution. At the age of two he contracted an illness, which was taken to be a fever and which lasted two years. I would not be surprised if this were simply a bout of tuberculosis which went away on its own. This sickly childhood left him weak all his life, subject to frequent stitches in his side, which were treated with bloodletting. In addition, he was dyspeptic, and hence inclined toward melancholy and hypochondria, a common illness in the Arié family. His extreme irritability translated into repeated and painful migraines, which made the slightest annoyance painful; the most insignificant incidents

7. Uzundje-Ova, near Philippopolis in Thrace, was the site of a large fair, which began to decline in 1873.
8. Ltq. is the abbreviation for Turkish pounds (the Turkish currency).

made him angry. Hence, his suffering, at times physical, at times moral, had very early impressed upon his fine and distinguished physiognomy the imprint of sadness and pain. The joys of this world were rare for him, at least until he had to leave Samakov, which is to say until he was about forty years old.

My character was to be modeled on his. I understood very early that life is a serious business. I do not remember committing any of those childish pranks that everyone keeps in his distant memory. From the age of four I was sent to the *meldar*,[9] where I had the following teachers in succession: Béhar Melamed,[10] who taught me to read; Harbi[11] Haïm, who taught me the prayers, the *perascha*,[12] and the *En-Jacob*;[13] Moïse Alcalay, who gave me a few notions about Hebrew grammar; and finally, Harbi Abraham Cohen, with whom I translated the Talmud from the age of ten.

We were also taught a bit of Turkish; in 1874 I began spending two hours every day at the Conak,[14] in an office, where I copied administrative documents, of which I did not understand a word. That is where my father came looking for me the day the Alliance school opened in January 1874. Everything I know in Hebrew and Turkish I learned during the first ten years of my life, for beginning in 1874, I devoted myself to French and neglected all the rest.

School exercises were not the only things I was obliged to do; exercises of piety occupied a large place in my small existence. Every day there were the three prayers at the temple, winter and summer, not counting the extra prayers, the *ticoun-hatzot*.[15] Very often during the month of Eloul,[16] I awoke before dawn to go recite the *sélihot*.[17] On

9. See n. 5 above, this chapter.

10. *Melamed* (Hebrew), "instructor."

11. *Harbi* (*ha-rabi*, Hebrew) is a title given to rabbis who have attained a high level of knowledge and who perform advanced rabbinical duties.

12. *Perascha* (*parasha*, Hebrew), the pericope, a weekly section of the Pentateuch.

13. *En-Jacob* (*Ein Yaakov*, "the spring of Jacob," Hebrew), the work of Jacob ben Salomon Ibn Habib (1445–1515 or 1516), a collection of *agadot*, "narratives," from the Talmuds of Babylon and Jerusalem. One of the basic books in traditional Jewish education.

14. *Conak* (*konak*, Turkish) here means the governor's palace.

15. *Ticoun-hatzot* (*tikun hatsot*, Hebrew) is the midnight liturgy.

16. Eloul (Elul) is the last month of the Hebrew calendar.

17. The *sélihot* (*selihot*, Hebrew plural), the nighttime liturgy of penitence practiced throughout the month of Elul and the first ten days of the month of Tishri (the first month of the Jewish year) until Yom Kippur (Day of Atonement).

Saturday, a day of recreation, I read the *Perascha, Targoum,*[18] *Perakim,*[19] Psalms, and then, after dinner, the *Zohar*[20] at the *midrasch,* in the company of a lot of old men. And you had to pay attention, not lose a word, not stand around gaping, for I was being observed and I got a slap— more than once, right in the synagogue—for allowing myself to daydream. That was the education of the time. It was harsh in general, but for us it was particularly rigorous. It is therefore not astonishing that my father's home has left me with only austere memories and that the joys of childhood remained almost unknown to me, as they did to my brothers and sisters.

One should not imagine, however, that being at home was like being in prison. The seriousness of our life was often enlivened by music. My father had a musical ear and sang well, though with a head voice. Every Friday night we rehearsed part of the *Pizmonim,*[21] from collections passed on in the family from generation to generation; I believe I remain one of the last repositories of these melodies, many of them harmonious. Rabbi Moïse Alcalay and Haïm Serouma, a singer from Sofia, added to this repertoire a few Turkish songs from the time, which we were taught at the *meldar* and, later on, at school.

Apart from these distractions, we had the habit of getting together in the winter to entertain ourselves, to play a game with empty cups, one of which concealed a ring. We accompanied ourselves with rather grotesque traditional Turkish songs, which greatly amused the spectators-actors. I often accompanied my father at these feasts, and played my own little role in them.

18. The Targoum (Targum) is the Aramaic translation of the Bible.

19. *Perakim* (*prakim,* Hebrew plural), "chapters." Here Arié is referring to the reading of the *Avot* treatise of the Mishnah, also called *Pirkei Avot,* "Chapters of the Fathers."

20. The *Zohar* (The Book of Splendor) is a mystical work written in Aramaic and is the principal source of the Kabbala. It is a compilation by Moïse de Léon, a thirteenth-century scholar, but was traditionally attributed to Simeon Bar Yohay, of the second century.

21. *Pizmonim* (Hebrew plural), liturgical refrains.

2/ Primary School (1874–1877)

At the beginning of 1874, within this narrowly circumscribed environment in which I was passing my childhood, a capital event occurred that was to have a decisive influence on my entire future: the opening of the Alliance school. On the initiative of my uncles, who directed community affairs, the Central Committee sent to Samakov one of its professors, M. Nissim Béhar,[1] who had recently married Mlle Melanie Rosenstrauss, herself a teacher.

Like all children my age, I was enrolled as a student and began to learn the French language. Since I was used to the study of Hebrew subjects, which were far more dry and arid, French was for me a game, a relaxation. I dedicated myself enthusiastically to my studies and from the first day became the top student. Until the end of my studies, I do not remember ever being second, in Samakov, Balat,[2] or Paris. The severe discipline to which my father had accustomed me was of great usefulness now. Self-control and constant work came naturally to me. I was never punished or scolded by my teachers for being lazy or negligent. I studied with passion. Mme Nissim encouraged me as much as she could; she became as attached to me as a mother and I adored her with all my heart. I was less fond of her husband, whom, in fact, I rarely saw.

Unfortunately, M. Nissim's stay in Samakov did not last long; in July 1875, he was sent to Balat-Constantinople. With two comrades, I accompanied Mme Nissim, her mother-in-law, and her two children, Henriette and Isaac (who died soon afterward), to the Vada, four kilometers from the city. Upon leaving her, my eyes filled with tears: "Don't cry," she said; "Only mountains never see each other again." Alas! Men too do not always see each other again. These words were the last I was to hear from her mouth. Less than two years later, she was to die in Constantinople.

1. Nissim Béhar (1848–1931) was an instructor at Alliance schools and a renowned pedagogue who pursued a long career in Jerusalem and the United States. He was considered one of the architects of the modern teaching of Hebrew.
2. Balat, a quarter on the Golden Horn (Istanbul) with a large Jewish population.

When I returned home, I was sad and dejected all day. I went to my room, covered my face with a book, and cried profusely.

She often wrote me from Constantinople, begging me to join her, promising me I would be like a son in her home, that she would teach me, that she would send me to Paris, all at her own expense. My father refused to send me. I have never known why.

M. Emmanuel Daffa, a young teacher fresh from college, succeeded M. Béhar. He was more concerned with his own pleasures than with his school. During the year he spent at Samakov, studies were greatly relaxed. Several months after his arrival, he took a trip to Volos,[3] his native town, and in his absence I directed the school.

If schoolwork left something to be desired, my leisure time was well spent. I borrowed many books from the library. My first readings were *Robinson Crusoe,* which I recounted to my mother chapter by chapter, something she enjoyed very much; *Paul et Virginie,* which left a profound impression on me and gave me a glimpse of what feelings of love could be; Plutarch's *Lives of Illustrious Greeks;* science books such as Cartambert's geography and Ganot's physics, whose meaning I struggled to grasp. As for children's literature, which is today the joy of our children, I didn't even know it existed.

The rest of my leisure time was occupied copying maps. I copied all the maps on the walls of the school and decorated our house with the result. In the series of moves the family made, these maps must have been lost in Samakov.

It was in that year, 1876, that I made my first communion.[4] On that occasion, I was taught a speech in Hebrew, which I recited at the temple. I have kept this speech among my papers. At the family meal that took place on that occasion, no one dared show any noisy rejoicing, since the revolution in Herzegovina was at its height, and our Turkish neighbors would not have looked kindly on anyone singing in a Jewish house.

M. Daffa was replaced at the end of 1876 by M. Isaac Schulmann, who also came from Volos. But by that time, the level of studies had dropped so much that I no longer had any comrades as strong as I was, so to speak. Thus I dispensed with doing most of the homework that was given. In spite of that, the year I spent with M. Schulmann was for me one of the most profitable; it was this professor who initiated me into the beauties of French literature. He acquainted me with almost all the classics from various collections, the most important of which was

3. Volos, a port city of Greece (Thessaly).
4. That is, his Bar Mitzvah.

Merlet. I learned a great number of pieces by heart. Everything there is to know about the great writers of the seventeenth century I already knew in Samakov. My later studies of literature in Paris were only reviews for me. But what formed my style and gave it the few qualities it may have today was an attentive reading of Fénelon's *Télémaque*. The study of this book taught me to feel the harmony of language. Today it is fashionable to denigrate this author. That is a mistake in my view.

And the war continued; the Russians, having crossed the Danube, were approaching. My maternal uncles, who no doubt had their reasons, decided to emigrate to Turkey. One part of the Arié family went to Lecce, Italy, the other to Constantinople. At the insistence of my mother, who feared the Russian invasion would be the end of the world, my uncles agreed to take me with them to Constantinople. Having said good-bye to my parents, I joined the caravan. We took the railroad to Sarembey in November 1877, and two days later we were in Constantinople.

3/ Constantinople (1877–1878)

My uncle Nahim had been in the Turkish capital since at least 1874. He opened a bank there with his partner, M. Baruch Cohen. Everything was thus set up to receive us. We moved into a house on Yazidji Street in Pera.[1] I wondered what would be done with me: I was not long in finding out. The role of a servant charged with running errands was destined for me. My instincts warned me that if I did not seek my own way, outside the protection of my uncles, I was lost. Without telling anyone, I went to Balat, where my former teacher M. Nissim Béhar was living, and informed him of my situation.

M. Nissim knew the affection that his wife, who had died the previous year, had had for me and how happy she would have been to welcome me, since she had called for me so insistently. He immediately proposed that I come stay with him and sent me to get my bedding. I returned to Galata[2] and presented myself to my grandmother to inform her of my resolution. She was greatly annoyed, but my resolution was made and I left.

On this matter, let me say that my maternal grandmother was always a stranger to us. She never showed the slightest affection and I doubt she ever loved anyone, even her own sons. As for me, I never received an embrace or a loving word from her. Later, she even broke off ties with my mother for refusing to pass on an offer for me to marry a cousin with a birthmark.

The stay in Balat was a fruitful period for me. I worked relentlessly, day and night. I belonged to the first class, which had no program properly speaking. We did what we liked and taught one another in tacit freedom. Here we were a little club of amateur students. Chatting took up as much of our time as study. This system has some advantages and many disadvantages. The greatest disadvantage of all was that I, who had remained completely innocent until then, was now present at ex-

1. Pera, the European quarter of Istanbul.
2. Galata, an Istanbul neighborhood with a large concentration of Europeans and Jews.

changes that were less than edifying. My comrades showed me obscene books, the likes of which I have never seen since. The consequences of these unhealthy excitations can be guessed.

At the end of the school year, I was nominated for the Ecole Orientale,[3] along with my friend Joseph Nar. Only he was admitted. But on the advice of M. Nissim, I left for Paris with my friends from Constantinople: Alphandary, Chéni, Haym, and Nar. M. Nissim himself was going to Paris. My uncle Nahim was kind enough to lend me twenty Turkish pounds for the trip.

We arrived in Paris on 18 September 1878, the eve of Rosch-Haschana.[4] My friends went to 4 *bis*, rue des Rosiers, where the school was located, and I headed for a hotel at 12, rue Mazagran. M. Nissim went to live at 4, rue du Plâtre. Since my purse was almost empty, I quickly moved, renting a room on rue du Faubourg Saint-Antoine for eighteen francs a month.

The day after my arrival, I began efforts to be admitted to the Ecole Orientale. I saw in succession, several times, Chief Rabbi Isidor,[5] MM. Goldschmidt,[6] Leven,[7] Charles Netter,[8] Veneziani,[9] and Loeb.[10] These efforts lasted a month, during which time I lived on the fifty francs that remained from my trip. Once the rent of eighteen francs was paid for the room, I still had thirty-two francs. I thus resolved to limit my food and lived during that entire time on a rather frugal diet: in the morning, a cup of milk and fifteen centimes' worth of bread; at noon, ten centimes' worth of bread and ten of chocolate; and in the evening, the same menu as at noon. I did most of my errands on foot. I don't know how many times I went from one end of Paris to the other in search of a member of the committee, only to find him not at home! I returned to my room dead on my feet and often went to bed with all my clothes on.

Finally, my efforts were crowned with success: thanks to M. Narcisse

3. Ecole Normale Israélite Orientale (ENIO), the Alliance teacher-training school.

4. Rosch-Haschana (*rosh ha-shanah,* Hebrew) is the Jewish New Year.

5. Lazare Isidore (1814–88) was chief rabbi of France beginning in 1867.

6. Salomon H. Goldschmidt was a philanthropist and president of the Central Committee of the Alliance from 1881 to 1898.

7. Narcisse Leven (1833–1915) was one of the founders of the Alliance and its president beginning in 1898.

8. Charles Netter (1826–82) was one of the founders of the Alliance and of the agricultural school Mikveh Yisrael (Hebrew, "the gathering or Israel" or "the hope of Israel"), in Jaffa, Palestine, in 1870.

9. Emmanuel Félix Veneziani (1825–89) was director of the Camondo Bank in Istanbul and member of the Regional Committee of the Alliance in the same city.

10. Isidore Loeb (1839–92) was a rabbi and French scholar and secretary of the Alliance between 1869 and 1892.

Leven and the late Charles Netter, I was admitted to the school toward the end of October. You can imagine how overjoyed I was to enter that school on rue des Rosiers, where I was to live with free room and board and instruction.

At the time, I was fifteen and a half. My childhood was not yet over and I had already felt the first difficulties of life.

During that year, my father's existence had been extremely difficult. Never, not before or after, did he suffer as much as in 1877–78. The Russians had entered Samakov in January 1878. The invasion caused no damage to anyone except my uncles, whose homes and stores, crammed full of possessions, were pillaged by the populace. Since the Russian garrison consumed a great deal of alcohol, my father thought it would be advantageous to establish himself as a vendor of spirits; but his bad luck led him to form a partnership with Béhor Eliézer Arié, my cousin, a notorious drunk. That association was a source of friction, disputes, injustice, humiliations, and worry; my father never spoke of it without getting overexcited, angry, often shedding tears. I was witness to all this, and I shall never forgive that rascal Béhoratchi.[11] Naturally, under these conditions, the business, which might have been productive, ended in disaster. Without telling anyone or going through the accounts or accounting for it in any way, Eliézer Arié closed the store and sent all the remaining merchandise to his home. Until this day he has never settled his account.

This business relation was the last my father had with my uncles. He was thirty-six years old and his position was not yet established. Fortunately, the regime had changed. The establishment of Bulgarian Customs near Samakov finally tore my father away from his native city and the tyranny of his brothers-in-law.

That is why the end of the year 1878 marked, for him and for me, the beginning of a new stage of existence. Better days would shine for us.

---

11. Béhoratchi is a popular form of Béhor. It was the custom in Judeo-Spanish to use popular forms for given names.

4/ Paris (1878–1881)

The dream I had had for three years, to be admitted in Paris, had been realized. For the moment, I was free from want and had a secure position for the future. At the time, I imagined that position brilliant; since M. Nissim had begun with a salary of three thousand francs, I believed that was the rule for all beginning teachers.

During my stay at the school, I lived perfectly happy and did not understand why my comrades complained about the rules of the institution, the food, the uniform, the little obsessions of the director, Marx. Marx was severe, of course, but I had been raised in a school that was far more severe. The food was mediocre? I had never had such good food. And so it was with everything else. Thus I became sincerely attached to the institution, to M. Marx, and truly felt gratitude toward the Alliance. It was all the more natural, then, that the director, professors, and more than one member of the Central Committee showed kindness toward me. I was the only one who was invited to the director's table on Saturday afternoons.

The relations among the students were agreeable. I must say in praise of the institution that morals were absolutely excellent, that I never heard an equivocal word there, and that our young people were studious, honest, and profoundly innocent.

The number of students at the school varied between twenty-two and twenty-six. Let me recall my comrades: Jacob Benchimol, Loria, Loupo, Béhar, Nabon, Fresco, Astruc, Carmona, David Arié, Ribbi, Bondy, Benveniste, Hazan, and Dalmédico, all older than I; Alphandary, Chéni, Nar, Haym, and Bassat, comrades in the same class as I; and those younger, Tchiprout, D. Lévy, J. Niégo, S. and J. Danon, Sabah, Navon, Taourel, Cohen, and others I do not remember.

The school regime was much more rigorous at that time than it is today. We were never allowed to go out on our own. But when we went out on Saturday or Sunday afternoon, we took advantage of the opportunity to slip away and catch a theater matinee. The school sent us to the theater once every two months at M. Goldschmidt's expense. The school also paid for the two stamps per month used to write to our parents. I had very little money in Paris. In three years, I received only fifty francs from my uncle Nahim and fifty francs from my father. I did not feel any need to have more money.

M. Sacki Kann was the school inspector. He came there often and was very interested in the students. We took turns being his guests on Saturday. He was in correspondence with most of the students who had left. The other members of the committee often came to see us and we also visited them during the high holidays. Thus, I had the opportunity to know well MM. Leven, Goldschmidt, Veneziani, Erlanger,[1] Rosenfeld,[2] etc.

After two years of study, I took the exam for the elementary certificate, which I passed with great success. During my third year, I was the head instructor and replaced the director when he was out of Paris. My duties brought me nothing but trouble because of the jealousy of my comrades, but I could not refuse to exercise them.

At the end of the third year, the Alliance needed new staff, and it was decided that my class would graduate. I was designated for the post of director in Ortakeuy[3]—Constantinople. And as chance would have it, the same five students who had made the trip to Paris in 1878 made the return trip together to Constantinople in 1881.

The journey on a Fraissinet boat lasted thirteen days. We stopped over in Genoa, Naples, Piraeus, Volos, and Salonika. In Constantinople, my uncle Nahim and my aunt Rachel received me with eagerness. I did no more than pass through the capital and left for Samakov, where my parents were in a hurry to see me again after four years of separation.

In Samakov, I found only my mother: two years earlier, my father had established himself as a commission agent in Vacarel, a village on the border between Bulgaria and Eastern Rumelia.[4] He was earning a good living and even saved a bit of money each year. My mother, who had given birth to my sister Sultana in 1879, remained in Samakov. When I arrived, my mother made a gift of the *séfer-tora*,[5] which she had promised to do the day the Russians entered the city, should we escape that

---

1. Michel Erlanger was a member of the Central Committee of the Alliance.
2. Jules Rosenfeld was a member of the Central Committee of the Alliance.
3. Ortakeuy (Ortaköy), a suburb of Istanbul on the European side of the Bosphorus.
4. Eastern Rumelia, a region in southern Bulgaria, was established as an autonomous province under Ottoman suzerainty in 1878 and was reunited with Bulgaria in 1885.
5. The *sefer-torah* (Hebrew, "the Book of the Torah") is a roll of parchment containing the Pentateuch written by hand. Making a gift of such a book to the synagogue is considered an important act of charity.

event unharmed. I was saddened to think that when there was a little happiness in the family, my father could not participate in it, and my eyes often filled with involuntary tears.

With my mother and Sultana, I went to Vacarel, where I found my father living in a peasant room with a clay floor. The lodging was poor but my father looked happy. He was freed from material preoccupations. He was to remain in Vacarel until 1885. My mother joined him permanently after marrying off Oro in 1882 to Nissim Joseph, called Yachar. Rosa and Elia were left behind with my uncle Samuel so that they could go to school. My parents later recalled with pleasure their memories of Vacarel, for they lived there happily. Business got better and better; my father's savings grew from month to month; everyone was healthy; there were no more worries. What more was needed?

I remained only three days in Vacarel and continued my journey to Constantinople, where I was expected in Ortakeuy. My father, who in some sense had caught only a glimpse of me, cried as he said good-bye; I promised him we would not remain separated for long.

I arrived in Constantinople in November 1881 and began my duties on the seventh of that month.

5/ Constantinople (1881–1885)

I n Constantinople I directed a small school for boys in Ortakeuy, founded by some notables from the neighborhood. A small school for girls was connected to it and directed by Mlle Rachel Lévy, who is today Mme Carmona. My colleague and I each received a salary of fifteen hundred francs. We had been placed under the supervision of M. Félix Bloch: his intermittent supervision did not weigh heavily upon us. In fact, M. Bloch soon became my friend, or rather, I became his favorite and was often one of the guests at his table on Saturday.

The premises the schools occupied were extremely run down: at the entrance, there was a hall that smelled of the toilet, which was in a cellar; on the mezzanine, there was a servant's chamber and the refectory; on the second floor, four rooms for the boys school; and above that, three rooms for the girls school, and a small room where I lived. The schoolyard was large and well ventilated. My room looked out on the yard.

The servant did my cooking, which was not complicated: a cup of milk and bread in the morning; a noon meal, often grilled fish; and a cup of curds in the evening. This diet continued for three years, and I found it adequate. But I tolerated it only because I spent merely a part of my time at Ortakeuy. Here is how I arranged my existence.

My uncle Nahim, who lived in Galata on Yazidji Street, had hired me to give lessons twice a week to my cousins Elise and Sara. I gave these lessons Tuesday evenings and Friday afternoons. As a result, I was in Galata from Friday evening until Sunday morning and on Tuesday evening. That was when I had something to eat and relaxed in town with my cousins Léon and, especially, Nissim. When I returned to Ortakeuy, I closed myself up in the school and rarely went out. Once a month, on a Monday evening, I went to have dinner and stay the night with M. Chalom Elia Cohen, my future father-in-law, whose cordial welcome drew me there. Apart from his family, I did not visit any Jews in Ortakeuy.

At home, I worked every evening until midnight. I studied German, which I was to set aside and take up again several times. I established relationships with the family of M. Koch, a German horticulturist, in order to have the opportunity to speak that language. Through the Kochs, I established a relationship with the Lalès family, who gave very jolly parties, and with a few Armenian notables. I also spent a great deal of time with Nedjib Pasha, division general, who presided over our annual balls, given on behalf of the school, and Monsignor Joseph, the Bulgarian exarch, who resided in Ortakeuy.

The first two years of my stay in Ortakeuy were no doubt the happiest of my life. I was young, healthy, and cheerful by nature; what I was earning was ample for me. In Ortakeuy, in addition to my work, I had the company of my colleague, Mlle Rachel Lévy, who was extremely pleasant. We were very fond of each other and would have married, were it not for the fact that I was still too young and her ways, which were a bit too free, displeased me.

At that time, the Alliance staff in Constantinople was united. Apart from pedagogical meetings, for which I served as secretary, the teachers often got together for picnics in the country, parties at one home or another, and reciprocal invitations. I had a wonderful time everywhere. My life seemed like a celebration: I intensely enjoyed it and felt an unqualified happiness at being alive. The years between 1881 and 1883 remain in my memories as the most radiant time of my existence, and I never think of them without deep tenderness.

In 1883 in Ortakeuy, at the home of M. Vitali Béhar, a member of the committee, we organized an awards ceremony that was a marvelous success. At that time, Mlle Lévy left Ortakeuy to marry Elie Carmona.

The same year, during the high holidays, the marriage of my cousin Elise to Moïse Behmoiras took place. I went to Adrianople to attend the wedding, which was celebrated with great pomp.

My uncle Nahim's business had not been thriving for a long time. Baruch Cohen had withdrawn from the partnership in time, and my uncle's ruin, temporarily postponed, soon became inevitable. In July 1884 he had to give up. My uncle wanted to commit suicide; he spent his days and nights crying and bemoaning his fate. Under these circumstances, I was of great help to him. I had studied the laws pertaining to bankruptcy, in treatises on accounting. I advised my uncle, who was a French subject, to conform to the law and file a petition. We made up this petition one Saturday, at night in his office. On Sunday, we went to see the lawyer Mizzi, whom we charged with the affair. On Monday morning, the petition was filed. I took my uncle to Kadiköy[1] to get him

---

1. Kadiköy, suburb on the Asian coast of Istanbul.

away from his screaming creditors, which included several Turkish women, and I remained with him for several days. The bankruptcy took its course and ended in a certificate. The creditors received 20 percent of their money. This poor good man never recovered from his fall.

Beginning at that moment, the charm of Constantinople began to diminish for me. With Elise married, I stopped giving lessons; my uncle readjusted my salary to one Turkish pound per month and deducted from what he owed me the twenty Ltq. he had lent me in 1878 for my trip to Paris. From that time on, I had scruples about asking for my aunt's hospitality and I no longer went to spend every Saturday at Galata. In Ortakeuy, Mlle Lévy had been replaced by Mlle Léa Cazès, with whom I did not get along. Finally, my aunt closed down her home and went to live in Samakov with my uncle Samuel. From then on, I no longer had any ties to Galata.

During the year 1884, my brother Elia was sent to Constantinople to continue his education. He took my upper class with his friends Frandji, Pilosof, and Ouziel, who were quite advanced. We returned together to Samakov for the holidays. My father decided that Elia knew enough and took him with him to Vacarel to help him in his business. I thus returned to Constantinople alone.

It was not possible for me to live alone at the school and be satisfied with the frugal food, which had been adequate as long as I had resources at my uncle's. I thus convinced a friend, M. Joseph Sémach, to come settle in Ortakeuy and I took room and board with him for two Ltq. per month. But Ortakeuy without Galata was very dreary. In addition, I had already been working for three years at the Alliance and still did not have a penny in savings. The fifteen hundred francs from the first two years and the seventeen hundred from the third had been just enough for my support. For the first time the question arose in my mind: "What will my future be?" For on no account did I want to spend my youth without setting aside some money for my maturity and old age.

I spoke about this to my friend M. Félix Bloch and shared with him my intention to leave the Alliance at the end of the school year if my situation had not changed. He then entrusted me with publicity work in Constantinople, paying fifty francs per year; I became choir director at the Galata temple for two Ltq. per month; I did some tutoring in town; I organized a branch of the apprenticeship program in order to have lessons to give in the evening to the apprentices, which brought me three hundred francs per year. This intense work kept me busy for more than forty-two hours a week, but I did not feel too tired and succeeded in saving almost my entire salary.

During the winter of 1885, M. Pariente came to inspect the schools. Despite the respect he showed me, I felt that his report on the Ortakeuy school had been unfavorable. And for good reason, in fact: what result can be expected from a school of sixty students that had only three classes? Having thus begun by disliking Ortakeuy, I stopped liking my school, where my efforts had been in vain and where, in fact, an unsympathetic committee (Capuano, Rossano, and Fresco Haïm) had replaced the founding committee. At Purim[2] came the Alliance jubilee: the choir I had formed at the Galata temple where the ceremony was celebrated did not perform to anyone's liking—the *hazzan*[3] sang off-key. I resigned as head of the choir. Soon afterward, in the spring, I lost my tutoring jobs.

In the summer that followed, M. Bloch hired me as inspector in his stead for a few schools. I visited those of Kuzguncuk[4] and Daghamami[5] for boys and girls (the director was Mlle Abélès, now Mme Nabon). But the outcry raised by the teachers, who could not accept the fact that the youngest of them was their inspector, was such that M. Loeb and M. Bloch had to give up on the plan, which, if it had succeeded, would have procured me rapid advancement.

At the end of 1885, I thus found myself facing this situation: my only resources were seventeen hundred francs in salary, at a school where I was marking time; no friends in Ortakeuy (the company of M. J. Sémach was rather gloomy); in town no family, no attachments; colleagues who had been giving me the cold shoulder to a certain extent since the inspection affair; and above all, no future on the horizon. And I was over twenty years old with four years of service!

During this time, my mother had had enough of the life in Vacarel, and my father went to settle in Sofia, leaving Elia by himself to oversee the commission business in Vacarel. Elia was only fifteen years old, but he managed perfectly well at Customs. My father rented a place in the shop of a quartermaster sergeant and took care of collections. He had acquired some capital in Vacarel, about six thousand francs, and separated from his partner, Isaac David, who had until that time provided him with the funds necessary for his business.

---

2. Purim is the feast of Esther, who saved the Jews from the extermination ordered by Haman, minister of Ahasuerus.

3. *Hazzan* (*hazan*, Hebrew), "cantor."

4. Kuzguncuk, a neighborhood in Istanbul situated on the Asiatic coast.

5. Daghamami, a neighborhood bordering Kuzguncuk.

SELECTIONS FROM LETTERS
TO THE ALLIANCE CENTRAL COMMITTEE

11 January 1884

. . . This week the chief rabbi of the neighborhood died in Ortakeuy. This was the all-too-notorious Sonsino, whose fanaticism against the schools has yet to be equaled.

In him, we lost one of the most relentless adversaries of the Alliance and its work of civilization. His successor will not be much more favorable to us, but he is far from having the authority of the octogenarian, now deceased, who, until the last moment, repeated to whoever would listen that the words "school" and "abomination" were synonymous.

On Sunday 6 January, everyone in Ortakeuy and a good portion of the Jews of Constantinople came together in the synagogue where the casket of the deceased had been placed. A rabbi, whom the dying man had taken care to designate three days before his death, rose to the podium and began the funeral oration. A summary of it follows.

After an exordium in Hebrew, which it would be pointless to evaluate, he began more or less this way: "Today, (the literal) Constantinople has fallen, the light has been extinguished in Israel, the crown taken from our heads, etc., etc."; endless jeremiads. Then he arrived at the main point of his speech: "He is no longer, alas! he who so abhorred all schools, where the law is forgotten, where students learn so many things contrary to Judaism. Yes, schools are abominations; yes, it is they that are attracting so much misfortune to us; it is because of them that an entire neighborhood was destroyed, that the books of the law fell prey to flames. Why, then, has the wind made so many boatloads of Jewish fishermen capsize recently? Is it not to expiate these crimes, to punish us for founding schools, that smoke has just asphyxiated twenty young children, twenty innocents? Sleep in peace, O holy man, who kept on your breast as a precious amulet the promise signed by the Camondos and the Carmonas,[6] by which they committed themselves not to open any school."

This worthy orator found nothing else to say in praise of the deceased. It is true that nothing else could have painted him with more truth.

---

6. This is an allusion to a conflict between reformers and conservatives over the founding of the first Jewish school on the European model in Istanbul in 1854. It ended with a compromise between the two camps in 1859. In the reformers' camp, there were notables such as Abraham de Camondo and Hezkia and David Carmona. See Rodrigue, *French Jews, Turkish Jews,* 47.

It is sad to have to note such hatred of all progress, such a war against all civilization, preached before such a dense crowd that said not a word, that by its silence seemed to approve to a certain degree these ideas for a return to the good old days. It is true, however, that protests after the fact by a few young men did come to moderate what was distressing in that speech. Everyone blamed His Eminence the *caïmacam effendi*[7] because he did not make this zealous orator step down from the podium. How could he not silence a man who has the cynicism to excommunicate all those who, in the future, have the misfortune of touching their beards, if only with scissors! (That was also in the funeral oration.) Why was there not a man courageous enough to say to a few stupid people in tears: "Today we found twenty-two property titles belonging to the neighborhood—your holy man pocketed the rent. Wait until he is buried and we will show you the Turkish bond titles found at his home, which came from his sale of untransferable property." There was so much to say!

But it is not up to me to judge Rabbi Sonsino.

What I want to bring out is the state of mind, or at least the state of the majority of minds in Constantinople. This circumstance gives a sense of what remains for us to do to uproot prejudice, which will not disappear for a long time yet. Our efforts may do a great deal, but time will do even more. . . .

Archives of the AIU, Turquie XXXVI.E.

7. *Caïmacam* (*kaymakam*, Turkish), "locum tenens" performing the duties of chief rabbi. At that time, this post was held by Moshe Halevi, who kept it from 1873 to 1908. *Effendi* (*efendi*, Turkish), "sir."

6/ Sofia, in Business (1885–1887)

During the high holy days of 1885, I came to Sofia to spend the vacation with my parents, then went to Samakov to see my sister Oro. I found myself in that city when, on the 6/18 September, the eve of Kippour,[1] the revolution broke out and united Eastern Rumelia to Bulgaria. A general mobilization took place, the Turkish border was closed from one end to the other, all the talk was of war with Turkey, and everyone was preparing for it with feverish activity. Business stopped cold, and since the two parts of Bulgaria had been reunited, the Vacarel Customs no longer had any reason for existence. It was eliminated and the problem of existence was once more raised for our family. But for the moment, everyone was thinking only of the war. There was a run for the border, the gendarmerie was forcibly detaining passersby. I had no desire to take up arms.

After having maturely examined the situation before us, my father and I resolved to send in my resignation to the Alliance, since my work in Constantinople no longer brought in any money, and in Sofia I was assured of room and board. Nonetheless, until peace and quiet was reestablished, I was to wait out the events in Constantinople. These events, in fact, grew more complicated: Serbia had just declared war on Bulgaria.

I had a French passport, which I was able to obtain thanks to the embassy recommendation, at the request of the regional committee of Constantinople; I thus left Sofia in the beginning of November to go to Constantinople via Lom, Ruschuk, and Varna. My traveling companions were Isaac David, scared to death like me, and Matché Melamed. The trip to Lom, on the route along the border, was stirring: salvoes of cannon and rifle fire succeeded one another; along the way, we came across large convoys of cattle cars hauling munitions. Consternation and despair were on every face. We did not exchange a word. We slept in Klissura, just before Berkovitza, in an inn where the wine was excellent. Thanks

---

1. Yom Kippur (Hebrew) is the Day of Atonement and is celebrated by fasting and prayers on the tenth day of Tishri (see also chap. 1, n. 17).

to Melamed, who was a joyful companion, it had its effect and we spent the night in merriment.

The next day we were in Lom, where I saw the Danube for the first time. We embarked on the boat *Orient,* which left us off in Ruschuk [Ruse]. We merely passed through that city and arrived in Varna, where we were the guests of a good family, the Cohens. Again thanks to Melamed, we spent delicious days in Varna and no less delicious evenings, where all we did was sing and drink.

Once arrived in Constantinople, I went to stay in a modest inn on Voïvode Street in Galata, and took my meals in a little Jewish restaurant. But the weeks went by and the border remained closed. I resolved to take advantage of my forced vacation to learn German properly and, with this goal in mind, took a room with M. Kralovitz. I began to be sorry I had handed in my resignation under these circumstances, but the die was cast and I did not want to back down. The weeks of waiting turned into months, and the little savings I had accumulated the preceding year melted away before my eyes. I took measures to enter the Régie[2] as an employee, without success. In my panic and naïveté I sent a plea to the sultan asking to be allowed to return to Europe to continue my studies. Of course, I received no response. I tried journalism and worked for *La Turquie,*[3] but without success, for journalism is a difficult trade that demands a long apprenticeship.

Thus I pined away the entire winter in waiting and inaction. Finally, in the spring, the border was opened, and I returned to Bulgaria. I stopped in Tatar-Pazardzhik [Tatar-Bazardjik], where the Vacarel Customs had been relocated. Joseph Ouziel and Jacob Manoah were already established there as commission agents. I signed a partnership agreement with them, with capital of 175 Ltq., of which 50 was provided by us, 50 by Ouziel, and 75 by Manoah. We had to borrow the 50 Ltq. from M. Maïr Alcalay of Samakov, since my father had just used almost all his money to purchase a house on Milin-Kamik Street, also in the Makedonia neighborhood.

We had thus secured our housing and a certain income, which the Pazardzhik business would not fail to bring us. I came to Sofia full of confidence, with the firm purpose of making my fortune there. We began by renting an office near the Saint-Kral church and I wrote a large number of letters to factories, whose addresses I had got in Constantino-

2. The Régie Co-Intéressé des Tabacs of the Ottoman Empire, constituted in 1883.
3. *La Turquie* (1866–[95]) was a political, commercial, and literary newspaper in the French language.

ple. In them, I offered to represent the firms in Bulgaria. Many refused, but many accepted as well. Among that number, there were several that were quite serious. I represented the New York and the Bottin of Paris. The business was well under way, but to succeed, a certain experience and some contacts were necessary. As a recent arrival, I had neither. I was counting on my father's possessing them. I was wrong.

Commerce is a field of knowledge one acquires primarily through practice. This field, like all things human, changes according to need. The salesman, and especially the commission agent, must above all else have a mind open to innovation. He must, in addition, possess a cheerful, easygoing, persistent, and patient character. A small dose of cunning, combined with the senses of a gunner, is also indispensable. Contacts are made in society: he must therefore go out into the world, be on the lookout, create friendships, make people care about him. Too much education is damaging rather than useful. Engrossing readings occupy the mind with unreal things, when it ought to be occupied with immediate contingencies.

Did my father and I possess those qualities? Obviously not. For myself, I had until then seen the world only through books. Neither the Ecole Orientale nor the teaching profession could have introduced me to the world of business. In addition, my four years of leadership in Ortakeuy had accustomed me to count on a certain consideration, which is generally not granted in commerce. I considered it humiliating to solicit orders and even more humiliating to be refused. And I was all the more sensitive to these mortifications in that the Bulgarians are not known for their refined manners. I thus confined myself to writing from the office when I should have chased after my clientele, as I have since learned one does.

It was my father who went on errands. The poor man was working as best he could and it was he who procured the few orders we received. But he too lacked many of the qualities needed to succeed, as one can see by the sketch of the commission agent given above. Thus the commissions from Europe hardly worked at all and two years later, the New York, for which we had generated no business at all, withdrew its representation and gave it to G. Georgoff, who was to find it a gold mine.

Worries once more overtook us. And when it came to marrying off Rosa, who was engaged to Tchelebon Madjar, we thrashed out the question whether we would have to sell the house to pay for her dowry (one thousand francs) and the trousseau. Fortunately, we were able to find a way out without resorting to that.

During the summer of 1886, the exchange rate of gold for silver was very high, and since it was not the same in every city, productive operations could be carried out between Sofia and the provinces. For this purpose, I entered into relations with M. Benjamin Rodrigue of Burgas, whom I had known in Constantinople. That gave me the idea of creating a partnership in Burgas similar to the one we had in Pazardzhik. I thus went to Burgas and concluded the matter. The circulars were sent out on 10 Ab 5646.[4] Elia moved to Burgas.

When I returned from this trip, I sent the Alliance a report on the communities in the cities I had passed through, which was published in the *Bulletin*.[5] In fact, I had maintained excellent relations with the Alliance, since I had a premonition that one day I would need to turn to it.

The Burgas business netted us some profits. It might have worked better if Benjamin Rodrigue and Elia had gotten along well. But it seems there was a certain incompatibility of temperament between them. Less than a year later, Rodrigue asked that Elia be called back, and the partnership was dissolved.

Pazardzhik and Burgas gave us our means of existence, but we were doing almost nothing in Sofia. Inaction weighed upon us and our mood grew more sour. I often left by myself to take interminable walks around the city to drown my sorrows. My health began to deteriorate and I lost—forever—the stoutness and good color I had had in Constantinople.

During the winter of 1886–87 I returned to Constantinople to attempt to establish some new relations. In Mustapha Pacha[6] I had three days of quarantine under the worst conditions of hygiene and sanitation, sleeping in communal rooms with between ten and thirty travelers from all over. But I was homesick for Constantinople and thought I would find a way out of our situation there.

In the matter of commerce, I did very little: I established relations with a certain Méchoulam for the importation of salted fish and fruit and with the Menassé firm for paper; and I believe that was all.

But during this trip an important event began to take shape. In Ortakeuy, I always went to see M. Chalom Cohen, whom I was fond of. During my stay in the capital, Rébecca, my future sister-in-law, became engaged to a son of M. Rossano. (This engagement was later broken.) The dancing party organized for the occasion was quite jolly. I danced almost exclusively with the second daughter in the family, Rachel, and from that evening on her grandmother predicted she would become my

4. Wednesday, 11 August 1886.
5. *Bulletin Semestriel de l'Alliance Israélite Universelle* (1860/65–1913).
6. Mustapha Pacha, city on the Bulgarian-Turkish border.

wife. She was not mistaken. The idea took hold in the Cohen family to take me as a son-in-law. I guessed their intentions but attached no importance to them: did my position allow me to think about marriage?

When I returned to Sofia via Burgas, business became more and more scarce. The railway station was almost finished, the Vienna–Constantinople line linked up, and Customs was established in Sofia itself. The Pazardzhik company was dissolved by force of circumstances. We formed another in Philippopolis, where Elia, called back from Burgas, was sent. In Sofia, I did some tutoring and contributed to the French part of the Stambolovist[7] newspaper *Svoboda*,[8] edited by Zacharie Stoyanoff[9] and Dimitur Pétkoff.[10] But that brought in very little money and the question of our existence once more became agonizing.

It was during that summer of 1887 that Emmanuel was born. In my father's mind, his name was an appeal to Providence, an invocation of heavenly aid. This aid was to come to us in the form of two jobs.

The Sofia school had been closed in 1885, and now the community wished once more to obtain an Alliance director. I served as intermediary between the Alliance and the committee, composed of Israël D. Lévy, Nissim Farhy, Joseph Madjar, and Joseph Machiah. When all the conditions of the Central Committee had been accepted, I announced my candidacy as director of that school and asked for three thousand francs in salary. On 15 November 1887, the Alliance informed me that my request had been approved and I immediately assumed those duties.

We could finally breathe easy! Even if my father no longer worked, the life of the family was ensured. From that moment on, I was forever freed from any material preoccupations and could save a bit of money each year. I still had many struggles to endure, a thousand difficulties in my career, but they were inherent in the teaching profession. The ques-

7. "Stambolovist" refers to the National Liberal party of Stefan Stambolov (1854–95), which was formed to fight Russia and restore Bulgaria to the Bulgarians. Stambolov was a Bulgarian politician who favored the return of Alexander of Battenberg after the 1886 insurrection and who preserved the regency when he abdicated. Having contributed to the election of Ferdinand of Saxe-Coburg-Gotha as prince of Bulgaria (1887), Stambolov stayed in power until 1894.

8. *Svoboda* (Freedom) was a journal that appeared between 1886 and 1899. It then took the name *Nov Vek* (New century), reappearing between 1918 and 1920.

9. Zacharie Stoyanoff (1850–89) was a revolutionary, politician, writer, and journalist.

10. Dimitur Pétkoff (1858–1907) was a politician and journalist; he was mayor of Sofia under Stambolov (1887–93), president of the National Assembly (1892–93), minister of public works (1893–94), and contributor to and editor of numerous journals.

tion of money no longer existed for me, ever again. I was twenty-four years old at the time.

All things considered, my resignation was a good thing for me: two years outside the service had procured me a raise of thirteen hundred francs, which put me ahead of nine-tenths of the teachers with more seniority than I, and I remained ahead of them until the end of my career.

For his part, my father gave up on the commission business and occupied himself with investing money for M. Maïr Alcalay.

As for Elia, in 1890, after two years in Philippopolis, he was hired as an employee at the Romanian insurance company Nationala. He owed this job to M. Baruch and began at 120 francs per month. Since then, he has had a good career in that branch of commerce.

And that is how he and I learned by experience that one cannot improvise being a salesman. That occupation, like all trades, requires an apprenticeship, which it is infinitely more useful to begin sooner rather than later.

That is the moral of the two years of my life I have just traced.

SELECTIONS FROM LETTERS
TO THE ALLIANCE CENTRAL COMMITTEE

29 September 1885

... I am writing to inform you that a serious difficulty prevents me from leaving Sofia for Constantinople.

You may know that I am a native of Samakov, and therefore of Bulgarian nationality. My name, however, is not listed on the civil registry because my parents did not put me down at the time of the creation of the Principality in 1878; at that time, I was in Constantinople, about to leave for Paris.

When I returned to the East and wanted to go to Bulgaria, I needed a passport: I got it in Constantinople for a few piasters. Also in that year, I got the Turkish passport I now have and that I did not have occasion to show when I arrived.

But then the troubles erupted. All eligible men between eighteen and forty years old were drafted, some into the active army, others into the militia. Obviously, I was not required to do military service, since my name is not on the registries; but if I presented my passport with its visa from the Bulgarian authorities, I would run the risk of being immediately incorporated into the army, given that this passport bears the unfortunate words "native of Samakov" in Turkish.

In addition, I do not think it prudent to attempt to cross the border without having a proper passport, since at the present time, the relevant laws are being applied with the greatest rigor. In fact, if an effort of this kind did not succeed, it would compromise the name of the Alliance, since I am one of its teachers, and would destroy, or at least unnecessarily interrupt, my career.

As you see, my situation is rather awkward, and I beg the Central Committee to examine it closely and give me its instructions.

In my humble opinion, if you will allow me to offer it, I believe that trying to leave Bulgaria at this moment would be a big gamble, which would best be avoided. Would it not be better to await the return of calmer times, the suspending of the state of siege in which we live, the disbanding of the army?

But it is impossible to foresee when order will be established in Bulgaria, and moreover, our classes begin very soon. Under these circumstances, I believe the best thing would perhaps be to have me temporarily replaced in Ortakeuy by one of my colleagues and to entrust to me, also temporarily, a job of some sort in one of your schools in Bulgaria. Everything will return to normal as soon as I can leave Bulgarian territory without danger for my future and with the authorization of the Central Committee.

In any case, I will wait here for the instructions you are kind enough to give me. Let me remind you of my address: Gabriel Arié, c/o Nissim Arié, Sofia.

Having learned that the privacy of correspondence is not very scrupulously respected, I am sending this letter through Mme Marx. . . .

Archives of the AIU, Turquie XXXVI.E.

15 November 1885

. . . I am writing to submit my resignation as Alliance teacher.

The reasons for this decision are related purely to my future. During my stay in Sofia, I have become convinced that I can earn not less than four thousand francs per year in commerce, starting immediately. Considering that I have a duty to my family and myself as well as to the Alliance and, in addition, not wishing to ask the committee to make any exception whatever in my favor regarding the established regulations (an exception that, in fact, I know I have not earned), I have decided to make this request of you and I dare hope you will grant it.

In asking for authorization to leave your service, I must, Mr. President, thank you and the Central Committee for the kindness you were good enough to show me for the four years I was able to devote to the work of the

Alliance. I shall always remember the benefits I owe you and shall make it my ambition to prove to you in the future that I am not ungrateful. Wherever I find myself, the interests of the Alliance will find in me a zealous defender. I will be happy if in the future you are kind enough to turn to me as to your former and grateful student and teacher. . . .

Archives of the AIU, Turquie XXXVI.E.

11 December 1885

. . . *Ten-Year Commitment.* You ask me what I think of the ten-year commitment that my parents or I supposedly made to you. I will take the liberty of observing that neither I nor my parents were able to make such a commitment, given that the regulations on the matter did not exist or, at least, had not yet been issued.

But supposing that I find myself morally committed by those regulations, issued subsequent to my entrance at the school, and to my entry into service, I believe the reimbursement of education costs would be adequate to free me from any promise.

Education Costs. You fix these at eight thousand francs. I believe this figure is a bit inflated, given that I did not stay in Paris for four years but for less than three years. I would thus be very obliged to you to calculate exactly the sum of my debt and, taking into account my four years of service, let me know the sum I should reimburse the Alliance. Obviously, I cannot hope to pay off that debt immediately upon entering my new career, but I can assure you that I will on my honor pay you what I owe as soon as that is possible and my means allow it. . . .

Archives of the AIU, Turquie XXXVI.E.

24 September 1886

. . . I returned a few days ago to Sofia and found your letter of 1 July here, to which I hasten to respond.

During my trip in Eastern Rumelia, I had the opportunity to visit most of the Jewish communities of that province. In Philippopolis in particular, I administered the examination of the students at the girls school and attended part of the examination at the boys school. The directors of these institutions will have spoken to you of the results of these examinations.

Here are some details on communities that probably have not had frequent relations with the Alliance.

Burgas: Situated at the extremity of the gulf of that name, on the Black Sea, Burgas is a pretty little town of four thousand residents, most of Greek ethnicity. The salt marshes near the town make the climate unhealthy, and without the winds from the north that blow regularly every day from noon until sunset, the town would be uninhabitable, or so I have been told.

Burgas is destined for a great commercial future: as soon as a railroad links it to Yamboli, or as soon as Rumelia is separated from Constantinople by customs barriers, Burgas will become the principal warehouse for southern and northern Bulgaria. This also means that the Jewish community of that city is destined to grow rapidly.

The first Jewish family settled there only in 1879. Today, there are more than thirty Jewish families from Karnabad and Yamboli. The community does not yet possess a temple, but last year it acquired a very good site, where the *talmud-tora*[11] will also be located.

The notables of the city, the leading lights of the place, are the Presentes, one of the richest Jewish families in Turkey. It was in the home of M. Presente—a true palace—that the prince of Bulgaria stayed when he passed through Burgas last May.

The community would be happy to inaugurate the new school site by opening a school; it would even be disposed to pay the Alliance the salary for a teacher, since money is not lacking here. What is lacking is unity. The proverb "Wherever there are two Poles there are three parties" is unfortunately true for our coreligionists in the East. It is the greatest obstacle opposed to their moral progress.

The president of the community, M. Presente, gave me the responsibility of proposing some capable instructor to him, someone from the Alliance schools, whom the community will commit to paying eighty francs per month. Having found no good instructor in either Philippopolis or Tatar-Pazardzhik, I will await M. Benveniste's return to Samakov to write him on this matter.

Karnabad: Placed midway between Yamboli and Burgas, Karnabad is a city in decline, though the annual fair held there still gives it a bit of life. There are about a hundred Jewish families there. The community is too poor to buy a schoolhouse. During the journey of Prince Alexander[12] in Rumelia, M. Samuel Presente of Burgas asked His Highness for pecuniary aid for the purchase of a schoolhouse in Karnabad. The prince, who was the guest of M. Presente, promised him that on his return to Sofia he would not fail to look into the matter. In fact, only a few days before the coup d'état of 21 August, the bailiff of Karnabad came to inquire about the situation of the Jewish

11. The *talmud-torah* (Hebrew) was a religious elementary school (see *heder, meldar,* chap. 1, n. 5).

12. Alexander I of Battenberg was prince of Bulgaria (1879–86).

community and to get an estimate for the construction of a school. A report was sent by him to the ministry in Sofia.

It is pointless to add that this report did not leave the ministerial cubby-holes, where it will probably remain until the blessed day when the revolutions leave the Bulgarians time to attend somewhat to their affairs.

In the meantime, the community of Karnabad will have to wait, and the Jewish children will continue to frequent their *talmud-tora,* which resembles all the *talmud-toras* in the East.

Aïthos (in modern Greek *Aethos,* eagle) or, in the vernacular, *Aïdos,* between Karnabad and Burgas, is a beautiful little town, possessing a good number of hot springs in the area, though no one has yet thought to analyze their waters. Aïthos has only about twenty Jewish families, and it is hardly probable that the Jewish population of that city will grow, given the proximity of Burgas, whose chances for the future are greater than any other city in the region.

Yamboli: I visited the school of that city, which will be one of the most beautiful constructions of Yamboli as soon as they manage to buy it. About which we must not despair "if God gives us life and the Alliance gives us money," as certain members of that community say.

Stanimaka, twenty kilometers from Philippopolis, is one of the richest cities of Eastern Rumelia because of the enormous expanse of vineyards, whose annual production reaches several million hectoliters of wine. The Jewish community of that city is small and very poor, its only revenue coming from the "seal." Here is what is meant by that. You know that the Jews of the East will under no circumstances buy wine produced by a Christian; they consider it a crime to taste that wine, which is *yaïn nessech.*[13] Jewish wine merchants are thus obliged to buy wine only in barrels bearing the seal of the community of the place; this seal is sufficient proof for the purchaser that the wine contained in the barrel was produced by a Jew. In Stanimaka, however, there is not a Jew who possesses an acre of land, and the Greeks, for a fee, have the seal of the Jewish community placed on the barrels. Owing to this procedure, to which the Jews lend themselves with a complacency unworthy of praise, the wine of Christians becomes potable for all Jews, regardless of their degree of piety. There is not a Jew in the East who is unaware of the crudeness of this trick, and yet all would have scruples about buying wine from a Christian! For that is how difficult it is to uproot a prejudice.

Despite its revenue from the "seal," the community of Stanimaka has not yet been able to finish the construction of its temple/school. When money is

---

13. *Yaïn nessech (yein nesekh,* Hebrew), "wine of libation."

lacking, the name of the Alliance is often pronounced. The Alliance would certainly have a great deal to do if it had to finish the constructions that communities almost everywhere have begun without preliminary studies, without securing the necessary funds, and with a confidence in the future that has no equal except in Muslim insouciance.

Tatar-Pazardzhik: The school committee of that city appeared entirely disorganized to me, with no kind of influence; if I am to believe my evaluations, the school in that city might very well soon encounter grave crises that could compromise its future. I believe the collaboration of MM. Varon and Moscona would be precious for M. Lévy, and that nothing serious and long-lasting will come about in Pazardzhik without the cooperation of those two men. It is the girls school that appeared to me to have the most to suffer from the incompetence of the current committee.

In all the schools I had the opportunity to visit, my former colleagues were kind enough to allow me to spend a few hours in their classes, which was very agreeable to me, and for which I am profoundly grateful to them. . . .

Archives of the AIU, Bulgarie XXII.E.153a.

7/ The School in Sofia (1887–1893)

I n November 1887, the draft board met in Sofia. The very day I came to the school, having been assigned there by the school committee, a gendarme came while I was taking the "owner's tour" of the classrooms and invited me to appear before the board. Obviously, I had been denounced by an enemy—still unknown—who was jealous to see me occupy a post in the public eye. But my decision was immediately made: I would do my military service and join the Alliance.

Escorted before the draft board, I was examined by the doctor and found qualified for service. I would have been drafted were it not for my myopia, which completely liberated me. A special decree *(prikaz)* declared that liberation, and the First Military District of Sofia delivered the necessary certificate to me on 14 October 1891. I still have the two documents among my papers.

The first plot hatched against me had thus failed, much to the vexation of its author.

At the time, the school in Sofia had five hundred students, divided into eight or ten classes. The staff, apart from the director, consisted of two teachers of Bulgarian, one instructor of French (Haïm Tagger, who has since become a distinguished businessman), and a half-dozen rabbis. In accordance with the Alliance, all secular teaching was to be given in Bulgarian. Even I studied and soon taught that language. The school committee was responsible for the financial management of the school. Little by little the teaching was reorganized, the level of studies raised, and at the end of the year, a very successful school celebration showed the progress that had been made.

Having improved the school, the community felt the need to put an enlightened rabbi at its head, one trained in a seminary in Europe. They chose Dr. Dankovitz,[1] rabbi in Strakoniz.[2] He was a man of about fifty, talkative, clumsy, clever rather than intelligent, incapable of action, preoccupied above all with keeping his job. I had known him through the

---

1. Shimeon Dankovitz was chief rabbi of Bulgaria between 1889 and 1891.
2. Strakoniz, city in Bohemia.

Alliance before he came to Sofia and I opposed his election. Naturally, Dankovitz did not forgive me that attitude later and tried to create all sorts of difficulties for me.

He was not the only one who opposed me. Among the adversaries who stood in my way, I will cite, in the first place, the entire Tagger family, namely, the late Mardochée and his brother Haïm, the late Conorté, Ezra my cousin, who played a preponderant role in 1893, and finally Nissim Farhy and Abraham Davitchon Lévy.

The first year I spent as director in Sofia passed without incident. Since my mother had suffered from rheumatism during the winter, my father, mother, and I went to spend the vacations of 1888 at the sulfurous waters of Bania, near Dubnitza. There, I used my leisure time to write a few notes about the past of our family. I later burned that manuscript.

Returning to Sofia, I began to think seriously about getting married. Since everyone must end up doing so one day, better sooner than later, I thought: you then have the chance to raise at least the eldest of your children and establish them in business, which ensures the future of the younger ones if you then have to leave them. And experience has proven that reasoning correct, since today, at forty-four, I have the satisfaction of having a son of seventeen who is apprenticed in business and who will eventually be able to replace me.

Two months later, through the intervention of M. Matchouno, the father-in-law of my uncle Nahim, I received a proposal to become engaged to Rachel, the daughter of my old friend from Ortakeuy, M. Chalom Cohen. Out of respect for proprieties, I awaited the arrival in Sofia of M. Isidore Loeb, then on an inspection tour, and asked his advice. M. Loeb approved of my plan and I telegraphed my acceptance to Constantinople.

M. Loeb's inspection left an excellent impression on him, which was very useful to me in my subsequent career.

During M. Loeb's stay in Sofia, Mlle Sara Ungar, whom the Alliance had sent to direct the girls school, arrived in that city.

On the evening of 31 December 1888, a ceremony took place at my home for the engagement *kinian*.[3] It was very successful, and when the

---

3. *Kinian* (Hebrew), "acquisition." On the evening of a formal engagement, it was the custom to draft a document containing conditions for the future marriage, which were first articulated orally before witnesses. Before a rabbi, the affianced couple formally committed themselves to respect these conditions, and both of them also promised to pay a certain sum in the case of a broken engagement. This ceremony, which took place in the home of the bride-to-be, bore the name *kinian*.

guests left around midnight I began my first letter to my fiancée, which was finished in the first moments of 1889.

My destiny had thus been decided a bit hastily. Here, as everywhere, chance played a preponderant role. A month later, the engagement would not have come about. Here is the reason.

Mlle Ungar, my new colleague, at the time thirty-nine years old, is one of the most distinguished, intelligent, and educated women I have ever known. Very quickly we established a good and solid friendship and were not long in speaking of what might have been, had we met a few weeks earlier. What might have been I know very well: we could not have gotten married, given the difference in age, but we would probably have remained single and lived together. In any case, we have maintained the keenest and most sincere of affections for each other, and Rachel, from whom I hid nothing, is a party to the relationship.

The winter passed for me the most agreeably in the world. During the spring vacation, I went to Constantinople to pay a visit to my fiancée. Those who knew me there found me very changed, and no one met me without immediately making this observation: "Look how thin you've become!" In any case, I had become extremely nervous and I remember I jumped at Rachel for trifles, which must have astonished her a great deal.

We fixed the wedding for the next vacation, and in the meantime, I spent my time adding a room onto our home, built at my own cost. In July, I returned to Constantinople to acquire the trousseau myself, as had been arranged. What a bother! All those errands in all those stores— what irritation! I do not advise any young bridegroom to take that route.

During this time, my father and mother had gone to Kyustendil for the hot baths. They came back to Constantinople for my wedding and were the guests of my uncle Nahim, who lived in Makrikeuy[4] because of my aunt, whose health was already compromised.

The wedding took place on 11 August 1889 (14 Av 5649) at the Jewish temple of Galata. The procession leading the bride from Ortakeuy to Galata was magnificent. At the ceremony, in addition to my colleagues, Chief Rabbi Moïse Lévy,[5] Elia Pasha,[6] and a few other friends were in attendance. M. Félix Bloch surprised me with a speech for the occasion at the temple.

---

4. Makrikeuy (Bakirköy), suburb of Istanbul.
5. Moïse (Moshe) Halevi was the locum tenens for the chief rabbi.
6. Elia Pasha Cohen was an admiral and an oculist at the palace and at the hospital of the navy in Istanbul.

When the ceremony was over, my wife and I went to Makrikeuy, where I had rented a room in a hotel. That is where we spent the first days of our marriage. After an additional weeklong visit with my wife's parents, we left. I remember that, when it came time to leave, I was the only one to cry. I will tell you why. Our life in Sofia was dreary. That stemmed from our hereditary character. My wife's parents had a very happy life; they were effusive and very affectionate toward one another. I was thus taking a young woman from an agreeable city and a loving environment into a world that was completely new to her, where she would be deprived of every joy, and I commiserated with her fate and was deeply moved by the sacrifice she was making of her youth.

Rachel's arrival at our house was, I believe, a disillusionment for her. The modesty of our style of life, our quiet existence, must have surprised her. We went to spend part of the Jewish holidays in Samakov, where we were the guests of my uncle Samuel. We spent about ten very agreeable days there. Our honeymoon was thus spent on trips that left us with good memories.

Upon our return, when I assessed our account with my father, it happened that, of the dowry and my earlier savings, there did not remain one red centime: the construction of the room, the trousseau, a little jewelry, the trips, and the loss I had incurred over a shop bought and expropriated soon afterward had absorbed everything. It was only after my wedding day that I began to save a little.

The city of Sofia had been changing over the previous year. At the impetus of the mayor, Pétkoff, the old houses were disappearing, and boulevards, streets straight as an arrow, were being created. In this general upheaval, all the synagogues but one were demolished, and the boys school met the same fate. The [community] committee was obliged to rent a house to hold our classes, and we began to study construction plans for a new locale, on the site of one of the expropriated synagogues. We decided on a plan whose execution was to cost 100,000 francs. The community provided 90,000. That sum came from expropriated temples; you can well understand we did not obtain it without difficulty from the community. I promised to have the rest paid by the Alliance. We made short work of it, and less than a year later had a school building as there exists no parallel in the East.

I would have liked to build living quarters for the director near the school, at the Alliance's cost. Rabbi Dankovitz opposed this on the pretext that the children of the director would communicate their illnesses to the students who frequented the school. The truth is that it is the students at the school who communicate the illnesses from the city to the director's children, as I later experienced in Smyrna. But in that as in everything, Dankovitz's tactic was to combat my influence and my interests.

The disappearance of the old neighborhoods had pushed the entire poor Jewish population toward Utch-Bunar. The children of these many families also required a school. I organized one in a rented building, but later we built a school building, which cost thirty thousand francs, again taken from synagogue funds. From that time on, I had two boys schools to direct and expected to be given the responsibility for directing the girls school as well.

It was during that [spring] of 1890, on 5 June, that Sandro (Alexandre-Moïse) was born. The delivery was difficult for Rachel, but the midwife who was called in did not have to intervene. My mother-in-law came from Constantinople, as she would come to help Rachel for the birth of all my other children. My father and mother were the godfather and godmother of my eldest, and I was very happy that my first child was a boy. It seemed to me that my love for my wife grew because of it, and I told her so, which astonished her.

Mlle Ungar played an active role in our happiness. A month later, during the vacation, she took a leave and asked to be transferred. She was assigned to Adrianople and I was given responsibility for directing the girls school. On 1 January of that year I had a 300-franc raise, and since I received another 400 francs for my time at the girls school, that brought my salary to 3,700 francs.

The first months of Sandro's childhood were spent without incident. But after four months, Rachel's milk dried up and we were obliged to put the child on the bottle. That gave him continual indigestion followed by spasms, which we relieved with castor oil. He also had several bouts of bronchitis, not counting all the other childhood illnesses, which kept us on tenterhooks. It was a very bad winter for us. Our house was not hygienic, since it was situated in the lowest part of the city. The cellar under my room was full of water three-quarters of the year. It is not surprising we were all sick and that the physician, Dr. Calévitz, was a regular guest at our home.

As a diversion, I went with Rachel and Sandro to spend the Passover of 1891 in Constantinople. It was Sandro's salvation: on the advice of my wife's parents, we took on a nurse, Estréa, and eliminated the bottle. Immediately, his indigestion ended and from then on the child developed normally. One mishap, however, came along to arrest his progress:

a rather serious pneumonia. Fortunately, he recovered, but the illness probably left its mark.

This change did us all a great deal of good. We were sometimes the guests of my uncle Nahim and of my aunt Rachel, then in the last stages of consumption, to which she succumbed the next October.

After the holiday, I returned by myself to Sofia, from whence I was to go to Paris to solicit the Alliance for its contribution to the construction costs for the school. I left Sofia on 19 May, taking with me a few photographs of the plans. I was very well received by M. Loeb and the members of the committee. It was at that time that I met M. Bigart,[7] who had joined the Alliance in 1886. At my insistence, and thanks especially to M. Loeb, who had consideration for me, I obtained a subsidy of ten thousand francs.

I came back to Sofia exactly a month after leaving. Rachel came home a few days later, bringing her nurse, who remained with us all summer. By the time vacation arrived, the illnesses of the year, the trips, and the preoccupations of every kind caused by the construction of the schools had made me lose a considerable amount of weight. To rest, I went to spend a few weeks at my uncle's *tchiflik*[8] in Bania.

Physical fatigue was not the only kind to undermine my health. A veiled malevolence was turning my mother against Rachel, whose life was becoming difficult. To have peace at home, I rented a little house of my own. My mother was very happy about this, but when my father learned of it, he upbraided my mother so much, and cried with such sorrow, that his distress troubled me deeply and I gave up my plan to move.

The school year [1891–92] opened in the new building. We did not arrange a ceremony for the occasion: I find nothing so vain, so tedious, as ceremonies.

A few days later, Rabbi Dankovitz, after a dispute with the president of the community, Abraham D. Lévy, had his contract terminated and, despite his pleas, was obliged to abandon his post and return to Austria, where he lived in obscurity. I did not regret his departure. During our entire stay in Sofia, he had been a constant adversary to me, not even taking the trouble to dissimulate his negative feelings. His departure thus brought me relief and I was left in peace for more than a year.

7. Jacques Bigart (1855–1934) was secretary general of the Alliance beginning in 1892.

8. *Tchiflik* (*çiftlik*, Turkish), "farm, farmhouse."

Winter came and with it the procession of illnesses that attacked us one after the other. My father in particular was growing weaker, with his old dyspepsia growing worse, and he had trouble bearing the weight of his clothes. We resolved to send him to Vienna to be treated. He remained more than a month and was the guest of his sister Rébecca Kaïmzioglu.[9] This course of treatment did him a great deal of good and restored his health for a time.

During the same winter, I was given the responsibility by the Alliance to inspect the schools of Philippopolis. I made an unfavorable report on Loria, who never forgave me, and a favorable report on Mme Graziani, the director. The Alliance found my reports remarkable and congratulated me for them.

When I returned, as usual I went to sit on the draft board to note the level of education among the draftees. The relationships I established on that occasion made it easier to have Elia and my cousin Sabat exempted from military service. The next year I obtained Tchelebi Alcalay's exemption, not without difficulty.

Around the same period, a disagreeable piece of news came from Constantinople: my father-in-law, until that time a small banker, had suspended payments. He was to live for ten years under difficult circumstances bordering on poverty, from which he recovered thanks only to the practical intelligence of his young son Léon.

During the vacation of 1892, I went with Rachel to spend a month in Kniajevo[10] and we moved into a small house with our two children, Sandro and Sophie-Jaël, who had been born in May.

In Kniajevo, I had a serious illness, enteritis, which left me very weak.

Then came the school year of 1892–93. The Alliance sent me two assistants, David Massé and Mlle Rachel Piza. The latter, whom I was not fond of, I was to find again in Smyrna.

Since my family had grown, I sought to augment my resources: the Alliance had refused me a lodging allowance, but I obtained four hundred francs for that purpose from the school committee, whose president was the late Samuel Kiosso. In addition, I committed myself to offering eight hours of lessons per week at the German school, for sixty francs per month. Of these eight hours, four were given on Saturday morning, my only day off.

9. Rébecca Kaïmzioglu appears on the genealogical tree possessed by the family under the family name Kuyumji.

10. Kniajevo, hot springs near Sofia.

Passover arrived and brought a serious accusation of ritual murder in Vratsa.[11] Of course, the communities of Bulgaria were deeply affected and had to band together to pay the costs of defending our coreligionists. With the help of their attorney Saïloff, they were acquitted. I obtained a contribution of five thousand francs from the Alliance for that purpose.

This incident made Bulgarian Jewry feel the need to organize, to give itself a leader. A general assembly of representatives of all the communities was convened in Sofia, to deliberate both on the Vratsa affair and on the election of a chief rabbi. The meeting took place in April 1893; it was presided over by Abraham D. Lévy, at the time at the height of his power.

The congress decided to elect Chief Rabbi Grünwald.[12] A central consistory was also organized and my father was elected a member. A photograph exists of all the members of the congress. In this photograph the emaciation of my physiognomy is clearly visible.

On the very day the congress ended, Rachel left for Constantinople with Sandro and Sophie. She remained for two months. Upon her return, we decided, with the agreement of my father, that I would move into my own home. I thus rented a house on Legay Street and bought some furniture. But I was not to enjoy either.

On 29 June 1893, a ceremony I had organized took place at the school to celebrate the end of the school year. After the celebration, Abraham D. Lévy, Nissim Farhy, and Ezra Tagger invited the audience to a general assembly. Imagine my surprise in the afternoon to learn that, on the pretext of saving money, the closing of the schools had been proposed! I understood that the true goal of the promoters of this so-called reform was to get rid of me. Isaac David fought courageously on that occasion against my adversaries, but he could not prevent the decision that had been made to close the schools. On that occasion, my cousin Ezra was

11. Vratsa, a city in northwest Bulgaria. During that affair, a classic accusation of ritual murder, Yohanan Benbasat, his mother, Sarutcha, and Haïm Levi, all Jews, were charged with stabbing an eight-year-old Christian girl to death in order to use her blood in religious rituals. In the city of Vratsa there were only a few dozen Jews. The murderer, a Christian, was found: he had committed the murder solely to incite the Bulgarian population against the Jews. The Jewish defendants were acquitted after two years of harassment. This affair illustrates elements of the antisemitism that reigned in Bulgaria during the period. Contrary to Gabriel Arié's testimony, this affair took place in June 1891 and not Passover 1893; it was merely the trial that began in February 1893.

12. Moritz Grünwald was chief rabbi of Bulgaria between 1893 and 1895.

even more relentless than Lévy and Farhi. What had I done to him? Nothing: the jealousy and meanness of that family toward us was always great; on that occasion, those people proved to be ferocious.

I became so sick with worry on that account that my health troubled my parents. I was having heart palpitations. What was I going to become? I thought. Would I open a private school in Sofia? Would I wait until the community's experiment failed, as I was certain it would, and I was once more placed at the head of the school? Would I seek a place in the government schools? The minister Jivkof[13] had offered me one in the provinces. It was with these fears about the future that I spent my vacation.

That summer as well, my father and mother were obliged to go to the baths of Kyustendil. I also went there, on the pretext of inspecting the students I had placed at the Alliance's cost in a normal school in that city. I found my father gravely ill. My arrival seemed to give him new life. A few days later, he was back on his feet and we returned to Sofia.

Upon our return, I received a copy of a letter full of insinuations, sent by the Alliance, that Abraham D. Lévy and Rabbi Grunwäld had written against me. That was too much. My parents, worried about the state of my health, urged me to leave Sofia and accept a new position. Tunis and Smyrna were going to be vacant, I wrote to Paris to ask for Smyrna, and my request was welcomed.

The schools in Sofia were dismantled; M. Moreno was hired to direct the teaching of Hebrew. The attempt did not succeed, and beginning the next year, on the initiative of Isaac David, the Alliance once more sent them one of its directors, Salomon Danon, who is still there.

My preparations for departure did not take long. I sold at a loss the furniture I had bought, lost the three months' rent on the house, and took with me only our clothes and bedding. In addition, I ended all the Alliance programs except the sewing workshop, which continued to function.

The eve of my departure was unforgettable. To celebrate my departure, since leaving Sofia was a deliverance for me, we invited all our relatives from Sofia to dinner. There was Turkish music, and I can still hear the sweet and melancholy tunes that a little hunchback sang to us, accompanying himself on the violin. Alas! I did not know that was to be the last night I would spend with my father. In thinking about it, anguish still clutches at my heart! If only I had known! How relentlessly I should have clung to Sofia, whatever the cost!

13. Georgi Jivkof (1844–99) was minister of national education between 1887 and 1893.

I left on 1 November 1893 with Rachel, Sandro, and Sophie. My parents, a few friends, and Chief Rabbi Grünwald accompanied me to the train station. My father, my mother, and Emmanuel made the trip with us as far as Philippopolis, where they were to prepare Régine's trousseau. At the train station in that city, we embraced, I kissed my father's and my mother's hand, they got down from the car, my father once more extended his hand, I took it and squeezed it for a long time; he was hiding his emotion under his sweet smile. "Good-bye," we said, and the train left. I had just been separated for eternity from my father. He survived our separation for only 128 days.

I was to occupy a position in Smyrna that was more advantageous than the one I had left; my enemies, in spite of themselves, had gotten me a promotion. But it is nonetheless true that the intrigues of Abraham Davitchon Lévy, Ezra Tagger, and Nissim Farhy had the result of separating me from my father, who had become my comrade, my friend, and whose weak system could not resist the blow. From that day on, life held no charm for him, he declined rapidly, and died before reaching his fifty-second birthday, on 9 March 1894—1 Veadar 5654. I did not have the consolation of closing his eyes.

I consider the three individuals named above responsible for my father's death, and in this respect, I do not forgive them the evil they wished upon me. I hope my children will not forget it.

It was a long trip from Sofia to Smyrna. After a quarantine of three days in Mustapha Pacha, a stop for two weeks in Constantinople, where we left Sophie with my wife's parents, and another quarantine for three days in the Dardanelles, we arrived on the *El-Kahira*, made by the Khédivié Company of Smyrna, from which we debarked on 21 November 1893.

SELECTIONS FROM LETTERS
TO THE ALLIANCE CENTRAL COMMITTEE

1 July 1888

. . . As I indicated to you on 25 June, the vice president of the rabbinate commission, M. Lévy, telegraphed from Vienna that Dr. Yellinek[14] very heartily recommends Rabbi Dankovitz and that, according to him, there would be a great advantage in placing him at the head of the Bulgarian communities; he concluded by asking for authorization to bring him to Sofia, at the cost, of course, of the commission. The commission first decided not to risk another

14. Adolf Jellinek (1820 or 1821–93) was a Viennese scholar and preacher.

useless expense, but in a second meeting, where only seven of the eighteen members were present, M. Dankovitz was granted the cost of a round-trip.

As soon as we received word of M. Dankovitz's departure, M. Farhi telegraphed you to ask for advice, on behalf of himself and me, on the conduct to follow at the time of the election. He received your response the same day: "Await information."

Today at two o'clock, M. Dankovitz arrived. A delegation of ten persons, including eight members of the commission, went to meet him a few kilometers from the city. I was there as well, in the role of everyone's interpreter; allow me to transmit a few notes to you on my first interview with M. Dankovitz. I hasten to add that I offer my evaluation for what it's worth, that is, as a first impression; a longer association with M. Dankovitz could lead me to change my opinion.

M. Dankovitz is a man of forty to forty-five years old, above-average height, wide shoulders, thick neck, a face more square than oval, small eyes hidden by large black glasses, a short and clipped beard, bald-headed, but adorned with a few locks of long hair that, in the disorder of the trip, were obviously not in the place destined for them. The bearing, gestures, speech, and manner of M. Dankovitz are all Germanic, by which I mean cold, heavy, a bit awkward. Not a lively movement, not a warm or even friendly word. After a few minutes of conversation, we discovered that M. Dankovitch is afflicted with deafness, only slightly it is true, but enough to disconcert the interlocutor at any moment if he is not forewarned. In addition, the honorable rabbi had a half-hoarse voice, which he said was the effect of the dust he had breathed in on the way, but M. Lévy affirms that his voice was husky in Vienna as well. Finally, to finish the physical portrait, M. Dankovitz is not at ease speaking, which will make it very difficult when he has to give a speech in a language yet to be learned.

Must I say it? The enthusiasm for M. Dankovitz has dropped considerably in the last few hours. The persons who went to meet him came back completely disoriented: we look at one another as if to exchange our impressions, but no one yet dares express his thoughts; the boldest say that before deciding, we would need to convene a meeting of all the taxpayers from the community to have the election approved. What does that mean? And why this appeal to the taxpayers if not because everyone is already afraid to take responsibility for a matter whose solution might not be to the taste of the community?

The opinion of those who did no more than see M. Dankovitz is thus not in favor of the rabbi. Having conversed for quite a long time with this rabbi, I can say something more about him. I have already said that M. Dankovitz expresses himself slowly; he studied French but he lacks practice in the language. He very much likes to speak in apothegms: Talmudic, German, Czech, etc., and to display his erudition at every turn. That may also be a German trait, but I was nevertheless shocked by that way of commending himself.

M. Dankovitz is not a stranger to a few members of the Central Committee: he told me he knew Chief Rabbis Isidor and Z. Kahn[15] personally, and that the chief rabbi of Paris even sent him a copy of his *Sermons et allocutions,*[16] a review of which M. Dankovitz published in *Israelitische Wochenschrift.*[17] Finally, he told me he had succeeded in forming a regional committee of the Alliance in Bohemia, which has thus far attracted about twenty members.

I would not care to hazard an evaluation of the capacities and knowledge of M. Dankovitz, first, because I am perfectly incompetent in the matter and, second, because it is not the extent of knowledge that is most important to us. For myself, I would willingly concede all his philology, his comparative pedagogy, and a half-dozen languages he speaks in favor of a bit less rigidity and more amiability. M. Dankovitz has not even smiled all day long! He may be a wellspring of science, but we would greatly prefer less depth and more surface polish and brilliance!

. . . We cannot yet foresee the solution to this affair—will M. Dankovitz be elected or not? That will be a question of pure chance and luck. For myself, I would not commit myself to voting for him: first, because the physical defects he has, especially his deafness, could get worse with age; second, because he did not inspire very good feelings in me; and finally, because for me all the documents he possesses do not have the value of a frank and warm recommendation from the Central Committee, which has been lacking until this point.

In conclusion, I will repeat that all these judgments are no doubt hasty; but since I propose to keep the Central Committee up to date on what happens during the week M. Dankovitz spends here, I thought I also ought to communicate the first impression, which, it is said, is often the best. In any case, I excused myself from going to the meeting of the commission and today even avoided the society of Jews: I am afraid I might let slip an unfavorable word about M. Dankovitz, which would be of great consequence, and just as I do not want to commit myself to voting for an unknown man whom

---

15. Zadoc Kahn was chief rabbi of Paris between 1868 and 1889. In 1889 he was elected chief rabbi of France, a post he held until his death in 1905.

16. Zadoc Kahn, *Sermons et allocutions,* 3 vols. (Paris, 1875–94).

17. *Israelitische Wochenschrift für die religösen und sozialen Interessen des Judenthums* (Breslau and Magdeburg, 1870–94).

I do not find at all appealing, I also do not want to raise the first hue and cry over a man whom, all things considered, I still hardly know. . . .

Archives of the AIU, Bulgarie XXII.E.153a.

19 July 1889

. . . I had the honor a few months ago of telling you about the demolitions that the municipality of Sofia planned in order to open ten new roads through the old Turkish city. This plan, of unprecedented daring in this region, was executed by our mayor, who unleashed a level of activity and a force of will seldom seen. Today, Sofia looks like a city in ruins: wide boulevards cross it in every direction; hundreds of Eastern-looking, low, dark, and dirty houses have disappeared, and with them many narrow and tortuous alleyways. The city will now be very well ventilated: already the new houses and stores are falling into line; in the streets, there are nothing but construction materials and busy workers; for three months all anyone talks about is constructions and plans. Everyone is building or will build; from every point of Bulgaria and Macedonia workers arrive in caravans and all find work; there are no fewer than five thousand masons and day laborers in Sofia today (and not a single Jew among them).

The transformation of the city will bring some changes in the economic and social life of our coreligionists. The Jews, in fact, occupy the center of the city; the cathedral and the principal churches, the market, and the park are, so to speak, in the Jewish quarter, and it is precisely that part of the city that is being regularized. The principal arteries, 58 meters wide, all lead to the cathedral, which will itself be in the center of a plaza that is 22,000 square meters in area. The Jewish quarter is thus entirely disappearing. As of today, in addition to the school, the community has already lost the Chalom [Shalom] temple next to the school, the *francos*[18] temple, and five or six prayer houses; all these buildings will be paid for, and the community will receive about sixty thousand francs in compensation.

While property owners see themselves thus dispossessed, the poor, those who have no property in the city, will receive from the municipality, at almost no cost, pieces of land outside the current city, in the new neighborhood called Utch-Bunar, where they can build houses and shops. As of this time, three hundred Jewish families have received land, and more than one hundred and fifty have already built on it and live there. A very strong current is carrying the Jewish population to that side of the city; there are already thoughts of building a temple there; a school will also be needed,

18. *Franco* (Judeo-Spanish) was the name given to Italian Jews in the East.

since children cannot come to the city from so far away. To that end, the municipality has donated three thousand square meters of land and the material from the demolished synagogues.

You see the consequences of this movement: the former property owners will no longer be such, but must themselves pay rent, while the poor souls who never dreamed of having their own homes will now have tenants.

The affairs of our community will be deeply affected by the upheaval; the school taxes will have to be divided up differently, the rate will have to be lowered, and it will be very difficult to collect them. . . .

Archives of the AIU, Bulgarie XXII.E.153a.

7 February 1890
[to Isidore Loeb]

. . . I am very happy that, in asking for an explanation regarding the Jewish history books I requested, you have given me the opportunity to speak to you on a matter about which I could not consult a man more competent than you. I must tell you it was solely for fear of being indiscreet that I did not speak of it in my first letter, despite the strong desire I had to do so. Here is the matter at hand.

On 31 March 1892 it will be four centuries since the expulsion decree against Spanish Jews, issued by Ferdinand the Catholic. If anniversaries, whether happy or sad, have any purpose, it is to offer individuals and peoples a natural opportunity to look into themselves, to reflect on their past, and to draw from these meditations lessons and resolutions for the future. No examination of conscience would be more useful to the Jews of the East than that inspired by the fourth centennial of 1492.

Unfortunately, the history of the Jews of Spain and Turkey is completely unknown to my coreligionists in this country; the students in our schools may know more about the Chinese and the Hindus than about their own ancestors. As for me, I confess that if M. Théodore Reinach[19] had not written his *Histoire des Israélites,* I too would have only an extremely vague idea about the Jews of Spain, left in my memory by fragments of readings. But I find almost nothing in that book on the history of my coreligionists in the East and can say I am completely ignorant about that. In the free time my various occupations allow me, I would like to study that history, to gather as many details as possible on my Jewish compatriots, from their arrival in Spain

---

19. Théodore Reinach (1860–1925) was a French scholar who wrote a very popular general history of the Jews: *L'histoire des Israélites depuis la ruine de leur indépendance nationale jusqu'à nos jours* (Paris, 1884).

until our own time. I would like to undertake this for my personal education. Later, if I believe I have enough material, I might be able to make myself useful to my coreligionists by bringing together and condensing these notes into a narrative, which I would publish in French and perhaps in Spanish. But that is still a very vague project in my mind. For the moment, I do not want to think that far ahead, and I will confine myself to studying for my own benefit. So much the better if, in 1892, I can give my compatriots a sketch of our history that would help them reflect upon themselves in the way I spoke of above.

I do not know if it will be possible to write this history, but I do know what the epilogue would be. Is it not the Alliance Israélite that, 360 years after the expulsion, has managed to repair the effects of that deadly measure and that, through its schools and apprenticeship programs, has undertaken to raise the moral, intellectual, and material condition of this persecuted people and has succeeded so well?

That is the purpose of my request for history books. I believe I already told you that, having studied German for four years, I can read that language and write it a bit and have neglected it for two years only to concentrate all my attention on Bulgarian.

Let us get to the choice of books. I have heard of Amador de Los Rios,[20] and he is also mentioned in the bibliographical note that follows M. T. Reinach's work cited above. It is also in that note that I saw two books cited, one by you, the other by Roenne and Lurion,[21] on Jewish history, and I thought, given their titles, that I would find some information on the Jews of the East. As for L. Philippson's *Marranen*,[22] it is a novel so praised by M. Dankovitz that I am curious to read it; M. Dankovitz did an abridged Hebrew translation of it, which has not been published and which I could not read in manuscript form, not knowing the cursive characters he uses.

It is understood, of course, that I intend to purchase at my own expense the books I will need.

You now know the goal I propose for myself and I will await your advice; and since you are kind enough to promise to help me in these purchases, allow me to take advantage of your offer; I will be infinitely grateful. . . .

Archives of the AIU, Bulgarie XXII.E.153a.

20. José Amador de Los Rios was the author of *Historia social, politica y religiosa de los Judios en España y Portugal,* 3 vols. (Madrid, 1875–76).

21. Roenne and Lurion: This reference appears in Théodore Reinach's book (see n. 19 above) as Roenne and Simon, *Die früheren und gegenwärtigen Verhältnisse der Juden* (1845) (see the new edition of 1900 of Reinach's book, p. 392).

22. Ludwig Philippson (1811–89) was founder and publisher of the journal *Allgemeine Zeitung des Judentums.*

3 June 1892

. . . The Bulgarian newspapers have been very occupied with the Jews for the last few weeks. Even if we do not mention the antisemitic newspapers *Tcherno More, Toundja,* etc., the more serious organs of the press such as the *Svoboda* and *Balkanska Zora*[23] write continually on the subject; it appears that a "Jewish question" is about to surface in Bulgaria. The cause of this movement is the frequency of Jewish bankruptcies in Sofia: in three months, twenty commercial Jewish firms have suspended payments or have been declared bankrupt. Since this economic crisis seems only to exist for the Jews—almost no Bulgarian firms have failed—and this state of affairs is very damaging to Bulgaria's credit abroad, the newspapers are vying with one another to explain that the proof that these bankruptcies are a form of speculation is that only Jews are involved. The government itself has been upset by this situation, and the minister of justice has just sent a circular to the tribunals inviting them to use all the severity of the law against the initiators of false bankruptcies, and particularly against Jews. On their side, the Christian businessmen of Sofia have formed a society this week and at this moment are elaborating a plan for a chamber of commerce, to protect themselves, they say, against the consequences of Jewish speculation.

Here, then, is a stain on the reputation of the Jews of Sofia, who until now have had a very justified reputation for exemplary uprightness in their trans-actions. We need not go into the causes for that collapse here. To be sincere and truthful, however, our detractors should remember that for three years the city of Sofia looked more like a construction yard than a place of business and that during that time businesses lay idle; that the sudden and total upheaval of the city obliged everyone to build homes, and most of the capital went into them; and that, finally, the rent on stores has become exorbitant, ruinously expensive. There are many other reasons that are not given.

But one must also say that our coreligionists are not doing everything necessary to avoid these scandals: they jump into business without allowing for a way out, without taking the expense into account, and perhaps some-times foresee with too much prudence the misfortune that will befall them.

Even though we deplore this state of affairs, which the press seizes on not without some pleasure, it is to be hoped that a severe repression of these abuses will put an end to this situation, which could be disastrous for the Jews. It is not without concern for the future that one sees the *Svobada* speaking of these bankruptcies as coming about exclusively among "foreign-

23. *Tcherno More* (Black Sea), provincial newspaper; *Tundja* (Tundja River; Yamboli, 1892–95); *Balkanska Zora* (Balkan Dawn; Philippopolis, 1890–1900).

ers, since autochthonous Bulgarians prefer poverty to dishonor." This is the first time the Jews of this country have been called foreigners. Another newspaper is in the process of publishing, over several issues, an article entitled "Are the Jews Dangerous to Us?" The subtitle of the article is "Regarding Recent Bankruptcies."

How will it all end, and what might we do to stop the evil?

Archives of the AIU, Bulgarie I.C.9.

1 May 1893

. . . There remains little for me to say regarding the work of the [communal] assembly. The last question on the agenda was antisemitism. It was decided to found a society in Bulgaria whose goal would be the following:

"The Fraternity Society has as its goal to defend Judaism against the attacks of which it is the object, and to lend moral and material support to Bulgarian Jews who suffer because they are Jews.

The society will reach its goal (1) by refuting, in existing newspapers or in special publications, any slander directed against Jews and (2) by organizing lectures and founding a newspaper to encourage closer friendships between Jews and their fellow citizens."

We then proceeded to the election of the first central committee; I was asked to be a member. I thought I should not accept for several reasons: first, because I do not have authorization from the Alliance; second, because I do not know how the government will look upon this association of Jews of the Principality; and finally, because the other members elected to this committee are very young and inexperienced, I would have to take responsibility for everything, and I do not really have the time.

It was decided we should ask for the government's approval of the statutes. I fought this proposal as being premature: antisemitism is not yet so threatening in Bulgaria that we should indicate to the government our intention to defend ourselves against our fellow citizens and to form a people within another people. Since I was alone in my opinion, the statutes will be submitted for the government's approval. . . .

Archives of the AIU, Bulgarie XXIII.E.153b.

17 July 1893

. . . The community and the most recent events:

The Jews are said to assimilate quickly both the good qualities and the faults of the peoples among whom they live. The Jews of Sofia seem not to have escaped that law. Bulgarians are willing rebels, adventurers; monotony in government bores them. Unfolding the newspaper in the morning, the reader from abroad must wonder: Are the Bulgarians at peace today? The history of our community resembles somewhat the history of the Bulgarians: it is made up of incidents, unforeseen events, jolts. I imagine that in opening the letters, you must also say to yourselves: Something new is happening in Sofia yet again!

This perpetual change in the community has been stimulated for several years by diverse circumstances: the schools and then the synagogues were demolished, a part of the Jewish population was transplanted from the city to Utch-Bunar, houses and temples had to be built; then we were given the luxury of a European rabbi who made the community live in intrigue and division for three years; then the schooling law came along with its procession of difficulties; then the election of a new chief rabbi; and finally, to top it all off, we now have the elimination of the Jewish schools. It seems so many jolts have shaken the community as to undermine its very foundations! Fine result!

. . . I cannot, Mr. President, think without some sadness about this deplorable future, about my efforts of six years annihilated in a day; I may have left behind the best of myself in those six years. All these sacrifices seem for naught at the present time. At least I have the satisfaction of having done my duty at every moment. In all the commotion that has agitated this community since my stay among them, I believe I have always been able to avoid the pitfalls and have never given reason for any complaint. I am conscious of having served the interests of Judaism and of the Alliance to the best of my ability and am still ready to serve them and begin the struggle again, on whatever field of action to which you are kind enough to send me.

Archives of the AIU, France IX.F.16.

8/ Smyrna, First Period (1893–1901)

At Smyrna, we were welcomed on board by Abraham Benveniste, the assistant at the school at that time. M. Pariente, my predecessor, did not see fit to trouble himself. He excused himself, saying he felt tired from the banquet the young people had given in his honor the night before. He had had two rooms prepared for us at the home of M. Mercado Benmaor, a good old man who received us very well and with whom we remained forever friends. When he died in 1902, I was to slip the sleeves of his shroud onto him, an honor that in Smyrna is reserved for the best friends of the deceased.

After M. Pariente's departure on 7 December 1893, we moved into his apartment, situated in the school building itself and containing three rooms and a kitchen. We set up a very modest household and I went to work.

The Alliance program in Smyrna was much larger than that of Sofia. It included a school for boys with three hundred students, the supervision of *talmud-tora* studies, an apprenticeship program, and the small agricultural school of Burnabat.[1] All these programs were administered by the Alliance director, without the meddling of any local committee. That complete independence was something new to me. It is one of the main factors for the consideration that the representative of the Alliance enjoyed in Smyrna.

The residents of that city are in general very sociable, which stands in contrast to the habits of the Bulgarians. We could extend our circle of relationships at will. But we soon realized that with the Jews of the region, any association quickly degenerated into a familiarity that was harmful to my prestige. As for visiting and receiving Europeans, our modest resources did not allow it. We thus restricted our relations to what was strictly necessary: the staff and a few notables, among whom I should note M. Haïm Polako, M. Gabriel Calef, and, later, Isaac David from Sofia, who moved to Smyrna. The general impression made on us

1. Burnabat, a suburb of Izmir.

by Smyrna was excellent in every respect, and we were tempted to bless our enemies from Sofia who had had us sent there.

My assistants were Abraham Benveniste, Joseph Sabah, my old school chums, and A. Halévy, a very lazy man and a nasty character. M. Aron Hazan, director of *La Buena Esperanza*[2] and professor of Turkish, was often useful to me; he left the school in Smyrna the same time I did, in 1906. In January 1894, the Alliance sent me Carmona, despite my protests. Having failed in Damascus, he was reassigned as an assistant. The events that followed showed how right I was to oppose Carmona's appointment in Smyrna.

Mme Jousselin had remained at the girls school after the departure of M. Pariente. We behaved very correctly toward her, but nothing more, given the little fondness she manifested toward us until her departure in 1897. Her assistant, Mlle Sara Sidi, was devoted to us until her transfer in 1901.

Such was the environment in which we lived. I was altogether happy with it and undertook to share this happiness with my father through letters, in which I described our entire life for him. He did not enjoy them for very long, unfortunately! He contracted pneumonia after catching a chill, and his debilitated condition could not overcome it. He died on 9 March 1894. The fatal news, telegraphed by Elia to Chief Rabbi Abraham Palatché,[3] was communicated to me by Benveniste on Saturday evening, 10 March. All the notables of the community came by that very evening to visit me and offer consolation for my suffering, which was great. I felt like a part of me was buried with my father in the grave. I spent a horrible week, and when I got up after the seven-day mourning period, my face was so altered that I was unrecognizable.

Thus passed away a man whom life had offered many hardships and few smiles. Philosophers would find a great deal to ponder in his case, on the utility of piety, of probity, of all the virtues that make up the upstanding man, when they do not procure him any satisfaction in this world. But my father never asked these questions, because he had an invincible faith in God; he believed in the immortality of the soul, in a future life, and he rendered up his soul to God with a prayer.

Peace and eternal respect to his memory!

During the entire year that followed, I regularly recited prayers in his

2. *La Buena Esperanza* (Good hope) was a Jewish newspaper in Izmir written in Judeo-Spanish. It was founded by Aron Hazan in 1871 and suspended publication in 1917.

3. Abraham Palatché (1809–99) was chief rabbi of Izmir from 1870 until his death.

memory, and for that purpose, I set up a prayer school in the morning, with regular readings of the *Perascha* on Mondays and Thursdays, from the scroll of the law. . . .

Two months later, on 2 May 1894, my third child, Ida-Jaël, was born.

And life resumed its course. That year, I worked with the greatest diligence. In July, very brilliant public exams took place, with Vali[4] Hassan Fehmi Pasha presiding, in the presence of the authorities and many notables. Then came vacation, but my activities did not end: I took a trip to Aydin,[5] where I organized a school and placed N. Cardozo at its head; took an inspection trip to Rhodes, where we had an apprenticeship program; and went to Magnesia, where Moïse Mitrani was soliciting my cooperation in settling various difficulties with the committee.

At the end of August, I left for Sofia via Salonika, and the reunion with my relatives, especially my mother, was as you can imagine. My mother did not recognize me: that is how thin and pale the sorrow, emotion, and fatigue had made me.

I had come for the wedding of Régine and Joseph Alcalay. The celebration was as you can imagine, that is, something less than merry, since the memory of my father was never far from anyone's mind. Poor Régine never had any luck, not even for her wedding.

We settled all the questions of inheritance with Elia. In any case, the inheritance consisted solely of a few little debts, which we paid, plus a house; the money from the sale of the house was set aside to pay for Sultana's wedding. What was left over went to Emmanuel. We burned all my father's business papers and sold the furniture. After the holidays, I returned to Smyrna, bringing with me my mother, along with Sultana and Emmanuel, who were fourteen and six years old at the time.

I returned to work with pleasure. I gave lessons every morning from nine o'clock till noon to the upper class, and the children benefited a great deal from them. Every afternoon was devoted to a different task: class exams, apprentices, visits to the Burnabat farm. It was while crossing the fields leading to the farm that I took cold and began to feel some pain on the right side, to which I attached no importance.

At home, my mother was naturally very dispirited. Her widow's sorrow sometimes escaped in episodes of hysteria accompanied by tears, shortness of breath, and screaming. I was very affected by them. One of these episodes had incalculable consequences for us. One evening while

4. *Vali* (Turkish), "governor."
5. Aydin, locality situated to the southeast of Izmir.

Rachel was taking a bath at home, my mother began to cry out. Frightened, Rachel hurriedly got out of the bath to come to her aid. The crisis passed, but the next day Rachel began to show symptoms of cystitis, the result of the sudden chill. The cystitis degenerated into nephritis. At that time, Rachel developed a long-term illness, which was to keep her bedridden for almost the entire winter. I had to take care of the children. One night when I was sleeping with Sandro, he fell asleep on my arm and, so as not to wake him, I did not move all night and left my right elbow uncovered. The bedroom was large and barely heated and the doors and windows did not close properly; thus, without my noticing it, a cold draft circulated in the room and froze my right elbow. When I woke up, it was frozen solid. I tried to respond, but it was too late: pleurisy had taken hold.

It was a wet pleurisy and lasted more than a month. Dr. Toledano and then Dr. Chasseaud treated me. It was a very dreary winter. Rachel and I were bedridden in the same room facing each other. On 15 February [1895] I had reached the climax of my illness. Then gradually resorption began and I got well. That pleurisy was the origin of my current tuberculosis.

Once we fell ill, my mother had no more hysterical episodes.

During my illness, I had promised myself I would settle family affairs and other matters as quickly as possible, to provide for any eventuality. The matter I had my heart most set on was Elia's marriage. I wished to arrange it myself and thus sought out a companion for him in Smyrna.

Near the school, there lived M. Salomon Faraggi, whose two eldest daughters I had seen in 1885, boarding at the home of Mlle Abélès (today Mme Nabon). Mr. Faraggi had been unlucky in business, and as a result, his daughters had to work for a living. They set themselves up as seamstresses. The younger, Léonore, made an excellent impression on me when she came to our home for some work. She was physically agreeable and I knew she was well brought up and that the family was honorable; her father's misfortune must have tempered her character. I made my decision and wrote to Elia to come see me at Passover.

Elia came, the two young people met, took a liking to each other, and became engaged. A dowry was out of the question, and I did not insist on one for Elia: as I have noted, I had not retained one penny of Rachel's dowry. I thought the best dowry for a woman was her character, her health, and her moral qualities, which were more certain to make a man happy than a few bank notes. Time has shown that I was not mistaken, since Elia's marriage was perfectly happy.

We spent the Passover vacation merrily and made several excursions.

Rachel and I were gradually recovering, and after the holidays I was able to resume my usual work at the school.

In April 1895, I opened a school in Karatash[6] and placed Carmona there. He remained for only a few months, because during the holidays I had asked the Alliance that he be transferred; given his odd character, his remaining in Smyrna had become impossible.

Another matter with which I concerned myself after my recovery was my lodging. Under no circumstances did I wish to remain in the place I was occupying, which had almost been fatal for us. I obtained an allocation of 6,500 francs from the Alliance to build, on the site of old hovels belonging to the school, a house for the director and a girls kindergarten room. I myself made up the plans for my future home, and with the help of an architect, M. Magnifico, the work was begun. Construction costs were 13,000 francs, twice the estimate. At my request, the Anglo-Jewish Association[7] and M. Goldschmidt, president of the Alliance, were kind enough to cover the deficit. The house was very pretty but could not be finished for the autumn, and it was only the next spring that we could move in. One detail: I wanted to plant trees in the yard. Sensing I would not remain in Smyrna for long, and wishing to enjoy these trees as soon as possible, I chose the variety that grows the most quickly, the eucalyptus, which in fact gave a thick shade from the first year.

The rudimentary agricultural school in Burnabat had been liquidated the preceding autumn, as being incapable of producing the slightest result. The property was then rented to an alumnus of Mikweh,[8] Goldenberg, who claimed he lost money there, and then to two Greeks, who are still there.

It was during that summer of 1895 that I began studies that were to lead to the creation of Or-Jéhouda.[9] To this end, I made several trips into the interior, principally to Aydin, where there was a small Jewish settlement. I brought aid to these settlers for three years.

The higher, or commercial, courses that I organized at the school also date from that time; they produced excellent results.

6. Karataş, suburb of Izmir.

7. The Anglo-Jewish Association, allied closely with the Alliance, was a British organization founded in 1871, originally for the defense of the rights of Jews through diplomatic means. It also undertook an education program in the Jewish communities of North Africa and the Near East.

8. Mikweh (Mikveh Yisrael) was an agricultural school founded in Palestine in 1870 by the Alliance.

9. Or-Jéhouda (Or Yehudah, "Light of Judah," Hebrew) was a school farm in Asia Minor founded by the Alliance in 1900.

During the vacation, I created the Cassaba school.[10]

My trip to study that school was made with Elia, who had come from Sofia to get married. The wedding took place at the school on 1 August 1895. The large corridor was decorated with greenery and banners, and lovely music was playing on the balcony. The ceremony took place before noon, in the presence of most of the notables of the community. After a luncheon at our home, the newlyweds left for Sofia via Salonika, where they were to stay for a few days.

It seems that Léonore brought good fortune to Elia, because during his stay in Smyrna, he received a note from M. Otto Bieligk, then agent of the Dacia-Romania, inviting him to return to Sofia as soon as possible to join the Balkan, a new insurance company he was in the process of creating. At the Nationala, where he had been for five years, Elia had already acquired a good position, five thousand francs per year, I believe. But at the Balkan, where he subsequently became the office head for fire insurance, he earned only slightly less than twice that. The five-year contract he signed in 1895 was renewed in 1900 and in 1905, this last time with the title of assistant manager of the company.

In February 1896, I created the Associations des Anciens Elèves [alumni association]. I felt it ought to become an effective instrument for the elevation of the community. The activities of that society were extremely useful and were published each year in bulletins. A bound collection of these bulletins is part of my small library. I was president of the association until my departure from Smyrna in 1904.

That year, my salary was raised from 4,000 to 4,300 francs. I felt the need to go to Paris to renew contacts, since I had not been there since 1891. I had no precise goal for this trip, but I felt I could only benefit from getting in touch with the members of the Central Committee. This trip and those that followed were also very useful in the work of the Alliance.

I left Smyrna on 21 March 1896. The secretaryship of the Alliance was in the hands of M. Bigart, who had replaced M. Isidore Loeb at his death in 1891. At that time, I met M. Bénédict,[11] with whom I established a friendship; our relations have continued to be excellent since then. He has subsequently done numerous and excellent favors for me.

I remained in Paris for eighteen days. I achieved two results: a planned inspection of the schools by M. Bénédict and the decision to buy a

10. Cassaba (Turgutlu), city about a hundred kilometers from Izmir.
11. Sylvain Bénédict was inspector of schools for the Alliance.

large farm in the *vilayet*[12] of Aydin. M. Bénédict's first tour took place the following May.

I also wanted to establish personal relations with the members of the Anglo-Jewish Association, and toward that end, I went to London, where I received a truly Scottish hospitality: the first day, Mr. Duparc had me visit the City, the Tower of London, the Jewish schools, etc.; the second day, Chief Rabbi Gaster[13] had me to his home for lunch and took me to visit a museum; the third day, Mr. Mocatta[14] took me to see Westminster Palace and Abbey, etc. Everyone was charming. I attended a council meeting (as I had also done in Paris). When I left London, Mr. Duparc was kind enough to write the committee that I did honor to the Alliance.

During my stay in London, I recall that I refrained from going out in the evening; it was in fact damp, and I was coughing a little because I had not recovered well from my pleurisy. I was afraid that some misfortune would befall me, as had happened a few months earlier to Dr. Grünwald, who died during a trip to London. This worthy pastor had, in passing through Paris, said a great deal of evil about me to M. Zadoc Kahn. Recall that at the time of my departure from Sofia, he had come to bid me good-bye at the train station. God rest his soul!

As had been decided in Paris, as soon as I returned I began traveling in search of a farm. The first one I saw was Oglan-Anassi. The memory of it has remained very sweet, I don't know why. I rode a horse there for the first time in my life. I would often repeat that exercise later.

Upon my return from that trip we moved into the new house, and I no longer heard Ida crying so often. It is extraordinary how much that child cried during her infancy: she could be heard throughout almost the entire neighborhood.

The kindergarten was also opened at that time. Mme Sara Danon was the headmistress for nine years; Mlle Rachel Crispine succeeded her. We began with four students; today there are a hundred and twenty, all paying.

On the advice of Dr. Condoléon, I took my family to spend the spring at the Burnabat farm, where we occupied two rooms. I had brought my sister-in-law Léa from Constantinople, and she spent the entire summer with us. We returned to Smyrna in the middle of June, with the arrival of the ex-

12. *Vilayet* (Turkish), "province, prefecture."

13. Moses Gaster (1856–1939) was a scholar, Zionist leader, and chief rabbi of the Sephardi community in London.

14. Frederic David Mocatta (1828–1905) was a philanthropist and important British community leader.

treme heat. The following years, I went regularly after Passover to spend a few weeks in Burnabat, but I went alone, which was not as pleasant.

The creation of the Aavat-Hessed lodge, affiliated with Bné Berith[15] in New York, which was to devote itself to so many intrigues against the schools and against me, dates from the same period. That organization tried to reform the administration of the community, and notorious regulations were drafted with that goal in mind: but Nissim Palatché, son of the chief rabbi, saw that these plans failed, and Haluf and Polako had to capitulate and withdraw from public affairs.

The end-of-year exams were presided over by M. Chayet, consul of France, and were attended by several non-Jewish teachers. All the notables were present. I had the Hebrew exams administered by a commission of rabbis and the Turkish exams by competent persons.

The holidays arrived, bringing their intolerable heat. I could not think of leaving Smyrna, since I had just taken a trip in April. I therefore remained, and remained alone, since Rachel had gone to Constantinople to attend the wedding of her sister Fortunée.

When the school year began, important changes had taken place in the staff. But in this account of our family life, I cannot insist upon the details of my school tasks. I have just sent the historical account of my activities in Smyrna beginning in 1893 to the Alliance, and it will be published in the *Histoire de l'Alliance,* now in preparation. This work may be consulted.

The winter of 1897 was marked by a full-scale attack on the school from the Aavat-Hessed faction. A school committee was absolutely demanded; I opposed it with all my force and was even willing to abandon my post rather than give in. Finally, I won my case and the communal council gave in.

Other events of that winter: first, the immigration of the Jews of Crete, which occurred following the anti-Turkish revolution on that island.[16] They came en masse to Smyrna, and I had to intervene in their favor with the Alliance: eight thousand francs were distributed to them.

15. Bné Berith (Bnai Brith) is a Jewish organization divided into lodges and chapters, on the model of the Masonic orders, founded in the United States in 1843. It had branches in the Near East, including Ahavat-Hesed, 1895–99 (Hebrew, "generous love").

16. In January 1897, a group of Greek Cretans, joined by Greeks from the kingdom, led an insurrection against the Ottomans and declared the rejoining of the island to Greece. At the end of the same year, after many vicissitudes, the sultan established an autonomous regime on Crete. It was to remain under Ottoman suzerainty but would be governed by a Christian designated by Istanbul and approved by Athens. The island was formally rejoined to Greece in 1912.

Second, following the disappearance of a Christian child, the Greeks refused to buy anything from Jewish peddlers, who were very numerous in Smyrna. The hungry Jews came to implore the help of the Alliance: I obtained three thousand francs for them.

Finally, on 1 January of that year, I received five hundred francs from the Jewish Colonization Association (ICA)[17] as a bonus for the reports I had already sent it. Beginning in 1898, I was to receive fifteen hundred francs a year from that organization, which, added to my salary and the interest from my savings, earned me more than eight thousand francs a year. Since I was spending only half that, I could save a great deal, and these savings were increased by the contribution Elia paid me to support my mother, Sultana, and Emmanuel. It was during those years that I managed to amass a little capital and to constitute dowries for my daughters.

My search for a farm to acquire did not end with the winter months. I visited the farm of Tchakyr-Oglu, which I reached by terrible roads via Bergama, in Tchandarlik,[18] where I also saw other farms. There I became ill and had no way to communicate with Smyrna, either by letter or telegraph. The rivers had overflowed and we ran the risk of drowning if we returned by land. We were obliged to return by land [*sic,* by sea], and to cross the infamous Gulf of Tchandarlik, famous for its storms, by boat. It was a very risky venture. Fortunately, the bad weather arose only when we were on the point of debarking.

I returned to Smyrna very tired from my trip and my illness. A few days later, I went to Tire,[19] to visit the property of Gumushlu. At the same time, I established the foundations for the creation of a school, which was opened the following summer.

In the spring, I made the same journeys once more in the company of M. Avigdor. But when it came time to go to Tchandarlik, I refused to go in any manner other than a little boat, chartered specially for that purpose. Rachel and Sandro accompanied me, and this time the trip was extremely agreeable. This new study led to the conclusion that the farm of Tchakyr-Oglu was the best suited.

Between these two trips, I concluded Sultana's engagement to Samuel Hemsi. My younger sister's dowry was to be taken from the sale of my father's house. What was left over was placed in an account opened in

17. The Jewish Colonization Association (known as the ICA) was a Jewish philanthropic association founded in 1891 by Baron Maurice de Hirsch.
18. Bergama and Tchandarlik (Çandarlik), Aegean cities north of Izmir.
19. Tire (Tireh), city situated southeast of Izmir.

Emmanuel's name, since Elia and I did not want to receive any of the inheritance.

Around the month of July, I began to feel extremely tired. I had a slight cough, was thin and haggard, and needed rest. I obtained a leave, which I was supposed to spend in Europe with Elia. But at the moment of departure, Ida contracted a grave illness that brought her within an inch of death. Even the doctor, who thought all was lost, had abandoned her. Fortunately, she survived and got well.

I had to remain; but since the heat had become oppressive, I took the first departing boat and went to Marseilles via Alexandria. It was a very interesting trip. I left Smyrna on the *Equateur*, debarked in Beirut, where I was for several hours the guest of Joseph Cazès, who has since been dismissed. From there, I went to Jaffa by a very heavy sea, and visited Mikweh, where M. Bénédict was on inspection. There I met M. Schalith, who later became an employee of the ICA, and then of Louis Dreyfus. I visited the Rishon colony[20] and admired the magnificent wine-making installation.

After three days at Mikweh, I rejoined my boat in Alexandria, where I visited the school and met Somekh for the first time. I was also curious to go see M. Tivoli, in whose home Mlle Ungar had been a teacher. Finally, after another five days of uninterrupted navigating, I arrived in Marseilles and went immediately to Paris, where Elia was waiting for me with some impatience.

At that point, neither Elia nor I was in especially good health; we were to go recover in the country. On the advice of M. Bigart, we went to Saint-Cergues near Nyon. Before leaving, I settled a certain number of questions with the bureau. In spite of M. Bigart, and with the cooperation of M. Schwarzfeld, I also received a sum of three thousand francs from Baroness de Hirsch,[21] for my sister-in-law Léa, who, thanks to that dowry, was able to marry Eliézer Mijan, widower of the unfortunate Flore, a cousin of Rachel's.

From Paris we went with Elia to Geneva. I remember we had a serious discussion about the possibility that Régine would divorce: her in-laws had gone bankrupt and her husband was unable to earn a living. We had been giving her thirty francs a month for two years, and we continued this aid until 1901. We then placed Joseph with a businessman, whom

20. Rishon, the Rishon Le-Zion colony south of Tel Aviv, famous for its vineyards.
21. Baroness Clara de Hirsch (1833–99) was the wife of Maurice de Hirsch (1831–96), businessman, banker, and illustrious philanthropist. She was also very active in Jewish philanthropic works.

we had lent two thousand francs interest-free. This loan was repaid in 1904, and since then Joseph has managed as he can, which is to say, poorly, and my sister lives in poverty.

The stay in Saint-Cergues was not agreeable. It is a wet, misty, cold region. Elia would have done better to follow the advice of M. Bieligk, who encouraged him to go to Dr. Lahmann's sanatorium near Dresden. He went there in the end but remained only a few days, so that one could say that for both of us, the time off was squandered. One agreeable day was spent in Evian, where we visited Dr. Sonnenfeld, director of the ICA.

With Elia gone to Dresden, I remained a few more days in Saint-Cergues, then left for Aix-les-Bains, where I wanted to see Mr. Mocatta. I spent delightful hours with him. He entrusted me with a mission to Corfu. I accepted it with pleasure, even though it delayed my return to Smyrna, where Mme Jousselin was preparing to leave permanently.

My stay in Corfu was very agreeable. From there, I went to Piraeus by crossing the canal of Corinth. There I rediscovered the heat I had fled. Finally, I returned to Smyrna, happy to find myself at home and to relax!

What useless agitation, tribulations, and fatigue! If only I had taken care of myself! I might not be where I am now.

The year 1898 was one of the most productive of my career, the year when I was the most active.

In the first place, in the interim I had been entrusted with the school for girls, where everything had to be organized, since Mme Jousselin had left things in the most deplorable state. At that time, I created the garment workshop.

In my school, I was deprived of the intelligent and devoted cooperation of my assistant, Mayer Lévy, my former student in Sofia. He was replaced by M. Tarragano, to whom I entrusted the bookkeeping. In fact, I made it a rule in Smyrna to always entrust the bookkeeping to an assistant. Later, the Alliance imposed that rule in all its schools, but it is far from being followed everywhere. Financial control is in fact nonexistent in the Alliance.

With our schools organized, I wanted to reorganize the *meldars*, where hundreds of children were languishing. I amalgamated five *meldars* into one institution, placed under my financial and pedagogical direction, and that was the origin of the [boys] school for the poor.

In Paris, I had obtained a subsidy of five hundred francs per year for a Cercle Israélite, which I proposed to found. This club was created and set up in a beautiful house in the Armenian quarter. What bother that founding was to cause me! How many meetings, worries, incidents to smooth out, how much trouble to maintain order!

But nothing stopped me, for the need for activity was irresistible. The number of members at the beginning was about two hundred.

Later, this club was transferred to an even larger locale. Every winter, balls were given that attracted a crowd of Jewish young people of both sexes. But with time, enthusiasm waned, the number of members dropped, and card games took on greater and greater importance; as a result, judging I could not continue to preside over a gambling den, I resigned as president in 1900. The club vegetated for another three years and was closed in 1903. It was replaced by a simple reading room, which inherited the library the Alliance had sent to the club at my request.

During my trip to Paris, I had also obtained an advance of two thousand francs, destined for small loans of capital to be made to the former apprentices. To oversee this fund, I set up a workers society.

Baroness de Hirsch had a neighborhood for the poor built in Salonika, and I asked and obtained a subsidy of fifty-five thousand francs to construct cottages for the Russian emigrants we had in Smyrna. To reduce my responsibility in the undertaking, I created, on the advice of M. Bigart, a special commission composed of the notables of Smyrna: MM. Haïm Polako, S. Marcus, Dr. Spierer, Simon Milch, etc. This was a mistake, because that venture, the only one I pursued in Smyrna with the assistance of a committee, turned out badly. We bought a piece of land on the mountain in Karantina,[22] without bothering to find out if there was any water. We then had to negotiate with the water company to have the pipes laid. Finally, the houses were built, and no one wanted to live in them: it was too far away. We finally rented them at prices so low that they did not even cover the taxes and maintenance costs. Following my proposal, the Alliance has just decided to sell these cottages.

I also received eighty thousand francs from Baroness de Hirsch for the reconstruction of the *talmud-tora,* on the condition that the community give twenty thousand. Since the community could promise only three thousand francs, the baroness withdrew her subsidy. Later, the *talmud-tora* was reconstructed using seventy thousand francs given by M. Edmond de Rothschild[23] and thirty thousand by the community.

I also received ten thousand francs to be distributed to help Russian

22. Karantina, suburb of Izmir.
23. Edmond de Rothschild (1854–1934) was a philanthropist known especially for having encouraged and financed settlement in Palestine.

emigrants, plus two hundred to three hundred francs per month for two years, to pay their rents.

Among the numerous gifts to individuals, I should signal a complete set of oculist's instruments with a value of one thousand francs, which went to Dr. Spierer, a good man, with whom I maintained the friendliest relations.

I also had to concern myself with another category of poor people: Thessalian Jews who, persecuted by the Greeks for having celebrated too noisily the short-lived return of the Turks to the country,[24] came to take refuge in Smyrna. I distributed three thousand francs to them and repatriated them.

Two happy family events took place that year: the birth of Narcisse and Sultana's wedding.

Narcisse (Joseph-Chalom) [Shalom] was born on 6 March 1898. His arrival in the world gave me infinite delight. The day of his circumcision was a great celebration, and I spared no expense.

Six days later, a son was also born to Elia, two months early. Michel always had precarious health, worried his parents very much, and finally died on 13 December 1905. I will say more about this poor child later.

Sultana's wedding was the occasion for a lovely demonstration toward me on the part of the community. Everyone who counted in the community of Smyrna, with the communal council in the lead, joined in that celebration, which was very beautiful.

Baskets of flowers filled the great corridor of the school, where the nuptial blessing was to take place. It was 5 June, Sandro's eighth birthday.

When the end of the school year arrived, I was truly tired. I was coughing a great deal and believed, in accordance with the doctor's opinion, that it was only pharyngitis. My thinness (I weighed sixty kilos) should have served as a warning to me. But in the fever of action, was I thinking of myself? Dr. Constans advised me to undergo treatment at Mont-Dore.[25]

I went to this resort via Marseilles, where I was the guest of M. Schamasch (a few months earlier, he had been my guest in Smyrna). Mont-Dore is full of tuberculosis patients. I stayed in the Serciron Hotel and underwent treatment for twenty-one days, which was extremely

24. At the time of the revolt on Crete (see n. 16 above, this chapter), the Ottoman army made major advances in Thessaly, to the point that there was some fear that Greece would again fall under Ottoman domination. Following a peace accord, the Ottomans returned Thessaly to Greece.

25. Mont-Dore, hot springs and winter ski resort in Puy-de-Dôme, France.

exhausting. Once, I even returned to the hotel in a faint. When I left, Dr. Tardieu recommended only laryngeal and nasal douches with saltwater. It was hardly worth the trouble to go to Mont-Dore for that. Those doctors! They're all such bluffers!

During my treatment, I received an invitation from M. Bigart to go see him and M. Leven in Villers-sur-Mer.[26] I thus merely passed through Paris, where M. Bénédict treated me as a friend, as he always did. In Villers, I was the guest of MM. Bigart and Leven; they were charming toward me. M. Leven always had a great deal of affection for me, and I returned it, as is proven by the name I gave my second son, Narcisse, and by the name Or-Jéhouda, which the farm of Tchakyr-Oglu would later receive. We discussed many questions in Villers, where I remained for two days; from there I returned to Paris with M. Bigart.

I went to relax for a few days in Switzerland, in Mürren at Interlaken, in view of the Jungfrau. It is a charming site that had only one drawback for me, the absence of society, since the public there was rather English. I can say that, for ten to twelve days, I did not even hear the sound of my own voice!

M. Zadoc Kahn was vacationing at the time in Interlaken and I went to visit him. He asked me to stay for lunch. Israël Lévy[27] was with him. It was 1 September 1898, the middle of the Dreyfus affair, Henry[28] had just committed suicide. What fever, what emotion! M. Z. Kahn could not contain himself for joy.

During that visit, I obtained a promise from M. Z. Kahn for a subsidy from M. de Rothschild[29] to found a soup kitchen in Smyrna. The idea for that project had been suggested in Mürren, where I read a chapter of François Coppée's *Bonne souffrance* (Good suffering) on Saint Vincent de Paul.

Via Interlaken and the Lake of Brienz, I went to Lucerne, a beautiful city which I found delightful. I went via Vienna to Sofia, where I spent a part of the holidays with Elia. In that city, Joseph Madjar gave me his three children to educate in my school in Smyrna. They were to remain for a year. I returned to Smyrna during the celebration of Succoth.[30]

26. Villers-sur-Mer, seaside resort on the English Channel.

27. Israël Lévy (1856–1939) was chief rabbi of France from 1919 to 1938.

28. Colonel H. J. Henry, author of the false additions to the dossier of Captain Alfred Dreyfus, committed suicide when they were discovered. This discovery led to the review of the case in 1899.

29. Alphonse de Rothschild (1827–1905) was a Jewish banker and philanthropist.

30. Succoth, the Feast of Tabernacles, commemorates the Hebrews' wandering in the desert and begins five days after the great fast of Kippur.

Mme Saporta, designated to take charge of the school for girls, arrived the same time I did. My relations with her were very correct, though I sensed that her home was the center of intrigues and slander, with which I did not concern myself, however. In particular, she spoiled my assistants Farhi and Guéron. But appearances were irreproachable and I did not ask for anything more.

My first concern upon arriving was the organization of the "popular" school [the school for the poorer boys]. Rahmané was named its director.

I made the inauguration of that school coincide with a celebration I organized on 24 November 1898 to commemorate the twenty-fifth anniversary of the founding of the Alliance school in Smyrna. The celebration brought all the notables of the community to the school. Speeches were given by Chief Rabbi Abraham Palatché, by M. Isaac Polako in the name of the alumni association, and by me. (Among my papers, I have kept several copies of the *Buena Esperanza,* which published my speech.) The Anglo-Jewish Association also published a translation of that speech, which had been quite successful, as an appendix to its annual *Bulletin* of that year. A collection on behalf of the Alliance ended the celebration.

Several weeks later, I inaugurated the soup kitchen, thanks to a subsidy of three thousand francs provided me by M. Alphonse de Rothschild. The poor could, for fifteen or twenty cents, have a two-course meal and a large piece of bread. This kitchen was in operation for two years. Then the baron, solicited for numerous similar charities created in Romania, suspended his subsidy, and the program had to be liquidated.

It was at that time I lost my faithful servant Abraham Abayoub. I gave him a beautiful funeral and obtained an allocation of four hundred francs for his widow.

In December of the same year, I was named by M. Emile Horner, delegate of Baron Albert de Rothschild of Vienna,[31] to be administrator of the [Jewish] hospital, conjointly with MM. Haïm and Isaac Polako, Simon Milch, Dr. Spierer, and Maulwurf. I was vice president of the council. Upon his return to Vienna, M. Horner sent an extremely positive report to M. Z. Kahn, which was communicated to me through the Alliance, on the administrative qualities he was kind enough to recognize in me.

Our actions at the hospital were extremely productive. The baron raised his subsidy from eight thousand to twenty-two thousand francs per year. Dr. Spierer was named its director.

---

31. Albert de Rothschild (1844–1911) was from the Vienna branch of the family.

On 1 January 1899 I received a raise of five hundred francs, which brought my salary to forty-eight hundred francs, a figure that has never been surpassed.

On the fifth of the same month, Chief Rabbi Abraham Palatché died. He was a man of great intelligence and vast Talmudic erudition. I had maintained the best of relations with him. His funeral was impressive and I was one of the pallbearers. The brass band of the musical society played at the funeral procession. That was the last time it was heard.

The winter passed very quietly. It was the calm before the storm. While we were discussing the possible candidates for the post of chief rabbi, a large faction, led by the late Nissim Palatché, proclaimed his son Salomon chief rabbi. Thus began a struggle, which was to last several years, between the Palatchists and their adversaries, known as the Colelists [from *kolel*, "community"]. From then on, the subsidies to the Alliance schools were paid only intermittently. My sympathies were naturally for the Colelists, and the Palatchists did not forgive me for it, making this known to me at the time of M. Bénédict's inspection in 1901.

The summer was very tumultuous. To add to my worries, I had to witness at home, between my mother and my wife, scenes of inexplicable sulking. I refrained from intervening, despite the sorrow I felt in not finding any peace at home after so many preoccupations at work. The day of 10 Iyar,[32] my birthday, was even sadder: my mother locked herself in her room and spent the whole day crying. Why? No one could say. That was too much. I wrote a letter to my mother to beg her to let me live in peace and proposed that she go to live in Sofia for some time with Elia, or in a house I would rent for her. This letter was dated 10 Iyar 5659. My mother treasured it as witness to her son's ingratitude.

In the following month of June, I was entrusted by the Alliance with an inspection of the Dardanelles, where M. Kowo and Mlle Adjiman were working.

We spent the vacation in Constantinople, in Halki,[33] where I rented a cottage. Elia also came to spend a month with Léonore and his children: Lucie, aged three years, and Michel, who was one year old. This vacation cost us a great deal of money and we did not get the pleasure from it we were expecting. Poor Michel, constantly sick, did not give his parents any rest. Halki, despite its forests of fir trees, is a very hot island, and the heat does not agree with me. We often received the visits of my relatives and colleagues. I was also the guest of these gentlemen more than once,

32. 10 Iyar 5659, 20 April 1899.
33. Halki (Heybeli ada), an island near Istanbul, famous as a vacation spot.

among others the Frescos and the Navons, and could then observe how much they all envied and despised one another.

The travels and the return to Smyrna were extremely tiring. As always, we were happy to rediscover the comforts of home, the abundant water that had been lacking in Halki, etc. That is always the way it is when one goes on vacation.

Emmanuel had gone to Sofia during the holidays with my mother, who had returned there. He came back with us to Smyrna.

The work of 1899–1900 began. I was obliged to again serve as acting director for the girls school, because Mme Saporta had become gravely ill.

In October 1899 there was an earthquake in Aydin, which caused great suffering in the Jewish quarter. I went to that city to bring aid. The Alliance started a small fund of ten thousand francs for that purpose, which, added to the twenty thousand I had earlier obtained from M. Goldschmidt, will be used to construct a school in Aydin.

The negotiations for the acquisition of Tchakyr-Oglu had finally ended. The farm was handed over to us for about twenty thousand Turkish pounds. I went to Akhisar[34] with my lawyer, Gabriel Calef, to examine the titles, and the property transfer took place on 11 November 1899. The name on the deed was M. Franz Philippson, vice president of the ICA.

From that moment and throughout the entire year, I no longer concerned myself with anything but the organization of that property. I had Saporta named provisional director, but the effective directorship was in Smyrna. This work was extremely agreeable to me: creating, organizing, and administrating are my greatest pleasures. All the services—farming, sharecropping, sheep pens—were set in place, and the working of the land was conducted with order, economy, and activity. I gave the farm the name Or-Jéhouda (from Maïr, son of Judah, father and grandfather of M. Leven).

From the outset, I concerned myself with the construction of a temporary school. M. Magnifico was my architect. The school cost twenty-four thousand francs, and the first students, about twenty of them, were admitted in autumn 1900.

I had our settlers from Aydin[35] transferred to Or-Jéhouda and prepared lodging for them. These good people are still there.

34. Akhisar, about a hundred kilometers north of Izmir.
35. The pogroms of the nineteenth century in Russia brought numerous Russian Jews to the Ottoman Empire. The sultan granted them lands in the region of Aydin, where some of them settled to work the land. At the founding of Or Yehudah, those who remained, about fifteen families, were transferred there.

Vali Kiamil Pasha was of great help to me under all these circumstances; I had him in my pocket, as they say. The Or-Jéhouda project, altogether due to his initiative, is one of those of which I am the proudest.

To complete the organization of the property, I negotiated with the Cassaba railroad company to have a train station built there, for which the ICA paid twenty thousand francs.

Carried away by the whirlwind of activity, I was no longer thinking of my health and was not attending to the little fevers that often kept me in bed for several days at a time. Rachel and my entourage certainly noticed them and redoubled their efforts to take care of me.

The greatest proof of love Rachel gave me was at the time of Jeanne's birth. My mother-in-law had arrived from Constantinople and was sleeping in Rachel's room. On Friday night, 29–30 March 1900, after dinner, we went upstairs to bed and I went to sleep in my room. Rachel was already experiencing labor pains, but she said nothing and calmly said good night to me. I fell into a deep sleep. She then sent for the midwife and prepared herself for the ordeal of childbirth. At dawn, I was awakened by comings and goings in the corridor. I perked up my ears and, suspecting something, jumped out of bed and went out. The voice of a crying newborn explained everything to me: Jeanne (Judith) had just been born. In order to spare me any emotion and not bother me as I slept, Rachel had forbidden everyone to wake me up. It would be difficult to be more devoted than that.

A month later, in April, Benveniste left Smyrna and went to Jerusalem, where he remains.

The summer that followed was marked by several trips I made into the interior: Aydin, Magnesia,[36] Cassaba. Always on the lookout for reforms, I conceived the plan of a synagogue with choir, and with this goal in mind, I hired a voice teacher for the school, M. Carreras, who later became Sophie's piano teacher. The students learned little about singing, but Sophie was to make great progress with this teacher, who showed great fondness for her.

Toward the middle of the summer, the plague made its appearance in Smyrna for the second time, and the city was isolated on all sides by quarantines. There was great suffering. I obtained a sum of eight thousand francs from various persons in Paris and London and distributed it in coupons for bread, rice, meat, and emergency cash. I also allotted each of my teachers 175 francs so that they could go live in the country. One of these gentlemen, Rahmané, showed his gratitude by writing a report

36. Magnesia (Manisa), north of Izmir.

against me to the Alliance: his school was functioning badly, and I had told him so, so he thought he would seek revenge by writing all sorts of rubbish against me. You just can't do anything for some people.

We ourselves went to spend the vacation in Budja,[37] in a pretty house I rented. Samuel and Sultana came with us. The evenings were deliciously cool. We remained there for more than two months and then sublet the house to Jacques Salzer, M. Polako's son-in-law. It was during our stay in Budja that I was named administrator for the community by the *vali,* along with three other persons. The debt I owed Kiamil Pasha did not allow me to refuse this perilous and troublesome honor.

We came back to Smyrna for Succoth. At that time, we received the visit of M. and Mme Antébi,[38] just returned from a trip to Europe. Antébi encouraged me to send Emmanuel to Jerusalem to prepare for a career in engineering. I accepted the proposal but soon realized I had been wrong to entrust my brother to that charlatan. The Jerusalem school is worthless, and that fact is very well known in Paris. It was a wasted year for Emmanuel.

The new school year of 1900–1901 was, as always, signaled by changes in the staff. The most important was the departure of Mme Saporta, who went to rejoin her husband at Or-Jéhouda, and her replacement by Mlle Marguerite Dalem, who came to Smyrna as director, with her sister Jeanne as assistant.

I had known these young women as children in Constantinople. Their father was my friend. Thus from the first day I considered them family and treated them as such.

While I was busy organizing the year's work, I received a mission from the Alliance to go to Athens, where a great number of Romanian emigrants had to be repatriated. This trip was agreeable. I settled all questions with M. Constantinis and had him extend six thousand francs in credit to the Alliance.

I continued to be part of the communal council of Smyrna. Having made a short trip to Or-Jéhouda, I learned on my return that the subsidies to our schools had been eliminated by my colleagues. Naturally, I refused to go to meetings as long as the subsidies were not reestablished. That is what my colleagues wanted. In my absence, they settled all the rabbinical questions, to be precise, the naming of Salomon Palatché as

37. Budja (Buca), near Izmir.
38. Abraham Albert Antébi (1869–1919) was the director of the trades school of the Alliance in Jerusalem.

head of Bet-Dîne[39] and that of Joseph Bensignor[40] as chief rabbi. The *vali* approved these arrangements, and having invited representatives of all the communities of the *vilayet* to the palace itself, he had a formal election take place in his presence. The vote was fifteen to thirteen in favor of M. Bensignor: I voted against him, and the Colelists themselves voted for! That shows the degree of intelligence among the Jews of Smyrna. This happened in December 1900. M. Bensignor is still chief rabbi of the community.

Three months later, on 1 April 1901, I proceeded to the inauguration of Or-Jéhouda. I invited Vali Kiamil Pasha, all the authorities of the city and of the *vilayet,* and five Jewish notables. M. Gaudin, director of the Cassaba railroad, gave me free use of a special train. The celebration, the dinner, everything was splendid: that inauguration cost the ICA two thousand francs.

During the Passover celebration that followed, I went to make my usual visit to Mme Benmaor, and that good woman placed a few cloves in my vest pocket to ward off bad luck, because my success meant that too many people were talking about me, and I had to fear the evil eye. Alas! How true her predictions were! From that moment on, I can say that my star began to fade; I had reached the apogee of my influence; now I could only descend.

That began with the Bergama school: unable to keep its commitments, it had to be closed. Then, Or-Jéhouda received Abravanel as director, and the bureau of the ICA gave him secret instructions to prevent me from interfering in any way in the administration. If the ICA had just told me that frankly, how many misunderstandings would have been avoided!

Instead of that, they wrote me a hypocritical letter naming me inspector of Or-Jéhouda. In M. Leven's mind, that letter was sincere, but the bureau, Mayerson[41] in particular, wanted to marginalize me, as I saw when he later wrote to M. Bénédict. That conduct toward me, when I had devoted body and soul to the ICA, had risked my life for it in Tchandarlik, was a crushing blow. I never recovered from it. The fact that Eastern communities are ungrateful, that their members are false and underhanded, can be explained and excused by their inferior intellectual state; what I could not allow was that a European administration

39. Bet-Dîne (*beit din,* Hebrew), rabbinical tribunal.

40. Joseph Bensignor (1837–1913) was chief rabbi of Izmir from 1900 until his death.

41. Emile Mayerson (1859–1933) was administrator of the ICA.

could be guilty of the same conduct. I suffered morally because of it, because it ruined all my preconceptions and destroyed my energy and my initiatives for the future.

During the next month, May, an incident occurred at Or-Jéhouda: Romanian students mistreated by Abravanel complained to their consul, who sent me a request for explanations. On that occasion, the ICA charged me with making an inspection at Or-Jéhouda. That was the last time I set foot on the school farm I had founded.

In June 1901, we had to seek treatment for Jeanne Dalem (today Jeanne Toledo), who was overcome by hysteria. The two sisters left the city on 29 June, embittered by everything they had had to suffer in Smyrna. The same year, Marguerite married a member of the family, M. Reisfeld, from Crowley (Louisiana).

I had asked for a leave to seek treatment for my throat, which was making me cough more and more. Since the Alliance had informed me that M. Bénédict would come to Smyrna for an inspection, I had to wait for him. Bénédict remained in Smyrna from 21 July to 4 August. He was satisfied with everything he did and wrote a sixty-page report to the Alliance in which he did not spare his praise of me.

The presence of Bénédict gave my enemies the opportunity to set out their grievances against me.

The community officially asked him that I be transferred. What did they have to reproach me for? For not having associated myself with the Palatchist scoundrels. Bénédict had no trouble demonstrating how ridiculous that claim was. But the fact remained that this attitude, on the part of a community for which I had attempted to do so much good, afflicted me deeply.

The fatigue, the emotion, the sorrow, and the oppressive heat of those two weeks weakened me considerably. Thus when, on 4 August 1901, I embarked with Bénédict for Naples, I was exhausted and my cough had taken hold permanently. It would never leave me again.

From Naples, via Italy, Switzerland, and Alsace, I went to Ems,[42] whose thermal waters have a reputation for curing respiratory ailments. I remained for twenty days. There I received the visit of Mlle Ungar, whom I accompanied to Koblenz.[43] I have not seen her since.

When my course of treatment was ended, I went to Paris, where it was easy to see that the intrigues of my enemies had not in any way altered the Central Committee's confidence in me. I was often the guest of MM.

42. Ems, city in western Germany (Rhine-Westphalia).
43. Koblenz, city in western Germany (Rhine-Westphalia).

Bénédict, Leven, Z. Kahn, and even of the bureau of the ICA, which offered both me and Pariente lunch.

In Paris, I was especially concerned about Emmanuel, for whom I obtained six hundred francs from the Alliance in order to place him at the school of arts and crafts in Châlons. Antébi was furious with this success and wrote a letter against Emmanuel to the Alliance.

I spent about three weeks in Paris, during which time I often went to see Mme Dalem, rue Saint-Paul. I left for Sofia the evening after Kippour. Marguerite and Jeanne Dalem came to accompany me to the railroad station. I remained in Sofia for a week, then went to Constantinople, where I met Emmanuel, just back from Jerusalem. I fitted him out and sent him off to Sofia-Châlons.

I debarked in Smyrna in a state of weariness and emaciation, which was noticed by everyone. My cough gave me no respite. I have the impression it was between July or August and October 1901 that the illness I now suffer from took hold.

SELECTIONS FROM LETTERS
TO THE ALLIANCE CENTRAL COMMITTEE

Aboard El-Kahira, *17 November 1893*

... Here we are, since day before yesterday, in quarantine facing the Dardanelles; we will remain here for three days before being authorized to continue our route to Smyrna. We must hope that no suspect illness is declared aboard. I will then have finally ended this trip, which has been very long for me and very costly for the Alliance.

During the week I was obliged to wait in Constantinople, I tried not to waste my time entirely; and I shall take advantage of the forced leisure of my floating prison to give you the impressions I had in seeing Turkey and the Turks again, and what I heard from the Alliance in Constantinople. I shall tell you of my visits to the Turkish school authorities, my interview with His Holiness the exarch of the Bulgarians, my conversations with some of my colleagues regarding the teaching of certain subjects of the curriculum, and will end with a proposal, which I am happy to have the opportunity to make to you before setting foot in Smyrna.

What strikes a Bulgarian entering Turkey is above all the air of freedom one breathes here. Under a theoretically despotic government, one certainly enjoys more freedom than in any constitutional country. That difference is particularly obvious for someone coming from Sofia: there, everything is specified beforehand, regulated; one cannot come and go, attend to one's affairs, or write a letter without running the risk of committing a thousand infractions of the laws and regulations; it is as if there is a policeman around every corner. Here, in contrast, one hardly feels there is a government; one of course sees its employees, more or less poor, but they seem to be on the job only to have a means of feeding their families and to serve the public for some small bonus. The affairs of government must go very poorly, but those of individuals go very well indeed.

The absence of an interfering police force, of crushing taxes, of very heavy critical duties, such things cannot be appreciated enough by the sultan's non-Muslim subjects. In particular, the Jews of the country can with good cause consider themselves the happiest of all their coreligionists in the world: enjoying all rights, they have almost no duties; they do not even have to worry about the antisemitic movement, which has flourished in almost all civilized states. Turkey could be a true Promised Land for our coreligionists if they knew how to profit from the advantages of their situation.

Unfortunately, the indolence of the Turks is shared by the Jews, who, it seems to me, do not like to trouble themselves, as they say; they certainly want their *kief*,[44] all their comforts, but on the condition that it come of itself, so to speak, or by working as little as possible. It is to this desire for money, combined with an entirely Eastern laziness, that I attribute the few scruples that the population seems to bring to its daily transactions. I have a certain number of friends and acquaintances in the business world, and I have seen them close up: well, it is appalling how they lie to one another, deceive one another, steal from one another. It is as if the moral sense is lacking in all of them.

It is impossible to suppose that the education given at the school could ever correct so many defects: the evil could of course be attenuated somewhat, but it seems to me that whoever would claim to moralize those masses, through schooling or otherwise, would be fooling himself. Too many elements conspire to corrupt them: the example from above, the absence of a government, Greek bad faith, Armenian baseness, indolence, the love of Eastern pleasures, all acting in concert before the eyes of that ignorant and essentially imitative population. That is more than enough to make the moral actions of the work of the Alliance in the East very difficult.

The atmosphere one breathes in Bulgaria is far more healthy and moral, and life far more active and honest; the progress and regeneration of our coreligionists are and continue to be far more rapid there. There the Alliance has very little more to do: in a few years, it will be able to (should I say it should?) liquidate its programs, as it did in Vidin and Sofia. In contrast, in

---

44. *Kief* (*keyf*, Turkish), "pleasure."

Turkey, the Alliance should remain at least as long as the Turks are there, plus another twenty years.

As a result of the necessity, the indispensability of the Alliance in that country, the organization is considered a major power. For myself, arriving from Sofia, where for six years I had to hide even the name of the Alliance from the authorities, as one would do for a dangerous society, I was keenly, and as you can imagine, very agreeably surprised to see the name of the Alliance Israélite known and respected everywhere. Turks, Greeks, and Armenians speak of "Alliance" schools, "Alliance" programs, "Alliance" directors, with a consideration I was far from expecting.

Two examples among a thousand: I present myself to the travel agency of the Egyptian Company to get my tickets; I ask to see the director. "Who are you?" they say. I show my card. Immediately, all doors are open to me, all the employees are endlessly polite, and I am given a 30 percent discount on the price of the ticket as director of the Alliance. (That is good to keep in mind for later trips I might have to make.)

Another example: I go to make a few official visits, which I shall speak of in a moment: everywhere I receive the warmest welcome as director of the Alliance Israélite. The official letters of recommendation I am carrying all mention my status as director of the Alliance. Please note I do not tell anyone what our society is: everyone in the area knows our work, and if I am to judge by the fondness everyone has shown me, both the public at large and high officials, all appreciate it at its true value.

My first and most important visit was to the staff director at the Ministry of Public Education. He appears to be well educated and speaks French fairly well. We talked about schools for a long time, and he seemed to take pleasure in the conversation. The letter he gave me for the director of public education in Smyrna is so flattering that I will forgo transcribing it here. Chukri [Şükrü] Bey (that is his name) asks his subordinate, among other things, to examine with the greatest attention all the proposals I might make to him, inasmuch as this teacher, he says, has very new ideas, which I encourage you to study, etc.

Chukri Bey hopes I will not have any difficulty with the authorities in Smyrna; but, he added, if in fulfilling your mission you encounter any obstacles of any nature whatever, you have only to write me: I will immediately have the minister recommend you to the *vali* (governor-general) himself. I forgot to tell you that Chukri Bey is the son-in-law of the grand vizier Kiamil Pasha.

I made another no less interesting visit to the director of non-Muslim schools, one Abdul Hassib. Through the letter he gave me for the *vali*'s assistant, I will have free access to the governor and can call on his support in every circumstance.

But even more useful to me is the confidential letter from the chief of general security for his agent in Smyrna; thanks to that official, I will be able to count on the cooperation of the police, should the occasion arise, for all questions that are not purely school matters.

Since you have known the East for so long, you also know that most matters come about through protection. I thought it wise, therefore, before going to Smyrna, to be recommended as highly as possible to the persons I might have dealings with.

To be altogether in the good graces of the Ottoman authorities, I began to study Turkish more thoroughly, which I already knew a little. The knowledge of the Bulgarian language did me nothing but good in Sofia; it allowed me to go everywhere, to associate with all the high officials, and to win their confidence and friendship. If I learn Turkish well, I believe it will only bring me closer to the masters of the country, for whom I will no longer be an outsider, and my mission in Smyrna will be all the easier and all the more productive.

I have never gone through Constantinople without making a visit to the exarch of the Bulgarians, whom I know from the time when I was director of the Ortakeuy school. His Holiness wishes to honor me with his friendship and keeps me with him for hours on end before allowing me to retire. I shall recount only the part of our conversation dealing with the Jews.

I spoke to His Holiness about the Vratsa affair. I asked him if, like those great popes who honored Catholicism by publishing bulls against the prejudice of ritual murder, he would not also be disposed to say, with the authority and competence proper to him, to all the Bulgarians of Bulgaria and Macedonia that ritual murder has never existed except in the imagination of envious fanatics. Here is the response of Monsignor Joseph I: "The belief in this prejudice has been passed on to the Bulgarians from the Greek Church. The Slavs did not believe that ritual murder existed, but the Greeks taught them this superstition, which as yet they have not been able to rid themselves of. I would willingly publish a bull on this subject if I had the liberty of my movements. But you know how M. Stambolov has limited my influence over the Bulgarian clergy: the synod of Sofia decides everything, and I must approve everything it decides. If you could obtain from the synod of Sofia a declaration that the belief in ritual murder is groundless, you can be sure I would sign such a declaration with both hands."

Regarding the possible consequences for Bulgarian Judaism of the fusing of schools that took place in Sofia, the exarch said this: "Do not fear that our teachers will proselytize: they themselves do not believe in anything and, more than all the others, make fun of religion and the Church, they to whom the laws have, alas, entrusted the mission of teaching the catechism. Your children will not learn Hebrew, no doubt, but they will learn no more about our catechism, for the good reason that the Bulgarians themselves are not learning it. I work very hard to maintain a bit of conservatism in our country, but I am not accomplishing anything: in a little while, you can be sure that the Bulgarians will be a people without religion. It is that conviction that makes me want Russian domination for Bulgaria: with the Russians as masters, we are at least sure that religion will not be lost."

And there we were back into politics.

When I rose to take leave of him, His Holiness repeated how sorry he was to see me leave Bulgaria, and was kind enough to add: "The best thing I can wish for my country is that it produce many men like you." I was abashed by so much kindness and left His Holiness, but not without promising to come back and see him every time I came through Constantinople.

At the exarchate, I found a great number of government workers from Sofia, whom I was very happy to see again: when one is abroad, one feels more connected to compatriots, who are almost like brothers. We discussed matters of the country for a long time, and then I left the residence of the head of the Bulgarian Church, with the feeling that this time I was bidding farewell permanently to Bulgaria and the Bulgarian language.

The first thing I had to do when I entered Turkey was to take a look at the program I will have to apply in this country, which differs slightly from the official Bulgarian curriculum that was required in Sofia. All the subjects we have to offer are perfectly determined by your 1883 curriculum; only details on the teaching of Turkish are missing. It would be very useful to me to know your views on this subject. . . .

If we must offer serious studies in Turkish at the Smyrna school, be persuaded, Mr. President, that I will spare no effort to soon be in a position to oversee the teaching myself. . . .

We will be in Smyrna the twentieth of this month. I shall write you immediately after my arrival to send you an accounting of my travel expenses and to ask for a little money as well. I will need it to set up my household. . . .

Archives of the AIU, Turquie LXXIV.E.

23 April 1894

. . . In keeping with the desire of the Central Committee, I have taken advantage of the Passover break to go to Aydin and to study on the site the question of the school the community of that city has asked you to open there. It is the first excursion I have made to the interior of Asia Minor.

And even though it lies outside my subject, allow me to express to you,

Mr. President, my admiration for that magnificent region, where nature has accumulated all the riches of a marvelous fertility, as if for its own pleasure.

The route from Smyrna to Aydin consists of a succession of gardens and fields, where the products of temperate skies are joined to those of the hot regions: olive trees, cotton plants, and blackberry bushes alternate with orange trees, lemon trees, and fig trees; immense expanses of rye and wheat give way to endless vineyards and vegetable gardens that produce as many as four crops a year. Thus we can understand why the practical Greeks chose these regions as the place to establish their settlements! One encounters the debris of Ionia's greatness at every step of the route taken by the railroad, and the ancient Ephesus appears there, as if to show what that country could be in the hands of an intelligent and hardworking people.

After three hours of travel, during which time we relived one of the most interesting eras of ancient history, we arrived at Aydin, the ancient city of Tralles. Let me say immediately that it is a dreary city, built at the foot of a hill; almost all the houses are at the bottom, because of the frequency of earthquakes. That explains why fires are so dreaded and so dangerous. The proximity of the Menderes,[45] which forms many marshes along its path, makes the climate of Aydin rather unhealthy: malarial fevers are endemic.

The population of that city is fifty thousand, of which thirty-seven thousand are Muslims, ten thousand are Greeks, and twenty-eight thousand [*sic,* three thousand] are Jews. The Jewish community is one of the poorest I know. One wonders how, in a country so fertile, where each of the twelve months of the year provides a new product for export, the Jews have not found a way to acquire a more prosperous situation. Eastern apathy and above all the extraordinary ignorance of these populations together explain the precarious material state in which they live.

Aydin impressed me as one of those regions depicted by travelers in Africa, where not a ray of European civilization has yet penetrated. It is a territory absolutely virgin of all intellectual culture (apart from the Greeks, who possess excellent schools and have all the commerce of the region in their own hands). In particular, the Jews of that city are extremely backward: their only means of existence is the sale of manufactured goods. There are also a small number of shoemakers and tinsmiths, but that is all.

Until last January there was not even a communal organization in Aydin; at my insistence, a communal council was elected, which has since been recognized by the chief rabbi of Smyrna. The first thing this council did was to turn to the Alliance to ask it for a school. Until now, here is what there has been in Aydin.

45. Menderes, river in Asia Minor.

The community possesses a school site composed of five rooms. Five old men, suitable for placement in nursing homes, have each taken possession of one of the rooms; there children from three to nine years old are piled up, supposedly to learn to read Hebrew; the rabbis are paid ten to forty centimes a week per student. A little while ago, some poor devil who sold something or other, not having succeeded in commerce, went off to become a rabbi. But where could he bring together the children? He went to the *talmud-tora* and, noticing a wine cellar, placed thirty-five to forty students there. They spend ten hours a day in darkness, because the two lamps that illuminate that underground passage give only the most dubious light.

Thus the *talmud-tora* is composed of six rabbis whose mission it is to torture thirty to forty children for ten hours a day. Spare me the pain of discussing the state of the premises, the hygiene of the students, the sort of thing one learns in that caravansary: anything I could say would not approach the truth. . . .

Thus, in Aydin, I found a *talmud-tora* more miserable than I had ever seen; a communal council that would certainly like to do something but does not know where to begin; an embryo of a school; a few young people full of ardor; no communal organization; no resources; no budget.

Under such conditions, it is obvious that the Alliance cannot dream of founding a school in Aydin.

But when one recognizes that before the organization of the work of the Alliance in the East, all communities there more or less resembled that of Aydin, and that a community of three thousand is declining more and more, to the point where one worries greatly whether it will ever be able to get out of that situation on its own, then it seems it is the duty of every Jew to consider the question a grave matter and to attempt to place that community on the right path. I have tried to do that in Aydin and I believe I have succeeded to no small degree. . . .

Archives of the AIU, Turquie LXXIV.E.

24 July 1894

. . . The example of a few coreligionists from Constantinople who attained the highest positions owing to their knowledge of the Turkish language is designed to encourage us in our experiment in that direction.

If you will allow me to rise to a larger consideration of the question, I may even add that, for the Jews of Turkey, this is the most favorable moment to seize hold of some influence over the affairs of this country. Did not the Greeks govern Turkey for three centuries? Since 1821, they have been set aside, and the Armenians are in turn losing the confidence of the Turks through their conspiracies, their revolutionary newspapers, etc. Why couldn't the Jews find themselves in a position to receive the inheritance of the Armenians? The Jews, at least until further notice, do not have nationalist tendencies; they are and will long remain faithful subjects of the sultan. If they knew the language of the country well, why couldn't they succeed just as well as the Armenians, since they are a hundred times more intelligent?

But let us come down from such heights. I was saying that it is up to the Alliance to take the initiative and to encourage members of the community to frequent the government schools for Jews. . . .

Archives of the AIU, Turquie LXXIV.E.

20 May 1895

. . . Last October, a M. Jélin[46] arrived in Smyrna. He was a student and then a teacher at the Alliance school in Jerusalem and is today a teacher in a Jewish boarding school in the Holy City. He is one of the most zealous members of the Bné Berith Society, whose seat is in New York and which, under different names, has spread its branches more or less everywhere, especially in Cairo and Jerusalem. M. Jélin came to Smyrna and succeeded in creating a lodge of that Freemasonry here. The avowed goal of the association is to "do good," but in addition, there is certainly a hidden goal, which I have not yet succeeded in discovering. Some, and they are the most numerous, claim that the members of Bné Berith are working toward the creation of an independent Jewish state in Palestine, while others think the society is the rival, or rather the enemy, of the Alliance, whose "anti-Jewish and antinationalist" actions it claims to combat.

What is admitted by members of the Smyrna lodge is that the members of the Bné Berith Society will acquire a preponderant influence in the community and will gradually seize hold of all minds and of all communal administration.

In the beginning, the lodge had twenty members: they now have close to forty, including several of the most intelligent rabbis and many educated and enterprising young people. The monthly dues are minimal. The members of the association get together every week, their deliberations are secret, and no one knows what is said there. Here is what has been done up to this point:

1. A reading room has been founded with the name Dorshei Leshon Ever,[47] for the propagation of the Hebrew language. This room is open and

46. David Jélin (Yellin) (1864–1941) was a pedagogue and promoter of the rebirth of modern Hebrew.

47. Dorshei Leshon Ever (Friends of the Hebrew language) was a society linked to the Haskalah (Jewish Enlightenment movement). The society's goal was the diffusion and renewal of the Hebrew language.

free to the public; only Hebrew newspapers and books are received and read.

2. Under the name Rofe Holim,[48] a service for home help for poor sick people has been organized. Jewish doctors, whether or not they are members of the organization, have offered their services at no cost to the Aavat-Hessed (the name of the Smyrna lodge). Medicine is provided free by the "Rothschild hospital."[49]

3. Aavat-Hessed has proposed that all Jewish students who frequent Protestant schools be withdrawn. On the initiative of that society, the chief rabbi and the communal council signed a document that was read in all the synagogues, in which it is said that, in the future, the following measures will be taken against those who send their sons or daughters to Protestant schools: their children will not be circumcised, their dead will not be buried, the poor will be given no assistance, not even unleavened bread at Passover. Of 150 children of both sexes who frequented these schools, 100 have already left them. (I have admitted 20, Mme Jousselin 16, the *talmud-tora* 15.)

4. Finally, the members of Aavat-Hessed are undertaking to relieve hidden poverty, to intervene in settling amicably the disputes that arise between individuals, and, in a word, to do as much good as they can.

At this time, they are working to found a school in Bédava-Bagtché, which is the most impoverished area of the city.

They have, then, covered a great distance in a relatively short period of time. I attribute this success to the method adopted, which seems to me identical to that used by Catholic missions: gentleness, persuasion, perseverance, an overly sweet manner of speaking, and, above all, great energy and deep convictions concealed behind a placid appearance.

What motive has been powerful enough to make these people, ordinarily so apathetic, become so active and skillful? There is obviously outside inspiration, some covert leadership. The Jerusalem lodge is kept informed of what is being done here, and in turn, it informs the central committee in New York.

Steps were taken to persuade me to join that Freemasonry. I responded that since the goal of Bné Berith is to do good, I thought I could make myself useful to my peers without enrolling myself in an association, and that, in fact, I am not part of any society on principle, preferring to conserve complete independence in the mission the Alliance has entrusted to me.

---

48. Rofe Holim (literally, "healer of the sick" in Hebrew) was a charitable organization.

49. Hospital founded in 1827, called "Rothschild" because Baron Albert de Rothschild of Vienna maintained it to a great extent and made up for annual deficits.

In giving you an account of the formation and progress of the Smyrna lodge of Bné Berith, I would be very grateful, Mr. President, if you would be kind enough to tell me what we should think of that society, since your knowledge of it is undoubtedly of long date, and what attitude we should take toward it.

Archives of the AIU, Turquie LXXIV.E.

28 November 1895

. . . Although I am away from Bulgaria and my Bulgarian coreligionists, I have not ceased to maintain fairly frequent relations with many of them. The news I have been receiving for some time is becoming increasingly grave. It seems that a movement has been created in Bulgaria in favor of mass emigration by the Jews to Palestine. Societies are forming under the name Carmel[50] to colonize the Holy Land. A M. Marcou Baruch,[51] who strikes me as a scoundrel, has founded a French monthly magazine in Philippopolis for the propagation of the ideas of emigration. This sheet, written in the style of a schoolboy who often played hooky, seems very dangerous to me both for the Jews of Bulgaria and for those of Turkey.

It tells the Jews of Bulgaria to leave that country. Mitakof[52] and all the other antisemites are telling them exactly the same thing in their publications. M. Baruch and M. Mitakof are thus in perfect agreement. And there is more: M. Baruch, with a criminal lack of awareness, praises the enemies of the Jews, exalts antisemites, blesses them. Yes, he tells them, persecute us, hunt us down, for in that way we will become conscious of ourselves, and we will go found a state in Palestine.

Those things and many others as well are found in the newspaper *Carmel,* which is sent not only to the Jews of Bulgaria but also to those of Turkey. Can you imagine the censor confiscating these brochures, in which it is a ques-

50. The Carmel associations were founded by Joseph Marcu Baruch and named after Mount Carmel in Haifa. The first of these appeared in Sofia in 1895. In Philippopoli, Baruch also founded a journal in French, titled *Carmel.* It lasted for only five issues, appearing between September 1895 and January 1896.

51. Joseph Marcu Baruch (1872–99) was a pre-Herzlian Zionist and is considered the founding father of political Zionism in Bulgaria.

52. In 1893, Nikola Mitakof published a periodical, entitled *Bulgaria for the Bulgarians,* dedicated to antisemitic propaganda. Beginning with the second issue, it was called *Bulgaria without Jews.* Publication was suspended in October 1894. It was taken over by another antisemitic journal, *Narodna Svoboda* (National freedom; 1894–95), for which Mitakof served as owner and publisher. His antisemitism was motivated by economic factors in particular; he represented the interests of strata fearing competition from Jewish capital.

tion of going to found a state in Palestine? But that has in fact happened; the censor in Smyrna confiscated a packet of these newspapers addressed to the agent of *Carmel*.

What is even more grave is that Jewish families are already leaving their country, their businesses, to go become plowmen in Palestine.

It is understandable that the Jews of Russia and Romania would emigrate, but it is inexplicable why the Jews of Bulgaria would leave a country where they are, from the material point of view, infinitely better off than those of Turkey. I believe an evildoer should not be free to commit his evil deeds. M. Marcou Baruch, after editing the journal *Hachophet*[53] in Algiers, after soliciting in vain a job as salesman in Sofia, became a journalist in Philippopolis, and is prepared to become an actor or a rope dancer if that does not succeed.

M. Baruch has no nation, but the Jews of Bulgaria do have one, and they should be advised not to leave it, but rather to commit themselves to remain there, to love it, to serve it, to make themselves its worthy sons through their honesty, their education, their work.

In the absence of an organization of the Jewish faith in Bulgaria, and of an intelligent spiritual leader who could stop the maleficent actions of Baruch, who could make the unfortunate, misled people understand the disappointments of all sorts they are setting themselves up for in leaving a country where their condition seems quite tolerable, I wonder whether the Alliance could not intervene discreetly to abate the evil. Through the intervention of its teachers, it could perhaps give advice and warnings to whom it may concern. It could even write directly to a few persons in whom it has confidence, to show them the danger they are posing to Judaism in Bulgaria.

I submit these reflections for your evaluation. More than once already, the Alliance has thought and acted for these overgrown children, the Jews of the East. Perhaps you will find in this circumstance that your intervention is not inopportune.

Archives of the AIU, Turquie LXXIV.E.

17 July 1896

. . . I am writing to respond to your circular of 1 June, relating to the moral direction to give to teaching.

In their monthly meetings, your teachers of Smyrna have had the opportunity to raise the questions discussed in that circular. Following various

53. *Hachophet* (*ha-shofet*, "the judge," Hebrew) was a newspaper with Zionist leanings founded by Marcu Baruch in Algeria during his stay in that country between 1893 and 1894.

incidents of school life that they had to examine, they were led to note that the new generation educated at the school is distinguished neither by its disinterested love of the good nor by its attachment to things Jewish. Moreover, it seemed to them that the conduct and education of our children are noticeably inferior to those we observed in the students educated in schools of other denominations. Linking these two facts, we asked ourselves if they did not have the same cause, and if that cause did not reside in the nature of our teaching. The discussion of this subject was opened when I went to Paris; there I had the opportunity to inform the Central Committee of my doubts about the effectiveness of our moral activities. Your circular now gives me the opportunity to develop my thoughts.

One must, first, exclude from discussion the goodwill and devotion of our teachers, who have always made the most praiseworthy efforts to elevate our pupils. None of us has deliberately neglected that part of our task. What we must wonder is whether the results have been proportionate to these efforts.

Before making an evaluation on that subject, let me recall how judgments on the matter can vary, depending on the temperament of the persons who make them. There will always be people who find that everything is for the best in the best of all possible worlds, and others who think we are headed for ruin. Let us attempt to place ourselves between the two extremes and examine the facts closely.

If we wanted to know the results of an apprenticeship program in a city, we would have only to count the number of workers who earn their living from the work we have taught them. Let us construct an analogous statistic concerning the students who have come out of our schools, and see how many young people it has made, not better educated, but simply better, more devoted to Judaism and its traditions. In Smyrna, of nearly two thousand students who have passed through the classrooms of our school, I have searched in vain; I do not find more than twenty on whose cooperation we can count for a useful and serious project. Three years ago, I created an Alliance publicity committee and it was from those twenty that I had to choose; I founded the alumni association, and it was again among those twenty from whom I had to recruit my committee; Mme Jousselin organized a school committee, and it was once more the same twenty young persons who formed it. It is clear as day that for an effort of a quarter-century of work, and for the half-million spent during that period of time, the result is meager.

And yet, see how difficult it is to agree on these questions! If I wanted to see everything through rose-colored glasses, I could tell you: "What! There isn't a generation trained by us in Smyrna? But look at the publicity committee, the alumni association, the girls school committee, isn't it exclusively alumni who work for these programs of general utility?" And I might say that, not to make you happy, but because in my soul and conscience I believed it was adequate.

But my conviction is that it is altogether inadequate. I can imagine that of the two thousand students on our registration lists, there will be many, let us say half, who did not stay at the school long enough to carry away a very profound mark of our actions, but there must still be half who spent four or five years with us. Of these thousand students, let us concede a failure rate of 50 percent, 60 percent, 90 percent if you like: there should still remain one-tenth, that is, one hundred young people with the manners, education, and sentiments we are seeking to inculcate in the new generation. I have already said that this core of one hundred young people does not exist in Smyrna; I have already been generous in granting there are twenty. What happened to the other one thousand nine hundred and eighty students? And why, from the moral perspective, have our actions been so sterile?

In my humble opinion, there is only one way to explain this state of affairs. It has to do with the professional instruction we ourselves received. Educated in France by French teachers, we long believed that our sole mission was to instruct; everyone knows that pedagogy is a new science in France, and the word "education" has been understood and applied there for only about fifteen years. It is therefore not surprising that, imbued with these ideas, we saw the principal goal of our mission from the outset as that of "instructing" the ignorant youth of the East. In producing good cipherers, good geographers, we thought we had done our duty. The official curriculum that was imposed upon us in 1883 was well designed to confirm us in that opinion, since the list of subjects to be taught was considerably extended; we thus had to cram more and more notions into the minds of our children, teach them things that even we did not know, such as, for example, the history of certain peoples of Europe, which we set out to study. The effort exerted by your teachers was immense, and like a spur thrust into the flesh of a steed, which makes him run faster and faster, the semester reports were returned to us with comments such as this: "Faster!—You're running behind!—Pick up the pace!" And we picked up the pace, and lessons followed lessons, and thanks to that breakneck pace toward knowledge, the level of instruction of our students was considerably raised. But when do you want us to find the time to concern ourselves with their education? We were instructing them at full speed, but we were doing little to truly educate them. And today, we must reap what we have sown.

What we have sown is instruction: the Jews of the East are no longer as fanatical, as imbued with prejudices and superstitions, or as ignorant as they were in 1870. In all the communities there are young people who speak

French, who know how to do arithmetic, and who possess a few notions about history and geography. It is a very appreciable result. But it no longer meets our ambitions. In 1883, you gave instruction a solid organization by providing us with a curriculum. You would now like to give us the means to fulfill the second part of our task, the education of our students.

Here again, the following response is easy. I could tell you that, in our lessons, we have never neglected to concern ourselves with the true education of our students, that every opportunity is good for moralizing, for elevating their hearts, etc. That is a lovely theory and a well-turned phrase; but for fear of allowing ourselves to be misled by words, let us consider the reality behind that phrase.

The subjects studied in our schools are very numerous; let us examine those that can serve for moralizing. First of all, let us strike from the list the subjects taught by indigenous professors, such as Turkish, Greek, and especially Hebrew as it is taught by our rabbis; let us also strike arithmetic, geography, and grammar, where it is difficult to find "matter for philosophy," as Molière would say; let us also eliminate physics, chemistry, and natural history, where, except for the notion of the infinite power of God, we hardly see any way that these sciences could contribute to the formation of the heart. That leaves history and reading, nothing more. Everyone is always saying that history is the best school for forming character, that one finds fine examples of devotion, abnegation, honor, and virtue. That is true, but one must not forget that, like the languages of Aesop, history is the best and the worst school for morals. For every example of devotion, how many others are there where ambition was the sole motivation that led to action, and for every man of honor, how many rogues! Are we to encourage students to do good by showing Christopher Columbus dying in prison, Joan of Arc at the stake, the massacres of the Crusades, and the religious wars? History, if you like, is from the first to the last page only the amplification of that beautiful maxim by La Fontaine: might makes right; the strongest and most deceitful is always the best. Far from making us love humanity, history is rather fit to make us disgusted with it, because since the beginning of the world virtue has always been unlucky, while force and lies have always been victorious. To moralize using history, one must very often falsify history, and you cannot ask us to do that.

But let us assume that all historical characters were models of virtue, or that we have purged our history manuals so as to be able to give them the subtitle "Morality in Action." In our lessons, we would still have to deal with the facts and events that do not lend themselves to any commentary: how could one draw the slightest useful reflection from the account of the Thirty Years War? And the unfortunate wars of Louis XV? And thus for most other events? The part to be given to the philosophy of history thus becomes excessively limited, and to count on it would be to comfort ourselves with the most disappointing of illusions.

That leaves reading. Yes, reading is the most effective means for elevating souls, provided, however, that one suppresses all the books where lessons about things and amusing tales occupy too great a place, for in truth, the fabrication of glass or of candles has only a distant relation to morality. We know by experience how difficult is the choice of such books. Nevertheless, it remains true that in reading we have an excellent way to educate our children.

The question is whether that is enough. Let us consider what, in this respect, the pedagogues throughout the world do. We find that schools everywhere are divided into two categories: religious schools and secular schools. In the first, morality is intimately linked to religion, and it is the priest or pastor who teaches it and who teaches it *ex professo,* in the form of catechism at school and of sermon at church. In the second, religion is completely eliminated, but morality persists and is the first among the re-quired subjects; on this point, the schools in Paris follow the detailed curricu-lum elaborated by M. Gréard. But I ask, are our schools religious or secular? If they are religious, who is giving religious instruction? It is not our teachers, and even less our rabbis. If they are secular, who, then, is teaching morality? No one, because it is a hazy subject that, it is said, should emerge from all our teaching. Hence your Jewish schools, situated in countries where the attachment to religious matters is so keen, are perhaps the only schools in the world where neither religious instruction, as in religious schools, nor morality, as in secular schools, is taught. We rely on random encounters in our reading manuals for the more important half of our task.

Please note again that one of the principal factors of education, the teacher's example, is reduced to almost nothing here. In other schools, the teacher has a class that he keeps from morning till afternoon, and it is impossible that in the long run his students will not model themselves on the teacher and manage to imitate him; for his part, he knows his class belongs to him from morning till afternoon, and he can observe his students all day long throughout the year and can correct them at every opportunity. But among us? Each of our teachers has at least three classes every day, and the 120 to 130 students with whom he deals are not attached to him exclusively: most often, the teacher of Turkish, Hebrew, or Greek undoes in four hours what the Alliance teacher was able to do in two or three. The moral action of example, upon which one can count in all the primary schools of other countries, is an important factor that is lacking among us.

As a result, how can you think that, with such disadvantages, education could have progressed among us to the same degree as instruction?

Up to this point, I have tried to point out the inadequacy of the moral teaching that can be drawn from our entire pedagogical organization. But it is not solely to this point that our attention was drawn in your circular of 1 June. You spoke to us above all of our alumni's attachment to their duties as Jews, to our ancient traditions, to the beliefs and the most respectable practices of our religion; you fear that our students are no longer concerning themselves with "all that," that for them religion and the faith are worthless old junk, to be relegated to the remotest corners of the Jewish quarter. Alas! We could dispute whether the education we occasionally give our students is adequate or not, but discussion is pointless when we seek to learn what is happening to religious feelings in our schools: everyone will tell you, all the teachers will admit to you, that the youth of the East no longer have faith, no longer have beliefs.

Allow me not to insist on this painful point; a combination of unhappy circumstances has led to the disappearance of faith, the loss of Jewish traditions. We are ceasing to be Jews in our hearts, even though we continue to be so externally. I know very well that the spirit of the time leads all men toward incredulity. In other religions, one sees powerful associations for spreading the faith, which redouble their efforts as materialist ideas are propagated and win back every day the losses of the day before; but I do not see what we Jews are doing to keep the repository of our traditions intact. At least in Europe, the sacred word is heard from time to time in our synagogues, but among us, what rabbi has ever spoken to us of religion, of our past, of our glory and our suffering? What, then, maintains faith in our heart, even supposing it was already there? And if no one has taught our children to know the Divinity, if they have never possessed faith, let us not be surprised that the young people who come out of our schools are ignorant of the fundamental principles of our religion, and that in deserting our temples, they have increasingly lost interest in our beliefs, in our past, and in our future.

Of course, as you say, we would have much to regret in our work if the result were to stifle faith in Jewish souls; on the contrary, our schools should contribute toward reanimating faith. But that will be a very difficult task. To succeed at it will take a sustained effort; a series of measures must be taken whose execution is more or less delicate. I shall limit myself to what, in my view, is immediately realizable; with your approval, I should like to attempt it in my school next year.

Methodology for the education of our students' character.

1. Since our schools are above all Jewish schools, and since religious education as given by our rabbis is inadequate, it is up to us to complement

that teaching ourselves. We can do so in the following manner. Religious instruction, prescribed by the 1883 curriculum we are obliged to follow, includes two separate parts. One is particular to the Jewish religion and has to do with the faith; it can perfectly well be taught by the rabbis. Let us entrust it to them. The other is shared by all religions and is called ethics. It cannot be taught by the rabbis; let us take charge of it ourselves.

I foresee the following objections: first, it is very difficult to give a lesson in ethics; and second, ethics should not be taught *ex professo.*

If we put forward the first objection, it will turn against us: you, the director, you, the teacher with a degree from Paris, you find it difficult to teach a lesson on family, on justice, on respect for human freedom, on brotherhood, on devotion, all matters that are contained, in the words of your curriculum, in "duties toward one's neighbor." And you want the school rabbi to teach all that? You have an infinite number of ethics manuals, which you have only to draw on to make up your course, and you find the lesson difficult? What must your rabbi say, whom you wish to assign the same lesson? (Just between us, the rabbi doesn't say anything; he is satisfied with not teaching.)

The second objection, that ethics ought not to be the object of a special course, is more serious. Let me assume with you that such is the case, but then I beg you to strike from your curriculum the words "duties toward God, toward oneself, toward the state, family, society, etc." For in the end, if these things are not to be taught, there is no point to putting them in the curriculum and annually assigning dates during which they are to be taught. If they were put into the curriculum, it is because they are absolutely necessary; who would dare strike these words from our curriculum today? As everyone knows, that would be sacrilege. We thus find ourselves faced with this dilemma: either we maintain the part of our curriculum I shall call social morality and we find a way to teach it, or else that teaching is not possible, and then we must strike from the curriculum these things we cannot teach.

Will you resolve to carry out that amputation? Probably not. Then the committee has the right to require that, in the religious schools belonging to us, in the smallest village schools throughout the world, we undertake to teach such things, under the rubric "religious" or "moral" instruction, the label matters little.

I shall not go into detail concerning the curriculum to be followed. M. Gréard has provided a master plan; the *Manuel général* published last year is a remarkable course in ethics, which could be adapted for the three levels of teaching; several other collections in my possession would greatly facilitate that task. With a little courage and a good will, the difficulty of organizing that course is not insurmountable.

2. The teaching I recommend would come to nothing were it not supported by very frequent moral readings; on this matter, our reading books could not be too carefully chosen. Those in which it is a question only of the vulgarization of certain scientific knowledge, those in which the author has sought only to amuse, to make children laugh, ought to be set aside.

3. Subjects such as singing and drawing, which serve to soften the heart and inspire a taste for the beautiful, ought to be required.

4. Moreover, the curriculum ought to be somewhat lightened; the teacher ought to have a little time to talk with his students during class. It is in these informal exchanges above all that the teacher holds the student's heart in his hands. With a curriculum as heavy as our own, teachers cannot slow down for such talks, they would be afraid of falling behind, of not finishing their courses, they are always being rushed; and that is no way to form hearts.

5. Our students do not pray; that is perhaps because our prayers are too long. Shortening them would not be possible, since the rabbinate would be opposed. But why not begin and end each session in the morning and afternoon with a short prayer in French that the children could understand? The chief rabbi of France was kind enough to promise to write two little prayers, which I requested from him for use in my school. I shall remind him of his promise.

6. You know that the poor fund functions with perfect regularity here; it teaches our well-off students to give to their less fortunate comrades. I have also taught our students to give to charitable works, and you know our classes are all on the list of Alliance members. To a certain extent, charity is also taught through practice. We shall study the question to learn if there is any way to establish a school savings bank here to accustom our students to save, an unknown virtue in Smyrna.

7. It is also through practice that we must teach our alumni to take an interest in their comrades; the creation of alumni societies in all the great centers would be highly advisable. The director would thus have in his hands, long after their schooling, the moral leadership of the young, and what he could not obtain while the students were at the school, he could obtain later, in the periodic meetings of alumni, in the lectures he makes to them, in the courses he establishes. An association of this type has existed here for six months.

8. Finally, and this has to do with the future, religious and moral instruction could be usefully introduced into the Ecole Orientale. It is a commonplace to repeat that one teaches well only what one knows well. In leaving the preparatory school, our ideas on these grave matters are still very confused. Why, for example, couldn't the Central Committee entrust one of the

numerous learned rabbis in the Paris community to go to Auteuil every Saturday morning to give a course in religious education to our future teachers? The current situation at Auteuil no longer allows our students at the preparatory school to ever hear the sacred word: that is an advantage we enjoyed when we were lodged on rue des Rosiers or at the seminary. If you wish our teachers to be good propagators of faith and virtue, their hearts must receive eloquent and authoritative words about them. Morality and religion are taught from conviction, so let us begin by convincing our agents themselves. Therein lies salvation.

It goes without saying that, in addition to all these special methods, there is occasion to provide the substance of capital importance for the formation of character: the daily practice of the good. In this respect, your circular does an excellent job of expressing the idea that everything is subject matter for morality and that every day presents opportunities for speaking of rectitude, kindness, tolerance, and charity. We must make an effort to take advantage of those opportunities.

In sum, if we wanted to embrace in a single glance the result of our moral role in the East, we would find (and here I once more repeat that in the world, some see everything through rose-colored glasses, while others see everything through dark glasses), we would find, I say, that from the religious point of view there has been a loss, and from the moral point of view, the results are inadequate.

One could remedy this ill by various means; I have set out a few of them and would be happy to know those that might be proposed by my colleagues. If that consultation is followed by a few practical measures, designed to give our teaching a direction more oriented toward education, religion, and morality, your teachers of Smyrna can consider themselves happy to have contributed toward encouraging it. . . .

Archives of the AIU, Turquie LXXIV.E.

12 January 1898

. . . I believe I saw matters clearly when I told you last year that Bné Berith would revolutionize the entire community and would seize hold of it. I thought it wise to keep you up to date regarding that society and to show you step by step the war it is waging against the chief rabbinate with its newspaper *Le Nouvelliste*,[54] forcing the chief rabbinate to name the communal council through elections, voting in a single voice to elect this council, in

54. *Le Nouvelliste* (*El Novelista,* Izmir, 1889–1923) appeared first in French and then in Judeo-Spanish.

which six members out of ten are its affiliates, drafting that infamous regulation where everything Jewish in Smyrna is to fall into its hands, pushing the council to move from paragraph 14 to paragraph 53, which concerns us, and, finally, launching the most serious assault on our institutions that we have ever experienced. Up to this point, all my predictions have come true. I am going to make others as well, which I owe to a false friend of Bné Berith:

1. The curriculum of the Alliance schools must be written by Bné Berith to considerably reduce French in favor of Turkish and Hebrew;
2. in case of resistance on the part of the Alliance, a competing school will be opened by the community where this curriculum will be applied;
3. all children of the members of Bné Berith will be taken away from us.

I shall make up a list of these children and send it to you, and when they are gone, you will be able to compare it with the list that I give you at that time. That will be the unimpeachable material proof that what is happening in Smyrna today is of foreign inspiration. I am convinced that M. Jélin of Jerusalem—founder of the Smyrna lodge—and the New York lodge are the soul of the movement we are witnessing. A word from New York is all that is needed for the face of things to change immediately.

As for the possible competing school, I am perfectly calm about the fate that awaits it. That experiment was already conducted in 1887–89; you have not forgotten Keter Tora,[55] which cost the community 300,000 piasters and produced nothing. You still have present in your memory the very recent experience in Karatash. Everyone to his trade: we can say without boasting that as for teaching, no one could do it as well as we can. . . .

Archives of the AIU, Turquie LXXV.E.

14 January 1898

. . . If the success of our work is the highest reward we can hope for, I can say that the founding of the Cercle Israélite has procured for me some of the keenest pleasure in my career as a teacher. In creating the alumni association, I had the honor of telling you that my final goal was to make all our former students into a group compact enough to act effectively, by means of the influence that their number and their superior education would give them over the destiny of the community. This day seems to be coming: The alumni association is not an entity, a philosophical abstraction, but is truly

---

55. Keter Tora (Hebrew, "crown of the law") was a traditional Jewish school in Izmir that the Alliance wished to modernize.

the gathering in a single house, during their leisure hours, of all our alumni, along with a quantity of others who, voluntarily or not, place themselves under our influence and are becoming ours. It is the awakening, after a long lethargy, of living forces that remained untapped; the youth of Smyrna are finally moving, speaking, acting, thinking. We can now follow their acts and deeds and lead them to converge toward good and useful works, which we have only to inspire.

The club opened on 9 January. Those who came felt they were in a club of long date rather than a new establishment: that is the extent to which order and even luxury reigned. In addition, from that first day, requests for admission have flowed in: there were eighty-seven of us at the beginning and there will soon be two hundred. The communal council came as a group to visit us; the chief rabbi sent us his congratulations in a very friendly letter; in short, the entire community is enthusiastic about a creation that appears to offer so many beautiful things!

It is only Bné Berith that finds no pleasure in this success, and for good reason. We shall impassively follow our own path, and so much the worse for the envious: their spite will be their best punishment.

An important detail: I have taken the necessary steps and have obtained from His Highness the governor-general written authorization for our circle to exist; no other club in Smyrna is legally authorized.

Archives of the AIU, Turquie LXXV.E.

25 March 1898
. . . Why haven't the lingerie shops given us any results?

I see two main reasons.

First, in the East, women have taste and coquetry only for what can be seen. Undress—in your mind—the first woman in silk who passes by: you will find under the most expensive satin and taffeta the coarsest sort of lingerie, which the most modest working girl in Paris would disdain. Just as the woman of Smyrna barely feeds herself so that she can decorate her drawing room with a thousand objects, a boutique of bric-a-brac that is opulent in appearance, she will prefer to go without an artfully embroidered cambric chemise in order to add one more ribbon to her dress. The passersby see the ribbon, what else matters?

The lack of an adequate clientele is one of the reasons our workshops are not prospering and that our student linen makers—if we are training any— have no future.

The second reason is that lingerie and embroidery are a matter of patience and bring in little remuneration, and it is not possible to introduce it into the cities: I am convinced that all fine lingerie, all the embroidery sold in Paris at the Louvre or the Bon Marché, comes from the country and only from there. A skilled peasant woman can, through her skill, earn 1.50 francs per day: a resident of the cities would never be satisfied with that.

The absence of outlets on the one hand and the low price of labor on the other mean that the craft of embroidery is among the least profitable in Smyrna, and I am in complete agreement with you when you propose to eliminate our lingerie shop.

What will we replace it with?

The same reasons I indicated a moment ago for suppressing the lingerie workshop could be put forward to prove that any dressmaking workshop would be a brilliant success in Smyrna. The exaggerated taste for clothes, the senseless luxury of this first echelle[56] of the East, cannot currently be satisfied except by Greek seamstresses, who drain the savings of all our households, from the poorest to the wealthiest. By training a few good seamstresses here, at least part of that money would remain in Jewish hands. The workshop itself would cost us less today, since our profits would reduce your subsidy by the same amount, whereas as of now those profits have been nonexistent.

. . . In Smyrna, we would not imagine placing girl apprentices as we do the boys. The Jewish quarter is very far from the Frankish quarter, and since I have more than once had to change the shop of my boy students because of the immorality of their employers, I will not assume the redoubtable responsibility of sending little girls to roam the streets of Smyrna: it would be better to have no apprenticeship at all than to run the risk of teaching our students mores that are fortunately unknown in our Jewish families. . . .

Archives of the AIU, Turquie LXXV.E.

8 June 1898

. . . We have had Russian emigrants and Cretan emigrants. We lacked only Thessalian emigrants, and they have just come to us.

The boat transports of the Turkish government, which are repatriating the Thessalian occupation army soldiers, have brought us a certain number of poor Jewish families—the rich were careful not to budge—who are leaving their country of origin, they say, to flee the persecutions, vengeance, and massacres that threaten them.

56. The *echelles* of the Levant were port cities of the Ottoman Empire through which commerce with Europe took place.

The causes of the Greeks' animosity toward them are many. Our coreligionists are criticized for

1. having welcomed the invading army with transports of joy and embraced the conqueror's cause in an open display;
2. having provided food to the Turkish army, who were without it at the time of the occupation;
3. having participated in plundering the repositories of Greek clothing and weapons and trafficked in stolen goods.

Let me just remind you of the trait called bravery on one side, treason on the other, which all the newspapers reported: this involved the case of the Jew from Larissa who warned the Turkish army that the bridge near Larissa it was about to cross was mined.

As they were announced, we all deplored the excesses of zeal and the incredibly reckless attitude of our Thessalian coreligionists during the war, and we foresaw what is now happening. But from a distance, we could hardly help them with our advice.

Now the damage is done and we can only seek to attenuate its consequences.

The number of poor families currently in Smyrna is thirty-eight, constituting one hundred and eighty-one individuals. Most are in a state of complete destitution. Those poor people have come to implore our help; I promised them I would intercede with you on their behalf.

My advice would be to repatriate them all. We have too many poor people in Smyrna, and these new arrivals would drag on in their miserable existence. I showed them that, under the circumstances, they also acted without due consideration and that, despite the persecutions they fear, their fate in Larissa and Trikkala[57] would be better than what awaits them in Smyrna.

Their response was that they would try to earn their living here or in the surrounding villages; if at the end of two or three months, they see they cannot live in this country, they will return to Thessaly.

For me, the experiment is already over and I know in advance the inevitable poverty to which these thirty-eight families, and those yet to arrive, are condemned. But to energetically stop this exodus and reverse the emigration current, we would need to know with accuracy if a danger truly threatens the existence of our coreligionists. To be certain of that, I believe a trip from Salonika to Larissa on the part of M. Matalon[58] would be useful. With

57. Larissa and Trikkala, cities of Thessaly.
58. The Alliance school director in Salonika.

the report on the situation he could send you, you would be able to see if we can take it upon ourselves to make all those emigrants turn around and go back, and you could send me your instructions on the matter.

In the meantime, since we must prevent these people from starving to death, I would be very grateful if you would extend the amount of credit to me that you judge useful for coming to the aid of all those unfortunate souls.

Archives of the AIU, Turquie LXXV.E.

20 January 1899

. . . About a month ago, the newspapers of Constantinople published an item claiming that M. Fernandez, president of the Regional Committee, submitted a request to the Porte asking for authorization to create a society in Turkey for the acquisition and cultivation of lands by the Jews.

This week, the same newspapers have informed the public that the request was rejected "given that, owing to the sultan's kindness, agricultural schools already exist in Turkey, where all Ottoman subjects, without distinction of religion, can be admitted. It is therefore not necessary to create Jewish agricultural schools."

You probably know these facts. I report them only to attract your attention to that "given," which could also be invoked against us when we want to set up the school in Tchakyr-Oglu. I do not know whether M. Fernandez made his official request with your authorization. I think that in his place I would have refrained, because, since the beginning of the Zionist movement, the government's refusal cannot be in doubt.

Last August I was charged by your dear president, M. Leven, to study that question, and I had the honor of sending him a report on this subject on 13 October of the same year, from which I transcribe these lines: "Since my arrival in Smyrna, I have concerned myself with the question you have charged me to study: Is it possible to have the Jewish Colonization Association recognized in Turkey—or else, could a civil society dependent on the ICA be created in Turkey with the capacity to acquire land?" Here is the response of Hakky Bey: "One must not even imagine having the Jewish Colonization Association recognized in Turkey: that would be absolutely impossible. It would be easier to get authorization to buy lands for an Ottoman society that would be constituted with the goal of encouraging agricultural training. There exist precedents, namely, etc. But for the moment, it would be preferable if you would refrain from taking a step in that direction. The Congress of Basel[59] and

59. The Congress of Basel was the first Zionist congress and was held in the city of Basel in 1897.

all the brouhaha surrounding Zionism have unfortunately indisposed the sultan and his ministers toward the Jews. I therefore advise you not to ask for anything at the present time: you would be heading for certain failure."

M. Fernandez was kept apprised of these developments, and he nonetheless made up his mind to renew the request.

The failure he was met with saddened me a great deal but did not surprise me at all: I was expecting it.

Why did he expose himself to it? That remains to be understood.

Archives of the AIU, Turquie LXXVI.E.

28 March 1900

. . . All those who have traveled in the East know the little meditation, order, and human respect (divine respect is out of the question) that reigns in our places of worship. In Smyrna more than elsewhere, this laxness surpasses anything you might imagine: people walking around, conversations, joking, noisy laughter, and even altercations are common and daily practices in our temples. In our synagogues of Smyrna, this disorder, which bears witness to the profound decline in religious feeling (which I do not confuse with the mechanical repetition of formulas and practices) on the part of our coreligionists, is combined with shameful trafficking, a shameless and unbridled exploitation of the faithful who go to the house of God to worship.

The synagogues in Smyrna, in fact, do not depend upon a central administration; they are autonomous, and the administrators do as they please, without rules or any supervision. Even if we assume there is not the slightest abuse anywhere and that gifts go precisely to their destination, it nonetheless follows from that system of organization that each temple has an interest in making as much money as possible off the piety of its faithful. Thus they have no scruples about overwhelming people with politeness, imposing *mitzwah*[60] upon *mitzwah* upon them, calling upon them to read the Tora, and extorting from them—the word is not too strong—as many offerings as they can. The merchants are no longer on the parvis of the temple, they are in the temple itself.

Like many others, I have been the victim of this ugly trafficking, and I do not know what it has cost me to have tried to attend services. To my memory, there has not been a single occasion when I managed to pray in Smyrna for free. Thus, in the face of this shamelessness, and even though, given my feelings as a Jew, I have paid a high price, I have opted not to go to the

---

60. *Mitzwah* (Hebrew, *mitsvah*; plural, *mitsvot*), "commandment."

synagogue except on great occasions: I am not rich enough to go every Saturday.

That lack of scruples on the part of the managers of our houses of prayer has had the consequence it had to have: our temples are nearly deserted, young people no longer set foot in them, and others gather in individual homes, where places for prayer are organized. There are a considerable number of these, dozens in fact. The tenor and dignity of such private meetings are easy to guess.

I propose to respond. In this matter, as in many others, the initiative must come from us. We have a lovely location, and one of our vast corridors can easily be transformed every Friday night into a place of worship; we can show the community in decline how services on Saturdays and holidays ought to be organized. We will pray with order and contemplation; auctioning off *mitzwoth* will be forbidden; and nothing will be sold or bought. For a fee of ten francs per year, a person will be guaranteed a place; an intelligent rabbi will give a short sermon every Saturday; the officiating minister will be assisted by a choir. I do not doubt that a host of people, our alumni in particular, who are disgusted by the state of mind of our religious authorities, will gather around us. Our school can thus become, not only a center of progress and modern civilization, but also a center of action for the reelevation of the faith. . . .

Archives of the AIU, Turquie LXXVI.E.

30 November 1900

. . . 1. The rabbinical crisis.

In April 1899, three months after the death of Chief Rabbi Abraham Palatché, a handful of people without scruples, vagrants and vagabonds, got together at the home of one of the sons of the deceased rabbi and proclaimed him chief rabbi. This group was soon joined by a few relatives and friends of the Palatché family, plus a certain number of people from the older generation, who played a role in internecine struggles that had earlier torn apart the community, and who were enchanted to find something to feed their maleficent activities. They formed a party, called the Palatchists, whose goal was to succeed by any means, even the most dishonest, in seizing hold of communal affairs and to govern them as it suited their interests.

The immense majority of the community rallied around the legal administration that held power, and the struggle proceeded with a bitterness, a passion, worthy of a better cause. It is pointless to recall the vicissitudes: the ruin of finances and of all institutions, the naming by imperial irade of Chief

Rabbi Eli[61] as locum tenens, scandals in the temples, armed attacks, frequent and ineffective intervention by the authorities.

The extraordinary thing is that most of the government agents, from the top to the bottom of the ladder, were and are in favor of the Palatchist party: Vali Kiamil Pasha, because the naming of Rabbi Eli was done directly, without his consent; others because they were bought with baksheeshes (deducted, naturally, from the communal resources paid to the Palatchists); and the rest because of a kind of superstition regarding a family that has given us two chief rabbis who are considered saints.[62]

. . . My calm was understood by the Palatchists; they realized that to remain masters of the domain, they had to strike me in the most sensitive spot, the subsidies to our schools. They would not have dared eliminate them in my presence; I would have had too many good arguments to oppose them, and they would have been beaten. What did they do? Exactly what a thief does when he sneaks into a house: they waited until I was gone. . . .

Archives of the AIU, Turquie LXXVI.E.

61. Joseph Eli was named acting chief rabbi of Izmir in 1899, performing that duty only until 1900. An irade is a decree of the Ottoman ruler.

62. These were Haïm Palatché (1788–1869) and Abraham Palatché (1809–99), both scholars of repute and authors of numerous books.

Gabriel Arié's father, Nissim Arié, in Samakov.

Gabriel Arié, fifteen years old, at the time of the liberation of Bulgaria, which had been under Ottoman domination for four centuries. He was still wearing the rez, traditional in Ottoman lands.

Gabriel Arié, at the beginning of his career
as an Alliance instructor, in Istanbul.

Gabriel Arié (*on the right*) with his brother Elia in Geneva in 1897.

Gabriel Arié, in Geneva in 1902,
soon after being diagnosed with tuberculosis.

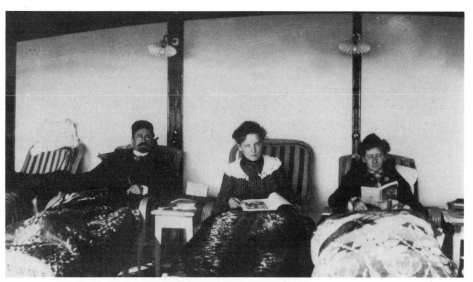

Gabriel Arié in 1903 or 1904
being treated in a sanatorium in Switzerland.

From left: Gabriel Arié, daughter Jeanne, mother Jaël, son Narcisse,
wife Rachel, and brother Elia, in Davos, Switzerland, winter 1909.

Gabriel Arié with his wife Rachel, née Cohen, in Sofia.

Gabriel Arié with his nephew Félix in Sophia in 1911.

The family of Elia Arié, Gabriel's brother (ca. 1914).
From right: Elia, Lucie, Edith, Léonore, Frida, and Félix.

Gabriel Arié and family

Gabriel Arié, beside his second wife, Rachel Crispine,
and surrounded by his family, on his seventy-fifth birthday.

Gabriel Arié in Sofia in 1926.

9/ Smyrna, Second Period (1901–1906)

From that moment on, I lost my resilience. I felt myself declining physically, and from the moral perspective, the ingratitude of the community took away any desire to continue to devote myself to it. What more could I have done, in fact, and with what resources? The ICA had transferred all the administration of Or-Jéhouda to Abravanel, and the Alliance was expected to reduce its subsidies to our schools. I thus had to confine myself to the role of a mere schoolmaster. That is what I did, and was profoundly bored.

Before vacation, I was approached by the Alliance to found a school in Rhodes. I sent Léon Sémach there, who was replaced in Karatash by Brasseur. Brasseur remained in that area for only two months, since the community had refused to make up for the school's deficit, and I had the establishment closed.

The community was also not paying its meager weekly contribution (25 francs) to the hospital. M. de Rothschild continued to send us 22,000 francs a year and planned to rebuild the building with 100,000 francs he wished to give. But, outraged by the community's indifference toward the project, he gave up the plan and, at the end of 1902, announced he was eliminating all subsidies. Of course, the community did not deserve these sacrifices. Today it pays 150 francs a week to the hospital and supports it solely with its own funds.

On the pretext of scarce resources, the community also eliminated its subsidies to the school. Then, to balance our budget and have done with the community, I had the Alliance eliminate an equivalent sum from the *talmud-tora* and other programs, and we had peace. The subsidies were later reestablished.

All these matters might have been worked out differently, but as I said, I had lost my resilience, the community of Smyrna no longer interested me.

My health preoccupied me more and more. Beginning on 1 January 1902, my cough became increasingly frequent, slight fevers often kept me at home, and the doctor we consulted diagnosed troubling symptoms left and right.

166

During that winter, Rachel took a trip to Constantinople to treat a problem with her hair, which was falling out. From there she went to Sofia, where she spent three days. During that time, Narcisse got sick, and I had to care for him alone with Mlle Naar (Julie), who had replaced Mlle Dalem.

At Passover in 1902, we put on a play at the school, which had considerable success. I remember I was so weak at the time that climbing the stairs to the school was hard work.

During the same celebration, I had to escort Alexandre Simon just about everywhere; he had come on a trip to the East, accompanied by M. Schalith.

In spite of everything, I again tried to do something: I formed a federation of alumni associations. But alas! There were hardly more than two or three of these associations, despite the Alliance's circulars.

Toward the middle of summer, at noon on Friday, 29 May 1902 to be exact, Sandro, having eaten an unripe plum, was overcome by gastric distress and lost consciousness. He remained in that state for quite some time and then came to. He escaped with only a purgative. But the emotion I felt because of his mishap was extremely violent. In fact, in my already weakened condition, that was more than enough to overwhelm me: that very evening, I developed a violent fever, which degenerated into a urticarial fever complicated by jaundice. The severe diet the younger Dr. Chasseaud put me on weakened me considerably: I could barely stand up, reading a letter tired me, a pen lay heavy in my hand, and my entire chest hurt. I looked like a zombie.

In the end, I went to see Dr. Condoléon for an auscultation. At the top of each lung, but especially the right one, he found "a little congestion," and advised me to go have it treated as soon as possible, to enter a sanatorium even. I had tuberculosis!

You can imagine my dejection and that of Rachel when the news was given to us. Nonetheless, I viewed the situation calmly, as when one is placed before the inevitable. In fact, hadn't I always sensed I would die young, like almost all my paternal ancestors? The wisest thing was to resign myself to my fate.

The leave I requested by telegraph from the Alliance was granted only two weeks later, at its meeting. I left Smyrna on 17 July 1902 via Trieste. Passing through Milan, Turin, and Mont Cenis, I arrived in Geneva and consulted Dr. Gilbert, who confirmed Dr. Condoléon's diagnosis. On his advice, I went to spend six weeks in Gimel[1] and then

1. In Switzerland, not far from Lake Leman.

two weeks in Glion.[2] I should have entered a sanatorium immediately, as Condoléon had told me to do, especially since the analysis revealed I was invaded by numerous bacilli. But everyone must submit to his destiny.

In the excursions I made to Geneva, I looked after Emmanuel, who had made little progress in Châlons. I soon learned his doctor in Sofia had found a heart defect and had advised him to interrupt his studies. Elia and I then decided to have him leave the Châlons school and to place him in Paris, at Pigier's, so that he could learn some bookkeeping. That expense was entirely superfluous, since he could have learned the same thing much more cheaply in Smyrna.

I left Geneva on 1 October, the day before Rosch-Haschana, and after a mechanical problem in Piraeus—the engine shaft broke—I arrived in Smyrna the day before Kippour, as discouraged as I had left.

I nevertheless resolved to take good care of myself, and to begin by renting a beautiful house in Cordélio,[3] near the train station, for sixty Ltq. a year. Mlle Naar came to live with us, and we all spent the winter together in the greatest intimacy, which led to a certain friction. The Alliance paid for most of my rent and authorized me to work only in the morning. My assistant D. Angel replaced me during my absence. From that moment on, I no longer gave lessons at the school, not even in bookkeeping.

Naturally, the level of studies at the school dropped. Similarly, the alumni association, whose sessions I could no longer attend in the evening, began to decline. A bad spirit, in fact, was slipping into that society, and I saw the time coming when I would have to separate myself from those young people.

During that winter of 1903, I tried to reconcile the two hostile factions of the community. But on the Colelist side, I ran up against unshakable opposition. The most intransigent of all was M. H. Polako, whose stubbornness in that matter lowered him somewhat in my esteem. I could thus estimate how far the love of the public good goes in a Jew of Smyrna, even a very intelligent one.

Toward the middle of winter, in December, Elia began to feel fatigued. The doctors he consulted in Sofia prescribed rest and fresh air in Egypt or the Riviera. I encouraged him to come to Cordélio and stay there rather than go alone to be cared for in hotels among strangers. I knew too well by my own experience how dreary those stays are when

2. Near Montreux in Switzerland.
3. An Izmir neighborhood.

one is alone. Elia would have done himself more harm than good. He thus remained in Cordélio for two months, gained a little weight, and the maladies he was suffering from disappeared. Not altogether, however, since all of us in the family have a hereditary defect of the lungs: but if we do not suffer exceptional fatigue, the seed we carry within us does not develop. That was not my case, unfortunately, but I hope the members of our family who read these lines, and their descendants, duly warned, will refrain from any excess of moral or physical fatigue, so as not to let the illness get hold of their bodies.

Elia left at the beginning of February 1903. Mlle Naar returned to her home at the school, to leave room for Emmanuel, whom S. Milch had promised to take on. Unfortunately, he did not keep his word, and while waiting to find an appropriate situation, I placed Emmanuel as supernumerary at the Anglo-Eastern Company with M. Axarli, who was indebted to me. Throughout the summer, I took all possible measures to place him, but I did not succeed.

The Passover celebration arrived. I spent more of it in bed than upright, to the point that I was unable to make the few customary visits. My illness was progressing and I was expectorating more and more. But I had resigned myself to anything.

I wanted at least to attend the celebration of one of my children, and since Sandro was to be Bar-Mitzva on 17 Sivan,[4] his Hebrew birthday, I taught him to read the *Perascha, U-ve-yom hakim et hamishkan,*[5] and organized a beautiful ceremony at the Cohanim temple. On that occasion, Sandro received gifts from my parents and a few friends. M. Bigart, M. Bénédict, and M. Wormser sent him interesting and magnificent volumes. What teacher's son ever received so many?

In May, I was obliged to take a trip to Constantinople. For several years, I had been working to obtain a firman[6] to construct the agricultural school of Or-Jéhouda. I had entrusted the matter to Uncle Nahim, to whom the ICA allotted four Ltq. a month, not counting what he could earn on the bribes he said he had to distribute. Finally, despite the favorable opinion of Vali Kiamil Pasha, my request was rejected. I had to go to Constantinople to obtain a promise from M. Isaac Fernan-

---

4. Sivan, May–June of the Hebrew calendar.

5. The passage beginning *u-ve-yom hakim et ha-mishkan* ("And on the day that the tabernacle was reared up") is Numbers 9:15. The day he reaches religious adulthood, the Bar Mitzvah is called upon in the synagogue to read a passage of the *Perashah* from the week of his birth.

6. Edict.

dez that he himself would undertake new efforts. I took Rachel and Narcisse with me.

During our stay in Constantinople, M. Bénédict came there on his way back from Egypt. He wanted to take a look at the schools and took me with him everywhere. How that must have enraged my colleagues! Together we took an excursion to Tchamlidja,[7] during which I swallowed an incredible quantity of dust! The heat in Constantinople was oppressive at the time, and I suffered a great deal.

M. Fernandez renewed the efforts, which this time bore fruit. The agricultural school is now built; I do not know if it is on the parcel of land contracted in my name. For that parcel, I gave a counterdeed to the ICA, a copy of which can be found among my papers.

This trip tired me a great deal. The heat and my worries of every kind made me waste away. What was I waiting for? I again set off abroad. Having established Samuel and Sultana in Cordélio, I bid farewell to my children on the wharf of the quay, where they were to take the boat back to Cordélio, and embarked on the *Ortégal*, which would take me to Marseilles. Rachel left me only after she had had dinner with me on the boat. Alas, that separation was to last for nine months, exactly two hundred and sixty days.

In Marseilles, I tried to conclude an agreement with M. Schamasch that would allow Emmanuel to join him as an employee with an interest in the business. We were to invest ten thousand francs. But Elia did not approve this plan and we abandoned it.

In Geneva, I saw Dr. Gilbert again, and this time he sent me to Corbeyrier-sur-Aigle,[8] at an altitude of a thousand meters. It is an isolated resort, very dreary. I was very bored during the six weeks I stayed there. As the height of misfortune, I went without mail, clear proof (among us) that something is happening. In fact, Narcisse was gravely ill with a gastric fever. He was cured thanks to the good old doctor Chasseaud.

In Corbeyrier, I received the visit of Elia, then on a business trip. He could stay for only three days. I accompanied him to Lausanne, where, after his departure, I spent a horrible night at the hotel and returned to Corbeyrier.

I found a letter from the Alliance there, sending me the copy of a letter from Léon Castro, a student of mine who had graduated from the

---

7. Çamlica, excursion site situated in the Asian part of Istanbul, known for its pine trees.

8. In Switzerland.

Ecole Orientale, in which he repeated all sorts of ugly insinuations about me. I responded as necessary to the Alliance and went to bed with a fever: such baseness exasperated me.

After a short stay in Gryon-sur-Bex,[9] I returned to Geneva to see Dr. Bard, who advised me without a moment's hesitation to enter a sanatorium and pointed me toward Montana-sur-Sierre.[10] It was 22 September 1903, the day before Rosch-Haschana. You can imagine how heartbroken I was to leave my family and occupations to go be locked up in one of those modern leper colonies, the sanatoria. I went to temple in the evening, where the service and sermon of Dr. Wertheimer moved me to tears. My emotion was even stronger as I left the temple and saw fathers and mothers embracing their children on the occasion of the new year. What were my children doing that evening of Rosch-Haschana? I dined alone at the hotel, in the company of a newspaper, and decided to leave the next day for Montana.

I arrived there the evening of 23 September. The loneliness I had suffered in Corbeyrier and in Gryon had been such that I was comforted at finding myself, in Montana, attended to by a doctor and nurse who showed a fondness for me. The sanatorium, situated on a plateau at fifteen hundred meters, is very small. The physician, Dr. Stéphani, is a good man, with whom I became friends.

I punctually followed the sanatorium regime, which is well known. After a stay of five months, I left Montana on 3 March 1904: I had gained ten kilos, and my lesions had diminished in size. But my bacilli, very numerous upon my arrival, had hardly been reduced by the time I left.

The only event that occurred in Montana was the visit I received from M. Bigart on 30 December 1903. It was a striking mark of friendship on his part, which I shall never forget. During my entire career, and particularly since my illness, the Alliance has been full of kindness toward me. Even though I did not ask for anything from them, they allotted me three hundred francs a month for six months, that is, all my expenses at the sanatorium. Of course, my full salary was also paid, as it will be until at least 30 September 1907.

During my absence from Smyrna, my mother had returned. Emmanuel was still without a job. To Elia I suggested the idea of opening an agency of the Balkan [an insurance company] in Smyrna and placing Emmanuel in it. Elia took a trip to Smyrna in January 1904 and entrusted the agency created there, first to E. Neumann, and then to

9. In Switzerland, not far from Saint-Maurice.
10. Swiss summer and winter ski resort.

Charles Mirzan. Emmanuel earned between 100 and 150 francs a month at these jobs.

After leaving Montana on 3 March, I came to Geneva, where I met M. and Mme Maïer, brother-in-law and sister of M. Bigart, who received me graciously.

From Geneva I went to Ospedaletti[11] via Turin to see Dr. Huguenin, who was said to be a specialist. I still had a foolish belief in doctors. I stayed in Ospedaletti until 25 March. There, I received word from Samuel[12] that, on the advice of his brother Marco, he was leaving his position at Aliotti's and was going to Marseilles to establish himself as a rug merchant. He asked me for an advance of fifteen hundred francs, which I gave him.

I left Marseilles on 27 March aboard the *Bosphore,* and having transshipped to the *El-Kahira* in Piraeus, on which I had traveled ten years earlier, I arrived in Smyrna on 2 April 1904, just in time to say goodbye to Samuel and Sultana, who were leaving for Marseilles. That trip cost me 5,200 francs.

When I returned, I was so aware of the fragility of the results obtained in Montana that my first concern was to write my will, or rather to recopy, with a few variants, the one I had already made in 1899. Soon, in fact, the Cordélio maladies appeared: fever, lassitude, insomnia. As usual, I went to spend a few days in Burnabat, but we were so poorly installed there that I preferred to come back to Smyrna, where I at least had my comforts.

My stay in Smyrna was to last only three months. I used this time to get the school running again, which was badly needed. Studies there had been very neglected. I realized this the day I carefully administered Sandro's exam. I was astonished how superficial his knowledge was. It was above all for his benefit that I reorganized the advanced course.

My activities during those three months were also directed toward another matter: I conceived the idea of a professional association of Alliance teachers. I received preliminary approval from some of my comrades, drafted provisional statutes, which I had approved by the Alliance, and sent my colleagues a circular (of 11 August 1904) to invite them to form the organization. Many accepted this plan, but the majority, with Antébi of Jerusalem at their head, wanted instead to form a union, to claim rights of some sort. It was not my business to enter into a struggle with the Central Committee. I gave up my idea. It has since been taken up and realized by the teachers in Tunis.

11. In Italy, on the Mediterranean coast, near San Remo.
12. This is his brother-in-law Samuel Hemsi, husband of his sister Sultana.

As had been agreed upon, I spent my vacations in Tcham-Cori,[13] near Samakov, with Rachel and Narcisse. While I was there the Alliance entrusted me with an inspection in Samakov, where Bassat was having some difficulties with the community.

Soon Léonore, back from Carlsbad,[14] joined us, accompanied by Lucie and poor Michel. That added a bit of variety to our existence. Elia, then in Pazardzhik [on business resulting from] a vast fire, also came to visit us for a few days.

The end of August was cold. Before returning, we decided to spend a few days in Sofia. We had cause to regret it. I took a chill and had to remain in my room for several days. Then it was Rachel's turn; she had a relapse of her nephritis on Kippour, 19 September. For that celebration, Elia organized the prayer service at home, because I did not want to be closed up in the temple. The prayers were said in an orderly manner, and I took pleasure in them. A week later, Rachel's nephritic episode had passed, and I could leave for Smyrna, taking Narcisse with me. In Constantinople, I found Sophie, who had spent her vacation in Salonika with my in-laws, and the three of us returned together to Smyrna on 28 September 1904.

I immediately began to organize the schools and settle my affairs before leaving for another trip to Switzerland. A presentiment told me I would never return to Smyrna. Thus, without saying anything to anyone, I made the necessary arrangements. While I was engaged in that task, I was visited by M. D. Cazès, who was taking a tour of the classes and who made himself very likable: that did not prevent him from telling the bureau that "things were not working" in Smyrna, on his return to Paris. What a hypocrite!

Rachel recovered fairly quickly and was able to return to Smyrna toward mid-October to help me in my preparations. I took all my books and personal papers from my office. I made up an exact inventory of everything belonging to the Alliance, and I handed over all services, accounts, and money to my assistant, M. Habib, whom I left in my place.

Having bid farewell to three or four friends, I once more took the path of exile, on Saturday, 12 November 1904. I kissed my children, who were altogether moved and surprised to have such a vagabond father, and embraced my mother, Rachel, and Emmanuel. My sadness was incommensurable. But I made an effort not to show it.

In Marseilles, I could easily take stock of the poor state of Samuel's

13. Tcham-Cori (Borovetz), winter ski resort.
14. The old German name for what is now Karlovy Vary in Bohemia.

business, and I predicted the outcome. In Geneva, I found M. Bigart at the train station and spent two days with him; I was often the guest of his sister there. He continued to behave as a comrade toward me. I note these words, which he said to me at the time: "The teachers find me severe: it will be very different when Bénédict takes my place."

I returned to the Stéphani sanatorium on 22 November, in worse condition than when I had left, resolved to try anything to get well. But the doctor had very few tricks left in his sack. He tried injections of phosote,[15] following Dr. Bernheim's system, and that did me no good. I was myself very discouraged, was sleeping badly, saw my expectoration increasing, my vision was affected, and I began to consider suicide in my mind. Moreover, I knew that in my absence Rachel would make the lives of my mother, Emmanuel, and Mlle Naar as disagreeable as possible, and vice versa. The presence of Elia, who came to Smyrna to transfer the Balkan agency from Neumann to Mirzan, was only a truce in that clandestine war, during which time neither my mother nor Emmanuel showed my wife and children the attention and affection they needed to tolerate their solitude. As I later told Emmanuel, I could see how they would treat my family were I to die.

As you can imagine, my state of health, combined with my worries, did not leave me much desire to live. Seeing that I was making no progress in Montana, I resolved, on the advice of Dr. Netter,[16] to come to Davos and place myself in the hands of Dr. Carl Spengler. On 6 February (1905), I began tuberculin injections. At the end of March, I was already doing much better, and by the end of May I thought I was cured. But everything began again in June, in my opinion following a change in the composition of the tuberculin.

The future of the family preoccupied me incessantly. I would have liked to place Sandro in commerce, which has more of a future than government work. I thought that, to do that, we would have to give him special preparation in a school of commerce, despite the opinion of the Alliance, which believed that sacrifice superfluous, since practice trained a young man better for business than a school's theory. I was wrong not to follow that good advice. I had Sandro come to Zurich, where I placed him at the Concordia Institute, about which I had heard good things. I went to settle him in myself on 10 May. He remained there until the end

15. This would be calcium phosphate used as a cough suppressant and given in subcutaneous injections.

16. Arnold Netter was a doctor and was a member of the Central Committee of the Alliance beginning in 1889.

of July, at which time he came to Davos to spend his vacation. Finally recognizing how right the Alliance's advice was, I kept him with me and had him take the courses at the Friedericianum school in Davos.

At the end of June 1905, Dr. Netter came to Davos for his health and for some studies. He examined me twice, found that I was in good enough condition to return to work, and sent a report to the Alliance to that effect. That surprised me, because I felt I had begun to lose ground. In the meantime, Elia came on 19 July, accompanied by Michel, whom he was taking for treatment. For several weeks, the child had been suffering from worrisome fevers. He stayed at Alexanderhaus.

We used all the time Elia spent in Davos to make plans but never managed to decide anything. Emmanuel and Sandro arrived on 25 and 26 July, and, examined by Dr. Carl Spengler, they were also found suspect or predisposed and underwent tuberculin treatments for three months.

Our little family in Davos soon grew with the arrival of Léonore, returning from Carlsbad, who was to replace Elia in looking after Michel. At the Ruheleben villa, I could see close up the endless care the child demanded. Only a father's devotion could submit to such exigencies. Unfortunately, all our efforts to save that poor martyr, so good, so sweet, were to have no effect. On Elia's order, Léonore left Davos on 22 September (1905) with Michel. I accompanied them as far as Buchs,[17] where I embraced Michel for the last time. The dear little boy was to die less than two months later.

A short trip I took to Passugg[18] to see M. Bigart, and another trip Elia took on business to Smyrna, allowed us to at last find a solution to the situation. Since the Alliance had granted me another six months' leave, we resolved to have part of my family come to Davos. First Sophie, then Rachel and Narcisse, came to join me (19 October). Emmanuel left again three days later to return to Smyrna. The observations I had made to him about his conduct bore fruit, and I must say that, like my mother and Mlle Naar, he was full of attention and affection for Ida and Jeanne, whom we had left in Smyrna.

The winter of 1905–6 passed without incident. My health improved and I no longer felt the maladies of the last days of summer. We were living in peace at Marugg's and we felt happy to be finally brought together. We had only one regret, that of knowing that Ida and Jeanne were far from us. My great distraction was the lessons I was giving Narcisse. The rapid progress he made filled me with joy.

17. In Switzerland.
18. In Switzerland.

The only preoccupation I had that winter was the renewal of Elia's contract at the Balkan around the first of January. Urged on by his colleague Michaïloff, Elia wanted to impose unreasonable conditions on the company, forgetting that it was Bulgarian and that he was Jewish. I acted in time to prevent him from going too far, and he signed a new five-year contract with the title of assistant manager.

My leave had expired in March, and I went to Paris to ask for an extension for another year and a half. This request was granted, and I remain on leave with full salary until 30 September 1907. Again this time, as in the course of my entire career, the Central Committee was faultless in its relations with me.

By a happy coincidence, the Alliance was at that moment discussing the regulation of the retirement fund. This plan, so unfavorable toward teachers, gave me the idea to immediately place Sandro in commerce, given that once I was gone, my family could hardly expect more than ten to twelve thousand francs in capital from the Alliance. Always with the cooperation of M. Bénédict, I succeeded in placing Sandro with Goldstück Heinze and Company, where he now earns sixty francs a month and where he can make a future for himself.

A presentiment had told me Emmanuel would remain without work, so I found him a temporary job in insurance for a hundred francs a month. The same week, Emmanuel was dismissed by Mirzan; he thus left the Balkan and came to Paris, bringing me Ida and Jeanne on that occasion. He has just left insurance and entered the jewelry trade like Samuel, who liquidated his rug business in Marseilles at a total loss.

I came back to Davos with the idea of remaining for a long time, left the Ruheleben villa, and after a month's stay at the Strela Hotel, we settled into the Schönau villa, where we can live as we like. Samuel, Sultana, and Sandro came in July–August to visit us for a few weeks.

Also during August, I went to take a short trip to Geneva, to see my old friend Polako. By chance, I also met M. Bigart, who led me to hope that the regulation on retirement would not be applied to me. We shall see.

Following the departure of my children and of Emmanuel, my mother also left Smyrna, and I invited Habib to occupy my apartment. But from then on, that assistant, whose character I had not had time to study, thought he was the absolute master, no longer consulted me about anything, and took my former adversaries as his advisors. The school was in a state of total decay. I did not feel I could let it be sacrificed any longer. Convinced that sooner or later I would have to be replaced, I preferred to put an end to that provisional situation and myself asked the Alliance to name my successor. For her part, Mlle Naar had gone to be married in

Salonika, so the Alliance named M. and Mme Nabon of Haskeuy [Hasköy]-Constantinople as directors. I now had only to sell my furniture and take my effects from the school. I did this through my father-in-law, who transported my papers, books, clothing, bedding, crockery, pots and pans, rugs, etc., to Salonika, where he is keeping them.

Before breaking the last ties that attached me to Smyrna, it was pleasant for me to reward a few of my coworkers; I placed Mlle Rachel Crispine in the dormitory and gave her a salary of sixty Ltq.; through the Alliance, I accorded M. Aron J. Hazan three thousand francs, and Rabbi Rabéno Albagli five hundred francs in retirement benefits; I had my student and assistant Haïm Couriel made part of the Alliance staff; and finally, I improved the situation of my other teachers and of my good and faithful *cavas*[19] Arif.

I was very sorry to leave Smyrna, despite the difficulties I had encountered there. These difficulties, inherent in my occupation, themselves pleased me. I am aware that I have done some good to that community, and you become attached to those who are in debt to you in spite of yourself. A little of myself remains in that city, where the greater part of my career was spent, where three of my children were born, and where all were raised. Smyrna is a little bit their home, they speak of it with tenderness, and when they evoke the memory of it, I share their emotion.

CONCLUSION

Thus was prematurely interrupted, and perhaps terminated, a career that, with a better state of health, might have had many a great day. If I embrace the whole of my existence in a single glance, I find in my memory an arduous childhood and severe discipline from my parents, who were constantly worried about their means of support. Then there were the studies, in Constantinople and Paris, which prepared me for the career of teacher. At eighteen years old, I began teaching in Constantinople and there experienced the four most beautiful years of my existence. Then came, after my resignation from the Alliance, the money troubles that began to affect my health.

I returned to service two years later, and the money concerns were replaced with preoccupations of every kind, in the midst of a difficult community, Sofia, which I left after six years. I came to Smyrna in 1893,

---

19. *Cavas* (*kavas*, Turkish) was a name given to certain members of the domestic staff of an embassy or consulate; in this case, it indicates a servant.

and for eight years pursued extremely productive work, which formed the apogee of my career. Then the seed of the illness I was carrying found the opportunity to develop after several episodes of emotional distress. By 1902, I could think of nothing but of conserving the little health remaining to me. After many attempts, I managed to settle in Davos with my family, and the mountain climate seems to maintain me better than any other.

So much for the past. It is brief, no doubt because it was too eventful. Life is not worth the trouble if it is purchased with so much worry. I do not say that as a reproach, because that would serve no purpose; I say it for the instruction and benefit of my children, who will read what I write.

As for the future, I dare not look to it. "The future belongs to God," especially when one is only hanging on to life by a thread. I thus limit my ambition to sparing my strength as much as possible in order to devote it to the education and instruction of my children for as long as possible. Their progress is my only consolation here. The Alliance and my brother Elia provide for my existence, Sandro is earning a living, my daughters' dowries are ensured, and I have no worries about Narcisse, who will know how to make his way in the world!

In a sense, I can consider myself a happy man, since, having come to the end of the day, I can rest a little and can depart with the awareness that I leave my children, in the absence of a fortune, the example of a life of work, probity, and devotion. I would be happy with them if, in their own lives, they found inspiration in these principles, even while avoiding the faults and excess of zeal to which I may have succumbed. It is to help them avoid the latter and to acquire the former that I thought it useful to recount to them in all sincerity what my life was.

Davos, November 1906

SELECTIONS FROM LETTERS
TO THE ALLIANCE CENTRAL COMMITTEE

1 February 1901
. . . I have the honor of including with this letter an article for the *Revue des Ecoles*.[20] It is understood of course that if you judge it damaging to any interest whatever, you may omit it.

I wrote it before I read in the newspapers that, in the French parliament itself, the Alliance Israélite was called an association of criminals. That is the

20. *Revue des Ecoles de l'Alliance Israélite Universelle* (1901–4).

reward we get for all the good we have done, indirectly, for the propagation of the French language and French influence in the East for the last thirty years.

We might have suspected these feelings existed, given the indifferent attitude taken toward our schools by all the representatives of France in the East, which give their attention and their smiles only to missionary priests. But let's not get into politics.

My article is signed with the initials HB.

Archives of the AIU, Turquie LXXVI.E.

25 February 1901

. . . I am enclosing with this letter the copy of a personal letter I am sending to M. Albin Rozet, deputy.

I have known M. Rozet for twenty-four years, and until this time have never ceased to be in constant touch with him.

I saw him for the first time in 1877 in Samakov, where he had come on a mission, accompanied by MM. Baron de Ring and Baron Coutuly (who later became ministers to Bucharest and Madrid). All three received the hospitality of my family during the few days they spent in Samakov.

I then rediscovered M. Albin Rozet in Constantinople, where he was an attaché at the embassy.

Finally, I never go to Paris without having the honor of a lunch with M. Rozet at least once.

I have exchanged many letters with this deputy, on various questions of instruction and other topics and, in particular, on the right to vote that Muslims who have remained in the country enjoy in Bulgaria (a few years ago, M. Rozet gave a great speech before the Chamber to ask that the same right be accorded to Muslims from Algeria).

Since the letter I am writing him today relates exclusively to the Alliance, I felt it necessary to communicate it to you, and at the same time give you the information above that explains and—in my eyes—justifies it.

Archives of the AIU, Turquie LXXVI.E.

25 February 1901

Monsieur Albin Rozet, Deputy

Paris

Mr. Deputy,

I have just read in the newspapers the excellent speech you gave to the Chamber regarding the question of Tunisia, and I wish to express gratitude for your warm and sincere defense of the Alliance Israélite.

In my humble opinion, the accusations directed against that society from the Chamber constitute an unpatriotic act; the deputy who dared make them has assumed a very grave responsibility in slandering us.

If he had had the opportunity to see up close the institutions we have set up almost everywhere in the East and in Africa, I would like to believe that, despite his hatred of Jews, he would have paid tribute to the work of the Alliance, work inspired by the purest, the most elevated, the most noble sentiments the human spirit is capable of.

The deputy's speech I am alluding to was unworthy of the French parliament; it has deeply wounded all the sincere friends of France in the East.

You have had the courage—alas! one must have courage today to plead the cause of minorities—to rise up against those blind attacks. Let me tell you, Mr. Deputy, how much your words comforted us, and how indebted we are to you for having avenged us for the undeserved insults they are trying to shower upon us.

All my coreligionists share these feelings, but my family and I feel a satisfaction that is all the more keen in that they are directed toward an old friend. The affection and respect we profess for him is now combined with keen and sincere gratitude. . . .

Archives of the AIU, Turquie LXXVI.E.

23 May 1901

. . . I wish only to clarify one detail: the knowledge of Turkish appears useful to me for the defense and development of the individual interests of the Jews of the East, or, to speak more clearly, useful for the development of their commerce, their business. The great mass of Jews in Turkey live only from their relations with the Turks: the Greeks, the Armenians, and the Catholics are too strong for the Jews to be able to fight them. I put aside any idea of pushing Jewish youth toward work in the Ottoman bureaucracy and do not recommend knowledge of the Turkish language except as an instrument in the struggle for existence. The exclusive knowledge of a Western language, excellent for raising the moral and intellectual level of our coreligionists, seems to me inadequate for raising them out of their current poverty. Live first and philosophize second; that is what Eastern communities everywhere ask us to do.

Archives of the AIU, Turquie LXXVI.E.

PART II

Journal
and
Correspondence

(1906–1939)

10/ Davos (1906–1913)

Notes constituting the rest of my memories, beginning in October 1906.

I n a first notebook, I noted the important events in my life until 1906. I now propose to continue the account and to note each year, as long as Providence will allow me, the important facts concerning my family and myself.

OCTOBER 1907

Since last year, we have continued to live in Davos. My health, though it has not worsened, has not improved either; the status quo has been maintained, which, in my condition, is a very appreciable result. I have left Dr. Carl Spengler, whose treatment no longer inspires confidence in me, and have placed myself in the hands of Dr. Philippi, who knows no more than his colleague, but who experiments less on his patients and treats them with more prudence. At this point, my illness seems to be arrested, my lesions encapsulated, and the doctor thinks I could go live on the plains, in the country, without any danger.

Everything would be going well, were it not for the fact that we have extremely serious worries regarding one of our children: last January (1907), Ida developed diabetes mellitus. After a violent beginning—260 grams of sugar per day—the illness responded to a severe regime. Then, despite the regime, the sugar reappeared, first in a concentration of a few tenths of 1 percent, then in 1, 2, 4, and 5 percent. That is where we stand now. The poor little girl is losing weight, getting weaker, her cheerfulness is gone, she has no appetite, most food turns her stomach. It is a pity for Rachel to see that beautiful child wasting away, a sorrow and perpetual heartbreak, and for me, to see her leaving us a little more each day, with no way to keep her from her fatal decline. The doctors are powerless against juvenile diabetes, which is more dangerous than tuberculosis.

To distract the child, I have just taken her to Paris, where I showed her to Dr. Netter. He could do no more, alas, than confirm the disturbing prognosis of his colleagues. We will fight with all our strength to save good, poor Ida, even as we weep for her endlessly in our hearts.

Last November (1906), Elia came to spend three weeks with us in Davos. During his stay here, he was informed that his eldest daughter, Lucie, was worrying the doctor somewhat because of her state of health, which had always been delicate, and that he recommended a change of air. A few days later, on 26 November, Lucie was brought to Davos, accompanied by Léonore. Since then, Lucie has remained in Davos, where her health is improving. Her stay among our children, who are generally cheerful, has had a happy effect on her character, which is rather disposed toward melancholy; the child eats, talks, laughs, and has fun, which she was not doing in Sofia. She participates in the lessons I am giving to Narcisse and profits from them a great deal, since she is intelligent.

The winter of 1906–7 was very long and harsh. Almost 6.5 meters of snow fell on Davos. Except for slight indispositions, we got through it well in general.

On 2 June, we received the visit of our relatives from Sofia: my mother, Elia, Léonore, and their two children Edith and Frida. There is no need to relate what good days we spent as a family. On 12 July, our guests left us, except for Mama, who was to remain until 18 August. Lucie also remained with us. The separation from her parents was quite painful.

During Elia's stay in Davos, we had Emmanuel come; for a year, he has been involved in the jewelry trade and was doing nothing there but waiting for clients in the café for jewelers. We realized this career as a broker was demoralizing for a young man and decided to look for a place for him as an employee in commerce. Emmanuel also recognized the need for a change. He returned to Paris and three days later, on 1 August, he was taken on by E. Bruckner, 16, rue Buffault, for a salary of 150 francs a month, soon to be raised to 175. He is still there.

Sandro also came to spend two weeks with us, from 10 to 25 August. He continues to be well looked upon by his employers at the Goldstück Company and now has a salary of 150 francs a month. Since 1 January of last year (1907), I have not had to make any sacrifices for him; he can provide for his own needs himself. It has been agreeable for me to note that he is developing well, is gifted with good sense, practical intelligence, and energy, and with that grain of philosophy that allows him to consider all the events of life, whether happy or unhappy, with calm.

Finally, Samuel and Sultana also came to spend the months of July and August in Davos. It was a pleasure for us and a great distraction for Sultana, who does not have many amusements in Paris.

The summer of 1907 was thus far from monotonous for us. By 25 August, all our guests had left us. I immediately began lessons for the school year 1907–8 with Narcisse and Lucie. Sophie is taking only German, and Jeanne, who made great progress last year, will study the subjects for the children's class this year. I am devoting an hour a day to her, and three hours to Narcisse and Lucie. Those four hours of regular work are the most agreeable of the day for me. For Narcisse, I am following the curriculum of the French *lycée* exactly; this year he is studying seventh-grade subjects.

In October, these classes were interrupted for about three weeks. Here was the occasion for that interruption.

My leave has lasted since November 1904, not counting a nine-month leave in 1903. During all that time, my salary of 4,800 francs has been paid in full. Last July, the Alliance asked me what I was planning to do at the beginning of the school year. I responded by requesting an extension of my leave. It was denied me, and the Central Committee announced that my retirement fund would be liquidated beginning 1 October.

The Alliance has, in fact, drawn up a regulation concerning retirement, which went into effect on 1 January 1907. In various ways, teachers had almost unanimously clamored for that regulation. I opposed the measure, foreseeing that a regulation would give us only minimum retirement pay, which was assured us in any case, but I was not heeded by my colleagues.

According to the newly established rules, the retirement capital will be raised to about 12,280 francs. That capital, converted into a life annuity at the rate offered by French companies, 5.76 percent, would yield me barely 700 francs a year in revenue. It is, as they say, too little to live on and too much to die on.

On 2 October, I went to Paris to examine the situation up close. From the beginning. MM. Leven, father and son, led me to understand that a supplement would be added to my retirement. But the other members of the committee I saw responded: The law is the law.

It seemed to me we had at least a moral right to retirement pay from the Alliance, and I wanted to assure myself of that. I thus consulted a lawyer on the matter and was assured that as for rights, we had absolutely none; any legal action against the Alliance on this account would be rejected without the slightest doubt.

My decision was thus made: with seven hundred francs in revenue, I cannot remain in Davos, where I am spending nine thousand. It would be extremely indelicate to ask Elia for such great sacrifices in my support. I thus formed the plan of going to live near Paris with Sandro, Emmanuel, and Samuel, since I calculated that a shared household would be less expensive for everyone. With that decided, I calmly awaited the decision of the Central Committee.

The session took place on 16 October. M. N. Leven, the president, began by praising me highly; his son, the chairman, proposed to add a supplement of two thousand francs to my retirement of seven hundred. M. Salomon Reinach,[1] who is kind enough to have a high opinion of me, proposed to keep me on at half-time and entrust me with writing the second volume of the *Histoire de l'Alliance* (the schools section) that is being planned.

This view was adopted. Beginning 1 October 1907, I am on half-time. My salary is taken from the general funds of the Alliance bureau. As for my capital of 12,280 francs, it is no longer increasing: the interest of 3.5 percent is taken by the Alliance, which credits it to the general funds. That decision is valid for a year.

I returned to Davos on 19 October and wrote to Elia to share with him my plans to move to Paris. He responded by formally opposing the plan in a moving letter that does him honor and that affected me deeply. He is afraid my condition will worsen in Paris and that I am risking my life for a question of money. He believes he is in a position to provide for his own needs and for mine as long as he remains at the Balkan.

All I could do was promise him to put off the plan until the end of next summer, since in any case, I must remain in Davos until September, when my lease expires. So many events could occur before then! We will thus discuss the question again next summer.

In the meantime, I have got down to the task the Central Committee has entrusted to me and will attempt to carry it out successfully. Along with the lessons for the children, that will be my occupation this year.

OCTOBER 1908

A year of misfortune and grief!

The winter of 1907–8 was a long martyrdom for poor Ida. Reduced to living solely on vegetables, overcome by an invincible disgust for all

---

1. Salomon Reinach, scholar and member of the Institut, was vice-president of the Alliance from 1887 until 1912.

food, she continued to lose weight day by day, to the point where she could no longer stand up. Toward the end of March, she was just skin and bones, and her blood sugar, despite an extremely severe regime, did not drop below 8 percent. There were premonitory symptoms of coma; the end was near. I had Sultana come from Paris to assist us in the sad times we were going to have to go through.

Poor Ida went to bed on Monday 6 April, nine days before her death. She was extremely weak. On the seventh, she began to lose consciousness often and barely recognized Sultana, who arrived on the eighth. Her condition then improved and the ninth, tenth, and eleventh were good days; she was eating well and we were allowed to give her hydrated food. On the twelfth, she began to complain of pain in her arm; this was alleviated with injections of camphor. On the thirteenth, the concentration of acetone was very high, and her temperature, which had always been very low, rose to 37.8 [°C]. On the fourteenth, she became extremely weak, the dyspnea became acute, and her heart grew weaker and weaker.

That state of affairs continued on Wednesday 15 April. Dr. Philippi had warned me that the patient would not get through the day. I brought the children into the bedroom so that they could see their poor sister for the last time, and I took my place at the patient's bedside. She never suspected her imminent death.

At 1:35, she again complained about her arm; she was immediately overcome by a strong convulsion, her eyes rolled back, she emitted a raucous cry, grimaced horribly, and did not move again: her unseeing eyes remained motionless; she had lost consciousness. The death agony began, interrupted every half-hour by convulsions. I was alone in the death chamber with our landlord, M. Clavadetscher. At 4:15 in the afternoon, the dying child gave a deep sigh and her breathing stopped. She was dead. Cadaveric pallor immediately came upon her. I went to join Rachel and Sultana in the other room, to weep for our poor Ida with them, and a nun took my place with the deceased. It was the day before Passover. A month earlier, Ida had said: "On the first evening of Passover, I shall be the one to set the table!"

On the first evening of Passover, she was dressed for the last time: a funeral shirt, linen she had embroidered herself for her wedding, flowers in her hands, flowers in her hair—she was as beautiful as an angel! Two nuns watched over her. We spent the day in the adjoining bedroom.

On Thursday 16, I went to take care of the funeral preparations. In the Davos-Platz cemetery, I bought a plot in perpetuity for three hundred francs (the deed of property is among my papers) and made all the arrangements. We spent the whole day crying, attended by M. Arman Aftalion.

At seven o'clock in the evening, the hearse arrived, carrying the varnished oak casket. Poor Ida was lain in it to sleep her last sleep. With Aftalion and Clavadetscher, I followed the coffin to the mortuary, where we set it down.

The burial took place on the eighteenth, at nine o'clock in the morning: I recited the Kaddisch[2] and an *achkava*[3] on the grave and then withdrew. The next day, a mound of earth indicated the place where our "Idica chérica,"[4] as we called her, was resting for eternity!

The grave bears the number 2074. It is located in the first row on the left as you enter the cemetery.

I erected an indestructible monumental stone, and I hope it will never need maintenance. But we must take care of it and see from time to time that nothing has deteriorated. The commune has the right to appropriate and resell abandoned graves after twenty years. We must not abandon Ida's! For the occasion of mourning, we received many touching testimonies of sympathy.

This blow was not the only one we had to suffer in 1908: the eldest of our children, Sandro, also gave us great worry. Because the doctor in Paris had noted a Pott's abscess, I went to Paris on 13 February; after ascertaining it was Pott's disease,[5] I took Sandro to Berck-Plage and entrusted him to the care of Dr. Tridon. He entered the clinic on 23 February. He is still there. After eight months of immobility, and numerous punctures, his abscess has disappeared. Recovery is taking place slowly: much time and patience are needed. They have said two years; we shall see.

Sandro had to leave the Goldstück Company, where he was already earning 175 francs a month. His employer, M. Rechner, promised me he would be rehired as soon as he was well.

Through the intervention of M. Bigart and Dr. Léon Zadoc Kahn, Baroness Edmond de Rothschild[6] has been paying 150 francs a month for Sandro's board since last June.

On 9 May, Rachel went to spend a month in Berck and returned

---

2. *Kaddisch* (*Kadish,* Hebrew), prayer that concludes each of the three daily cycles of the Jewish faith. The prayer is also uttered for the dead by those in mourning.

3. *Achkava* (*ashkavah,* Hebrew), prayer for the peace of a dead person's soul.

4. *Idica chérica* (a mixture of Judeo-Spanish and French), "dear little Ida."

5. Pott's disease is tuberculosis of the spine, the most common tuberculosis of the bones.

6. The wife of Baron Edmond de Rothschild, a famous philanthropist.

completely reassured about Sandro's condition. At the same time, it was a diversion from her own suffering.

As if these blows of fate were not enough, my mother's vision has been affected since last February: her eyes are covered by cataracts, which she inherited from her mother. (Note that in the matter of inheritance, our parents and grandparents left us only their illnesses.) One of the two cataracts is mature and will be operated upon immediately; the other will be put off for a few months.

I was to go to Vienna to attend to my mother during the operation, but for the last few weeks my health has not been stable. For the moment, I must refrain from tiring myself in any way.

During the last year, my health was satisfactory, despite the severe shocks I experienced. I was confined to bed only four times, for a total of sixteen days. I was able to work six or seven hours a day for the whole year: lessons for Narcisse and Lucie (eighteen hours a week), lessons for Jeanne, and tutoring, which brought in eight hundred francs, compared to fifty francs last year. It would seem that work contributes toward keeping me healthy. What is harmful to me is physical fatigue, long walks especially.

My historical account of the Alliance has advanced: I have completed two-thirds of the work and will probably be in a position to hand in the finished version within the year. This occupation interests me more and more. The Alliance has renewed its allocation of 2,400 francs to me for 1908–9.

On 31 May, with the consent of M. Bigart, or rather at his inspiration, I sent all the Alliance teachers a circular inviting them to take advantage of the seventy-fifth birthday of M. N. Leven, which falls on 15 October 1908, to demonstrate our feelings of respect and gratitude toward our president. Each school was to sign an address to M. Leven. These addresses, bound in a luxurious album, will be given to the president on 15 October 1908.

As we do every summer, we had visits to Davos. I have already spoken of Sultana's visit, which lasted four months, until Samuel found work (work he has just left to go back into the jewelry trade).

Elia arrived on 25 July, after a long trip to France, Spain, and Italy. He remained until 18 August. His stay could not have been very enjoyable for him since neither Rachel nor I was very cheerful. It was only a visit of condolences. It did him good in that Dr. Philippi was able to warn him that he is headed for illness and must take the most serious measures to ward it off. Elia left for Sofia with the intention of giving up all his bad habits, particularly tobacco and gambling. If only he can keep his word!

He took Lucie back to Sofia; she seems to have recovered here. He also took Sophie, who will spend some time in Bulgaria.

From 14 August to 19 September we were visited by M. and Mme Béja of Salonika. They stayed with us. The visit of Mme Béja gave us pleasure, but her husband was a stranger to us. He remained one.

During the last year, Emmanuel received a raise from Bruckner, to two hundred francs.

Narcisse and Jeanne entered public school in Davos, Narcisse in seventh grade and Jeanne in second. They will learn German there and will also find distractions they are missing at home. I am giving them French lessons.

Such was the year 1907–8, which ravaged us in so many ways. I dare not predict what 1909 will be like and what I will have to record in the following pages. God's will be done!

OCTOBER 1909

By the grace of heaven, this year was much better than last.

My health has remained the same, with a slight growth in my lesions. That is inevitable: if you don't get well, the illness always progresses. According to Dr. Stéphani, who has just examined me on his way through Davos, my right chest cavity is a bit enlarged, and the condition of the rest of the lungs has not changed. I have given up on medication and even on doctors, having lost all faith in any medication other than air, rest, and food.

In May and June, I tried living on the plains, moving to Saint-Cloud, near Paris, for two months. The result was negative: the thermometer was always above thirty-seven degrees, sometimes rising to thirty-nine degrees. That experiment is decisive: I can live only in the mountains. I will remain here as long as I can, sparing my strength as much as possible.

This year, the number of days I had to stay in bed because of an elevated temperature was fifteen, of which nine were spent in Paris.

For the first time since I've been sick, I had to record a bit of blood in my spittle in October 1909. That happened when I returned from my trip to Chur, of which I shall speak later.

This relatively satisfactory state of health is due, I think, to the diversion provided my thoughts by the work the Alliance has entrusted to me.

By April, I had completely finished the history of the schools. I took the manuscript to Paris personally (on 25 April). M. Leven and M. Bigart, who read it, found it very good. M. Leven asked me to help him compile the first volume, *Histoire générale de l'Alliance,* which he had promised to write and of which he had finished only about a hundred pages. I accepted, and after drafting a plan for the book, which was accepted, I took on the task of writing the second half of it, from the chapter entitled "Antisemitism" to the end. At this point, I have almost finished the last part of my manuscript for the Alliance and will send it out in a few days.

For the two months I spent in Paris at the request of M. Leven, I received a thousand francs, which allowed me to procure a pleasure trip and a month's stay in Berck for Rachel and the children.

Relatively little tutoring this year: I barely made seven hundred francs from it.

My trip to Paris was primarily intended to defend a plan I had submitted to the Central Committee regarding the creation of a *Bulletin des Ecoles,*[7] essentially pedagogical in nature, a bulletin for which I would serve as the primary editor. Written in a spirit of tolerance, freely open to the discussion of all ideas, the bulletin would put a little life into the school programs of the Alliance, which are so much in need of an infusion of new, younger blood. The creation of the *Bulletin* was adopted by the Central Committee (session of 2 June 1909), but with what reservations! The collaboration of the teachers will not be solicited, for fear they might express subversive ideas—admittedly, after the experience of the *Revue des Ecoles,* that fear is no chimera—but a *Bulletin Mensuel* will be published by the secretariat. It will be composed of three parts: 1) official news concerning the staff; 2) school news, excerpted from correspondence; and 3) reviews of the pedagogical press.

I am responsible for compiling this third part, for a salary of 2,400 francs, which will continue to be paid to me, in keeping with my registered letter of 7 June 1909, in which M. Bigart set out the decision of the Central Committee. As a result, my retirement of 700 francs has been converted into a permanent salary of 2,400 francs.

I must add I had much to be satisfied with in the attitude of all the members of the committee and of the secretariat toward me.

During my stay in Paris, I made two visits to Sandro, who is still immobilized in Berck. He is doing better, the doctor says. He has been there for almost two years. What patience he must have, and what a school for courage for the rest of his life. We have been promised he will be able to stand up this year: May it be so!

From 17 May to 17 June, Rachel, Narcisse, and Jeanne were in Berck,

7. *Bulletin des Ecoles de l'Alliance Israélite Universelle* (1910–13).

which made everyone happy. Rachel in particular came back with less gloomy ideas; ever since the death of our poor Ida, she had not even smiled.

She herself had to undergo the ordeal of another attack of her nephritis this year, from 14 to 18 December 1908. Fortunately, she has recovered from it.

At such times, we felt keenly the weight of loneliness, since Sophie was also gone. But what is there to do? I invited my mother to come spend some time in Davos, to keep us company, but she refused.

The operation my mother was to have on her eye took place on 15 October 1908. It seems to have been only partly successful.

Narcisse went to the public school in Davos. I do not think he has made much progress, but he is well enough prepared to enter the first *Realklasse*,[8] where he is one of the better students.

As for Jeanne, I preferred to keep her at home, where I, and then Sophie, gave her the lessons I feel are appropriate for her age: let her first acquire a good foundation in French, and we will consider German later.

A joyous event marked the last year: the birth of a boy to Elia. On 15 November 1908 (21 Hesvan)[9] my nephew Félix-Salomon was born, may God bless him! One of our dearest wishes has come true.

As he does every year, Elia came to spend his vacations—20 July to 15 August—with us. The regime he has submitted to is succeeding marvelously: his health has improved and he has gained ten kilos. I am now reassured about him.

He brought Sophie back to us, after an absence of eleven months. Since her return, we no longer feel lonely.

For several years, my sister Rosa has had tuberculosis. When she felt very ill, she consented to being treated. Alas! It was too late: after trying the sanatorium in Wienerwald[10] and treatment in Rheinhall,[11] she spent six weeks in Davos on my advice. The climate was too harsh, the altitude too high for her weakened heart, and I had to take her back to the plains in all haste and wait for her husband in Chur. He took her to Merano, where she is now. Her illness has not progressed very far, but she is not strong enough. If she can regain some of her strength in Merano,[12] she may still be saved. Let us ardently hope so for her and her large family.

8. *Realklasse,* modern high school class *(realschule).*
9. *Hesvan (heshvan,* Hebrew), October–November of the Hebrew calendar.
10. Wienerwald, outside Vienna.
11. Reichenhall, not Rheinhall, in Austria, southwest of Salzburg.
12. In the Tirol.

Her weakness has caused me deep emotion, and it is to this I attribute the trickle of blood I had when I returned from Chur.

Sophie turned seventeen. Two marriage proposals have been made to me on her behalf. One came from my father-in-law, who saw fit to ask for a colossal dowry in terms worthy of a professional go-between. I refused the offer without telling him what I thought of the way he had proceeded, but since then I do not write him, having understood exactly the degree of interest he has in me.

As for the second, it comes from one of my best former students from Smyrna, but the matter cannot be seriously discussed until the candidate is in a position that will allow him to raise a family. Until then, I have reserved all my freedom to act.

Emmanuel continues to be well regarded at M. Bruckner's and earns 250 francs a month. He is advancing and behaves well. But there is too much mystery in his private life. I hope he has not become involved in some *liaison dangereuse!*

Sultana is finally enjoying a little peace of mind, with her husband's business back on its feet; they have moved into a little apartment and say they are happy.

Régine is also managing on what her husband earns and on the rent for her house. We have arranged with Elia to give her two thousand francs to help her buy a cottage for herself.

We have made many other plans with Elia. But in these notes, I want to record only those that are realized.

It will be important to settle our mutual financial situation with him this year. Since I cannot accept being a burden to him, and since it has been demonstrated that I cannot live anywhere but in Davos, we must find an arrangement where I can live independently, so that no one can ever reproach my children for having eaten anyone's bread but their father's.

JANUARY 1911

The year 1910 was marked by dramatic alarms, great worries, and, fortunately, ended in joy and happiness.

On two occasions, the worries were caused by Narcisse's health. He took a chill on 31 January at an ice-skating match he attended, and on 2 February came down with pneumonia complicated by pleurisy, which lasted until 21 February. His robust constitution and the care of Dr. Buol succeeded in conquering the illness.

He had barely finished convalescing when on 15 May, he developed appendicitis. On 28 May, he had to have an operation. We thus transported the patient to the Davos hospital, where Dr. Meisser successfully operated on him. On 16 June, Narcisse left the hospital, and a few days later, he was completely recovered. During those few days, we were severely tested.

Since that time, Narcisse no longer goes to public school, where, in fact, he was making little progress—it was not his fault but that of the curriculum and teaching methods—and I have undertaken to give him the instruction he will need later on, as I am doing for Jeanne.

The shock suffered by Rachel during these two illnesses provoked, or perhaps aggravated—one never knows—polyuria, which I always knew she had to a greater or lesser degree. Having analyzed her urine on 25 June, I discovered more than 10 percent sugar in more than two liters of liquid. A diet was immediately set in place and the sugar dropped to .5 percent. On 7 July, she left for Vienna to consult Professor von Noorden. She returned on the fifteenth with no sugar, and since then has continued a more or less severe diet and is feeling better. Her general condition has improved a great deal.

Between 28 and 31 July she again suffered an episode of nephritis provoked by a chill. Dr. Schindler of Zurich, who is treating her, is having her follow a diet to destroy what remains of the nephritis.

In general, my health was satisfactory. In the last fifteen months, I spent fifteen days in bed, of which nine were after Narcisse's operation and the emotion and fatigue I endured.

During the entire year, I did not see a doctor or take any medication.

The history of the Alliance I wrote is still in M. Leven's cardboard boxes. He is ill and cannot go over it, and I do not know if it will ever be printed. What a shame that would be, and how much trouble I would have taken for no reason!

I was happier with the *Bulletin des Ecoles,* which appears regularly each month and gives me great satisfaction, without making me too tired.

There was also a great deal of tutoring this year, as I earned eighteen hundred francs from it.

As I had proposed, I tried to create some business relations with the East, which would supplement my income, allowing me to balance my budget from my work alone. To this end, I went to Saint Gall,[13] where I

13. Saint Gall, city in northeast Switzerland, near Lake Constance, known for its embroidery and lace industries.

procured samples of lace and embroidery, which I sent to various correspondents in Turkey and Paris. It was a wasted effort: the article is second-rate and the competition from German factories would allow for only meager profits, which would not make up for the risks. I must seek the income supplement elsewhere.

At this time, Elia and I are studying the possibility of transforming the house in Sofia, of which we share ownership, so as to make it produce a higher revenue than it now brings in. The question is under study by various architects.

A great subject of preoccupation this year was the renewal of Elia's contract at the Balkan. This contract was renewed for five years under excellent conditions, which assures Elia of quite an ample existence.

As soon as he signed the contract, Elia came to spend his month of vacation in Davos. He has also had many fears regarding the health of Félix and of his other children. His health has been affected, and in 1910 he lost almost all the gains he made in 1909. The stay in Davos restored him in part, but he must continue to take care of himself.

The rather dreary winter and spring we went through had a negative effect on Sophie. I thought it wise for her to change her surroundings, and on 7 June, as soon as Narcisse was out of danger, I sent her to France, where she remained in Berck with Sandro for two months (he is still there; his return has been promised us in 1911) and in Paris with Samuel for four months. This change did her the greatest good, physically and morally. She returned to us on 1 December.

On the seventeenth of that month, she became engaged. Not to my former student from Smyrna, whose name I did not even mention last year, since his candidacy did not seem at all serious to me, but to my cousin Ezra Arié from Sofia. I am very happy about the prospect of that union, which will keep Sophie within our family, will give her as life companion a young man about whom everyone is agreed in saying the greatest good, and who loves her. The wedding is fixed for April 1912 at the earliest.

Rosa left Menton in April and returned to Sofia in a very precarious state of health. The odd thing is that she recovered in Sofia. She has just returned to Menton to spend the winter months there.

While she was in Menton, she called for Mama, who went to join her in February. A month later, she went to Paris, and on 10 May, Mama was with us in Davos. She stayed until 18 December and then returned to Paris. From there, she is to once more go to Rosa's in Menton, where she will spend the winter.

Emmanuel is still at Bruckner's under the same conditions.

In December 1910, he wrote me to sound me out regarding the opportuneness of a marriage, which I could not approve. I responded sharply that I disapproved of such a plan. He sent me a letter that was quite uncalled for, and obviously did not mince his words. He immediately regretted writing it, using his overexcitement as an excuse. I accepted his apology: the essential thing was to prevent him from ever compromising his future.

In August, he came to spend two weeks with us.

Samuel and Sultana also came, once in December–January for two weeks and once in July–August for six weeks.

JANUARY 1912

The year 1911 was good in every respect.

The doctor did not come to our house. Rachel and the children were healthy. Sandro finally left Berck on 15 June 1911: he first went there on 23 February 1908. He is spending a transitional year with us to complete his convalescence and will begin work again in 1912. His illness will have cost him a delay of at least four and a half years in his career. But since he is cured, we are very happy to forget that sad past. We are thus able to find ourselves reunited in Davos for a year, with all our children, before they leave us to follow their destinies.

Our home is much more cheerful now, all the more so since we also have Lucie this year, who has come to continue her education with me and who is taking some of the courses I am giving Jeanne and Narcisse.

Narcisse is also going to Friedericianum School for certain subjects: German, English, geometry, algebra, and geology.

My health has remained the same. On the advice of Dr. Hollos of Szeged,[14] my student, I have begun tuberculin treatments, which I continue with Dr. von Muralt. The results are not yet noticeable. Number of days spent in bed: twenty.

At Elia's house, everyone was perfectly healthy.

Our great preoccupation this year was the realization of the plan we had come up with to rebuild our house in Sofia. For Elia, this was a source of continual worries for six months, because in Bulgaria the landowner has to oversee all the details himself. Work began on 24 April, the cornerstone for the addition was set in place on 12 May, and the inauguration occurred on 28 November 1911.

14. In Austria-Hungary.

Out of a single two-storey building costing 85,000 francs and bringing in 8,000, we made a full block containing six shops and five apartments, currently bringing in 20,000 francs and costing in all 200,000 francs. As revenue, the invested capital draws in scant interest, but Elia has a comfortable and hygienic home for himself, and that is the reason that decided us to undertake this reconstruction. The house is, in fact, likely to appreciate in value and the revenue may increase.

To give Elia moral support in that burdensome task, I went to Sofia with Rachel and Narcisse and remained there for three months (12 April–14 July). Sophie and Jeanne were sent to Paris to be with Samuel and Sultana.

My stay in Sofia was extremely agreeable: I had not seen the Bulgarian capital since 1904; I found many changes there, much material progress. But in the education of Jewish youth of both sexes, there has rather been a move backward: the company of those young people is not at all agreeable.

The decline of the various branches of the Arié family continues; there remain only remnants of the fortune left by my mother's brothers and cousins. All those people have remained with the mind-set they had under Turkish domination in 1877: they feel out of place in Sofia.

Thus I found pleasure, not among them, but at home with Elia's family. His children are charming, and little Félix was a joy.

At the end of the year, I made a second trip to Sofia (28 November–2 December) to help Elia take care of a host of little projects, from purchasing the furniture to moving in and inaugurating the building, which was very joyous; our closest relations were invited to the inauguration.

I returned to Davos with Elia, who spent his annual month of vacation with us.

I took advantage of our stay in Sofia to send Rachel to Constantinople, to give her parents her love one more time. They are getting old! She spent two weeks there.

I said earlier that in December 1910 I arranged for the engagement of Sophie and Ezra Arié, whom I did not know but "about whom everyone is agreed in saying the greatest good." This young man came in February to visit us in Davos and spent a month here. The impression he made on me was bad, and we were all disappointed by his almost total absence of breeding and education. How could Sophie, so discriminating, so intelligent, share her existence with such an individual? That impression did not change during the three months I spent in Sofia, where we had the leisure to observe him. Thus, at our return, we took advantage of a rather cavalier letter he wrote me, and we broke the engagement, giving Sophie back her freedom. She will marry a man with character, one who offers some guarantee of happiness by his social situation and level of education, which were lacking in that suitor.

No change occurred in the situation of the other members of our family during 1911: Samuel is earning a good living, Régine lives in perpetual poverty in Sofia, we pay part of her rent, Emmanuel is still at Bruckner's, Rosa has recovered somewhat, she married off her eldest daughter, Sabrina, but the youngest fell ill suddenly and has just arrived in Davos to be treated. Her father is accompanying her. What a burdensome inheritance ill parents leave to their children!

JANUARY 1913

The year 1912 has seen the unfolding of one of the most important political events of history: the war of the Balkan people against the Ottoman Empire and the end of Turkish domination in Europe. This significant event will profoundly alter the social and economic life of the entire peninsula. Our family interests will also be affected, and in an altogether favorable manner.

The great event that marked 1912 for us was Sophie's marriage. She left for Salonika on 8 May to visit my brother-in-law Léon and was engaged on 28 August to M. Salomon J. Carasso. The wedding was to take place a few weeks later, and Rachel and Jeanne went to Salonika on 4 September. But the apprehensions caused by the war, the sudden occupation of the city by the Greeks on 9 November, obliged us to put off that event until 15 December. I cannot go to Salonika, since all communication has been cut off, and at this point, I do not yet know my son-in-law. Everything that has been written and said about him makes me hope he is an intelligent man—honest, serious, a self-made man. Sophie is enchanted with him, and I hope he will make her perfectly happy.

Rachel and Jeanne returned to Davos on 2 January, and I am very happy about that, since my isolation in Davos for four months had begun to weigh upon me.

Another happy event was set in place in the last days of 1912: the naming of Elia as general director of the insurance company being formed: The Balkan Phoenix. Extremely advantageous conditions have been granted him by the consortium of banks launching the business. It will be organized immediately after the conclusion of the peace. The excellent position that has fallen to Elia is a well-deserved climax to twenty-four years of assiduous and intelligent work, combined with scrupulous probity.

The matter was settled in Vienna, where I also went with Narcisse between 16 and 20 December.

The week Sophie got married was thus altogether auspicious.

I also had the joy of seeing Sandro return to work. After a stay in Berck, from 3 June to 19 July, and the assurance from Dr. Tridon that he is fully cured, Sandro left on 7 August for Sofia and, on the twenty-third of the same month, joined the office of M. Isaac R. Arié. He is there still. I do not think he will remain there for long: he will probably follow Elia to the Phoenix.

Having finished the school year at Friedericianum, Narcisse resumed his studies with me: we finished the courses in contemporary history and Jewish history, a course in literature, and another in bookkeeping. He continued his studies in German and English, and at Passover, I shall probably place him at the school of commerce in the city of Freiburg-im-Breisgau.[15]

Jeanne continued her studies with me as in the past. She has developed well physically and her robust health brings me much satisfaction.

My state of health was a little less good this year. Number of days with a temperature higher than normal: twenty. Twice, during three-day periods, I had some red or pink spittle. Finally, the left side, which had until now been almost unaffected, was infiltrated at the top. This series of mishaps incited Dr. von Muralt to interrupt the tuberculin treatment. Greater caution is now necessary than it was in the past.

In Elia's family, everyone's health was good, except for a scare with Félix in February. He had bronchial pneumonia. Léonore repeated a course of treatment in Carlsbad, and Elia came to spend his vacation, from 11 July to 7 August, in Davos.

When he returned to Sofia, he took Lucie back with him. She had stayed with us for about a year.

Elia came back through Davos, from 2 to 4 December, on his return from a trip to Europe he had made to solicit the large Jewish associations on behalf of the victims of the Balkan War.

As we do every year, we had the visit of Samuel and Sultana, who stayed in Davos from 27 August to 21 September.

In response to the kindness Mme Béja showered upon Sophie in Salonika, we invited Mathilda Naar to Davos; she stayed from 26 August

15. City in western Germany (Baden-Württemberg).

to 4 September. This stay did a great deal of good to my health. What a good girl, what a heart of gold!

I have not seen Emmanuel this year, who has had nothing to do with us for the last six months because we could not lend him the twenty thousand francs he needed to launch a business we considered extremely risky. In the end, he apologized for his incomprehensible attitude. It is too bad that that boy, who has a good heart, cannot resist the impulsiveness of his character.

Tchelebon and his poor daughter Elise also stayed in Davos for three weeks in January and February. That child, who was sent to Vienna to study, caught galloping consumption, which the air in Davos could not improve. She has returned to Sofia and will die soon.

Rosa remains the same.

No change either in Régine's situation.

Mama continues to enjoy excellent health. She still insists I should go back to Sofia. What would I do there? And where would I find a climate comparable to that of Davos, an existence so calm, and independence in the world such as I have enjoyed here? Apart from Elia's companionship, nothing attracts me to Sofia.

SELECTIONS FROM LETTERS
TO THE ALLIANCE CENTRAL COMMITTEE

29 September 1905
. . . Greetings and Happy New Year!

I am writing in response to the official letter extending my leave. . . .

I received your letter on 30 August. Is it really necessary for me to write to withdraw my "paper" from the dossier of the *Revue?* M. Bigart told me said review is truly defunct this time. May it rest in peace! Before I saw M. Bigart, I told you that, given the state of mind of some of the staff, it was better to cancel publication. Now it is done. It is true there are still the Tunis pamphleteers to spread the good word, but after a few issues, the *Bulletin* will meet the same fate as the *Revue:* remember the debut of that last rise and fall! That is all there is.

You ask for the remedy to the wind of revolt and insubordination that is so troubling our dear president. To find the remedy, one must seek the causes of the illness, and the causes are many. Let us try to understand a few of them.

We must first recognize what could be called "the spirit of the times." In every field of social activity, the master is increasingly the enemy. In the last analysis, the highest salary possible for the least work possible is the goal of every trade union in the world. Raised in Paris, the revolutionary center par excellence, nourished on modern literature and progressive newspapers, our future teachers, on leaving the school, already have no illusions, and no enthusiasm as a result. It is already in school—yes, you hear me right—that plans for desertion are formed in these precocious skeptics. A person's word, devotion, and sacrifice are just old saws. When you work six or seven hours a day, not counting supplementary employment, to earn 116 francs a month, there is no devotion that can hold you there, and you resolve to leave the service before even entering it.

Unfortunately, there is no counterweight to oppose to these ideas of revolt brewing under every uniform cap. From this perspective, the transfer of the school to Auteuil, though a gain for the students' health, was a loss for the Alliance. On rue des Rosiers, we often saw members of the committee at the school, since everyone passes by rue de Rivoli. But who goes by rue d'Auteuil? One must not demand the impossible from committee members; a trip to Auteuil, in the midst of life in Paris, is a sacrifice few people can make. Thus many teachers no longer feel the way their elders did, like the coworkers and often friends of M. Charles Netter, M. Veneziani, M. Leven, or M. Zadoc Kahn, whom we saw so often, but rather like the employees of an administration like any other, tramway or telegraph for example. And they behave like these employees. There is no reason for them to do otherwise.

On the other hand—since all the wrongs do not lie with the teachers, and the committee must be honest enough to recognize that—for twenty-five years, the fortune of the Alliance has increased more than tenfold, its budget has more than quadrupled, and the teachers' salaries have remained the same. The fact that the Alliance is using its new resources to develop its programs is entirely legitimate. But the fact that from this new wealth not a crumb has been distributed to the teachers in the form of a universal raise in all salaries is, as the saying goes, "vexing."

In 1881, twenty-four years ago, my comrades Alphandary, Chéni, Nar, Haym, and I left school at a salary of fifteen hundred francs apiece. Today the beginning salary is fourteen hundred francs. The hundred-franc decrease is nothing, what matters is that life throughout the world is much more expensive than it was a quarter-century ago. Ask M. Neymarck or another economist among your friends, you will find that fourteen hundred francs in 1905 are worth only eleven hundred francs from 1881. And yet, even with the fifteen hundred francs of 1881, we could barely survive. I remember that, for several years in Ortakeuy, where I began, my dinner was composed invariably of a plate of curds and a piece of bread. This diet tired me, and I went in search of supplementary resources to live on. In addition to lessons to the students in an apprenticeship program, which I created in Ortakeuy for precisely that purpose (see the *Bulletins* of 1883 and following), I became secretary of the regional committee (five hundred francs), head of music at the Galata temple (five hundred francs), and I even gave lessons in Pera to a Russian chiropodist, and God forgive me! to an actress, whom I taught to recite her lines properly at coffeehouses. That is what I did to survive when the Alliance paid me fifteen hundred francs per year. With my seven hours of courses daily, you can see the amount of work that constituted.

It could be that, with the ideas of the time contributing, my young colleagues of today find this way of life rather harsh. Moreover, there is no choir at the Chiraz temple, no artist in Tiberias whom one could teach to sing "with heart and hand." In the majority of posts, the teacher finds no supplementary resources to bring a little comfort to his life. "Joie de vivre" is for most a bitter joke. So then what? So then their character grows bitter, the seeds sown in *Crainquebille*[16] and *Le Père Duchesne*[17] develop, and since no personal ties of a moral nature attach teachers to members of the committee, revolt brews, then bursts forth in seditious cries. And as soon as a teacher can, he takes his leave.

I beg you, do not allow yourself to believe that the question of retirement plays a role in this movement. The unrest created around retirement pay is artificial. Just consider the age of those who resign or are insubordinate: they are between eighteen and twenty-five years old, the best years of life, when you think that old age will never come. No, what torments young people is the present: *Primo vivere* is on all their lips.

I do not claim to exhaust the analysis of the multiple causes of the evil you deplore in two or three pages. It is enough for me to have indicated the principal ones: an education that is too liberal, I was going to write "libertarian," the elimination of any moral action from the committee on its future agents, and the inadequacy of salaries, especially the beginning salary.

All the rest of the "demands": vacation, work hours, transfers, and other such gibberish we read in the circulars and *Bulletins,* are empty phrases not worth discussing or refuting.

It is possible to modify the spirit and the regime of the Ecole Orientale (have you noticed the spirit of the women teachers has remained excellent?). It is not impossible to put the committee back in touch with the students of the school. (I talked about this at great length with Dr. Netter and will also

16. *Crainquebille* is a satirical story by Anatole France (1901).
17. *Le Père Duchesne* was a revolutionary periodical published by Hébert in 1789. Very popular for its content and crude style, it was suppressed by Robespierre.

speak to you about it.) But it must above all be possible for the committee to raise salaries, even if it has to stop program development for a certain period of time, or even cut it back a little. A little and well, not too much and badly, is a principle that is valid, and not only in pedagogy.

We shall come back to all these questions. If you like. . . .

Archives of the AIU, Turquie LXXVII.E.

13 October 1905

. . . I was thus telling you that I saw the principal causes for the loosening in ties between the Alliance and its staff to lie in the administration of the school, in the absence of any contact with the Central Committee, and in the manifest inadequacy of the beginning salaries.

It is quite pointless to reproach the spirit of insubordination that is invading our staff, as it is invading every social class. Leading free men is becoming an increasingly difficult matter. The engineer in his factory, the captain on his boat, the entrepreneur at his work site are obeyed only if they virtually apologize for the liberty they take in giving an order. It would be surprising if our future teachers, raised in that breeding ground for revolutionary culture called Paris, were more respectful of discipline than the students of every category who, at the drop of a hat, shout down the professor or go on strike at the hospital.

In a very praiseworthy sentiment of liberalism, the school has been opened wide to Paris and Parisian life. Moreover, students of foreign upbringing and origin have been introduced into the establishment. Finally, the institution is now for both boarders and day students. As a result, students have been subjected to the most various influences; the outside air has invaded our house in great gusts and has swept away the atmosphere we used to breathe.

We must return as soon as possible to the old traditions, decrease the students' unsupervised outings to the boulevards, eliminate the Sorbonne courses, place the agronomist day students somewhere else (at the trade school, for example), no longer accept Romanian students: in short, close off the school as much as possible to foreign influence. Less knowledge and more attachment to the work would be better for the Alliance. One slightly violent circular was enough to turn the heads of many working teachers, whom we might have thought more levelheaded. What kind of destructive influence will excitation of that kind have on minds still being formed! To be permeated by the spirit of the Alliance, it is not enough simply to eat one's soup at the Alliance's expense; other conditions are also necessary. In the first place, students must be removed from that spirit of revolt that is brewing, in France more than in any other country, and in Paris more than in the rest of France. The seminaries where missionaries are trained are closed schools: our women teachers in Auteuil and Bischoffsheim[18] are subject to the regime of a closed school; under that regime the first generations of teachers were raised by M. Trenel and M. Marx.[19] We have experimented with the other sort of regime, and there is nothing to do but return to the old system.

Do not accuse me of preaching against freedom and for obscurantism. The faculty with which the Alliance has equipped the Ecole Orientale is extremely remarkable; there is no fear that the minds of our students will grow narrower under such masters. What I ask is not that the level of studies be lowered but that these studies take place exclusively at the school, that it be closed to foreign students, and that day students not come into Auteuil every evening, bringing all the gossip of Boul'Mich[20] and elsewhere with them.

Distancing students from the deliberate influences that weaken their vocation before it has developed is our first task. Linking future teachers with their future leaders is our second. How to bring this about?

We must not hold out the hope that men as busy as the members of the Central Committee will often find the time to take the train to visit Auteuil. M. Bigart and yourself do not come often either. One student, more mischievous than the rest, told me one day that, when he sees a member of the bureau at the school, it is generally from the back, as he leaves the director's office. I do not want to say anything about your back, you've a fine one of course, but all the same the contemplation of that part of your person is not enough to inspire love for the work of the Alliance in these young people. They need more.

You did not know M. Sacki Kann, secretary general of the Alliance. He took on the task of inspecting the Ecole Orientale and winning the affection of the students. He knew that that affection would be transferred to the work itself. How many memories my comrades and I have kept of his tender kindness! Every Saturday a certain number of students were invited to his table. Afterward, we took a walk together as comrades. Sometimes M. Crémieux[21] surprised us at his nephew's and we had the joy of hearing that man speak to us as

18. The Bischoffsheim Institute was one of the Paris schools in which future women teachers were trained.

19. The normal school was first located at the rabbinical seminary in Paris, under the direction of Chief Rabbi Trenel, and was then transferred to rue des Rosiers; its first director was Maurice Marx.

20. Boulevard St. Michel, where students congregated.

21. Isaac Adolphe Crémieux (1796–1880) was a French politician and jurist and became president of the Alliance in 1864.

he knew how about our future duties, about the Alliance and its role in the future. These times will never return.

But they might be restored to us in part if, in the choice of committee members, one took into consideration the needs of the Ecole Orientale. When couldn't the committee add one or two personalities who are less busy than the others, to serve as general inspectors of the school? MM. Alvarez, E. Manuel,[22] and Rosenfeld often filled that role in the past; we saw them many times occupying the professor's chair and very effectively completing the special education that M. Marx was responsible for giving us.

On the other hand, one might divide up the task M. Sacki Kann alone used to assume. That method is successfully practiced at the Bischoffsheim school. You know that in that institution, a few patronesses share the supervision of students and serve as their protectors; they sometimes have them come to their homes, showing them their friendship in various ways, even getting a little gift for them from time to time, a complimentary outing, etc.

With the exception of the packets of chocolate and the ribbons, to which our boys in Auteuil would be impervious, all the rest of the system could be applied to our school.

Each member of the committee is an advocate of a group of students whose progress he closely supervises. To that task, each might—if possible— add that of adopting three or four students, who would go to see him often, whose guardian he would be during their stay in Paris, and with whom he would later remain friends, a protector destined to temper what is sometimes painful in the necessary administrative rigor.

If you should find it too much to keep your eye on three or four young people, I shall do as Abraham did in pleading for Sodom[23] and say: leave the students in the first and second year, leave those in the third year even, and merely divide up those of the fourth year. There are hardly more than a dozen, and each of you will get only one student, a single pupil, whom you will have to follow closely. And be certain that the young teachers will return the interest and regard you show them in Paris, in their zeal, devotion, and abnegation for the work. When you have brought them closer to you, they will feel more solidarity with the Central Committee; they will stop considering themselves ignored and soon-to-be-forgotten agents. That tie of affec-

22. Lévi-Alvarez and Eugène Manuel held seats on a commission responsible for the pedagogy at the ENIO.

23. Arié is referring to Abraham's intervention on behalf of Sodom in order that the righteous not be destroyed along with the wicked (Genesis 18:16–33).

tion will be far more solid than the promises made before a notary public, the absolute ineffectiveness of which you will not be long in seeing, owing to the way justice works in the East.

But all that is not yet enough. In leaving the school, the teacher must be able to live without too much deprivation. Poverty, it is said, is a poor counselor, and devotion has no hold when one is faced with the alternative between going into debt and depriving oneself of the necessities. A modification in the pay scale, which will keep the staff from want without throwing the finances of the Alliance into disarray, ought to be studied. . . .

Archives of the AIU, Turquie LXXVII.E.

5 November 1905

. . . You are kind enough to inform me that the question of retirement pay is also placed on the agenda. I am not unaware that the majority of my colleagues are in favor of regulation. That is no reason for me to rally behind their opinion. I have no foolish attachment to universal suffrage. A majority is not an argument; I have already seen majorities do extremely stupid things. Although I declare myself ready to follow my colleagues out of a spirit of camaraderie, I believe I must be able to make known to the commission the reasons I think regulation would be contrary to the interests of the majority of teachers, and therefore I beg you to be kind enough to add to the dossier the article I sent you for the *Revue* last April. The commission will then see why I fear an effect contrary to what you expect from the planned regulation.

I am responding, finally, to the third paragraph of your letter, in which you express doubts about the effectiveness of a raise of two hundred francs in the beginning salary. It is possible that two hundred francs is a small thing: you will grant more if you can, but it is urgent to do something in that direction. Just today I received a letter from a colleague, whom I had more or less brought up to date regarding my correspondence with M. Bénédict. He says: "Thank you for preaching on behalf of our parish! A raise in salary would give us courage in performing our tasks. All the colleagues I have seen during the vacation were crying poverty, and the great majority are correct. I wish you good success."

I also hope for this success, even as I wish, in the interest of discipline and the future, that precautions be taken so that it does not seem to constitute an encouragement to the calls for revolt that have recently been heard in our ranks. . . .

Archives of the AIU, Turquie LXXVII.E.

25 October 1907

. . . As I undertake the work that the Central Committee was kind enough to entrust to me, I would like, first, to decide with you on a plan for the book and to propose for your approval the method of proceeding that seems most rational to me.

Since the transformations brought about in the East through the action of the schools are perceivable only after a fairly long period of time, it seems to me that only the historical account of the older schools would be interesting. And since, in each region, the history of one school is exactly parallel to that of neighboring institutions, there is no interest in noting for each of them the vicissitudes, struggles, and triumphs that characterized our actions there. These repetitions would be tedious.

We will thus choose, in each country or region envisioned, one typical school among the oldest of them; we will develop its history and will then briefly mention the programs later created around the mother school, if I may call it that, as if we were saying: This produced that.

One exception must, in my view, be made for Persia, where the presence of the directors of the Alliance had immediate and incomparable results, without precedent in the history of the Alliance. Of course, the prestige our organization enjoys in the East invested and continues to invest your directors with a real authority with the public powers, but nowhere is that moral authority as effective and as beneficial as in Persia, and this perspective deserves to be emphasized. (Who knows whether our future representatives in Abyssinia will not have an analogous role to play, as protectors of a population that is ten times larger than that of Persia?)

Then there is Algeria. Either I am ill-informed or our actions in that "extension of France" are temporary and precarious. Are they worth speaking about? If these programs are one day to be liquidated or put back in the hands of the communities, is there any interest in recording the passing of our directors through these French departments?

Finally, the agricultural schools must necessarily have a place in this comprehensive book. We have exchanged a few ideas on this matter verbally: of course, reservations are to be made concerning the results obtained; we shall make these reservations, but we shall nonetheless recount the persevering efforts of the Alliance for the last thirty-eight or forty years at Mikweh and elsewhere. It is undeniable that one-tenth the effort would have produced miraculous results in Canada, the United States, or even Egypt.

If these general considerations are accepted, one could adopt the following divisions for the planned book, subject to correction:

1. Tetuan and Morocco.
2. Baghdad.
3. Adrianople and Thrace.
4. Salonika and Macedonia.
5. Sofia and Bulgaria.
6. Smyrna and Asia Minor.
7. Constantinople.
8. Tunis and Tunisia.
9. Cairo and Egypt.
10. Tehran and Persia.
11. Jerusalem and Palestine.
12. Mikweh and Djedeïda.[24]
Conclusion or preface summarizing the book.

What would be the best method of proceeding? Obviously, one must begin by reading the correspondence and the minutes. But since the schools have long taken up the preponderant place in our daily tasks, reading the correspondence from all your schools for the last forty or forty-five years—a half-million letters—has become a formidable task. Moreover, even if someone had the courage to do it, he would hardly be more advanced once he had finished reading, since he would then have to be locked up in Bicêtre.[25]

Through mere force of circumstances, the work will have to be divided up. I therefore propose that once the above program has been approved, I establish relations with my comrades from the various regions. In appealing to the goodwill, egotism, or self-interest of each one, depending on the case, I hope to find collaborators everywhere and stimulate them to help me examine the dossiers, perform a first task of screening, and perhaps even draft entire chapters.

It may often happen that we are lucky enough to find a man of real ability such as M. Yomtob Sémach, whose account of Baghdad is remarkable. Others will send us compilations of reports such as the one I have in my hands, where the author spares no detail, noting for posterity that at some awards ceremony, the students performed *Le dîner de Pantalon*,[26] and that on a particular day, the correspondent from a local paper, defunct for twenty years, honored the school with a visit. But flights of fancy of that kind will be

---

24. Djedeïda (Djedeida) was an Alliance agricultural school established in Tunisia in 1895.

25. The mental asylum in Paris.

26. Pantalon (Pantaloon), a stock character of Italian comedy *(commedia dell'arte)*.

welcomed: we shall put them back in the crucible, and from the two hundred pages sent to us, we will endeavor to draw out twenty or so that have some interest.

When a colleague has consented to give me his cooperation and take on some work, I shall inform you of it and shall ask you to be kind enough to sent him some dossiers.

I would be very obliged to you, dear Monsieur Bigart, if you would give me your opinion on the questions I have raised in this first letter. Others will follow: since the secretariat ought to be the definitive author responsible for our publication, it is natural that I should write often to its head. From whom I shall gratefully receive advice and directions. . . .

Archives of the AIU, Suisse A.

10 November 1907

. . . I have received your letter of 4 November and have taken note of its content.

Here, now, are some other questions.

Would you agree to preceding the history of each group of schools with the succinct history—one, two, or three pages—of the community itself: probable time the first Jews arrived, immigrations that followed, dominations undergone in turn, principal events to be noted, rabbis and prominent persons the community produced.

M. Abraham Danon[27] could do a very good job on that part. About twenty years ago, he wrote a history in Hebrew of the Jews in Turkey; he then pursued his study of that subject in his newspaper *Yosef Daat*.[28]

Another writer, M. Salomon Rozanès,[29] one of my childhood friends, now in Ruschuk, has just published the first volume of his *History of the Jews of Turkey* (did you receive it for the library?), also in Hebrew. Various societies of Jewish studies have contributed toward the printing costs of this book. I had in my hands a large part of the manuscript, which is very interesting. My friend Rozanès will also collaborate with us.

Once we have collected all these accounts, we could submit them for criticism to M. Hartwig Derembourg[30] or M. Théodore Reinach, so as not to

27. Abraham Danon (1857–1925) was a *maskil* (a proponent of the Jewish Enlightenment movement), Orientalist, and pedagogue.

28. The Hebrew and Judeo-Spanish journal *Yosef Daat* (Growth of knowledge; Hebrew) survived only from March to December 1888.

29. Salomon Rozanès (1863–1938) was a Jewish historian from Bulgaria.

30. Hartwig Derembourg (or Derenbourg; 1844–1908) was a French Orientalist and Arabist.

risk publishing historical heresies, or—if they are unavoidable—so as to publish them only with their stamp of approval.

If you agree to this proposal, I shall get in touch with MM. Danon and Rozanès.

I enclose a letter for M. Joseph Halévy.[31] I would be obliged if you would send it to him. Not that I could not find his address if I looked hard for it, but I think it might be useful to exert a little pressure on him, in having him get my letter through you. His account will form an excellent introduction to the history of the school in Adrianople, which I am going to write by reworking M. Loupo's manuscript.

I also inquire with this mail whether M. Hirsch[32] would not want to write part of his memoirs for us: with Charles Netter, he was the creator of Mikweh. Netter died and was buried there, and M. Hirsch buried two of his children there. M. Hirsch could recount better than anyone the genesis of the agricultural idea and the first efforts to realize it. The reports of MM. Niégo and Avigdor[33] will then provide us with the elements necessary for drafting the following chapters relating to recent events, which are always less interesting than the trials and errors at the beginning.

As you see, I am writing to the old men first, those who were actors during those heroic times you discuss in your letter. Of those heroes, there are still a few who remain, thank God; we must hurry to question them—life is so short!—and to collect their memories. It is at this price that we will have the chance to place some living sections in our book, living because lived, which will make reading it easy and agreeable. If we do not take that precaution but limit ourselves to summarizing or reproducing documents from our archives, I fear we will make a cold, glacial historian's work and, as a result, a work that no one will read: twenty *Revues Historiques* whose pages have not even been cut exist to bear witness to that.

The day I left Paris, you were to write to MM. Fresco and Salomon Danon to ask them where they are in their work. I would be very obliged if you could tell me what responses you have received. . . .

P.S. If the name of the Swiss locality where you said life was less expensive than it is in Davos returns to your memory, please be kind enough to let me know. The fact that I have not been able to discover it by myself proves I do not yet know the geography of this country.

Archives of the AIU, Suisse A.

31. Joseph Halévy (1827–1917) was a famous Orientalist.
32. Samuel Hirsch (1843–1925) directed Mikveh Yisrael between 1879 and 1891.
33. Joseph Niégo (1863–1950) took over for Samuel Hirsch at Mikveh Yisrael until 1903. Samuel Avigdor was assistant director of the same school from 1890 to 1893.

3 February 1908

. . . *Palestine:* I asked you for more documents on this matter, since my intention was to treat Jerusalem and the holy places more extensively than the other parts. First, Jewry as a whole is interested in Palestine: the chapters on Adrianople and Baghdad, for example, may be leafed through by a few curious souls, but everyone will stop at the pages evoking the profound poverty that reigns in the City of David and the persevering efforts you are making and that must be continued for several generations for the revival of that population.

Second, it seems to me that the societies emulating the Alliance, which are gradually settling in Jerusalem, would not be sorry to buzz about self-importantly and erect themselves as the standard-bearers and sole saviors of Judaism. In setting out for the public at large, and in some detail, the extent of your work and the immensity of your sacrifices in the Holy Land, we will perhaps take away the desire of some to measure themselves against the Alliance, and in any case to criticize its actions in that country. I am especially alluding here to the Zionist organizations, to whom it is important to show that the Alliance was in reality the first Zionist society formed within contemporary society, and that it has undertaken to rebuild, not the walls and fortresses of Zion it is true, but rather its soul and character. . . .

I have just received a letter from M. Rozanès informing me that he sent you a copy of his *History of the Ottoman Jews* (in addition to the one he gave you through M. Angel); he sent me the second of the two copies, you will receive it with this mail.

Each of these volumes costs seven francs. I am thus sending M. Rozanès fourteen francs and would appreciate it if you would credit that sum to me.

M. Rozanès tells me that the entire work will comprise six to seven volumes, and that it will take at least three years of work for each volume. You should know that M. Rozanès is a very busy businessman and can devote only his evenings to his historical work. He is a self-made man who attended only primary school, in Balat, where he was my comrade. He inherited from his father, a great Hebraist, his love for Hebrew letters and history.

Archives of the AIU, Suisse A.

11 December 1908

. . . My work on the Alliance schools is reaching its end. Beginning with the new year, I shall begin to revise the completed chapters and will send them to you one after the other at brief intervals. I would like to know beforehand your opinion on the following points:

    1. MM. Loupo, Fresco, Confino, Sémach, and Danon have written, respec-

tively, chapters on Adrianople, Constantinople, Persia, Baghdad, and Bulgaria. We have judged it impossible to publish the work of my first colleagues, and I have rewritten it from beginning to end. The last three of these chapters, as excellent as they are, seem to me to contain tedious passages and digressions. Examples: unpleasant dealings between M. Confino and a converted Jew in Ispahan, and the defeat of the latter; political history of Bulgaria from the ninth to the nineteenth centuries; the avarice of M. Marx, who well deserves we remember only his good qualities, etc.—Am I authorized to make alterations in the reports?

2. Since my work has been remunerated by the Central Committee, it goes without saying that no article written by me will be signed. The work supposedly comes from the secretariat. As a result, I did not feel obliged to cite my sources of information, which are the archives and *Bulletins,* the property of the Alliance, nor to place passages from them that are incorporated into my studies in quotation marks—I hope that is correct.

. . . When we have finished with the history of the Alliance, I will ask you to entrust another task to me. I am thinking about resuscitating the *Revue des Ecoles* in a more modest form, without the backing of the secretariat, under conditions I shall reveal to you when it is useful. There is no diocese, however impoverished, that does not have its religious weekly, no society of the subprefecture that does not have its periodical publication, and the Alliance, which has twelve hundred teachers in its service, which receives six to seven thousand letters and reports per year, cannot find the means to support a poor little pedagogical bulletin? . . .

Archives of the AIU, Suisse A.

15 January 1909
. . . I do not believe the discussion of the spelling of the words *juifs* and *israélites* is purely byzantine, and I ask for your permission to return to it.

When it is a question of French Jews, whose denomination the laws ignore and whose religion is considered an opinion on the same level as a philosophical conviction, there is no doubt that one must write *juifs* and *israélites* as one writes *protestants, cartésiens,* or *pythagoriciens.*[34]

But there are countries where the Jews constitute a nation, formally recognized as such by the state. Turkey is one of these. The new Turkish constitution,[35] even while proclaiming the equality of citizens of every denomina-

34. That is, uncapitalized.
35. In July 1908, the Young Turks took power following a peaceful revolution and reestablished the constitution of 1876, which had been applied for only one year.

tion, specifies that the rights and privileges of each of the "nations" of the empire are to be maintained. These nations have leaders at their head: patriarch, exarch, and chief rabbi, who are the sovereigns of these states within the state. It is too bad for Turkey that it has thus favored the populations of races foreign to the Turks over the Muslims, but neither the Greeks nor the Armenians nor the Bulgarians would give up their privileges—which are civil and political as well as religious in nature—for all the constitutions in the world.

The Jews have benefited from these advantages to the same degree as the Christians. In the eyes of the Turks, they form a "nation"; as a nation, they have been granted a place in national representation. They thus form a portion of that great Ottoman family, distinct from other portions, which are called: Turks, Greeks, Armenians, Druzes, Maronites, Bulgarians, Wallachians, etc. In my opinion, it would be a grave error to abandon, out of love for equality, the external signs that distinguish the nationality of our coreligionists in the East from other rival or enemy nationalities. (Consider the Serbs, who, having never been recognized as a nation, are preyed upon by their Albanian neighbors and have almost been exterminated by them. There is no Serb deputy in the Chamber.)

The security and future of our coreligionists in Turkey—and by extension those of other Muslim countries—require that, until further notice, they consider themselves and we consider them an ethnic entity. We should thus say, in speaking of them, *les Juifs, les Israélites.* Algeria, which has been assimilated to France, naturally escapes that definition. There are only *juifs algériens.*

So much high politics for a capital letter, you may ask. Well yes, you know we live only by words, and words are made up of letters. . . .

Archives of the AIU, Suisse A.

11 June 1911

A small event, which could have very fortunate consequences for our coreligionists in Bulgaria, is about to take place.

The Treaty of Berlin[36] and the Bulgarian constitution guarantee full political rights to all Bulgarians without regard for religion. In fact, however, the Jews of that country enjoy only some of those rights: for the thirty-three years that Bulgaria has been in existence, the Jews have never sent a deputy

36. The Treaty of Berlin (1878), signed following the Russo-Turkish War (1877–78), granted the Balkan states new territories and new statutes. The Bulgarian nation-state was born with that treaty.

of their religion to the Sobranié,[37] all public offices are refused them, there are at best two or three Jewish officers in the Bulgarian army, and the military school has long been closed to our coreligionists. In the army of government employees of all kinds who trim the budget, there is not a justice of the peace, not a telegraph operator, not a railroad worker, not the most modest copyist of the Jewish religion.

The Jews are nonetheless voters with the same status as Christians and Muslims. If the governments have treated them with some scorn until now, it is because, trained to obey by long centuries of Ottoman absolutism, our coreligionists took it as an invariable rule to always vote for the party in power. Since the balance of their votes was always ensured to the various governments that succeeded one another, these governments, divided on so many points, were at least agreed on this: the support of Jewish voters is ensured us whatever our attitude toward them, so why bother with them?

It seems this state of affairs is about to change. For a certain number of years, the Jews have been more actively interested in the political life of the country: we see a certain number of them joining the clubs of the different parties, and they are gradually developing the ambition to stop being second-class citizens.

This sentiment has just made a sudden and remarkably unanimous appearance on the occasion of the elections for the great Sobranié, which will take place on 18 June. That assembly, which will meet in Tirnovo on 22 June to revise certain articles of the constitution, will include about five hundred deputies, to wit, one deputy per ten thousand residents (ordinary Sobraniés have about two hundred and fifty deputies, that is, one per twenty thousand residents). Since the community of Sofia has thirteen thousand members, our coreligionists of that city thought they had the right to a deputy for the great Sobranié. Since voting proceeds by lists, the chief rabbi and the consistory[38] approached the head of government about two months ago, asking him to include at least one Jewish deputy on the list of government candidates. The reception of this overture was polite but reserved and changed a few weeks later into a categorical refusal.

On the initiative of a few of our coreligionists who belong to different political parties, a meeting was convened to examine the situation. On that occasion, all quarrels between Zionists and anti-Zionists were forgotten, and it was decided that everyone would walk hand in hand to see that a Jew, whoever he might be, won a mandate at the next grand Sobranié. A commis-

37. The Sobranié was the Bulgarian parliament.
38. The consistory was the central community organization of Bulgarian Jews, formed on the French model in 1890.

sion of six members was constituted, representing the six principal political parties, with the mission of going to the club of each party to request that a Jew be put on its list. Four of the groups granted the request at once; the nationalist party, to which M. Gueschoff, council president, belongs, evaded the issue once more, but soon pulled itself together at the thought of losing at least fifteen hundred votes of the three thousand that Jews have in Sofia, and finally gave in. M. Gueschoff, who was at the head of the Sofia list (and who was a candidate elsewhere as well, since simultaneous candidacies are allowed), withdrew to give way to a Jew. The nationalist club designated M. Haïm Farhi, president of the school committee, as its candidate.

Thus, for the first time since Bulgaria has been in existence, there will be Jewish candidates at legislative elections, including one supported by the government.

Archives of the AIU, Suisse A.

15 March 1912

. . . For some time, the Bulgarian press has been manifesting antisemitic tendencies. A notable from Sofia, Dr. Navon, published an "open letter" to the Bulgarian central consistory in a Jewish newspaper to call its attention to the peril that threatens the Jews. Given the state of public opinion, M. Navon believes pogroms are possible and even imminent in Bulgaria. He thus advises the consistory not to let attacks against Judaism go without response.

In response to that article, M. Ehrenpreis,[39] chief rabbi, believes the consistory can in effect defend the Jews in the press, but for that, money is needed, and we are lacking in resources. Money is also needed to compile and publish writings designed to spread a knowledge of Judaism, its doctrine, and its ethics throughout the Christian population.

I am afraid both M. Navon and M. Ehrenpreis are on the wrong track. A consistory, an official organization presided over by the chief rabbi, that would spend its time in polemics would quickly be discredited. As for the works on Judaism recommended by M. Ehrenpreis, one can be sure that no Christian would read a single line of them.

Antisemitism will progress quickly in Bulgaria; that is certain. But it will be the fault of the Jews themselves. I wrote as much in an "open letter," which I also sent to the central consistory of Sofia. I believe I should communicate the following passage from that letter (in translation) to you:

"To ward off the peril that threatens the Jews, flat denials in the newspa-

39. Marcus Ehrenpreis (1869–1951) was chief rabbi of Bulgaria between 1900 and 1914.

per are not enough. If Dr. Navon will permit me to use a medical term, the remedy proposed by him is only a palliative. And even this palliative, used as he recommends, would in my opinion do more harm than good. The truly effective means to defend Bulgarian Jewry is to elevate it morally and intellectually, so that it will acquire the esteem of the Christian element. I do not think I am mistaken in asserting that after thirty-two years of freedom, Bulgarian Jews have remained, from the intellectual point of view, not only very inferior to their fellow citizens in other cities, but also inferior to their coreligionists in the Turkish empire. Those who have visited Constantinople, Salonika, Smyrna, Beirut, and other cities with large Jewish communities will not contradict me, once they have compared Ottoman Jewish youth to Bulgarian Jewish youth. How many Bulgarian Jews speak and pronounce correctly the language of the country? I would be very surprised if we found even ten. Ten out of forty thousand! And this in a country where for thirty-two years all the primary schools, all the secondary schools, and the university are open almost without cost to Jews!

"I recently had the opportunity to read a few Bulgarian comic newspapers. I saw with regret that the subject that comes up most often in the satires and jeering published by these newspapers is the Jew with his incorrect and poorly pronounced language. How much esteem can the Bulgarian reader have for a people whose members, after thirty-two years of free education, do not know how to articulate a single correct sentence in the official language? To have the right to be part of a nation, certain conditions are required, among the most important a thorough education in the language, history, and traditions of the country. Without a serious Bulgarian education, the Jews may legally be the equals of their fellow citizens, but they will still be considered a foreign element by them, and will be treated as such, by public opinion first and by the laws second.

"To acquire the esteem and sympathy of the Bulgarian people, the Jews must not go begging for the kindness of their fellow citizens. They must deserve it. And they will deserve it only when they have succeeded in raising the intellectual and moral level of their children. That is the task of the schools. As the schools go, so goes the future of Bulgarian Jewry. Thus, before seeking to combat the external causes that sow antisemitism in Bulgaria, we must make the internal causes disappear, those that depend upon the Jews themselves. The almost universal ignorance in which the current Jewish generation in Bulgaria is growing up contains in germ all the future calamities that Dr. Navon foresees and predicts for Bulgarian Jews. It is this malady we need to cure, and that is the primordial question, the vital question with which the central consistory ought to be preoccupied before all others."

Archives of the AIU, Suisse A.

12 March 1913

. . . The profound transformation of eastern Europe that is occurring before our eyes will bring about a radical change in the age-old conditions of existence for our coreligionists in the Balkan countries. It will also not be without serious effects on the respect the Alliance has acquired in those regions through fifty years of effort and sacrifice. This may be a unique opportunity to examine with attention what precautions ought to be taken to ensure a prosperous moral and material future to that portion of Eastern Jewry, and at the same time to safeguard any attack on the institutions of the Alliance located in the new territories that have been detached from Turkey.

Logically, the Alliance ought to have examined these questions in concert with the constituted authorities of Bulgarian Jewry. But a few incidents of very secondary order have unfortunately chilled, if not in fact suppressed, the relations between your society and the central consistory of Sofia. As a result, for matters of little interest and, what is more regrettable, for pointless reasons of protocol, the communication between the Alliance and the representatives of one hundred thousand Jews, who may perhaps be one hundred and eighty thousand tomorrow, has been interrupted at this decisive, I will even say solemn, moment of their history.

Placed by my career at the Alliance, and by my Bulgarian origin, between the Central Committee, which has always been kind enough to lend a benevolent ear to my suggestions, and the central organization of Bulgarian Jewry, where I count friends with a preponderant influence, I felt it was incumbent upon me to intervene to dissipate the misunderstandings and prepare for a collaboration whose effects could be as useful to the prestige of the Alliance as they are beneficial to my compatriots. That is why I solicited a mandate from my compatriots, which was eagerly granted me, to come speak to you in their name.

In speaking of two hundred thousand Bulgarian Jews, I include in that number those of Salonika. It is possible that that city will temporarily remain attached to the Greek kingdom. But be assured that as soon as peace is signed, Bulgaria will actively prepare for a new war against its ally of today, in order to conquer Salonika. It is not possible that the native city of Saint Cyril,[40] who gave Bulgaria its alphabet, which has become the Slavic alphabet, and Saint Methodius,[41] who Christianized the country, should forever

40. Saint Cyril, called the Philosopher or Saint Cyril of Salonika (827 or 828–69), was the evangelist of the Slavs. Tradition attributes the invention of the Cyrillic alphabet to him.

41. Saint Methodius (825–85) was an apostle of the Slavs, along with his younger brother, Saint Cyril.

remain a Greek city. Whether Salonika is linked to Slavism sooner or later, the Bulgarians need the Alliance and the collaboration of the Jews. It has already been twenty-five years since the great minister and patriot Karavelov[42] told me: "We need you in order to establish ourselves in Macedonia and Salonika: Spread Bulgarian propaganda among your coreligionists in that city." King Ferdinand[43] and his government are asking us for the same thing today and are ready to grant us in exchange all the liberties and exemptions for the commune and the schools that we request of them.

The circumstances are thus exceptionally favorable to ensure a regime in the new Bulgaria that is propitious for the material and moral development of the populous Jewish communities that are or will be located here.

I say nothing of their civil and political rights, since those rights were assured them by the Treaty of Berlin, whose provisions, reproduced in the constitution, are generally respected.

But what good does it do the Jews to possess rights if the inferiority of their education makes them incapable of exercising them? Bulgarian legislators have concerned themselves very little with non-Orthodox communities and schools, and when they have concerned themselves, it was rather to obstruct their expansion. For thirty years, the Jewish schools, caught in the net of bothersome regulations on the pretext of hygiene, have merely vegetated. The children who frequent them have succeeded in learning Bulgarian less well than in the public schools (which are open to them), Hebrew less well than in the old *talmud-tora,* and a foreign language less well than the little coloreds of the Congo. Rabbi Israël Lévy, who has visited these schools, will tell you if there is the slightest exaggeration in this judgment.

If we do not take care, that decline in the intellectual level of our coreligionists of Bulgaria will affect the Ottoman Jews, which the recent war has annexed to Bulgaria. And then, in twenty or thirty years, in the southeast of Europe, there will be a Jewish population of more than two hundred thousand in such a state of intellectual inferiority in relation to the other populations that surround it that the question will be raised whether that collectivity does not constitute an undesirable element in the country, and whether the civil and political rights it possesses ought to be maintained.

42. Petko Karavelov was the brother of the Bulgarian writer Lyuben Karavelov. The former was anti-Russian and in 1883 became premier of the liberal cabinet formed by Prince Alexander of Battenberg, after the dismissal of Dragan Tsankov from that office. He thus came to power from the opposition, even while preserving his intransigent position toward the prince.

43. Ferdinand I (prince of Saxe-Coburg-Gotha) was king of Bulgaria (1861–1948). In 1908, taking advantage of the Young Turk revolution, he assumed the title of king or tsar of the Bulgarians.

An analogous problem was raised a few years ago regarding the Gypsies, numerous in Bulgaria, who originally enjoyed all the rights of citizens. Because of the inferiority of their culture, these rights were taken away from them. One has only to take a walk in the Jewish quarter of Sofia called Utch-Bunar to recognize, in the crowd of ragged and wild children one encounters in the streets, the seeds of the Gypsies.

Bulgarian Jews must not fall to the level of the Gypsies.

It lies within the role of the Alliance to foresee that catastrophe and to prevent it from occurring.

The Alliance can do it. It is equipped for that.

The other Jewish associations can flood Bulgaria with gold. That gold melts or disappears like smoke.

I am coming to Paris to invite the Alliance to work for lasting programs.

. . . It would be both politic and humane not to exclude the Jews of Bulgaria, who are suffering from the war, from a share of the resources placed at the disposition of the Alliance by the Balkan fund. Poverty is only increasing as the war drags on. The Passover celebration, which is approaching, will further increase the distress of the nine or ten thousand unfortunate souls listed by the central aid committee in Sofia. I think I am being very moderate in soliciting for that work of charity an allocation of ten thousand francs for the month of March and twenty thousand for the month of April and for Passover needs.

I can assure you that these two measures of kindness would reestablish the cordiality of relations between the Alliance and the leading circles of Sofia, which is indispensable for carrying out the shared and long-term work defined above.

There will then be occasion to examine the text of a proposed law to submit to the Sobranié concerning the organization of the Jewish communities and schools of the kingdom. . . .

In the meantime, you might begin your reentry into the schools with the two following measures, which are both educational and charitable in character and whose adoption would go straight to the hearts of the unfortunate and would immediately raise the popularity and prestige of the Alliance:

1. Reestablish the food program in the schools, which will benefit, in the first place, the children (of both sexes) of soldiers who died in the war or who are afflicted with infirmities.

2. Reestablish the boys' apprenticeship program, giving preference to war orphans.

You could also create at little cost an apprenticeship program for the girl orphans of Sofia.

All these apprentices would benefit from the food program.

Finally, I propose to ask you, Mr. President, in your role as president of the ICA, to be kind enough to place on the agenda of the council of that society the question of loan associations to be founded in Bulgaria to raise up thousands of families that the war has reduced from prosperity to poverty, and to use your high influence to produce a favorable outcome to that request.

I will then ask the Alliance to itself take on the responsibility for administering these associations, for reasons easy to imagine and necessary for the consolidation of its school programs.

For the proper administration of these programs, I can commit myself to constituting, wherever necessary, committees offering all the guarantees of honor and activity desired.

After the war, these committees will be the natural intermediaries between the Alliance and the communities for the education programs to be created, whose urgency I have tried to show you. . . .

Archives of the AIU, Suisse A.

16 April 1913

. . . You have been kind enough to accede to my request to place my daughter Jeanne, thirteen years old, with Mmes Weill and Kahn[44] in Neuilly, under the conditions these ladies set forth before the Alliance regarding room and board for your student teachers. I thank you again and come to inform you that, next week, my daughter will leave for Paris, will prepare the prescribed wardrobe, and, on 1 May, will present herself at the school of Mmes Weill and Kahn. I would be grateful if you would inform them of her arrival.

In addition to the studies required for obtaining the elementary certificate, which my daughter will try to master without overworking herself, I would also like her to take piano, dance, and needlework lessons.

I would be very obliged if you would let me know the total fees I will have to pay per trimester, and what deduction will be taken for the part of vacation my daughter cannot spend at the school.

Finally, I will ask you to be kind enough to pay all the fees on my behalf and charge me in installments.

I will inform Mmes Weill and Kahn of the names of my daughter's correspondents in Paris (my brother and sister). . . .

Archives of the AIU, Suisse A.

44. Until the inauguration of the Ecole Normale Israélite Orientale for young women in 1922, the education of women teachers was entrusted to three different institutions, including that of Mmes Weil and Kahn in Neuilly.

11/ The Balkan Wars and World War I
(1913–1918)

N othing attracts me to Sofia, and yet I have come here, and here I am settled into one of our apartments on Pirot Street with Rachel and Sandro. What folly it truly is to makes plans and to trace out in advance the route one will follow in life! The leaf is no more the plaything of the wind than man that of destiny!

I was living peacefully in Davos at the beginning of 1913 when, in March, I went to Paris to solicit funds from the Alliance for the Bulgarian victims of the Balkan War. I thought these funds were necessary, but such was not the case. M. Salomon Reinach proposed I come to Sofia to represent the Alliance here. Since I wanted to try living on the plains, I accepted a temporary mission and I came.

We arrived in Sofia on 28 April and were Elia's guests for six months. I had imposed this period of time to test the effects of the climate before spending money to move into our own place.

The summer was relatively cool and I was just as healthy in Sofia as I was in Davos. Number of days with an above-normal temperature, six; salmon-colored spittle, three times, for periods of three days. Weight, seventy-eight.

The Second Balkan War, which took place between the allies, took almost all of Bulgaria's conquests away from it. My mission in Sofia no longer had any object and the Alliance was going to put an end to it. Then, in November, the Union des Associations Israélites in Brussels, with F. Philippson serving as president, delegated Dr. B. Kahn, secretary of the Hilfsverein,[1] to review with me the accounts of the aid committee. Dr. Kahn found the administration very much in order and me very incor-

---

1. The Hilfsverein der Deutschen Juden, founded in 1901 by German Jews, undertook a program parallel to that of the Alliance, but on a smaller scale, in eastern Europe and the East.

rect. There resulted a conflict between us that Dr. Kahn made public in *La Luz*,[2] the Judeo-Spanish newspaper of Sofia. By order of the Central Committee, I was obliged not to respond, so as not to give too much offense to M. Philippson, who could suppress the Alliance's annual grant of three hundred thousand francs from the ICA. But the Central Committee approved my manner of conduct and thought all down the line, and has retained me in my mission, which is well remunerated.

In the meantime, I have begun talks with the Zionists for the Alliance's return to the school in Sofia. If only I could reorganize these institutions, what satisfaction I would have!

Since I was to come to Sofia for only six months as a kind of test, I could not bring Narcisse and Jeanne with me to Elia's: I thus sent the first to Norwich [England] and the second to Paris.

Narcisse spent eight months in England and did excellent work at Bracondale School. His director, Mr. Francis Williams, took a great interest in him and prepared him for the Cambridge Junior examinations. We will know in a month the results of these exams. At this point, Narcisse is on vacation in Paris, at Sultana's, and is getting to know the museums, theaters, and universities there. He will return to Sofia in February and, after studying Bulgarian a bit, will go to work in Sandro's office.

As for Jeanne, I placed her in Neuilly, at the Weill and Kahn Institute, and will send her back, since she likes it and would have nothing to do in Sofia.

The goal that I proposed upon leaving Davos to settle in Sofia, at the risk of my health, was to found an independent firm for Sandro and Narcisse. This goal has been accomplished. We found the partner we needed, a M. Moïse Mévorach, with whom we came to an understanding. Since 25 January 1914, the Mévorach and Arié firm exists; it concerns itself with commissions and representation. Narcisse will join soon, and one day the two brothers will be partners and will try to earn a living at the business.

Thus, in the space of fifteen months, I'll have married off Sophie, established Sandro on his own, and put the final touches on the education of Narcisse, who is beginning his commercial apprenticeship. My duties as father are almost completed.

Sophie is very happy with her husband. But I have not seen her since her departure from Davos in May 1912.

The catastrophe that struck Bulgaria ruined all the plans for enter-

2. *La Luz* (The light; Judeo-Spanish) was a newspaper representing the interests of the chief rabbinate, published between 1906 and 1918.

prises that were forming and also scuttled the plan for the Phoenix of the Balkans, for which Elia was to be director. But Elia has been named director of the Balkan.

Since my arrival in Sofia, I have been giving an hour of French lessons to Edith and Frida every day. Their education has been very neglected.

In Paris, Emmanuel is happy in his career; I will give him a financial interest in Sandro's business. Samuel is also earning a good living. In April, I helped him make up a will in which he leaves everything to Sultana; the future of my young sister is thus ensured.

Régine's existence is calmer; her husband is earning a good living; we contribute only to her rent.

Rosa remained the same until October. Since then she has had a relapse and has been in the Kniajevo sanatorium for two months. Her condition worries me a great deal.

What will 1914 be like?

JANUARY 1915

The year 1914 was marked by the most horrendous, the most cruel war that humanity has ever seen. The European conflagration, which has been brewing for years, broke out, and today almost all of Europe is in flames: on 28 July, Austria declared war on Serbia; on 1 August, Germany declared war on Russia; on 3 August, Germany on France; the same day, England on Germany. Then Japan went up against Germany, and Turkey against the Triple Entente. Not to mention Belgium—which is entirely occupied by the Germans—or Montenegro. The other states of Europe, including Bulgaria, are biding their time or preparing. No one believes this war of the giants can be ended in 1915.

This year, 1915, has begun very badly for us. My poor sister Rosa died on 28 December 1914/10 January 1915, that is, 24 Tébet [Tevet] 5675, after a year of horrible suffering, despite the most devoted care lavished on her at the H. Ivanof sanatorium in Kniajevo and at her home.

Four days earlier, M. Narcisse Leven, president of the Alliance, died in Paris. A saint has passed away, one of the men I most admired. He showed friendship for me and did me the honor of working with me in the elaboration of the plan for the two books of *Cinquante ans d'histoire*. What will become of the Alliance now?

The mission that society entrusted to me in Bulgaria ended on 28 February. The epilogue to my dispute with Dr. Ehrenpreis was his departure; he left Bulgaria in September to occupy the post of chief rabbi in

Stockholm. Neither his publications against me nor the public meetings he organized to embarrass me could save him: he had to leave his job, accused of falsifying accounts. I believe that execution will be the last of my activities in Jewish public affairs.

At present, I am spending my leisure time writing a short book entitled *Histoire du peuple juif,* a summary of Graetz.[3] The *Bulletin des Ecoles* has ceased to appear since the war.

Another affair that preoccupied and agitated me a great deal this year was the settling of accounts with my brother Elia. I must note with regret that my brother disputed, aloud and in writing, my share in the co-ownership of our house at 20 Pirot Street in Sofia. He finally acknowledged his error and, in his letter dated 2/15 August 1914, wrote me: "To have peace, I do hereby make the solemn declaration that I recognize your right to the ownership of half of the house and that I am ready to provide you with a formal deed of property for that half as soon as you have deposited the exchange value, and you may take up to five years to do that; unless between now and then by common agreement we have sold the house to a third party."

That arrangement was confirmed by the statement of his accounts, which he handed over to me on 31 December 1914, where the net worth of the house is shared equally between him and me.

Thus I or my heirs have until 2/15 August 1920 to give Elia what is required above my current investment of capital, in order to get the deed of property for half the building, or else to sell the building to a third party and deposit half the profit over 240,000 francs, the current price of the house in our accounts.

Of course, the letter from Elia cited above does not have the value of a notarized document, but he will no doubt be honest enough to consider it such, if between now and 1920 I should pass away.

The Mévorach and Arié company did not prosper: with the outbreak of the war, the company was dissolved and Sandro returned to the Balkan, where he will remain until the end of the war.

Narcisse returned to Sofia on 12 February and since June has been employed at Mayer and Aftalion's.

Jeanne also returned from Paris on 23 July, ten days before the war broke out.

Thus the chapter regarding expenses for the education of my children is definitively closed.

Sophie is very happy in Salonika. Rachel and I went to see her at her

3. Heinrich Graetz (1817–91), the famous Jewish historian.

home and remained for two months (April and May). We brought her back to Sofia, where she stayed for two months (June and July). Salomon came to get her in July. He also came in September on business.

Another great event this year was the wedding of Emmanuel. On 21 December 1914 in Geneva, he married Mlle Lucie Nestor Weill. It is a marriage of love, with a very large dowry on the side, which doesn't spoil a thing. It even seems the family will already be growing in September.

My health was good for the entire year of 1914. But I got off to a bad start in 1915: following a chill, I had to stay in bed or in my room for almost the entire month of January, so that I did not see Rosa die or attend her funeral or participate in the mourning.

All my fatigue and emotion for the year 1914 must have disturbed my body. But I am not sorry to have struggled if I have ensured bread for my old age and, after me, for my wife.

Sofia, 31 January 1915

JANUARY 1916

The war that has plunged Europe into a bloodbath for the last eighteen months is still far from ending. The year 1915 was marked by great events, which I noted day by day in a special notebook. Here are the most important: in Russia, the Germans occupied all of Poland and part of properly Russian territory. In Turkey, the Anglo-French forces tried to seize the Dardanelles: they have just abandoned that undertaking after nine months of enormous effort and sacrifice. Bulgaria entered the struggle on 1/14 October. In concert with the Austro-Germans, it erased Serbia from the map and inflicted bloody defeats on the Anglo-French, who had come to the aid of the Serbs. It is now preparing to chase them out of Salonika. A conquered Montenegro asked for peace. Italy has been fighting Austria, its ally just a little while ago, for the past eight months, but to no avail. The destitution the war brings is incalculable.

As we await the end, the cost of living is rising at a distressing rate. Certain essential articles have doubled or tripled in price.

During the year 1915, our family grew by one member: on 26 September, a boy was born to Emmanuel. He received the name Pierre, *Bessimantov*.[4]

---

4. *Bessimantov* (*Be-siman tov*, "may it be a good sign, an auspicious event"), congratulations on the occasion of a happy event: an engagement, wedding, or the birth of a male child.

Emmanuel, Lucie, Samuel, and Sultana were able to return to Paris and are busy with their affairs.

My health has been satisfactory. I was able to go to Shumla for an inspection entrusted to me by the Alliance. To improve my health through a little change of air, we went to spend three months—June to August—in the countryside at Kniajevo, and we shared a house there with Elia's family.

I have completed my *Histoire du peuple juif.* Just as I was about to send it to the printer, the Bulgarian mobilization occurred, which interrupted communication with France. The execution of this project is necessarily delayed until after the war.

This year, I engaged in a bit of commerce, in partnership with my cousin Rahamim Arié. It was all the more necessary in that, on the one hand, the Alliance has reduced my small salary by half for the duration of the war and, on the other, the revenue from our house has hardly exceeded the rent received, given the moratorium law. The few operations I engaged in for the purchase and sale of certain commodities have allowed me to cover my expenses. It should be the same in 1916. Moreover, Sandro and Narcisse have each been contributing a hundred francs to household expenses since 1 January.

Sandro has just received a raise, to three hundred francs, at the Balkan. Narcisse had to leave Mayer and Aftalion's in May because of overwork, and he has just joined the Balkan. He will receive two hundred and thirty francs per month beginning in January. It is a great joy, as I feel my own strength declining, to see that my children are ready to support the family with the product of their work.

During the entire year, I have not seen Sophie and Salomon. The troubles in the Balkans prevented any easy communication between Sofia and Salonika. Currently, all relations between those two cities are interrupted. Who knows when it will be possible for me to see my dear daughter again?

Jeanne is developing quickly and is gradually learning to keep a good house.

Oro and her husband have settled definitively in Sofia. Their son Joseph has just finished his studies in law and will establish himself as a lawyer.

Joseph, my brother-in-law, is mobilized and attached to a hospital in Sofia. Emmanuel, Elia, and I contribute toward the majority of the household expenses for Régine and her family.

Sofia, 7/20 January 1916

JANUARY 1917

The war in Europe continued this year more relentlessly than ever. The desperate efforts of the Germans since February 1916 to seize hold of the fortress of Verdun were foiled by the heroic resistance of the French. The French, with the cooperation of the English, even advanced a little on that side and on the side of the Somme, where the most murderous battles of the war broke out.

In Russia, a Russian offensive led to a retreat by Austro-Germans in Bukovina and Galicia. The Central Powers proclaimed Poland's independence.

On the Italian front, the Austrians advanced from the north side.

In Macedonia, the Bulgarians lost Bitola [Monastir].

The most salient event of the year was Romania's entry into the war against the Central Powers (28 August) and the occupation of most of the country by the Allies. Dobruja is in the hands of the Bulgarians as far as the Danube. The war continues.

The peace offer made on 12 December by the Allies to the Entente was rejected, as was the mediation of President Wilson.

The Central Powers have the advantage in arms everywhere. But their economic situation is worsening from one day to the next. For Bulgaria, an agricultural country, here are a few prices: bread, 0.42 per kilo; sugar, 12 levas;[5] coffee, 24; salt, 0.45 (nominal); meat, 3; oil, 16; soap, 12; cheese, 5; butter, 9; flour, 120 (per sack).

In 1916, my expenses were 80 percent higher than they were in 1915.

Fortunately, my resources increased to an even greater degree: not from the Alliance, from whom I remained without news all year long, but from business.

My partnership with Rahamim Arié lasted barely four months, since the poor man died on 13 August of stomach cancer. But I continued my commerce with a broker, Léon Farhi, and since last November have been working without a permanent partner. The result of this beginning is satisfactory: I covered my expenses and more than doubled my capital.

Since 1 August, I have been taking Sandro with me to the office; I have just made him a partner in my business, giving him a share of the profits.

Narcisse left the Balkan on 1 July and joined the Balkan Bank. He is currently in Ruschuk for a few months.

---

5. Leva, Bulgarian currency (abbreviated L.).

The state of my business has allowed me to no longer take contributions to household expenses from Sandro and Narcisse, beginning 1 July.

I finally stopped feeling out of place in Sofia. Now I am involved in business activity and have a social position, which I was lacking, and am busy from morning till evening.

My health has not suffered from this new regime. I was confined to bed only once this year, after the emotion caused by Sandro's temporary enlistment, along with all Turkish subjects, in the Bulgarian army (March 1916).

Rachel has also been healthy and is happier since our material situation has improved and the future seems secure.

Jeanne divides her time between domestic work, sewing with a teacher, and the piano.

I have not had news of Sophie since July, I hear from Emmanuel, Sultana, and their families only rarely.

At Elia's, nothing new has happened. On 1 January 1916, he got a raise of eight thousand levas per year at the Balkan.

Mama had her seventieth birthday yesterday, which we celebrated with a fairly large family reunion (21 January 1917).

This year, three members of our family passed away: Rahamim Arié, whom I mentioned, Uncle Samuel Arié, who died on the twenty-seventh, the eve of Purim, and Isaac Moïse Arié. May they rest in peace!

JANUARY 1918

The war continues: it has escalated from a European war to a world war. The United States of America, almost all the countries of Latin America, and China are at war with Germany. Since February 1917, the seas have been furrowed by German submarines, which sink all the ships they find, whether enemy or neutral. About 600,000 tons thus disappear under water every month.

On land, 1917 was marked by the following events: on the western front, slight progress by the Anglo-French forces (six hundred km of terrain conquered). In Italy, invasion of the Austro-Germans as far as the Piave; in Russia, retreat of the Russians all along the line, loss of Riga and neighboring islands. No change on the Macedonian front. Turkey lost Arabia, Palestine (including Jerusalem), and Mesopotamia, all of which were taken by the English.

In Russia, a revolution overturned the Tsarist regime and proclaimed a republic.

The Kadets (KD),[6] who led the revolution, reportedly with the co-operation of the Entente, were overturned by the socialist revolutionaries and they in turn by the maximalists, with Lenin and Trotsky at their head. Those two are in the process of concluding a separate peace with the Central Powers. The capital point of that agreement is the parceling up of Russia into small states, the richest of which will inevitably fall into the lap of the German confederation.

This state of affairs is causing growing suffering and deprivation throughout the world. Food and clothing are reaching unheard of prices. Here are those of Sofia: bread, 0.95 L.; meat (600 grams per week per person), 3.50 L.; white cheese [Bulgarian feta], 8; hard cheese, 20 L.; sugar, 20 L.; flour, 6 L. per kg; coffee, 80 L.; tea, 120 L.; oil, 40 to 60 L.; one chicken, 15 L.; 1 egg, 0.45; soap, 30 L.; butter, 30 L. Most of these goods can be obtained only with coupons.

It is not surprising that under such conditions my expenses were twice what they were in 1916, and surpassed 33,000 L.

Fortunately, the state of my business has allowed me to meet these expenses and to double my capital in spite of them. I was also able to give a large sum to Sandro and Narcisse for their contribution to my business and thus to lay the foundation for their future fortune.

The first half of 1917, I was busy with commodities, the second with securities.

Narcisse is backing me up from Ruschuk, where he is serving as director of the Balkan Bank. It is excellent schooling for him.

I was more and more involved in business activities and was able to found, with the cooperation of the major firms of Sofia, a joint-stock bank with capital of five million levas. This is the Eastern Bulgarian Bank. I am vice president of its board of directors. The director is M. S. Serrero, who was recommended to me by Mme Béja. The bank opened on 1 October 1917.

Elia has also seen his situation change. With the cooperation of the Hamburg and the Hungarian Bank of Budapest, he founded the Bulgarian Phoenix, with capital of four million. He thus left the Balkan, where he had spent twenty-two and a half years, and has become director of the Phoenix under splendid conditions. I participate in that institution as a shareholder possessing three thousand shares and as member of the board of directors.

The Ottoman Colony of Sofia was also founded, and I have been named president, at the consul's proposal.

6. The Kadets (KD) were the liberal Russian party opposed to the tsar.

Everything has thus worked out in Sofia as we wished. Even my health has improved this year, and despite intense work, I have felt neither tired nor ill.

Unfortunately, my dear Sophie lost her house and furniture in the fire that devastated Salonika on 18 August. I will replace all that for her after the war, *inschalla.*[7]

Emmanuel, Samuel, and their families continue to be well in Paris. No change in the state of our family in Sofia.

Sofia, 10 January 1918

SELECTIONS FROM LETTERS
TO THE ALLIANCE CENTRAL COMMITTEE

15 May 1913

. . . The Balkan War will bring a profound transformation of the social and economic life of the regions occupied by the Allies. If the fate of our coreligionists in Salonika, Monastir,[8] and Üsküb[9] is undecided, that of the Jews of Adrianople,[10] Demotica,[11] Dede Agach,[12] Kavalla,[13] Kirk-Kilissa,[14] and some other smaller cities of Thrace is already permanently sealed: those thirty to thirty-five thousand Jews are already part of Bulgaria and will be called upon without delay to fulfill their duties as Bulgarian citizens.

During the first years, the existence of the annexed regions will be somewhat difficult: age-old habits are not modified from one day to the next, and it is certain that members of the generation over thirty-five years old will go to their graves without having changed their mores, their language, or their dress in the slightest. There is thus no reason to be concerned with them. The younger generation, now in school, will have no trouble adapting to the new way of life. But what will happen to those between fifteen and thirty-five years old? Will they be classified among the older generation, half-Eastern, half-French in culture, with nothing in common with the ways, customs, and

---

7. *Inschalla* (*inşallah;* from Turkish and Arabic), "God willing!"

8. Monastir (Bitola), Macedonian city, part of Yugoslavia beginning in 1918.

9. Üsküb (Skopje), city in the former Yugoslavia, capital of Macedonia.

10. Adrianople (Edirne), in Eastern Thrace (Turkey, Europe).

11. Demotica (Didymotikhon), in Western Thrace, currently Greek.

12. Dede Agach (Alexandropolis), seaport city of (present-day) Greece, on the Aegean Sea, in Thrace.

13. Kavalla (Cavalla), seaport city of Greece (Macedonia).

14. Kirk-Kilissa (Kirklareli), in Eastern Thrace (Turkey, Europe).

language of the new masters? Or will they make an effort to advance assimilation by twenty years, an assimilation that has now become inevitable?

The establishment of Bulgarian culture in Thrace will be arduous, long-term work. That province is Turkish, Greek, and Jewish, but it is not Bulgarian. Just because geographical conditions have led the Bulgarians to exert their principal military efforts there, it does not in any way follow that the war was undertaken to liberate Adrianople and the coastline of the Aegean Sea, where there are not ten thousand Bulgarians: the center of Bulgarianism is not there but in Macedonia, and primarily in the cities now held by the Serbs (hence, for the Bulgarians, the prospect of a new war of liberation brewing). In the province of Adrianople, the future belongs to the element that will adapt the most rapidly to the new conditions of existence in the region. One must not count on the Turks: by its proximity, Constantinople will prove too great an attraction for them to be kept in the country. The Greeks have never gotten along with the Bulgarians, whom they hate and distrust too much to condescend to form closer ties with them. That leaves the Jewish element, whose facility for assimilation is well known. That assimilation should begin, not tomorrow, but today.

It is altogether pointless to waste time with superfluous regrets for an abolished past. One must live first, and begin resolutely to learn Bulgarian, the language of the country. Without a knowledge of it the Jews will long remain second-class citizens and will rapidly lose the economic prominence they hold in certain sectors. The schools will do what is necessary to prepare for the future. But what about the present?

In order to put the young people who have already left school in a position to struggle to advantage for their existence, it is, in my opinion, urgent to create, in all the cities where you have schools, evening and Sunday courses where men between fifteen and thirty-five years old can come to learn the language of the country. Teachers would be hired on your behalf; the fees required of the students would no doubt be sufficient to pay the salary of these teachers, but if there were a deficit, the Central Committee could cover it. Not a single student, salesman, bank or administration employee should fail to attend these courses.

That program of immediate concern currently takes precedence, it seems to me, over that of the schools.

I would thus like to propose that the Central Committee prescribe that its directors in the cities occupied by the Bulgarians organize evening and Sunday courses in their schools without delay for all those who wish to study the Bulgarian language.

If your directors cannot find the necessary teachers in the cities themselves, I shall be available to procure some for them. . . .

Archives of the AIU, Bulgarie I.C.22.

Sofia, 22 May 1913

. . . In the three weeks I have been in Sofia, I have had the time to gather impressions and to reflect on what I have seen and heard. I believe I am today in a position to propose to the Central Committee a solution to the difficulties the Alliance has encountered in this country for the last ten years, and to those of the same kind that await it in Adrianople and the other Turkish cities annexed to Bulgaria. This will be the object of the present report.

1. The state of mind I noted in the Jewish population is in fact as I had imagined. As with political questions, Jews are organized into parties for questions of education. These parties possess a central committee and local committees, clubs, and newspapers. The most active parties are:

a) The Zionists, who have managed to bring almost all the educated young into their ranks. They are already divided into two rival parties: the ultra-Zionists, partisans of violent methods, and the moderates, who find scandals repugnant. The ultras have two newspapers: the *Schofar*[15] (in Judeo-Spanish) and the *Michpat*[16] (half in Bulgarian and half in Judeo-Spanish); the moderates publish the *Chalom*[17] (also bilingual, in the same languages), from which I sent you an article the other day. These two parties, divided on certain points, are one in their hostility toward the Alliance.

b) The Bné Berith, who meet in secret assemblies and have only words of peace and harmony on their lips. M. Ehrenpreis is the high priest of the order and M. Angel is his assistant. The activities of that association remain mysterious; what one sees of them is a food program, which does not operate and allows children of the school to fall down from starvation— literally—and an apprenticeship program, in preparation say some, while others claim it has seventeen apprenticeships. When I manifested a desire to work with these two programs, they almost answered: "No Trespassing." I did not insist.

c) The members of the Bulgarian Jewish Union, read Alliance Israélite Bulgare, our friends, who have one journal, *La Luz* (in Judeo-Spanish). This group includes the majority of the bourgeoisie and has subsidiaries in the principal cities of Bulgaria. It is probable—and regrettable—that this organization has remained unknown to you until now. As I shall explain further on,

15. *Schofar* (*Ha-Shofar*, "The ram's horn," Hebrew; Philippopolis, 1901–41), organ of the Zionist Federation of Bulgaria, suspended publication between 1913 and 1918.

16. *Michpat* (*Ha-Mishpat*, "Justice," Hebrew; Sofia, 1912–20) was the newspaper of the Zionist organization of Sofia.

17. *Chalom* (*Ha-Shalom*, "Peace," Hebrew; Sofia, 1913) was the organ of the Theodor Herzl Zionist Society of Sofia.

we shall depend upon it to defend the positions that remain ours in Bulgaria and to acquire others if possible.

2. The opinion of the Unionists—that is what we will call our friends—who are also the largest contributors to the expenses of the communities, is that the 65,000 francs per year that the Jewish communities of Sofia currently cost (50,000 provided by the community and 15,000 by the municipal council) are wasted, and that the results of the teaching in these schools are practically nil.

Let us briefly recall the causes of that sterility:

The mediocrity of the staff, recruited haphazardly, poorly paid, and with no pedagogical preparation;

the incompetence of the director, who was never anything more than a poor instructor, and who is a docile instrument in the hands of the committee that pays his salary;

the absence of any supervision. For three and a half years, neither M. Ehrenpreis nor any rabbi or member of the community has set foot in the school;

the demoralization of the staff, which is participating in the party struggles, writing in the newspapers, etc.

But the most important of these reasons is the following:

Following the Zionists' takeover of the schools, the level of studies has dropped a great deal, as the Alliance mission noted. Since then, all parents who care at all about the education of their children have had only one concern: get their children out of that undisciplined, unclean, and ignorant environment and place them in public or private (Catholic, German) schools. Within a few years, the Jewish schools have found themselves deserted by the entire wealthy population. The effect of that exodus is to leave only the children belonging to the lowest classes of society in Jewish classrooms. Currently, the appearance of the children attending the Jewish school—whom I observed during a recess—is that of the students of the *talmud-tora* in Smyrna before its reorganization. You will find very few whose attire reveals any means among the parents. We know that everywhere the schools of the poor are those that give the least results—unless the resources of knowledge and devotion are provided them. In this case, they are entirely lacking.

For all these reasons, the schools of Sofia can only vegetate.

Thus every thoughtful father has already resolved to his own satisfaction the question of schooling: he refrains from sending his son to the Jewish school. Do you want proof of this?

In 1892, when I left Sofia, there were about a thousand students in the schools. Today there are twelve hundred, but the community, which consisted of six thousand in 1892, numbers fourteen thousand today. Simple arithmetic demonstrates that the Jewish schools are today missing . . . eleven hundred students. The statistic that I requested from the appropriate source, and that will be provided me in a few days, will demonstrate, I hope, that this calculation is accurate. You will see that we find those eleven hundred students in public and private schools.

These observations lead us to ask the following questions:

1. Is there any reason for the Alliance to wish to take on the instruction of the children who are attending the community school, given that the population of that school is recruited exclusively from the poorest class?

2. If the answer is affirmative, is the thing possible?

3. If it is, does your curriculum fit that clientele?

To the first of these questions, the entire past of the Alliance responds in the negative. What does your society do when it undertakes the regeneration of a community? Does it try to penetrate into the *talmud-tora,* where the children wallow in more or less total ignorance? No. It rents a site, constitutes a faculty, and announces it is opening a school. The clientele arrive gradually, and much, much later, the community, finally enlightened by its own interests, itself requests either the incorporation of the *talmud-tora* into the school (Adrianople) or its reorganization (Smyrna, etc.).

Alas, ten years of Zionist agitation have nearly transformed the Jewish schools of Bulgaria into *talmud-tora*s. Like the *talmud-tora*s in backward countries, these establishments are defended—not by fanatical rabbis whose religious convictions are profoundly respectable because sincere, but by a group of agitators who are just as fanatical, led by a few lamebrains wanting to advertise themselves, to fish in troubled waters, men without faith, without scruples, without morality. Why would the Alliance follow a method in Bulgaria it has never used elsewhere and begin with the reformation of the *talmud-tora?*

Moreover, even if we wished to adopt that method here, we could not. An absurd provision of Bulgarian schooling laws makes the election of school committees open to the popular vote. We know how the popular vote functions even in countries whose civilization is much more advanced than Bulgaria's. What it is in the Jewish communities of this country, your representatives must have told you often. They must have described to you the vile means of corruption used by the demagogues to get themselves elected to the councils and committees. Can we lower ourselves to do battle with such weapons? Which of your agents respects himself so little that he would use such means for propaganda on behalf of committees that favor our views? And once he had succeeded, what guarantee would there be that this success would be repeated in the next elections? Under those conditions, your schools would always be on the alert and would be unable to establish a long-term program of studies. Your constructions could only be short-lived, and, in building on that regime, you would be building on sand.

There is yet another consideration: everywhere you have abandoned a school, the Hilfsverein has established itself. Oh, it is a very modest establishment, and the place the Hilfsverein occupies in these schools is quite simply the place of the poor: four hours a week in each of the three upper classes, without any interference in the direction of the studies. But even so, the Hilfsverein can print in its reports that it has established its influence in such and such a school, which was abandoned by you. Are you in favor of appearing to push it out of the positions it has conquered? I confine myself to asking the question.

Let us suppose, however, that all these objections have been set aside, all these difficulties overcome: Why would you take back these schools? To apply your program there, whose essential point is the intensive study of a foreign language? What purpose can that language serve for a thousand poor children, for whom tools would be much more necessary than higher education and a foreign language? We must look toward the future, and that future does not lie in the hands of the current sons of porters and beggars but rather in the hand of the sons of the bourgeoisie; and not a single one of them still sets foot in the Jewish school.

My conclusion on this point will thus be the following: as long as Bulgarian schooling laws reserve the leadership of the schools for men elected by universal suffrage, and as long as Zionism has not disarmed in relation to the Alliance, it seems to me there is no reason for the Central Committee to seek to return to the schools it has abandoned.

3. The Zionists, their appetite whetted by their success in the former Bulgaria—as I know through a very reliable Zionist source—are preparing to undertake the destruction of your schools in the annexed Turkish cities as soon as the peace is signed. The procedure will be the same: the constitution of Zionist committees, propaganda in the newspapers and in public gatherings and meetings, votes for motions expressing the so-called popular will, denunciation to the authorities of supposed illegalities; in short, everything you have seen working against your programs for the last ten years will be repeated in Adrianople, Kavalla, and elsewhere. And since the Adrianople turf resembles all turf, and is just as accessible to the bad suggestions of the demagogues, the days of your schools are numbered if serious and immediate measures of defense are not taken.

In my view, these measures can consist only in the transformation of the character of your schools. They must move from "private communal" schools to simply "private" schools, placed not under the extremely severe regime the law exercises over private schools of all kinds but under the infinitely more liberal one that has been guaranteed to French schools in Bulgaria, most often those supported by the missionaries, as a result of an agreement concluded between Bulgaria and France on 15 April 1910.

I wanted to learn about the advantages and immunities guaranteed to Catholic schools by this treaty, and with this goal in mind, I requested an audience with M. de Panafieu, minister of France in Bulgaria. That diplomat was kind enough to receive me on the twenty-first of this month and gave me the warmest welcome. M. de Panafieu, who has been in Sofia since 1896, is very well informed about the Alliance, the Zionist obstruction, the reasons that made you abandon certain schools (he was very surprised that you left Samakov for no reason), and he deplores the withdrawal of the Alliance, which is a withdrawal of French influence. He is convinced that your schools in the annexed cities will know the same fate as those of Sofia and elsewhere and says this is a unique opportunity to try to save them from imminent disappearance.

M. de Panafieu was consulted on this subject about two months ago by the minister of foreign affairs in France—you probably raised the question with him—and he pronounced himself in favor of immediate and energetic action. He received no response to his suggestions, and he found that I had arrived just in time to realize them. The minister of France wishes to work here with all his strength.

. . . I mention that our schools are destined for Jews, to exclude any suspicion of proselytism. The government, in fact, would have shown itself even more tolerant and liberal toward the Catholic schools if it had not had the fear, often justified, of seeing Orthodox Bulgarians embrace the Catholic religion. I believe that the government, which, in general, has very little concern about the Jews, will grant us what we want, provided our schools remain exclusively Jewish. . . .

What is the Bulgarian government's frame of mind regarding this subject? I think I can say it is excellent. . . .

4. If we manage to obtain the advantages and immunities we are requesting from the Bulgarian government, beginning with the next school year Alliance schools can be reopened everywhere: in Sofia, Ruschuk, etc. No longer community schools but our own schools, paying schools, where I believe we could attract the entire bourgeois clientele. . . . There is no reason to suppose that what has succeeded for us everywhere else will fail in Bulgaria. Even if we managed to attract only two hundred of the Jewish children who are today attending Catholic school, and who go there only to learn French, that would be enough.

After which, the Zionists can keep their schools, which will fall more and more to the level of the *talmud-tora*. When the bourgeoisie has a Jewish school to instruct its children, it will willingly let the Zionists direct the schools they hold, according to their whim. Zionist agitation will have no object and will fall away by itself, and perhaps one day we will again be invited to return to the communal schools.

These are plans for the future, which I merely point toward and which it is premature to develop further. Today I do no more than sketch out a plan of action.

5. This plan includes, among other things, the organization, let us say the recruitment, of the Bulgarian Jewish bourgeoisie into an association similar to those of the Zionists, the Bné Berith, or the Pères de Famille (in France), with committees in each city and a central committee in Sofia. During the recent struggles between Zionists and anti-Zionists, the anti-Zionists formed such an association, which I mentioned above: the Bulgarian Jewish Union. The war and other circumstances, including the absence of any cooperation, be it moral, on your part, have resulted in some neglect of that organization. We must take it up again and extend its activities to the annexed communities, where your directors must be the soul of these organizations, founded solely to defend the Alliance, its schools, and all its programs.

To the plan of attack devised by the Zionists to destroy our schools, there is truly occasion to respond with resistance measures. Those measures cannot be limited to the protection of the French government. In the country itself, we must depend on enlightened public opinion, must guide it, put it on guard against sophism and the lies of men without scruples. The time is past when the Alliance was alone in the world in working for the renewal of Judaism. Daughter societies have been born that plot to seize hold of your clientele, and they often succeed. Philanthropy, like commerce, has become competitive. At the risk of seeing our field of action shrink like Balzac's *peau de chagrin*, the Central Committee must be cognizant of these new mores and conform to them.

Thus I propose to give new life to the Bulgarian Jewish Union, for which I shall solicit your cooperation in good time. For the moment, let me express the hope that at the beginning of the next vacation, the directors of your schools in Bulgaria can be convened in Sofia for a conference, during which time we will decide by common agreement on the measures appropriate for safeguarding your interests. On the same occasion, we could discuss a certain number of questions of a pedagogical nature and prepare for the school campaign of 1913–14. It goes without saying that the decisions made would be submitted for your approval.

This, Mr. President, is the guiding principle that, in my opinion, would be

the most advantageous to follow to maintain and develop your school programs in Bulgaria. With the existing law, this is impossible. We must therefore correct that law with a diplomatic agreement. I humbly submit that the
Central Committee should devote all its efforts and influence to the task of
obtaining that agreement. . . .

Archives of the AIU, Bulgarie V.B.116.

Dated: 11 March 1914

> *Notice on the Conduct of Bulgarian Jewish Military Personnel during the
> Two Balkan Wars, 1912–13*

Of a total Jewish population of approximately forty thousand, about five
thousand Jewish young men were enlisted.

The exact number of the dead and wounded, and the list of officers and
soldiers decorated for valor, will be published in a few days, or so it is believed;
at that time, I will communicate to you the statistics relating to the Jews.

The Jews most distinguished themselves in Lüle Burgas[18] and in Chatalja.[19]

At the height of the battle of Lüle Burgas, which, as we know, lasted three
days, a company of the Engineers was in Bunar-Hissar.[20] From that location,
someone needed to go to the train station of Lüle Burgas to get two boxes
containing telegraph and telephone instruments. The captain said: "Which
of you, my children, wants to go on bicycle to bring me the two boxes? Who
wants to sacrifice himself? I will not oblige anyone to perform that difficult
task." Four soldiers stepped out of the ranks and said: "We are ready to leave,
my captain." They left and brought back the boxes. Of these four brave men,
two were Jews.

During the entire war against Turkey, the Jews were most often placed on
the front line and sent on reconnaissance, because of their knowledge of the
Turkish language.

In Chatalja, the Jews particularly distinguished themselves, especially
those of the third regiment of Vidin. On the evening of 9/22 November
1912, the night before the armistice, three hundred Kurdish volunteers attacked the outposts of the third Bulgarian regiment. Colonel Panof, to save
the honor of the regiment, himself attacked the advancing Turkish army and
forced it to retreat. The colonel fell, killed by a bomb; next to him lay three
soldiers, all Jews.

18. Lüle Burgas (Lüleburgaz), in Turkey, Europe, southeast of Edirne.
19. Chatalja (Çatalca), in Turkey, Europe, west of Istanbul.
20. Near Lüleburgaz.

Almost all the Jewish doctors were called to the front lines to bring help to the wounded. Division hospitals were entrusted to some of them. Most were presented to be decorated.

Jewish medical orderlies, most often sent to the front lines, always distinguished themselves by their devotion and the intelligent swiftness with which they brought help to the wounded officers and soldiers.

Many delicate and secret missions were entrusted to Jews, who performed them with success and bravery.

To our knowledge, among the host of military men accused and sentenced for lack of bravery or for dereliction in military duty, not one Jew has yet been found.

Many Jewish soldiers were decorated. General Koutintchef, receiving the list of decorated soldiers one day, and noticing a good number of Jews at the top, expressed his great satisfaction. He and Generals Tochef and Radko Dimitriev often declared that the opinion they had of the pusillanimity of Jews at war had to be modified after the events they had witnessed during the Balkan Wars, where the Jews proved they were the worthy descendants of the Maccabees.[21]

Archives of the AIU, Bulgarie I.C.27A.

8 October 1918

. . . It is with a feeling of inexpressible happiness that, after more than three years of forced silence, I reestablish contact with the Central Committee of the Alliance. I owe that favor to the obligingness of Colonel Trousseau, head of the French military mission in Bulgaria, who is kind enough to take on the task of transmitting my correspondence to Salonika, from whence it will be sent to you through the mail. I would be obliged if you could please address your response to M. Salomon J. Carasso in Salonika, who will remit it to the French military authorities, to be sent to me in Sofia. Colonel Trousseau was kind enough to make the necessary arrangements on this matter in Salonika.

Allow me, in this first report, to give some rapid notes on the situation of the Jews in Bulgaria during the three years that have just passed.

Material situation: The material situation of the Jews has improved considerably. As a result of the blockade imposed on the Central Powers, including Bulgaria, manufactured goods and all articles imported from the colonies and from abroad have reached fantastic prices. Here are some figures: coffee

21. "Maccabee" was the surname given to Judah (ca. 200–160 B.C.E.), son of Mattathias, and later applied to his whole family. Mattathias and his five sons were Jewish warriors who led the revolt against Antiochus IV Epiphanes (about 165 B.C.E.).

is currently sold for 150 francs per kilo; sugar, 30 francs; olive oil, 70 francs; iron nails, 10 francs per kilo; tin, 250 francs; calico, 40 to 70 francs per meter, depending on width; man's suit, 1,200 to 1,500 francs; package of spun cotton (2.5 kilos), 500 francs; spool of thread, 1,000 yards for 60 francs. And so it goes.

As a result, all businessmen with stocks of merchandise obtained ten, twenty, up to fifty times their value by selling them, depending on the item. It is obvious, to take only the lowest of these figures, that private fortunes increased by at least tenfold and that, as a result, small shop owners who had ten to twenty thousand francs in capital are today possessors of a few hundred thousand francs, and middle-class businessmen with a business worth one hundred thousand or more are today all millionaires.

The rise in the price of imported objects had repercussions on the price of articles produced in this country, since the peasant, to cover his costs, also had to raise the price of objects produced by the soil, but as a speculator more unbridled than the rest, he raised them by an even larger ratio. Thus, a kilo of flour now sells for 12 francs; butter costs 45 francs; rice, 18 francs; grapes, 8 francs; dried beans, 10 francs per kilo; one chicken, 25 francs; one egg, 65 centimes; one kilo of tobacco, 40 francs (instead of 1.50 francs).

The consequence of the war for Bulgaria was thus a general increase in wealth. What will remain of that apparent prosperity when the barriers that isolate the country are lifted, I shall attempt to explain in one of my next reports. You don't have to be a genius in political economy to foresee the financial cataclysm that awaits us and the poverty that will replace these artificial and short-lived fortunes—except that of the peasant, who is and will remain very rich.

For fifteen minutes—this expression should be taken almost literally—the Bulgarians, the Jews included, are the possessors of immense fortunes. Amidst that apparent prosperity, what was the poor man's share?

Charitable Works: The poor man's share, as it concerns the Jews of course, was small, solely because of a lack of organization. The Jew is charitable, and provided he is asked, he gives without a second thought. For the three feast days of this month, the central synagogue collected 75,000 francs in gifts. Where is that money going? No one knows anything about it. Does there even exist a communal administration? No one could say. Before America entered the war, Sofia received a large monthly subsidy for the poor from New York. Whom did that money go to? I did not attempt to find out, since I could no longer communicate with you.

We must nonetheless mention an admirably organized and well-directed program, the Jewish Orphanage, founded three years ago to house war orphans, and which now houses fifty children, twenty-five boys and twenty-five girls. Its budget for the current year is about 100,000 francs. I shall speak again of this establishment.

Schools: The two school buildings of Sofia (for boys and for girls) were requisitioned by the military authorities at the beginning of the war and are still serving as hospitals. The Utch-Bunar school remained open. I will not deign to speak about it.

As for your Samakov school, it should have been closed long ago. Almost the entire community of Samakov emigrated to Sofia. . . .

The directors of the schools in Shumla and Gümüldjina[22] have given no sign of life for a long time.

Recent Troubles: You know from the newspapers that about ten days ago, battles took place at the gates of Sofia between the mutinous Bulgarian troops and the city garrison. The Jewish community was exposed to a grave risk at that time. If the mutineers had gained the upper hand, we would have witnessed a horrifying pogrom. On the list of persons designated to be murdered, there was an Arié. I do not know if it was I or one of my relatives. You will see by my next report that with the collusion of an employee of the municipality, the break in the Bulgarian front and the capitulation of Bulgaria were about to be attributed to the treason of a Jew. . . .

Archives of the AIU, Bulgarie V.B.121.

2 January 1919

. . . I am writing to inform you that I have received your letter of 3 November, in which I learn that your newspapers have not said anything about the troubles that accompanied the Bulgarian retreat and that placed our goods and lives in such great danger. If you have not been more faithfully informed about what happened on this side of the barricade during the war, you know only one face of the great war that is ending. It may be interesting for you to know how things occurred in one of the belligerent countries, the smallest of all, but the one whose departure from the arena was the signal for the end of the cataclysm that desolated the world for four years.

Departing for once from our rule to deal only with questions of interest to Judaism in our correspondence, I shall today concern myself with the war generally, as it was felt, seen, and understood in Bulgaria. Since the beginning of that war, I have noted my impressions daily in a journal, as I experienced them. And since I wrote only for myself, these writings, in the absence of any other merit, will have that of sincerity. To be truthful, then, I have only to summarize in a few pages my notes of four years.

22. Gümüldjina (Komotinē), city in Western Thrace, in present-day Greece.

It was only against its will that Bulgaria mobilized on 23 September 1915 and went to war with the powers of the Entente, under force and duress. Duress from whom? From its king Ferdinand, and one day we may know the secret promises he made to Germany. We who were the eyewitnesses of that policy, we know the violence that monarch did to the feelings of his people. To act against the immense majority of the country, Ferdinand began by naming as prime minister a man of rare incompetence and imbecility: Dr. V. Radoslavov.[23] History will blame this evil man for crimes of all kinds: to defend himself, he need only give one excuse, his intellectual mediocrity. Was he even aware of the harm he was going to do to his country?

The people, with their sure instincts, sensed they were being led to their ruin. Thus, when the Chamber was dissolved and Radoslavov ordered new elections, the country voted against him, a rare event in Bulgaria, where the government that holds the elections generally wins the majority. The Chamber elected in that way was dissolved before it convened. For a second time, elections took place on the deceitful platform: "A vote for Radoslavov is a vote for peace." With the cooperation of about ten Muslim deputies from Gümüldjina and Xanthe,[24] whom it had under its thumb, the government finally had the minimum small majority necessary to govern.

With the elections hardly over, a general mobilization was decreed. Here I copy from my journal (13/26 September 1915). "The mobilization is going forward without any enthusiasm. The impression is that we are headed for a new adventure, a catastrophe. The Russophiles are in anguish. A large number of officers have been dismissed because of their political opinions in favor of Russia."

We may well ask why, if that is the case, the Bulgarian people did not react, did not revolt. There are two reasons. The first lies in the passivity of oriental peoples. For five centuries, Bulgaria bent to the Turkish *kourbache*,[25] and it continues to obey. Have we not observed the same passivity in the Turkey of Enver and Talat?[26] The second reason lies in a series of decrees—laws Ferdinand published almost at the same time as his war manifesto, and in which capital punishment was established against a host of crimes and misdemeanors that the military codes punished with prison

23. Vasil Radoslavov (1854–1929) was a Bulgarian politician and Russophobe, several times minister and prime minister.

24. City in Thrace, situated northeast of Kavalla (Greece).

25. *Kourbache* (kirbaç, Turkish), "whip."

26. Enver Paşa (1881–1922) and Talat Paşa (1874–1921) were "Young Turk" leaders, architects of the Young Turk revolution (1908), and members of the triumvirate beginning in 1913.

alone. To lead troops into combat who did not want to fight, he forged Draconian laws so severe that if the Germans themselves had not later demanded they be softened, Bulgarian bullets would have claimed more victims among the Bulgarians than enemy cannons. It is under that iron discipline, a military reign of terror, that the Bulgarian armies were forced to fight against the Russians, the French, and the English.

The war began. For three years, the Bulgarian army knew only success. Indeed, the valor of the Bulgarian soldier is incontestable. Poorly shod, poorly dressed, poorly fed, he headed for the front and stopped only at the gates of Salonika. That happened in a matter of months. But the so-called position war dragged on for another two years, and while the army was defending the borders with weapons at its feet, a gnawing ill, a redoubtable ill, attacked the very body of the nation.

There was, from the top to the bottom of the administrative ladder, something like the command: "Enrich yourselves!" Anyone from near or far who had anything to do with the government clique pounced on the occupied provinces and exploited them thoroughly. A system of unheard-of corruption was established in the country, and from the ministers to the most modest scribe, everyone began to steal, speculate, rob his neighbor. Thus, in two years, scandalous fortunes were constituted, due for the most part to plunder. Moreover, the Germans who were occupying Bulgaria as allies began, by legal and illegal means, to export food and other products in volume, sucking the lifeblood of this country down to the marrow, to the point that life became much more expensive here than in Germany itself. And when soldiers left their trenches on leave and came to visit their families, they were obliged to notice that while they were fighting over there, those who had remained in the cities were making a fortune and couldn't care less about the increasingly expensive life. With time, the situation worsened. Many soldiers saw the nest egg they had left behind disappear and their families suffer the worst deprivation. They themselves were more and more malnourished, while the German comrades fighting beside them were incomparably better supplied. Thus there arose friction, jealousy, and quarrels between the allies, which at times degenerated into battles and bloodshed. Discipline began to grow more lax, and it was not rare to see leaders obeying the orders of their soldiers.

In May 1918 the situation had gotten so bad that a revolution was to be feared. Ferdinand felt a change in minister was called for, and he dismissed Radoslavov. Whom to replace him with? All the leaders he consulted were unanimous in once more condemning his policy, but no one wanted to accept the responsibility for liquidating his adventure. Out of a high sense of patriotism, M. Malinov,[27] head of the (Russophile) democrats, agreed to assume the responsibilities of power. But it was too late. For two months, the soldiers at the front had been telling the authorities that they would have to conclude the peace by 15 September at the latest. After that date, they said, they would throw down their weapons and go home. The ministers went to the front to exhort the army to be patient, but to no avail. At that time, M. Malinov opened unofficial peace negotiations. These were still in progress when the fatal date of 15 September arrived.

Far be it from me to diminish in any way the valor, courage, and abnegation of the Allied armies, and of the French army in particular. But one may suppose that if Bulgaria had had an honest government, if Radoslavov had not introduced the virus of outrageous corruption into the Bulgarian people, if the population remaining behind had shown evidence of a feeling of duty equal to that which animated the army, the war would not be over, because the troops of Dobro-Pole[28] would not have voluntarily opened the front on the day and hour they had fixed for more than four months. The most effective of the allies of Franchet d'Esperey was M. Radoslavov himself, who, after three years of war, could no longer oppose the Allied troops with anything but an army gangrened by lack of discipline and by the rage of seeing they were being sacrificed, not for the country's interests, but for the interests of certain members of the ruling party and their friends, who were enriching themselves by millions under cover of a war of liberation.

The troops, animated by this thirst for revenge against the government traitors and criminals, headed toward the capital. They came within ten kilometers of the city on 29 September. If they had entered, Sofia would have been set afire and bathed in blood. A battle began near Kniajevo (eight km from Sofia) between the insurgents and a few troops who could be hastily pulled together. It lasted two days and two nights. We lived through those tragic hours, the horrors of civil war, and we were witness to them. It was during those days that M. Malinov dispatched his mission to Salonika to sign the armistice.

Three days later, Ferdinand, after an attempted coup against his ministers—orchestrated with the cooperation of the Germans—was obliged to sign his abdication and to leave, protected as he fled by the darkness of night. You know the rest.

27. Aleksandur Malinov (1867–1938) was prime minister in 1908–11 and in 1918.

28. Dobro Polje, village south of the Vardar River in Macedonia. On 15 September 1918, during the offensive of Franchet d'Esperey, the Bulgarian front, which held the position of Dobro-Polje, was overtaken by the Serb and French troops. The follow-up offensive led to Bulgaria's capitulation (29 September 1918).

And now we have a country ruined through and through, burdened by debts, which several generations will not be able to pay off, disgraced in the eyes of the entire world because it dared raise its hand against the Russian nation, which had liberated it. This is a great crime. According to the Bible, the man who raises his hand against his father or mother deserves to die. That may be the sentence being prepared for the Bulgarians. But if I had the honor of pleading the cause of this people before the Supreme Court of Versailles, from which "empires shall rise again," it would be easy for me to show, through a host of documents, that the only great guilty party was not the Bulgarian people but the too changeable monarch to whom they entrusted their destinies. Ferdinand alone, and his imbecilic minister Radoslavov, lost Bulgaria.

I believe that if ever the Bulgarian people are punished for the crimes of their former king, they will not tolerate without revolt a punishment they believe they do not deserve. How will they manifest their anger? That is difficult to foresee.

A new peace of mind has begun to take hold with the abdication of Ferdinand I, whose departure was a relief for the country. Another reason for confidence in the future is the presence on the Bulgarian throne of a young king who takes after his mother, a princess of Bourbon-Parma, in the qualities of his heart and mind as well as in his physique. The popularity of Boris III[29] rises daily, and one can already predict that, thanks to him, Bulgarian public opinion will energetically turn away from any attempt at Bolshevism. Bulgaria, delivered from an ambitious monarch, will henceforth be an element of stability in the Balkans. On one condition, however: that it be treated equitably.

For the future tranquility of the East, it is desirable that Europe know the truth and that, if Bulgaria must be condemned, it at least not be condemned in absentia. Unfortunately for the future of the peace that is being prepared, Europe has begun by placing Bulgaria in solitary confinement: Not the slightest communication is allowed between Sofia and Paris or London.

I do not think I am mistaken in supposing that this report may be the first impartial political document on Bulgaria to arrive in Paris since the beginning of the war. I thought it would be interesting to send it to you, and you may make use of it as you wish. I would have no objection if you judged you ought to communicate it with the French government. . . .

Archives of the AIU, Bulgarie V.B.121.

---

29. Boris III (1894–1943) was king of Bulgaria (1918–43), the son and successor of Ferdinand I.

12/ The Interwar Period (1919–1939)

O n 29 November 1918 we had the sorrow of losing my mother, who passed away on Friday night, 25 Kislev, at 7:40. She had been bedridden since the first day of Rosch-Haschana. She first felt ill at the temple, where she fell away in a faint. Brought back to the house in a carriage, she went to bed and never got up again. She succumbed to cancer of the intestines, which quickly spread to the stomach. She had a long death agony, lasting eight days, during which time she suffered a great deal.

The funeral took place on Sunday, 1 December (27 Kislev), in the midst of a large gathering of people. She was buried next to my father, in keeping with her last will. May her soul rest in peace!

A happy family event also occurred this year. Lucie is married. She became engaged in February to one Robert Aron Cohen, who lived in our house. The engagement was broken in April. In May, Lucie left for Constantinople with her father, and there met M. Vitalis Canetti, named agent of the Hungaria by Elia. The young people took a liking to each other, got engaged in September, and were just married on 5 January. Elia and Léonore, who left on 15 December to attend the wedding, are still in Constantinople.

The year 1918 saw the end of universal war. The signal of capitulation was given by Bulgaria, which, under orders of a part of the army in revolt, signed the armistice in Salonika on 29 September, while Sofia was threatened with plunder and fire by the mutinous troops. There was fighting in Vladaya[1] and Kniajevo. Immediately afterward, the Germans evacuated Bulgaria, and the troops of the Entente occupied the country. They are still here.

Turkey and Austria capitulated within a few days of each other, and Germany itself signed the armistice on 11 November, to decide the conditions for peace. At this point, they are deliberating.

1. Near Sofia.

246

The conditions of peace imposed on the defeated nations are expected to be very harsh. For Bulgaria, a poor county, there will be a long period of ruin and destitution. Our future looks dark. Some are already thinking of leaving the country. I can no longer leave Sofia, where I am kept by many interests: the Banque d'Orient and the Bulgarian Phoenix, where I have large investments, cannot be left in strangers' hands. My private business affairs, undertaken in partnership with Sabat Arié, Isaac Arié, and Zacharie Alcalay, will continue to require my presence in Sofia for a long time: we cannot so easily liquidate the large stock of merchandise we have. The future looks dark.

It is all the darker in that Bolshevism is not yet vanquished in Russia and is spreading in Germany (where revolution is at its height, following the abdication of William II),[2] in Romania, and elsewhere. It is threatening Bulgaria, where we have only enough provisions for another month. The food one finds is about 50 percent more expensive than what I recorded in this notebook last year. Our expenses are thus rising before our eyes; they reached fifty thousand francs in 1918. For 1919, we must foresee a higher figure, plus the taxes to be paid on the war profits of the last four years. How will we manage? My worries on that matter are great.

Sandro has continued to serve me well in my business. Narcisse returned permanently from Ruschuk and is at the Balkan Bank in Sofia, a temporary position as he awaits something better. Since the armistice, I have had frequent news of Salomon and Sophie, who have struggled valiantly to reconstitute their home and fortune, which was lost in the fire of 1917. Finally, Jeanne has become a beautiful young lady and is waiting for her Prince Charming. Rachel has completely recovered since the Banki[3] course of treatment she underwent this year. My health, already a little less good after so much emotion, can still be considered satisfactory.

Emmanuel and Samuel seem enchanted with their businesses.

Sofia, 7 January 1919

YEAR 1919

Fifteen months after the armistice of 11 November 1918, Europe remains as troubled as ever. The peace between the Entente and the defeated countries is as harsh as was feared, entire provinces have been

2. William II (1859–1941) was emperor of Germany (1888–1918).
3. West of Sofia, known for its hot springs.

detached from Germany, which is also required to pay a formidable indemnity by way of reparation; Austria is reduced to a skeleton state made up of six million residents; Hungary is also only an embryonic state, and Romania, Czechoslovakia, and Yugoslavia have been enlarged at its expense; Bulgaria is losing all the acquisitions it made after the Balkan Wars and during the world war, plus some purely Bulgarian districts it has possessed since 1878. A war indemnity is also imposed upon it, but to tell the truth it is not too heavy.

This peace, which puts a very natural desire for revenge in the hearts of the defeated, does not satisfy the victors to any greater extent. None believes it is compensated adequately for its sacrifices. The discontent is thus universal. It is growing all the more because the cost of living has increased so much and great suffering is the result. Paper currency, which was printed in considerable quantities everywhere, is now depreciating everywhere. The only countries of Europe that have preserved a healthy currency are Spain and Switzerland. In Switzerland, 100 French francs are currently worth 47 Swiss francs; 100 marks are worth 8 francs; 100 Italian liras, 40 francs; 100 rubles, 8 francs; 100 crowns, 2.40 francs.

The ruin that is resulting from that collapse of prices is pushing the popular masses of every country toward revolution. In Russia, Bolshevism is stronger than ever and is spreading and gaining ground in Asia; its agents are propagating it in all the European countries, including Bulgaria, where the doctrine has numerous advocates and strong representation in the Chamber. After the danger of war, whose consequences we are seeing, humanity is threatened by a graver peril, Bolshevism.

Our existence continues under the rule of those fears; we are uncertain of tomorrow, worried, without pleasure or joy.

Yet perhaps the devil is not as evil as we believe and things will turn out better than we hope!

During this year, I liquidated the entire stock of merchandise I had and even bought and resold another. The war tax I feared cost me little. The commodities I had in Switzerland with the Banque d'Orient have been sold; there is only the difference to be paid. The situation is thus more clear than last year.

To settle these affairs in Switzerland, I took a trip to Europe this year, which lasted eighty days (1 September–20 November). I visited Italy, Switzerland, Germany, and France. I returned with some contacts for the Banque d'Orient and for me. During that trip, I saw that hundreds of young men who left the East have succeeded in Italy and France. In particular, I saw Emmanuel's prosperous situation in Paris.

I thus resolved to attempt a commercial enterprise outside Bulgaria for Sandro and Narcisse, and to that end, I have just founded—on 2 January 1920—a branch in Constantinople, which Narcisse will manage. We shall be concerned with representation and the sale of merchandise for [our] own account. This branch was organized during a trip I made with Narcisse to Constantinople (15 December 1919–1 February 1920).

My plan to create an insurance business for Elia in Constantinople is delayed for the moment, since the unprecedented cost of living in Constantinople would probably absorb all the anticipated profits and more. (For the record, here are some prices in Sofia, and those in Constantinople are on the average four times as high: bread, 4 levas per kilo; meat, 25; milk, 8; rice, 35; butter, 70; oil, 45; one egg, 1.20; and so on.)

This summer, we received the visit of Salomon and of Sophie, who successfully underwent an operation for appendicitis. She returned to Salonika on 15 September with Rachel, who came back on 20 November, and with Jeanne, who is still there. Sultana and Samuel also spent a month in Sofia, and I accompanied them as far as Milan. Only Sandro did not leave Sofia; he continues to assist me well in every way.

Sofia, 6 February 1920

YEAR 1920

The situation in Europe has changed little in a year. Uncertainty about tomorrow continues to reign in the world. Germany has pulled itself together and refuses to execute the Treaty of Versailles.[4] A conference has been convened in London for 1 March in order to come to an agreement with the Germans: a new war could be the outcome.

The Treaty of Sèvres[5] has been recognized as inapplicable: there was a gathering in London to modify it in favor of Turkey. Bulgarian Thrace was occupied by the Greeks, who are also in Adrianople, Smyrna, and Asia Minor.

Bulgaria has continued to be governed for the last two years by the

4. The Treaty of Versailles (28 June 1919) was signed between the Entente and Germany, ending World War I.
5. The Treaty of Sèvres was signed 10 August 1920 between the victorious powers, their allies and partners, and Turkey. It established the dismemberment of the Ottoman Empire. The treaty remained without effect.

Agrarian party, with Stamboliyski[6] at its head. That is better than being governed by the Socialists or Communists.

The world economic situation is critical. The fall in prices, which are rapidly returning to prewar levels, is causing enormous losses everywhere. A large portion of the fortunes acquired during the war will be lost. The crisis is particularly grave in the East.

It is under these conditions that my business developed in Constantinople this year. Narcisse worked alone for four months, during which time he established relations with the Edwards and Sons Company of Constantinople, and I have become its collaborator here, along with its representative, L. Cunningham. In April 1920, Narcisse became partners with Salomon Toledo and did quite good business with him. He suffered losses in the business only with C. Schamasch of Marseilles, because of the drop in prices and especially because of Schamasch's negligence regarding shipments. He also had quite productive business at exchanges with a few banks in Sofia.

Here I engaged Bitouche Sidi as an assistant, with whom we worked well and realized good profits. Unfortunately, we had noticeable losses as well and will especially have some in an alcohol deal concluded with the T. Balabanof Company, on behalf of P. Cosmaoglou of Constantinople. Everything I own could well be swallowed up by it. Nonetheless, my life has been so full of ups and downs that I still hope to get out of this safe and sound. And if I lose everything, I will be where I was when I went into business, and shall begin again.

What gives me patience is the terrible automobile accident I was in on 17 January 1921 in Constantinople, which I survived only by a miracle of chance. He who saved my life when I was underneath the car will give me the energy necessary to get out of the present difficulties in an honorable manner.

During my stay in Constantinople with Rachel, Jeanne found the Prince Charming I spoke of here two years ago. She chose a companion for herself freely, in the person of Djemil Policar, a dentist in Burgos (Spain), and I gave my consent. Returning to Sofia on 30 January, we celebrated the wedding on Thursday, 10 February 1921, with the requisite solemnity and with a great gathering of friends. I had the great sorrow of not seeing Sophie and Narcisse at that celebration: she was

6. Aleksandur Stamboliyski (1879–1923) was the founder of the Agrarian Union and established a peasant dictatorship in 1920, which limited the possession of landed property to thirty hectares and reduced industrial and financial revenues. He was overthrown and assassinated in 1923.

held back in Salonika by an indisposition, and he was kept in Constantinople by the alcohol deal.

Djemil and Jeanne left us on 20 February 1921 to return to their home in Spain: my blessings and best wishes accompany them there.

My task as head of the family is almost over. There remains the matter of marrying off Sandro and Narcisse: if the situation clears up a bit, that will be the easiest thing in the world.

In May 1920, I was admitted to the Bulgarian Freemasonry; I am part of the Sgovor (Harmony) Lodge.

Here, to conclude, are the exchange rates in Geneva at the end of February 1921: 100 French francs, 43.60; 100 liras, 22; 100 marks, 9.85; 100 Austrian crowns, 1.31; 100 Czech crowns, 7.50; 100 levas, 7.

Here are some prices in Sofia: bread, 5 levas per kilo; milk, 8; meat, 25; rice, 18; wood, 180 per cubic meter; one worker's daily salary, 80 levas.

Sofia, 4 March 1921

YEAR 1921

Yet another great event in our family: on 1 January 1922 I had the joy of marrying off Sandro to Gentille Policar. Their mutual feelings for each other took root during Jeanne's wedding and developed over the months that followed; the engagement took place on 23 September, and here we are united to the Policar family by a double tie.

May the good Lord shower his favors on the new couple. Sandro and Gentille will live with us.

Jeanne is very happy in Burgos; she is especially so since she has learned she will be a mother, in February or March. Rachel had to go to her; she left yesterday, 9 January. Her absence will thus last four to five months.

At her return, she will have to prepare for another trip: it seems that Sophie too anticipates motherhood. That is the effect of the treatment she underwent this year in Franzenbad,[7] where she spent two months, after a stay of one month in Sofia.

The economic crisis I indicated last year has worsened. In the West and East, there is only one cry: Poverty! In countries with healthy currencies, there is unemployment and the sale of merchandise at a loss; in countries with weak currencies, which includes Bulgaria, there is the high cost of living, which leads to abstention from buyers and stagnation in ex-

7. Franzensbad, not Franzenbad, city in Thuringia.

changes. Add the rise in direct and indirect taxes and you will understand the worry and insecurity that reigns in the commercial world.

I have had my share, a large share, in the losses experienced by salesmen this year. The greatest of all came from that unfortunate alcohol deal in Constantinople, which is not yet liquidated, since my suit against Cosmaoglou is still in process. But I long ago resigned myself to the inevitable, persuaded that with time, work, and a little luck, everything can be repaired.

My company in Constantinople was liquidated in June 1921. Narcisse returned at that time, and while waiting to find a stable occupation for himself, he worked for six months at the Franco-Belgian Society. Beginning on 1 January, he joined the Bulgarian Phoenix as secretary. He will be able to make a career for himself in insurance.

My relations with the Baker and Edwards firms are now defined by contract, as of 11 May. Although Constantinople gave us many disappointments, it also procured our collaboration with two companies, which have given me all their confidence and from which we will draw a good profit.

We finally liquidated our consortium with Sabat, Isaac Arié, and Z. Alcalay. Although I feared a large loss from it, I in fact realized a slight profit.

My situation has thus improved, and I was right not to despair.

The Banque d'Orient also had losses to sustain, which it has in part corrected with the purchase and resale of a building. Given the continuous rise in fees and taxes, we felt it preferable to liquidate that establishment. It will be done in 1922.

The Bulgarian Phoenix has affiliated itself with the Riunione Adriatica of Trieste. The business has been prosperous until now. Unfortunately, the last days of December have brought us some enormous fire and maritime disasters.

Last December, I was named member of the board of directors for the French Chamber of Commerce in Sofia.

My health and Rachel's have remained fairly good during the last year, but I now feel a bit more tired and would like to spare my strength from now on, since I shall soon be sixty years old.

Elia arranged for the engagement of Edith to Sami Behmoiras, who is a good and intelligent boy.

Régine married off her daughter Valentine, who got divorced two months later.

So many events in ten months!

And the life struggle continues.

Sofia, 10 January 1922

YEAR 1922

Two great family events marked the year 1922: the births of Rosita and Maurice.

Rachel left Sofia on 9 January and stopped in Paris for three weeks, where she was welcomed by Sultana and Emmanuel as they would have done for their mother. She then went to Burgos, where, on 2 March, Jeanne gave birth to her daughter, Rosita, my first granddaughter. Rachel returned to Sofia on 5 May.

Nursing and the solitary and monotonous life Jeanne leads in Burgos have tired and irritated her. She is now in Paris, where distractions and family life are restoring her before everyone's eyes. Djemil will have to leave Burgos, for Jeanne can no longer tolerate the solitude.

On 13 August Maurice was born. In a sense, Sophie brooded him for the last seven months. The delivery was difficult, but since Sophie has been rewarded for it, she now seems the happiest of women! Rachel stayed in Salonika for about two months on that occasion.

I myself took a trip there in April, and on that occasion could see the precariousness of Salomon's situation. The military catastrophe in Greece, which has led to the collapse of the drachma, could not have improved it.

On that occasion, I began business relations with the Salomon S. Mordoh Company, which have had excellent results and which, I hope, will continue. Unfortunately, the cocoons I sent suffered great damage on the seas, which brought a huge profit to Mordoh but cost a great deal to the Bulgarian Phoenix, where they were insured.

The Cosmaoglou lawsuit—that nightmare—is not over. I had to take a trip to Constantinople on that subject in August. The matter must now go to Sivas[8] on appeal.

The general situation of the business was splendid for me this year. I was able to recuperate all my earlier losses and am happy to see that my program of work, perseverance, and economy has produced the expected results. Now I see the future with more confidence than ever.

My relations with M. Cunningham, the director of Baker and Edwards in Sofia, could not be more cordial. B. Sidi now remains at Baker's all day, where he performs the duties of salesman.

Narcisse is still at the Bulgarian Phoenix, where he will learn the business. One day he will be its assistant manager and later—as late as possible—its director.

8. City in Turkey, east of the Anatolian plateau.

Sandro and Gentille are living with us in the most perfect harmony.

Oro arranged for the engagement of her daughter Elise, but the engagement was broken.

Emmanuel and Samuel are becoming more and more prosperous in Paris.

Edith married Sami on 2 April.

Sofia, 6 January 1923

YEAR 1923

The year 1923, when I turned sixty years old, saw the realization or liquidation of several family matters.

The most important of all was the arrangement with Elia regarding the ownership of the house in Sofia. Having nearly reached the point of filing suit to settle the question, I considered the scandal it would cause and granted Elia an additional sixth of the house, in compensation for the advances in gold he made to me, and which I reimbursed, or so he claims, only in paper. On 14 July 1923, he finally transferred a third of the ownership of the house on Pirot Street to me, keeping the other two-thirds for himself. The deed of property is deposited with my other papers.

Since 15 August 1923, Elia has been the director of a new insurance company in Constantinople, the Orient, founded by the Riunione Adriatica of Trieste. On 11 November, he left Sofia permanently with his family, after renting his apartment to the Zaria Institute.

Nonetheless, he retains his title as general director of the Bulgarian Phoenix and most of the salary attached to it. I am performing the duties of director, and it is probable that these temporary jobs will end in 1924, and that I will share the effective directorship of the company with Narcisse.

In view of that eventuality, which will no longer allow me to devote my time and attentions to the Baker Company, my contract with it, which expires on 11 May, has been voided. That will lead me to dissolve my partnership with B. Sidi as of the same date.

Another consequence of that change will be the near closure of my private office. Sandro, who was particularly concerned with it, accepted Emmanuel's proposal to come work for him in Paris, where, between salary and commissions, he is assured of 25,000 francs per year. Sandro and Gentille left Sofia yesterday, on 6 January. Will I ever see them again? My separation from him was painful. But truly, for the eleven years he spent in Sofia, Sandro had little joy. I hope he will live more happily in Paris and will develop a taste for initiative in business, more than he did with me. His departure deprives me of my best friend in Sofia.

The year 1923 also saw the realization of my pet project for ten years: I was finally able to publish my *Histoire juive,* which was written in 1914. I had to take care of the matter myself during my stay in Paris in March and April. The Jewish press has given the book an excellent reception. King Boris, to whom I sent a copy, sent me a very flattering letter through his secretary.

As I just said, I took a trip to Europe this year: I was the guest of Emmanuel and Sultana for a week in Nice, then went to Burgos, where Djemil has had to liquidate his dentist's office, since his degree is not valid in Spain. In fact, Jeanne could not have continued to live in Spain, where she is too isolated. During my visit in Paris, we decided to send Narcisse to stay with Emmanuel. Since Narcisse is kept in Sofia at the Phoenix, Sandro has just left in his stead.

As for Djemil, after trying for six months to work in Paris in the jewelry business, where he was not successful, and three months in Constantinople to obtain his license to practice, which he did not obtain, he will return to Sofia, where he will decide what he will have to do to earn his living. In the meantime, Jeanne and Rosita have been staying with us since August.

In 1923, the business went very well and my capital is increasing before my eyes.

Unfortunately, my lawsuit in Constantinople was definitively lost on appeal. But there is so much that is unforeseeable in life! Just wait.

Sofia, 7 January 1924

YEAR 1924

During the year that is ending, my situation and that of Narcisse at the Bulgarian Phoenix were solidified, and we have the new business well in hand. Elia's departure did not compromise the development of the company, and our authority, both in Sofia among the circle of insurers and in Trieste, has continued to grow.

For the first time, Narcisse had to make up the balance sheet himself in 1923. He went to Trieste to discuss it with M. de Frigyessy, on whom he made a good impression. At Elia's proposal, Narcisse was named assistant director at the Bulgarian Phoenix in September 1924.

My contract with Baker was voided and replaced with another, under the terms of which I remain attached to the company as advisor.

As a result, my partnership with Bitouche Sidi no longer had any purpose, and I also dissolved it on 11 May 1924.

Sandro ended his first year with Emmanuel in Paris. Beginning in January 1925, he will have to manage by himself in Paris, in the brokerage and sale of pearls.

Djemil was not successful there: after trying commissions in Paris, a job with a banker in Nice, and after vainly seeking to live by his profession in France, at the end of December he returned to Bulgaria, where his brother Marco gave him a place in his office. For the moment, he is boarding with us, along with Jeanne and Rosita.

After twenty years of work and difficulty, Samuel has just sunk into the most deplorable of catastrophes in Paris: he suspended payments on 3 November, with liabilities of 2.5 million. Thanks to the sacrifices agreed upon by his brothers and by Emmanuel, he will be able to pay 35 percent of his debts. Sultana gave up all her jewels; on the threshold of old age, she remains without resources. That is a dreadful prospect for a woman without children.

That bankruptcy and the crisis raging in France have to have affected Emmanuel's situation. I saw him and Lucie this summer during a ten-day visit they made to us in Sofia toward the end of June.

Immediately after their departure, we undertook some repairs in our apartment, which has become more spacious and more agreeable to live in.

With the repairs completed, Rachel left for Salonika on 15 August, where Sophie gave birth to a daughter, Yvette, on 5 September. The news she brought me regarding the situation of Salomon's business is not heartening.

The Orient is developing in Constantinople, and would develop even better without the thousand obstacles to all financial and commercial enterprises set in place by the Turkish government. I saw Elia three times this year in Sofia.

Everyone's health was good this year, at least relatively. Rachel and I hope to take a trip for relaxation this summer: she and I need to go to the country to recuperate.

Life in Bulgaria is becoming more and more expensive, but thanks be to heaven, I have no more money worries. What I earn is more than adequate for my needs.

Sofia, 1/14 January 1925

YEAR 1925

The year 1925 and the beginning of 1926 have been filled with very important events for our family.

On 23 and 24 March, M. Frigyessy, accompanied by M. Léonzini, came to Sofia to examine on site the balance sheet for the Bulgarian Phoenix in 1924. What he saw here amply satisfied him: from Constantinople, where he went after his stay in Sofia, he sent word to us that my salary and Narcisse's were to be doubled. That surprise was all the more agreeable in that we had not even dreamed of asking for a raise in salary the second year of directing the Phoenix.

M. de Frigyessy's confidence in us was again manifested with the instigation of representation for the Riunione Adriatica in Bulgaria, of which I was named the holder. The authorization to do business was granted us by the tribunal in July 1925, and operations began the next month.

Finally, and this is the most important, M. de Frigyessy decided to build a palace in Sofia for the Bulgarian Phoenix and the Riunione, like those that large insurance companies everywhere possess. To that effect, on 25 May 1925, we bought the Panach establishment belonging to N. Nanof, for the sum of 13 million levas, all costs to be our responsibility. We were going to make some modifications and add on another two floors, but we realized it was more practical to demolish everything, down to the foundations, and build an entirely new building.

The demolition work began on 5 June, and by mid-August the construction of the palace had started. It will include a restaurant in the basement, stores on the ground floor, a mezzanine, and six floors. It may be the tallest building in Sofia. The plans were drawn up by the architect Fingof, the plan for the façade by the architect Lehmann from Prague, and general supervision was entrusted to the engineer Koestner from Prague. Directing that project gave me a great deal of work in 1925 and will give me a great deal in 1926 as well. But I will have the satisfaction of leaving behind a lasting memory of my time in insurance, and of housing the Bulgarian Phoenix in the heart of the city, in a location that will do it honor.

Another important creation due to my initiative is the Union of Insurance Societies of Bulgaria, to which twenty companies (thirteen indigenous and seven foreign) now belong. I was named president of the union. The Bulgaria, the Balkan, and the cooperative society of employees chose not to belong out of egotism, since they did not take the initiative in founding it. They will come around in time. The union has already manifested its existence with useful mediation in Parliament, requesting important modifications in the law in preparation regarding the oversight of insurance companies. It publishes a bimonthly newspaper, *L'Assureur.* . . .

Our authority in the circle of insurers has thus grown again.

The effects of age and the excess of work have manifested themselves in troubles that, at the end of the year, imposed a prolonged rest vacation on me. With Rachel, I went to spend a few weeks in the south of France, in Hyères. I spent a delicious vacation there, which the presence of Sultana and Emmanuel with Lucie made even more beautiful. Before that, I made a short business trip to Trieste, and then to Paris, where I had the pleasure of seeing Sandro settled into a pretty apartment on 37, avenue Victor Hugo.

As a matter of fact, Sandro is expecting a baby any day now.

Before our trip to Hyères, Rachel underwent treatment in Vichy in July and August, which was very helpful to her.

The greatest and happiest event of the year took place just a few days ago: on 23 February of this year (1926), Narcisse became engaged to Frida, and the next day, the fiancée arrived in Sofia, accompanied by Elia and Léonore, who are now at our home. I have been cherishing this hoped-for union for several years and am very happy it could be realized. I foresee much happiness for the young couple. The wedding will probably take place on 1 August.

Djemil did not stay long with his brother Marco but had to leave the end of May. Since then, he has been practicing his profession as a dental technician and lives in two rented rooms in Elia's apartment.

Emmanuel made up for the losses of recent years and is solvent again.

Samuel is also earning his living traveling in Italy on behalf of the Habib Company. Sultana is accompanying him in his wanderings. What a difficult life!

Sandro's profits in Paris have not been brilliant, and I am not yet assured he will be able to support himself much longer in Paris. Let us continue the experiment for another year.

The results produced by the Orient were excellent this year. The company is well launched. I am happy for Elia.

Sofia, 4 March 1926

YEAR 1926

The most important event of this year was Narcisse's wedding, which took place on 27 June in Sofia. For the occasion, I would have wished that all our relatives from abroad could have come to Sofia to attend this family celebration: only Sophie and Sultana could respond to our invitation. Sophie arrived in Sofia on 27 March and left the end of August with her two children, Maurice and Yvette; Sultana stayed with us for two months, from June to the end of July.

The religious ceremony, celebrated at the temple, was followed by a reception at our home and, in the evening, by a family dinner, at the end of which the newlyweds left for a trip to France, from which they returned on 6 August. They then proceeded gradually to move into their apartment, above mine, and in November began to do their cooking at their place.

A few days after the wedding, Elia and Léonore left for Carlsbad; they returned the end of August, but Léonore was very weakened. When she went back to Constantinople, her illness worsened; it became harder and harder for her to get proper nutrition, to the point that an operation was judged necessary. The patient was transported to a clinic, where she is still; the operation took place, but the hoped-for improvement has not come about. They are now talking about another possible operation, which would not be without risk. Thus, for the past two months, the entire family, here and in Constantinople, has been living on tenterhooks. As I write, the doctors are more optimistic. May their prognosis become true. That is my sole wish for this new year 1927.

For the rest of the family, there is nothing very cheering to signal. The commercial crisis that rages everywhere in Europe has touched us all: Sandro is vegetating in Paris but does not want to hear of returning to Bulgaria; he may be right. Emmanuel is also complaining that his business is becoming difficult. It is also difficult for Samuel, who is condemned to travel perpetually in Italy; his errant life tires Sultana a great deal, since she is no longer young.

Djemil also did not succeed in his career as a technician and wanted to go abroad to look for work. That was pure folly. He understood the error he would be committing in chasing after adventure and finally decided to accept the post of agent for the Riunione, which I have been offering him for a long time. He will earn a living there.

The law on the oversight of insurance companies was voted in on July 1926, and the administrative regulations for its application are about to be published. Thus, the law will soon begin to be applied. That is additional work and responsibility, but we will have to accept it. Our union of companies, of which I continue to be president, succeeded in obtaining several improvements on the original language from the Chamber.

The same difficulties and the same obstacles also exist in Constantinople, where Elia's task is neither easy nor agreeable. The profession is becoming harder and harder.

Our building on Dondoukof Boulevard is about to be finished. We will be able to move in as of February. It has become a palace, the most beautiful architectural monument in Sofia. But renting it out is going very slowly because of the crisis: I am rather worried about the results of the enterprise. But that is a task for tomorrow. Sufficient unto the day is the evil thereof.

I was not able to take a vacation this year, but my health and Rachel's are satisfactory.

Sofia, 1 January 1927

YEAR 1927

My most ardent wish, which I expressed at the beginning of the year, did not come true: Léonore has not gotten well. After spending several months in a clinic and undergoing a series of painful operations, her condition has not improved, stones continue to obstruct the common bile ducts and her bile flows only partly to the intestine, with the other part evacuated by a fistula, which has remained open for more than a year. During a period of improvement, she was able to take a two-week trip to Sofia during the celebration of *tischri*.[9] We will probably have to turn to the intervention of surgeons abroad.

But what a life for Elia!

A great misfortune has struck Sultana: Samuel abused the confidence of the Habib brothers, for whom he was traveling in Italy and, as a result, was the subject of a complaint and was sentenced to sixteen months in prison. He is serving his sentence in Florence. Sultana's life is shattered. She remains without resources and without support. Even the furniture has been sold. She cannot procure more without it being immediately seized as well. She has made a request for a legal separation. We will have to organize her existence and provide for her. It is hard for Sultana, after twenty-nine years of marriage.

9. Tishri, the month of the Jewish high holidays.

Sandro is expecting a child in February. Our hope that he would take up his jewelry business again has not materialized. Thus no brokering. Sandro has tried various articles of commission but has not been successful. He has just started a small hosiery business. That can only be one more expedient. This is still a grave question for me to resolve during the year that is beginning.

Jeanne is no happier: I gave Djemil a job at the Bulgarian Phoenix with a beginning salary of four thousand levas. With the commissions he got and the interest on the money he possesses, he could have led a peaceful life, sure of the future. But because we put his work table in another room and rented out the little room he occupied, he resigned on 8 September and left his job in an uproar, criticizing Narcisse for our "hypocrisy" and "duplicity." Since then, we have broken all relations with him and see only Jeanne and Zitta. Djemil plans to go to France to find work. When he has spent his last leva, Jeanne and her daughter will necessarily be under my charge, and I will have to welcome them, but between me and Djemil there can be no new relation: the experience of seven years has established the moral and intellectual value of that man for me.

Let us add, to complete this cheerless family portrait, that Régine has been gravely attacked by rheumatism for three months and will have to stay in bed or in her room all winter. Tchelebon Madjar is not doing well either: they have just discovered fairly advanced arteriosclerosis in him. He is leaving for Vienna for treatment.

My health is good, but I feel a bit tired. The vacation I am taking this winter in Hyères will mend me no doubt.

Rachel felt very well during a vacation of three months that we took this year to Krasno-Sélo,[10] but in September she developed an abscess on her foot, which worried us a great deal and from which she has not completely recovered. Two insulin treatments she has had since have helped her recover and gain back a few kilos, an appreciable advantage for a diabetic.

The Phoenix palace is completed and our company moved into it in April of this year. We occupy the second floor and part of the third. The entire site, from top to bottom, is rented out, a result I had not even hoped for. The return is still small, but during this period of crisis, one could not hope for better.

During this year, the Phoenix increased its capital from 2 to 6 million levas. The Hamburg and Mutzenbacher sold all their shares to the

10. Suburb of Sofia.

Riunione, which makes the Phoenix the property of the Riunione. This change will bring about some modifications in our organization, which will be studied during the year that is beginning.

The state's oversight of insurance companies has been applied and for the moment is not bothering us: on the contrary, it seems to be contributing toward making the business more healthy.

In Constantinople, Elia's task continues to be difficult, but that is the fate of all companies working in Turkey.

On 7 January I leave for Hyères with Rachel.

Sofia, 1 January 1928

YEAR 1928

Great changes have occurred during this year in the material and moral situation of our family.

On 10 February 1928, Sandro became the father of a daughter, who was named Huguette-Ida. A few months later, on 1 July, he established himself at 23, rue de Clignancourt, in a hosiery business, buying the stock under good conditions. This new occupation, independent and stable, ensures his existence in Paris. He and Gentille seem very happy with his present condition. . . .[11]

Maurice and Yvette are such adorable children, so intelligent and well brought up. That is happiness in reserve for Sophie.

All the clouds that darkened the horizon of my family in 1927 have fortunately dissipated in 1928. I shall add that Rachel's health has remained good, despite two or three bouts of flu, including one—from 9 September to 1 October—that was grave enough to worry the doctors. During this year, she had two insulin treatments, with the best results.

My health has been good in general.

During this year, we took both a winter and a summer vacation. On 7 January, Rachel and I left for Hyères; after a long stay of six days in Trieste, where I had to go on business, then one day in Venice and two in Nice, we arrived in Hyères on the eighteenth and lodged at the Hôtel des Etrangers. Two days later Sultana and Georges, Emmanuel's son, joined us there.

This cohabitation was not agreeable and spoiled all the pleasure we had promised ourselves for our trip. The quite innocent author of my

11. Two pages are missing from the journal here. We have eliminated two paragraphs that remain incomprehensible because of that omission.

dispute with Sultana was Samuel, then in prison in Florence, whom I pitied and whom Sultana wanted to see hanged, as she said.

We left Hyères on 27 February and spent a week in Paris, where we were the guests of Emmanuel, who was full of consideration for us. We left Paris on 6 March and I wrote numerous letters to Emmanuel, to which he did not respond. When I wrote him in June to ask the reason for his sulking, he responded on 10 July with a letter full of insults, which can be found among my papers. There is no doubt that Sultana put him up to it.

I shall refrain from judging that behavior. Perhaps one day Emmanuel and Sultana will be sorry for being so ungrateful and mean.

Samuel got out of prison after nine months of detention and is living in Florence on the allowance his family is giving him. He is legally separated from Sultana. She makes and sells yogurt in Paris.

Our summer vacation was taken in Krasno-Sélo, from 11 June to 9 October. We were there in the company of our daughters and their children. This stay did us all good, except that toward the end, in September, Rachel developed a grave stomach illness, from which she fortunately recovered quickly.

Régine underwent a course of treatment in Banki and feels the good effects of it this winter.

Fortunately, Léonore is completely cured and the wound is closed. In the summer she underwent a good course of treatment in Carlsbad, accompanied by Elia.

Félix went to Paris to study law. He needed to complete his general education with more extensive studies.

Our affairs at the office have developed in a satisfactory manner.

In all, the year 1928 was favorable to us. On 31 December, we concluded it with a family celebration, during which Rachel and I celebrated the fortieth anniversary of our engagement.

May we enjoy in peace the few years of life that Providence may yet hold in store for us!

Sofia, 6 January 1929

YEAR 1929

30 June 1929
Alas, no!

The wish I made at the end of 1928 did not come true.

An irreparable misfortune has struck me.

My home is destroyed.

My life, or what remains of it, is shattered.

My poor dear wife is dead.

My beloved Rachel has been taken from me.

The family celebration we had last 31 December was to be the last.

And from now on grief has entered my heart.

It will never again leave.

From now on I am a stranger on this earth; nothing can interest me here anymore, since I no longer have beside me my faithful companion, my adored Rachel, who was as necessary to me as the air I breathe.

I could only live with her here.

Night and day, whether she was present or absent, I called her untiringly: Rachel, Rachel!

She will respond no more.

Sometimes she asked: "Why do you call me all the time?"

To see her, to hear her, to speak to her, to feel her near me were for me ever renewed sensations of pleasure.

But no more.

The only moments when I am alive are those when I imagine her in my thoughts, thin, svelte, smiling, elegant, kind, coming and going in her house, her eye on everything, taking care of everyone, thinking of everyone but herself. And when that image has left me and I return to cold reality, what a void, what distress, how my heart aches!

Dearest Rachel, why did you do this to me?

Why did you leave before me?

Hadn't I arranged your life so that, after my death, you would live independently, in comfort, like the noble woman you were?

Wasn't I counting on you to wipe away the sweat from my brow when my final hour came?

How am I going to live from now on?

How am I going to die?

Alone!

No, I do not wish to remain alone. I want to join her, and as soon as possible.

My home is no longer my home, our home. My home now is the little enclosure surrounded by wire mesh, which I prepared for us and where you have already taken the first place.

The second place is waiting there for me. That is where I long to go, near you, my dearest, to sleep our eternal sleep together, O my adored Rachel, the best, the most holy of women!

How did this catastrophe happen? Here it is in a few words.

We had been at the countryside since 3 June. In a villa chosen by my poor dear wife, on the road to Gornia-Bania. The place is peaceful and relaxing. We were planning to spend an agreeable summer season with Narcisse, Frida, and their little Gabico.[12] We spent fourteen delicious days there. On Monday 17 June I was awakened: my poor Rachel felt ill. She had two or three bowel movements, vomited copiously, and felt relieved.

On Tuesday 18 she took a laxative. She felt the effects only in the evening. But the day had gone by peacefully.

On Wednesday 19, she felt a little apprehension. Was it the effect of indigestion? The next morning we called a doctor who had already treated her, Dr. Stoïtchef.

On Thursday 20, the doctor noted a strong odor of acetone throughout the house and immediately prescribed high doses of insulin. Dr. Pipano was brought to the house in short order and injected seventy units of insulin into the patient, who was already semicomatose. In the evening, he injected another sixty units of insulin. Dr. Kirkovitz, also brought to the patient's bedside, calmed us a little and also advised injections of camphor, which the local physician gave. He remained at the house overnight, for the profile of the illness was growing darker by the hour.

On Friday 21, Dr. Angelof, another doctor who had taken care of my poor dear wife, was brought in. He reassured us; was he being frank with us? Perhaps, since the year before Rachel had had the same illness, in a much more serious form, and had recovered. He told us that when the patient got back her appetite and began to eat, we could consider her in convalescence.

When Dr. Pipano came by for the insulin injection at about one o'clock, he noted the beginning of pneumonia at the base of the right lung. That aggravated the situation. He advised the patient to lie on her side, which she did with her habitual courage.

But already at that time, I noted a frantic pulse, a glassy look, and delirium. I said to Narcisse, who was beside me: "Mama is lost."

At about three o'clock the patient declared she was hungry.

That was a joy for all. Hadn't Dr. Angelof said two hours earlier that we could recognize it as a sign the crisis had passed? Our joy was to be short-lived.

12. Gabico, Judeo-Spanish diminutive for Gabriel (little Gabriel).

On three occasions, from 3:00 to 11:30 in the evening, we gave her rice and vermicelli soup, curds, and cherry compote, which she took with pleasure. She chatted with us, made plans, joked.

At 10:00 in the evening, Dr. Pipano came back and noted that the pneumonia had moved to the left lung as well. Cyanosis was invading her face, her legs were frozen and covered with bruises. Her heartbeat was 130–40. All he could do was give his insulin injection, recommending that his local colleague, who was to spend the night in the house, multiply the camphor injections in case of lesions.

About 11:30 in the evening, still on that fatal night of 21 June, she asked that the carafe of water and a glass be set near her bed, so that she could use them by herself during the night, in order not to disturb anyone. We did as she wished.

She turned toward the wall and fell asleep.

Narcisse and I withdrew to the room next door to get a little rest. It was midnight.

My sister Oro, Frida, the maid Marica, and Dr. Ivantchef kept watch over the patient.

At 1:10 in the morning, we were awakened by a noise: we hurried into the patient's room: a cadaverous pallor had already invaded her, the doctor was listening to her heart, my sister was sprinkling cold water on her face, nothing moved. She had died in her sleep. Her heart, the heart that beat only for her husband and children, had stopped.

She had closed her eyes forever.

And I was a widower!

The night was horrendous for us.

Nonetheless, we had to take care of the thousand details of the funeral, since we were by ourselves in the country and no one was there to help us—as we had at the death of poor Ida in Davos.

On Saturday, the twenty-second, the entire city was informed of the misfortune that had struck us. The women came to keep watch, then relatives and friends.

At 7:00 in the evening, we transported the remains of the dear departed to the house, which had received the funeral decorations suitable for the occasion.

The funeral took place on Sunday, the twenty-third, at 10:00, amid a great crowd of people. For the absent children, I had a photograph taken of the casket as it left the house.

And I had the sorrow of seeing the body of my poor dear adored Rachel buried in the earth. At sixty years old, that body conserved the youth of an eternally young and beautiful nymph.

The rest is without importance.

The seven days of mourning[13] are past, the ceremonies are over. We return to the countryside, everyone goes about his business, life requires it, and I remain alone with my sorrow.

I called Sofia so that Sandro, Sophie, and Jeanne would come spend a few weeks or months with me. The family as a whole must come together around the grave of our dearly beloved and cherished departed!

Dead! Cry mine eyes, cry my dearest children. Our family's sun has gone out.

You too will return to your young families, who clamor for you, and you will have, or ought to create, joy around you, for that is the order of nature.

As for myself, I have reached my sixty-seventh year and am deprived of the love and support of my dear and faithful companion: life can be only agony for me from now on.

A single thought sustains me, and that is that this agony must have an end, and that at my age it cannot be far off.

31 July 1929

The children came: Sandro and Jeanne (with Zitta) on 17 June, Sophie (with her two children) on the nineteenth. You can imagine their meeting with me, their entry into the house in mourning, their visit to the cemetery, our whole family united—on 21 June—at the bedside of our dear departed.

On 22 July the religious ceremonies for the end of the first month of mourning took place.[14] Alas! That is also the first stage of forgetting. Yes, the dead are condemned to be forgotten, but I, who miss her every minute of the day and night, how could I ever forget her?

Since the children have been here, we often make a pilgrimage to the sacred tomb. I decorated it with real flowers, I made a flower bed, fresh and pretty like her. I placed a bench beside it, and that is where we go to spend hours at a time in silent conversation with her. I feel at home there and would like to stay forever. Life alone is intolerable for me. In the presence of the children and grandchildren, I suffer less, but when they go away, one after the other, it will be awful. Sandro is already

13. *Shiva* (*sheva*, "seven" in Hebrew; its Judeo-Spanish equivalent is *Los syete*) is the traditional seven days of mourning observed for the death of a loved one.

14. A religious ceremony is observed one month after the death, for the peace of the departed's soul.

preparing to leave on 8 August, since on the sixteenth he must hand over his store on rue de Clignancourt to Sultana, to whom he sold it. Fortunately, Sophie and Jeanne are staying longer: until the end of September at least.

Between now and then, perhaps the solution will be found to the terrible problem facing me: how shall I organize my existence? Who, at my age, will take care of me, with my infirmities? Who will attend to me when I am ill?

Rachel, my dearest Rachel, why did you leave before me? You who were so devoted, how could you abandon me? What shall I do from now on? What shall I become?

16 September 1929

Twelve weeks have passed since my poor dear Rachel left me, and the wound in my heart has only grown. Time, it is said, heals all wounds: I have not seen it so far. Each day that passes makes life harder for me, more intolerable. Neither the presence of the children and grandchildren, nor that of Elia, who came to spend a week with us, have distracted me. My thoughts are constantly, exclusively, with my adored Rachel, and to better see her in spirit, to better be with her, I leave the entire company behind and lock myself in my room. Solitude suits me best.

In fact, the children are leaving one by one: Sandro left for Paris on 16 August, Sophie and her children this morning, and Jeanne and Zitta are leaving us day after tomorrow. On the nineteenth, we are also leaving the fatal country house of Gornia-Bania and will return home to Sofia. Here the series of my difficult trials will begin. What shall I do? I don't have any idea yet and will abandon myself to my sad fate!

Yesterday we buried Rachel Isaac Arié: I relived every phase of my martyrdom of 22 June.

13 October 1929

Today is the eve of Kippour. What days we have experienced since our return to the city, what a lugubrious aspect my house has when she is no longer here to brighten it with her smile. I live alone in my apartment; dine alone at my table, where for forty years she sat across from me; eat lunch alone in a restaurant at noon. I did not want to share Narcisse and Frida's table, since I would have been disturbing them. But I am their guest Friday evening and Sunday noon.

Rosch-Haschana was a sad holiday: each of us withdrew to a corner on the first evening to cry in our own way. We had dinner at my house and it was like a funeral meal. In fact, tears stream from my eyes at every opportunity: at the table, in my bedroom, in the street, in the tram. As soon as I think of her, my heart swells with sorry and my eyes blur. Today it is ten weeks since we put her in the ground, and I suffer for her more than the first day.

I used the ten days of penance to prepare a grave for myself next to my beloved, where I shall sleep my last sleep. I built it of concrete and linked the two graves with reinforced concrete. We will thus be as in a single dwelling, separated only by a wall a few centimeters thick, and there we will lie next to each other forever. The thought of being together again comforts and consoles me. My adored Rachel, when shall I rejoin you? Why do I continue to live without you?

14 November 1929

Things cannot continue like this. Life in solitude has become intolerable for me. Either I should put an end to it or I must choose a help for myself, someone who will take care of my infirmities, run my household, and break the silence of my long days and longer nights. A governess? In a small city like Sofia that is impossible without compromising myself. A wife? The idea is odious to me.

After long reflection on every question, and on the advice of the children themselves, I called Mme Rachel Crispine to Sofia. Everyone knows her from Smyrna: she was a good friend of my poor dear Rachel, and I asked her if she would consent to share my existence, such as it is, it being understood that the memory of the dear departed would continue to reign as sovereign in my home and heart.

She accepted.

And she left again for Cairo to end the school year at the Milkdrop Orphanage, where she is the director.

6 December 1929

Did I do the right thing in taking that dear girl away from her career, from her environment where she is adored by everyone, to tie her to my sad valetudinarian's existence, that of a sad and disillusioned man whom nothing distracts any longer and for whom life is a burden?

I often have scruples about that.

But perhaps her own existence, under the appearance of material and moral satisfaction, was as lonely and sad as my own!

Winter is beginning. The fog forces me into reclusion. I do not even have the distraction of business. What a life!

31 December 1929
Sad anniversary! Fatal year's end!

With what joy we celebrated the fortieth anniversary of our engagement with the beloved of my heart! How busy she was for a week, so that the celebration would be splendid! As if an obscure instinct told us both that the celebration would be the last of our life together.

That is why, today, I am more than ever filled with her memory, why I isolate myself in my apartment in mourning, why I cry bitterly for her and for myself. Yes, the poet spoke the truth: "The only good left to me in the world is to have sometimes cried."[15]

She's been dead for over six months, and I am still alive!

The days are one thing; they are short and the office work brings me a little distraction. But the nights, the long, sleepless winter nights—I sleep barely three or four hours in two or three attempts. In the silence of an apartment, alone with my thoughts, with an inexpressible apprehension in my heart, it's terrible. This is agony! How long will I be able to bear it?

This week I sent some souvenirs of her to the children: to Sandro, diamond earrings, bought in 1926; to Sophie, her astrakhan coat, bought in 1928 and worn only a year; to Narcisse, her onyx ring; to Jeanne, her pendant, also diamond, bought in 1926 for Narcisse's wedding.

I gave two dresses, including a silk one that had not even been worn, to my niece Marguerite Alcalay, who has just gotten married, I mean to say engaged.

The year 1929, which was so fatal for me, brought little consolation to the members of my family in their businesses. In this respect, all were more or less hard hit.

My brother Elia must leave his enviable situation in Constantinople, where he founded the Orient in 1923, and where he also directed the affairs of the Riunione in Turkey. The insurance business in that country has become less than lucrative, there is no longer an individual post of director at the Riunione for the Orient, and my brother has been transferred to Trieste with the title of director. A step backward in his material situation, but an important moral advancement,

15. These lines are taken from a poem by Alfred de Musset entitled "Tristesse" (Sadness): "Le seul bien qui me reste au monde / Est d'avoir quelquefois pleuré."

offset by the necessity of separating from his family, his daughters and grandchildren, to live rather isolated with Léonore and Félix in a foreign country. It is hard at his age, but it is better than if he had been retired.

Sandro sold his business on rue Clignancourt to Sultana and has just bought another on rue de Meaux. May he succeed!

Sophie continues to live near poverty, and I also had to send a subsidy to Salomon this year.

Jeanne has again settled into a new business, which Djemil just bought in Paris, rue du Four. For him as well, one can only wish for success, and also for good relations between husband and wife.

Narcisse has seen his situation at the Phoenix improve. He certainly deserves it.

Sultana has reconciled with Samuel and quarreled with Emmanuel for reasons of self-interest. She no longer sees him. She is responsible for the end of my relations with Emmanuel, whom she turned against me with intrigues and shameful lies. At the request of my poor Rachel, I wrote to forgive her for her behavior toward me, but my quarrel with Emmanuel remains.

And here we are at the threshold of 1930: what will we register in its history? One no longer even dares wish for happy events. Happiness for us, when the dearest treasure of the family is no longer here, when she is being destroyed and disintegrated down there, all alone, under the cold tombstone?

22 JUNE 1930

Today is the anniversary of the death. Twelve months have passed since she is no longer, and I have just relived hour by hour the terrible days of her illness and death, from 17 to 22 June 1929. I think that, were I to live another hundred years, those events would remain engraved in my memory as on the first day. Never during her life did my poor dear Rachel live as close to me as since she has died; never did she dominate all my thoughts, all the minutes of my life, as since she has lain there, under the tombstone.

I wanted that stone to be simple, harmonious, beautiful, distinguished, as she was herself. It may be the most elegant in the entire cemetery, as she was the most elegant of women.

The tenth of June corresponded to 16 Sivan, the Hebrew date of her death. We celebrated her first *Jahrzeit:*[16] all the relatives attended, more than sixty people. Narcisse's apartment seemed transformed into a chapel, with at one end, the large portrait of Rachel in the mourning frame: she was like the goddess of the place, and the three-branched candelabra burned before her. During the ritual prayers, Dr. Sémach Rabbiner gave the eulogy of the deceased. It was a very impressive ceremony and the tribute made to her was worthy of her.

How I missed Sophie, Sandro, and Jeanne that night. But I know they were with [us] in their thoughts.

And while we were plunged in the bitterness of our memories, Mlle Rachel, now called Renée Crispine, was on her way from Cairo to Belgrade, where I must go join her to celebrate my wedding to her on 27 June.

The necessities of life are implacable.

At least no one knows the date of that event, and my children will have knowledge of it only when it's over.

Day after tomorrow, I will go to pray and cry on her grave and ask for her permission to organize a possible life for myself, until I can come to rest for eternity in the place destined for me beside her.

3 JANUARY 1931

The wedding took place in Belgrade on 27 June. We returned the same day to Sofia. And life has been reorganized and goes smoothly.

No important event to signal in the life of the family this last six months.

31 December 1931

Another year has gone by. And during that year, my adored Rachel did not leave my memory for a day, for an hour. Whatever the moment of the day or night, she is present in my mind, her image never leaves me, my thoughts are always with her, and my eyes never tire of contemplating her portrait. It seems to me that her gaze answers my own and that we understand each other at a glance, without speaking, like before. I sense it will be that way until my last breath.

My existence has become as regular at before, and from the material point of view, I want for nothing. My health is holding up. I have not

16. *Jahrzeit* (German), anniversary of a death, a religious ceremony celebrated in memory of a loved one or of a famous person, on the anniversary of his or her death.

been ill, but my chronic bronchitis is getting worse, and my breathing is becoming more and more painful. The treatment I underwent this summer in Reichenhall, accompanied by Renée, brought little relief, and my asthma tires me a great deal.

The entire year 1931 was bad for business throughout the world. Sandro and Salomon felt it particularly, and I had to come to their aid by agreeing to large advances. In contrast, Djemil's business is prospering.

I don't know anything about Emmanuel and Sultana. Elia is at Trieste, which he doesn't like because of the lack of society. Régine is fine; Oro lost her daughter Douda.

31 DECEMBER 1932

Monday, 31 May of this year, was almost the last day of my life: following a chill I took on 8 May, at the ceremony for setting the first stone of the Jewish hospital (a project for which I serve as president) or perhaps at the outing to the national theater on the evening of the same day, I was attacked by the flu, which added acute bronchitis to my chronic bronchitis. At the date indicated above I developed an edema in the lung: I felt my last hour coming and recited the Chéma.[17] The rapid mobilization of four doctors, led on by Narcisse, saved me: numerous shots were given and extensive bloodletting—6,700 grams—was performed. My heart, which was beginning to stop, began to function again and continues, though at a much slower rate, forty to fifty pulses instead of seventy to eighty as in the past.

Toward the end of June, I went to Banki with Renée to spend my convalescence in the fresh air. I remained until 15 September and have recovered fairly well.

But there remains from that crisis an aggravation in my bronchitis and a weakening of the heart, which does not allow me any fatigue, especially from walking. I have lost all my resilience and remain alive only through continual efforts.

It is for this reason that, in October, I presented my resignation to M. de Frigyessy, as representative of the Riunione in Bulgaria and as delegate of the board of directors at the Bulgarian Phoenix, offering only to maintain general oversight of those two companies. My resignation was

---

17. *Chéma* (*shema*, "hear," Hebrew), first word of the credo of the Jewish faith, which formally affirms divine unity: "Hear, O Israel: The Lord our God is one Lord" (Deuteronomy 5:6).

accepted as of 1 January 1933, with a request that I follow the affairs of the two companies for the important questions, for which I am to be allotted a salary equal to two-thirds of the current one.

Alerted by the gravity of my illness, Sophie came at the beginning of June to spend six weeks in Sofia, and Jeanne arrived with Zit[t]a in the middle of July, to remain with me until 20 September. I am awaiting Sandro's visit in January.

On the same occasion, Emmanuel and Sultana asked my forgiveness for the offenses they had committed toward me. I willingly consented to forget and have reconciled with them.

Elia and Léonore also took advantage of a business trip to the East to come to Sofia and stay here for two weeks. They may come again one of these days for the engagement of Félix, whom they would like to marry off.

Before all this moving about, Renée went to see her relatives in Cairo, at the end of February. She came back on 8 April, bringing her sister Régine with her, who stayed with us until the end of June, or more exactly, the twenty-sixth of that month.

This year, so sad for us, ended with a great loss: my brother-in-law Tchelebon Madjar passed away on 23 December, without being confined to bed. He succumbed to pulmonary tuberculosis, which he had been treating for close to forty years, and which he bore without complaint and with an admirable stoicism. May his soul rest in peace!

Business has not improved this year. On the contrary: the country is growing poorer before our eyes and the state's coffers are empty, but I am past the age when material questions worry me. I have had a large share of cares and pains in this world. The time is come for me to rest a little, before the hour of destiny sounds, when I will go to rest my bones beside those of my dear and unforgettable Rachel.

31 DECEMBER 1933

The year 1933 marked a great date for me: the seventieth anniversary of my birth, which I celebrated on 10 Iyar/6 May with the family, and with a modest ceremony at the temple, at the Minha prayer.[18] It was a Saturday. My brothers and children joined in the celebration through the dispatches they sent. In truth, I never thought I would reach this age, given my precarious state of health for the last thirty years, and I thank

---

18. *Minha* (*minhah*, Hebrew), prayer recited between noon and sunset.

God for having let me live a little longer, for the good of my children, to whom I am still necessary.

I devote most of my attention to maintaining my health and go to the office only once a day, and when Narcisse is absent. I naturally grow weaker and weaker as the effect of age, but I know I am ready to leave at any time.

One great object of preoccupation, which had been tormenting me for ten years, disappeared this year. Sandro's fate is finally settled in a satisfactory manner. During the trip he made to Sofia in January, we were able to talk at length about his situation in Paris, which was growing worse year by year and, with the crisis contributing, was becoming an untenable life, despite the substantial help I have continued to send him for the last five years. He understood that his future was not in Paris and agreed to liquidate his store and return to Sofia. He has been here with his wife and daughter since the beginning of July, and I gave him a job at the Bulgarian Phoenix, where I hope he will make a career for himself. He has finally found his way. And since he is not lacking in goodwill, or in intelligence, he will rapidly become a very useful assistant to Narcisse.

In Elia's family there was also a happy event. Since their transfer to Trieste, Elia and Léonore's lives have been very sad: a little youth and life was needed in the house, and Félix was also bored in that unsociable city. It was agreed that Félix should marry. He came to Sofia at the beginning of January to see the fiancée we had chosen for him: Mlle Mathilde Nissim Mitrani, granddaughter of Tchelebi Alcalay. The young people liked each other, got engaged, and on 12 March the wedding took place in Sofia. Elia, Léonore, Lucie, Vitalis, and Edith came. The couple are well matched and seem very happy.

Toward the end of the year, Félix was entrusted with an inspection in Morocco and Tunisia, and he acquitted himself of his mission very well.

Everyone's health is good in Sophie's family, but Salomon's business is far from improving. I supplement what is lacking as much as I can. Fortunately, she has children who are admirable for their intelligence. They are her sole hope for the future.

Jeanne and Zit[t]a are doing well, and Djemil is happy with his business.

Narcisse has taken the direction of the Phoenix and the Riunione in Sofia well in hand and makes all sections work, despite the large reduction in staff we have made and the introduction of new branches of insurance: accident, liability, automobile.

Among my brothers and sisters, everything seems to be going very well. In Trieste, Elia and Léonore now have a very agreeable life, thanks to their charming daughter-in-law. Oro is doing well, and her son Joseph has just acquired a house in Sofia. Régine's daughter Marguerite has also bought a pretty apartment in a cooperative. Sultana is living quietly in Paris, where Samuel is earning a good living. Emmanuel is also managing and does not appear demoralized by the crisis. The children of Tchelebon Madjar proceeded to the division of their father's inheritance without the slightest conflict.

This year as well our family registered a loss: Yomtov Arié succumbed to his old heart malady.

31 DECEMBER 1934

The year that is ending was drab, morose, and difficult for everyone. Grave political events occurred in Europe: the assassination of Alexander, king of Yugoslavia,[19] and of Louis Barthou[20] in Marseilles, a plebiscite in Saarland, pacts between various states, and massive rearming in every country all seemed to presage imminent war. The world economic situation, which has been getting worse every year since 1929, worsened yet again, and trade between nations has been reduced to half what it was five years ago. Unemployment is rising and is attacking countries that had been exempt, such as France and Bulgaria. The ruins are piling up and poverty is becoming universal.

In Bulgaria, that situation led to a coup d'état:[21] on 19 May, the Mouchanof ministry was overturned by the military party and replaced by a government that dismissed Parliament, dissolved all political parties, and now reigns by decree. This change has not improved business, the crisis has worsened, everyone must wait and see to know what tomorrow will be like.

A large number of articles produced in this country have become state

19. Alexander I (1888–1934) was king of Yugoslavia from 1921 to 1934.
20. Louis Barthou (1862–1934) was the French president at the time of his assassination.
21. The failed insurrection of the Communists and Agrarians, in September 1923, began an era of terrorism and counterterrorism, with Communists, Macedonian revolutionaries, and Fascists killing one another. In 1931, the cabinet formed by the democratic leader Aleksandur Malinov, who transferred his power for reasons of health to his colleague Nikola Mushanof, represented the last hope of saving the constitutional system and Bulgarian democracy. On 19 May 1934, nationalist officers of the Zveno group ("ring" in Bulgarian, a pressure group created in 1927 and supported by the military factions of the country) put an end to that hope. As a result, Bulgaria headed toward an authoritarian regime.

monopolies, and the state is gradually taking the place of the commercial class; cereal, tobacco, salt, alcohol, gasoline, cotton, hemp, etc., can be bought and sold only by the state. We are expecting the monopolization of insurance. If it comes about, the problem of our existence, of our livelihood, will be raised.

This uncertainty about the future leads many Jewish families to contemplate liquidating their businesses in Bulgaria and moving to Palestine.

It is under the reign of such worries that the year 1934 passed.

No change in the state of my health. I stay alive only by taking precautions: no going out during bad weather, various injections, tonics, permanent supervision by a doctor. Nonetheless, on 1 June I again had a heart attack, warded off by immediate bloodletting, though less extensive than in May 1932.

In the summer, we went to Banki (1 July to 15 August), but this time our vacation was enhanced by the presence of my sister-in-law from Cairo, Mme Régine Adéreth, and her four children: Lydia, Ninette, Max, and Gaby. What a charming family!

Sandro, Gentille, and Huguette vacationed on the beach of Messemvri[22]—what a change for them after Paris!—Narcisse, Frida, and Gabriel in Constantinople—first in Fanaraki[23] and then in Tcham-Cori—and Jeanne and Zit[t]a in the Pyrenees.

Only Sophie could not leave in the summer, since her husband's resources are extremely limited. I must constantly increase my subsidies to alleviate her poverty; I am raising them to 54,000 drachma per year as of next 1 January. A very heavy burden for me, but what can be done, given Salomon's incompetence?

Elia and Léonore have just made an extremely agreeable pleasure trip to Paris. They are expecting a grandson from Mathy next summer.

Régine has just arranged the engagement of her daughter Marguerite. This is the third time. Let us hope it will be the last.

Emmanuel and Samuel are managing in Paris, as is Djemil.

31 DECEMBER 1935

The year that is ending was marked by two deaths and a wedding in our family. My cousin Sabat Arié left us on 9 March 1935, taken by pneumo-

22. Mesembria, on the Black Sea, about thirty miles south of Varna.
23. Fanaraki (Greek name for present-day Fenerbahçe), vacation spot in the Asian part of Istanbul.

nia. He was eight months younger than I. He was an upstanding man and a hard worker. He established the large family his father left to him. He attained a very enviable material situation, which he lost during the last three or four years of his life, and he died poor, surrounded by the respect of all.

His sister-in-law Mazal, wife of the late Rahamim Arié, succumbed on the twenty-second of this month during a liver operation.

Marguerite Alcalay finally married on 20 February. Elia and I contributed fifty thousand levas apiece to round out her dowry. We made this sacrifice out of filial respect for our father and mother rather than out of family attachment, which Marguerite and her family have never shown us.

No change has occurred in the situation of the other members of the family: business is becoming more and more difficult for everyone, including the Bulgarian Phoenix, but Narcisse is struggling to hold on with marvelous energy. I help him with my advice as much as my strength allows. Sandro has finally obtained a situation that allows him to live, without turning to me for advances. Sophie remains almost entirely my responsibility. Jeanne, Emmanuel, and Sultana are managing well in Paris.

Summer was the occasion for the usual comings and goings. I spent six weeks in Banki, Elia four weeks in Gleichenberg[24] and ten days in Sofia, where he was my guest, Sandro two weeks in Genseken[?], Frida six weeks in Porto-Rose near Trieste, and Narcisse two weeks in Tcham-Cori.

The year is ending under the weight of dark worries for all. On 6 October Italy began a war of conquest against Abyssinia. In doing so, it violated the pact with the League of Nations, to which it and Ethiopia belong. The efforts at conciliation undertaken in Geneva did not work out, and financial and economic sanctions were applied to Italy, the aggressor. . . .[25]

31 DECEMBER 1937

Having nearly finished my seventy-fifth year of life, it seems an opportune time to look back on the past and on the present situation of my family.

24. In Austria, southeast of the city of Graz.
25. Two pages are missing from the manuscript.

I have just finished my active life, entrusting the total direction of my businesses, the Bulgarian Phoenix and the Riunione, to Narcisse, and my private affairs regarding the administration of the house to Sandro. From now on, I shall devote my time to taking care of my health and to a few studies, principally Hebrew.

Begun in 1881, when I left the Ecole Orientale, my active life will have thus lasted fifty-seven years, during which time I had to overcome difficulties of all kinds, the principal one coming from my state of health, which forced me to leave the service of the Alliance and to spend nine years in Davos. When I returned to Bulgaria in 1912, I hesitated for two years about the new path to take, during which time I wrote my *Histoire juive*. Then I launched a business. I founded the Banque d'Orient, which we had to liquidate in 1919, and the Bulgarian Phoenix with Elia. He was its director and I the delegate of the board of directors. In 1923, I took over the representation of the Riunione Adriatica for the Sicurità in Bulgaria; between 1925 and 1927, I built a palace for those two companies, the Phoenix Palace, which is one of the most beautiful monuments in Sofia. Since then, my tribulations have ended and my existence has been secure. It will continue to be so, I hope, until the end of my days, better than it would have been in the service of the Alliance, and in that respect, my departure from the Alliance was of great benefit to me.

During this tormented existence, I had the sadness to lose a daughter of fourteen in 1908 in Davos and then my dear and good wife, Rachel, in Sofia in 1929. Her memory is engraved on my heart and shall never be effaced.

Nonetheless, I remarried in 1930, unable to live alone in my old age.

My children are well established: after some attempts at commerce in Paris, which cost me a great deal of money, Sandro finally has a good position at the Bulgarian Phoenix and earns his living there; Narcisse has a brilliant position as director at the Bulgarian Phoenix; and Jeanne is very happy in Paris, where her husband, Djemil, is prospering. That leaves only Sophie, whose husband, Salomon, has not done very well in Salonika; I must support her with regular allocations.

In sum, I have reason to be satisfied with my health, which causes me worry but not torment, and with my excellent material situation, which causes me no concern, and with my children, who are following the path of honor and work. Can one ask for more out of life? No, and that is why I am ready to leave them when it pleases God, praising Providence for having all in all given me the good life in this world.

31 DECEMBER 1938

The year 1938 was remarkable both in terms of my personal existence and in terms of our family. In personal terms, it marked the seventy-fifth year of my life. That is an age I did not expect to reach, after the grave illness I suffered from for several years, which forced me to leave my job at the Alliance and to take an early retirement at age forty-four. Beginning in 1907, I had to manage with the very meager retirement the Alliance granted me. It is true they added two thousand francs per year, a salary that remunerated me for my work as editor of the *Revue des Ecoles* [*sic, Bulletin des Ecoles*], which I had had the idea of founding on behalf of the Alliance. During the few years I spent in Davos, my expenses were paid by Elia from our revenues on the Sofia house, which we had bought together. That account was settled between us after my return to Sofia in 1913.

At that date, I went into business for myself, which lasted until 1923, when Elia founded the Orient insurance company in Constantinople, leaving to me the direction of the Bulgarian Phoenix, which we had founded together in 1917. Beginning at that time, I gave up my commercial affairs, devoting myself entirely to directing the Bulgarian Phoenix, where I had Narcisse named director in 1926, on the occasion of his wedding.

In 1925, the Riunione, having established representation in Sofia, entrusted that post to me, which I exercised simultaneously with that of delegate of the board of directors at the Bulgarian Phoenix, with Narcisse remaining as director and Elia named general director.

Toward the end of the present year, since Elia had to give up all his positions at the Riunione following the measures taken in Italy against the Jews, the Riunione gave Elia the positions in Sofia that I had occupied, at the Bulgarian Phoenix and at the Riunione. I was thus retired by those two companies, beginning on 31 December 1938, and Elia was given the two places left vacant by my departure. Therefore, the commercial chapter of my activities is definitively closed. The pensions I receive from the Bulgarian Phoenix and from the Riunione, joined to that [of the Alliance], much reduced since the devalorization of the French franc, will allow me to live in the future under a much more modest regime than in the past.

These preoccupations are minor compared to those affecting my brother Elia, who, as a Jew, must bear the antisemitic treatment inflicted on all Jews in Italy: in the first place, his Italian nationality is being taken away from him, from his son Félix, and from all members of his family, beginning on 12 March 1939, and he is obliged to leave Italy before that date. He has submitted to that necessity and has come to live in Sofia with his entire family, to try to reclaim his Bulgarian nationality, which he gave up when he went to live in Italy. At this moment, he is taking very active steps to [have] his Bulgarian nationality restored to him, to his son Félix, and to his wife and daughter-in-law. Will he succeed before 12 March? That is the subject of our greatest worry, which does not leave a moment's rest to anyone in the family. The question of a livelihood, though of primary interest for him and for Félix, arises only in the second place, and no one can yet say how Elia and his son will be able to provide for their needs, despite the great financial assistance the Riunione is prepared to give them.

As you can see, 1938 is ending with dark prospects for us. Until now, circumstances have always favored us. We want to hope that, at the end of our existence, chance will not abandon us, and we are beginning the first days of the year 1939 full of confidence in the future.

I do not wish to conclude with the thought that the present jubilee year is ending in such somber tones. In May 1938, I had the joy of receiving, on the occasion of my feast day, very heartfelt congratulations from the Central Committee of the Alliance Israélite, from most of my colleagues, and from many friends. All these letters form a magnificent dossier that will be found among my papers. I do not believe that any Alliance teacher possesses one more flattering or richer.

On that occasion, Sultana, Sophie, and Jeanne came to spend two weeks with us, which remain among our best memories. Sandro and Narcisse already live in Sofia, only Elia and Emmanuel were missing from the celebration. I have the joy of having Elia and his family near me, and for a long time no doubt. Fortune may also bring us those who could not come to that gathering.

For her part, Renée, who had not seen her family for two years, took a pleasure trip to Egypt, which was also a health trip. She returned to a climate to which she is accustomed, to be treated for the many infirmities that afflict her from head to foot, and these words should be taken literally. She came back quite well recovered from many infirmities, and I hope such a trip can be repeated often.

Let us hope that our days will continue so that we may at least hear news of one another if we cannot meet, and that the years 1939 and following may be years of blessings for us all, Amen!

P.S. On 22 October 1938, or 27 Tichri 5699, Frida gave birth to a magnificent boy, who received the name Elie. His godparents were

Narcisse and Lucie, since Elia and Léonore could not leave Italy at that time.

[Gabriel Arié died in 1939 at the age of seventy-six.]

SELECTIONS FROM LETTERS
TO THE ALLIANCE CENTRAL COMMITTEE

28 March 1919
. . . I am writing to inform you that on 23 March a Congress of Jews of Bulgaria met in Sofia for the purpose of examining the situation created for Jews by the current war and the resolutions it is appropriate to take at a time when the statutes that will decide the future of all peoples of the world for a certain period of time are being elaborated in Paris.

Present were the following: delegates from all the communities of the country, from the central consistory, from all Zionist organizations, from the lodges of Bné Berith, from all charity societies, and from the Jewish organizations of social democracy. I was also called as representative of the Alliance.

The congress was presided over by Dr. Calef.[26]

After two days of debate, during which time several speeches were given, the following agenda was adopted.

Resolution
"The National Congress of Jews of Bulgaria, meeting 23 March 1919 in Sofia, having examined the new situation created for Jewry after the war, has unanimously decided to present to the Peace Conference in Paris the following demands, and to insist that they be met.

"1. The participation of the Jewish people, which forms a united nation, in the League of Nations, with the same status as any other nation.

"2. The institution of national guarantees that ensure the indispensable conditions for reconstituting a national and political center for the Jewish people in its historical homeland, Palestine, in which all civil, political, and national rights of the nonnative peoples will be safeguarded and supported.

"3. The assurance of civil and political equality to the Jews of every country through the constitutions of the respective countries and through international guarantees.

26. Dr. Yehoshua Calef (Caleb) (1875–1943) was a Jewish nationalist from the outset and a leader of the Zionist movement in Bulgaria.

"4. The recognition of the cultural and national internal autonomy of Jews wherever they live in compact masses and in smaller number.

"5. The representation of delegates of the Jewish people at the Peace Conference in a number equal to that of other peoples."

This resolution will be transmitted to the Peace Conference in Paris and communicated to the representatives of the various regions of Bulgaria, to the Jewish delegation of Paris, and to the press.

You will note that this resolution does not mention, as did that voted in by other countries, that the Palestinian state shall be placed under English protectorate. We limit ourselves to asking that this state be placed under international guarantees.

M. Calef informed me of the talks that have opened in view of the return of the Alliance to Sofia. There is probably some communication from you on this matter in the mail. The question is very complicated: on the one hand, the community numbers nearly eighteen thousand and could provide the schools with two thousand children; on the other, the extraordinarily high cost of living would require that teachers be paid four times what we paid in the past. One must thus foresee a minimum budget of 250,000 levas. We will study that question at the opportune time. I doubt we can resolve it through correspondence.

This is also true for the matter of the chief rabbi. I have already informed you that the salary foreseen is 36,000 levas per year. Many precautions will have to be taken to guarantee the future spiritual leader full independence and regular payment of his salary. . . .

P.S. M. Sylvain Lévi's[27] declarations in *Le Temps* on 23 February provoked great discontent here. A meeting of protest was planned for tomorrow, 30 March. In the meantime, *Le Petit Parisien* for the fifth of the current month brought new declarations from M. S. Lévi, which were judged more orthodox (not in the religious sense). That put minds at ease, and the meeting was canceled.

Archives of the AIU, Bulgarie I.C.28.

27. Sylvain Lévi (1863–1935) was a famous Orientalist. At thirty-one he occupied the Sanskrit chair at the Collège de France and was elected president of the Alliance Israélite Universelle in 1920. He also distinguished himself by his anti-Zionist positions during the Peace Conference (1919–20) in Paris. His declaration to the Council of Ten (1919), where he enumerated the problems raised by the establishment of a Jewish national center in Palestine, elicited strong reactions from the Zionist leaders.

7 August 1919
. . . *Jews of Bulgaria:* We are in the habit of saying we are satisfied with our fate in Bulgaria. Here, however, is a circular published by a Socialist newspaper, dated 2 August.

"By order 80 of the military district of Sofia, on 27 March 1917, given in virtue of order 95 of the general staff of the army at the war ministry, it is prescribed:

"1. that all Jews in service to the general staff be removed from their duties.

"2. that all Jews fit for armed service and occupied in the service of the rear guard be sent to the front.

"3. that all Jews unfit for armed service and occupied in the cities be sent to the rear services at the front.

"4. that the names of all Jews who were sent on missions to purchase supplies in Romania and Bucharest be communicated. Indicate at what moment, for how long, and by whose order these missions were entrusted to them. In the future, no mission of this kind may be entrusted to Jews."

On 31 March of the same year, Dr. Sakaroff, Socialist deputy, currently in the Madrid castle with the Bulgarian delegation, challenged the government on this matter. The minister of war responded that he would give orders to have this circular rescinded.

I do not know whether the circular was rescinded. But it is certain that when this paper arrived in the various corps, no leader took it into account, for two reasons. The first is that antisemitism is not a state doctrine in Bulgaria, as it is in certain countries of eastern Europe. One does find some anti-Semites in certain administrations, and that includes General Christoff and General Guirguinoff, who signed the above order. But these persons are known for their anti-Jewish sentiments and an order with this intent coming from them has little authority. The second reason is that the Jews are infinitely more resourceful than the Bulgarians; thus, when a leader has a delicate mission to entrust to a soldier, he knows the Jew will give him complete satisfaction. And since in war it is a matter of succeeding first of all, no one bothers to leave a service pending out of denominational considerations.

There is, moreover, this characteristic fact: General Christoff is one of the military men called in to be judged by the Entente and punished for his crimes, while Dr. Sakaroff, the spontaneous defender of the Jews, has the honor of pleading the cause of Bulgaria in Paris, before the Peace Conference. Always divine retribution. . . .

Archives of the AIU, Bulgarie V.B.121.

17 September 1920
Dear M. Chief Rabbi,[28]

I am honored to inform you that from 29 August to 4 September a congress of Jewish communities of Bulgaria met in Sofia with the following agenda:

1. Elaboration of statutes;
2. Election of a chief rabbi;
3. Election of the central consistory.

The congress was composed of fifty-four delegates, including fifty Zionists. A delegate from the Ministry of Religion attended its deliberations.

The statutes, which are henceforth the charter for Bulgarian Jewry, have been adopted. They are in press and I am not yet familiar with them. They should be submitted to the approval of the government, and if it does not approve them, we will disregard it, and they will be considered obligatory by the Jews of this country. Such was the decision of the congress.

As for the election of a chief rabbi, the former consistory published notices in European newspapers (including *Le Temps*) soliciting candidates. Three candidates presented themselves. The congress, unable to pronounce on the matter, charged the new consistory with studying them and submitting to it a proposal with justifications at its next session, which will take place as soon as this study is finished.

The central consistory was elected. It is composed of seventeen members, of whom six reside in the provinces and seven in Sofia. Those of Sofia form the permanent committee of the consistory. The congress has done me the honor of electing me as a member of that institution.

At the second session, which took place yesterday, the consistory examined the candidates presented for the post of chief rabbi of Bulgaria. Of three, they set aside two: M. Marmorstein, a rabbi recommended by a society of young people in Paris, author of a short book in Hebrew; and M. Rappoport, forty-six years old, rabbi in Zurich (he must be a rabbi of some little group of Zurich Jews, since the rabbi of that city is M. Littmann, whom I know). The information on M. Rappoport is not good.

We are thus presented with a single candidate, M. Dario Disegni, rabbi in Verona, born in Florence in 1878, married in 1903, father of four children, completed his studies at the Italian seminary, doctor of letters, assistant rabbi in Turin from 1906 to 1909 and rabbi in Verona since 1909, chevalier in an Italian order. He is recommended by several personalities and, in the last

28. The chief rabbi of France, Israël Lévy.

instance, by the Italian legation in Sofia, on the order of the Ministry of Foreign Affairs in Rome, which attaches an easily conceivable political importance to the election of an Italian candidate.

Before pronouncing on this matter and deciding to have the candidate come to Sofia so that we may see and hear him, we each resolved to find out about him from his friends and acquaintances in Europe.

May I permit myself to ask you to please gather confidential information from a few Italian colleagues on the aptitudes, character, and past of Dr. Dario Disegni and to communicate this to me. The future and progress of the Jewish communities of this country will depend in part on the felicitous or infelicitous choice we make. You will render a great service to our Bulgarian coreligionists if you will be kind enough to enlighten us on our choice and to help us with your advice.

It is unfortunate that the French rabbinate cannot provide us with a candidate. I am convinced that if M. Georges Picot, our minister of France, was aware of what is happening, he would immediately cable the government in Paris to ask the central consistory and the French rabbinate for a candidate for the post. I do not wish to place you in a difficult position and have refrained from speaking of the matter to the French legation. But I am profoundly sorry that it is Italian Judaism, so anemic, so insubstantial, that is providing a chief rabbi for the country, instead of French Judaism, which counts so many men of talent in its rabbinical corps. I am sorry for Bulgaria and for the influence of French prestige in the East. . . .

Archives of the AIU, Bulgarie I.C.23.

28 November 1923

. . . The antisemitic turmoil that characterizes the political and economic crisis from which all of Europe is now suffering has left Bulgaria unscathed until now. Various indications, however, seem to show that this favorable situation of Bulgarian Jews is about to end. At this time, there reigns among our coreligionists of this country an uneasiness similar to that which seizes hold of animals on the eve of great seismic activity. Pogroms are expected, and the insurance companies are solicited by Jewish big businessmen for insurance contracts against plunder and riots. In a circular dated 14 November, number 13249, the Ministry of the Interior invited all prefects and subprefects, the police prefecture of Sofia, and General Security to take measures toward protecting Jews in case of trouble. For its part, the police of Sofia requested this week that the community indicate the hours when the Jews gather in their temples for prayer. Finally, several of our coreligionists, both in Sofia and in the provinces, have received word from Bulgarian friends that armed attacks are being planned against our coreligionists. These rumors are consistent enough that the correspondent for the *Times* in Sofia, Mr. Collins, asked me for a meeting, during which he offered to make columns available to us in the *Times* and in various American newspapers he represents, to reveal to Europe the machinations being planned against us behind the scenes. I thanked him and begged him to do nothing for the moment.

To understand the causes and origin of this movement, we need to go back a few months and take a quick look at Bulgarian politics.

The disarmament imposed on Bulgaria by the Treaty of Neuilly[29] created a new social class in this country: that of unemployed officers, several thousand in number. The depreciation of the leva has reduced to almost nothing the pensions allotted to all these military men, who for the most part have fallen into the darkest poverty. There are some who had been solicited by colonels who, in order to survive, have had to accept lowly jobs in offices, even positions as porters. If you recall that in this rough, poor country, neither an aristocracy of birth nor an aristocracy of money has yet been formed, and that therefore the only relative nobility before the war was that of the sword, you will realize the exasperation that has taken hold of all those officers, reduced to champing at the bit in silence. The half Agrarian, half Bolshevik government of Stamboliyski has done nothing to improve the fate of that mass of déclassés, which it made responsible, along with the bourgeoisie, for the war and the misfortunes that followed.

The revolution of last 9 June[30] is the result of that state of affairs: it is the work of former military men, allied with the Macedonian organization. The government that has emerged from it, formed of honest but obscure personalities, without personal influence or prestige, is under the orders of a coalition that claims it is renovating Bulgaria, just as Fascism is renovating Italy. Today, almost all the posts of prefects and subprefects are occupied by former military personnel, the minister of foreign affairs is an officer, and the Bulgarian legations abroad are in the hands of the Macedonians. The merciless repression of the Communist movement of last September[31] is due more to the officers than to government initiative.

The antisemitic movement taking shape and the popular explosion that

29. The Treaty of Neuilly was signed on 27 November 1919 between the Allies and Bulgaria. That country gave up territories to Greece (Western Thrace), Romania (Dobruja), and Yugoslavia (in Macedonia). The treaty reduced Bulgaria's army to twenty thousand men.

30. The overthrow of Aleksandur Stamboliyski and his assassination (see n. 6 above, this chapter).

31. See n. 21 above, this chapter.

is feared are also due to the officers. The extremely high cost of living from which this country suffers is attributed by these simplistic men to the maneuverings of the Jews, who are supposedly the authors of the depreciation of the leva in the stock market; in commerce, of which they hold the greatest share, they are said to be the agents responsible for the rise in the price of everything. "While the old servants of the state, who got killed en masse at the front, are suffering from hunger, don't we see the Jews displaying an insolent luxury everywhere, filling the theaters and pleasurehouses, spending freely in the cabarets and at other similar establishments? We must reestablish the balance: Instead of six Jewish stores for every Bulgarian one [they have counted them up, it seems, but that's wrong], we must invert the ratio and leave only one Jewish store for six Bulgarian ones. Down with the Jews!" It is this reasoning that prevails in the environment, and that is the reason for the existence of the circular cited above.

In the presence of such a danger, which does not appear to be imaginary, we have not remained inactive, though we are acting with the greatest prudence and discretion. Here are the measures that have been taken:

1. Through our personal relations with the influential ministers and politicians we are now securing the full support of the government in case of trouble.

2. Through a secret circular addressed to all communities, the consistory invited our coreligionists to watch their conduct in public and, especially, to refrain from any display of luxury, from the frequentation of pleasurehouses, etc.

3. Lectures along those lines will be given this week in sites where Jews habitually gather: temples, (Zionist) Bet-am,[32] Bné Berith, and other places.

4. No charity ball will be given this winter on behalf of Jewish programs. We will limit ourselves to making collections.

5. Finally, an adequate organization, upon which it is superfluous to insist, is planned to resist the authors of trouble should it come about.

In this atmosphere where it so difficult to breathe freely, the letter the king sent me, which the Bulgarian press as a whole published, could not have been more timely; it was like a ray of sunshine and hope, and I am thanked on every side as for a *Kiddousch achem*.[33]

The purpose of this communication is not to ask you to take any measure

32. *Bet-am* (Hebrew), "house of the people."
33. *Kiddousch achem* (*kiddush ha-shem,* Hebrew), "sanctification of the divine Name."

whatsoever in favor of the Jews of this country. On the contrary, I must beg you carefully to refrain from any intervention and from any indiscretion. One or the other would provoke fits of anger here whose effects could be terrible. I simply wanted to bring you up to date on the current state of mind, so that if an explosion erupted, you would know in advance what provoked it. May our fears come to naught! In any case, we are keeping watch.

Archives of the AIU, Bulgarie I.C.30.

2 February 1924

. . . It is with a keen feeling of relief that I can announce to you the end of the nightmare that the Jews of Bulgaria have lived through in the past four or five months.

Yesterday morning, I received the visit of a police officer, who gave me the following speech: "I come on behalf of the Ministry of the Interior to inform you that it is forbidden to give any subsidy whatever to persons who might come to request them from you in the name of unauthorized organizations, such as the Macedonian Revolutionary Organization.[34] These contributions are forbidden by law, and those who make them are punished as accomplices, in the same way as those who solicit them."

This communication was made to many other Jews.

You know what this is about from the rumors that have reached you from various sources. Here is exactly what happened.

Last September, a commission of three Jews convened a meeting of thirty persons, I among them, to inform us that a delegate of the Macedonian Revolutionary Organization (ORM) required a sum of 20 million levas (3,250,000 francs) for their work from the Jews of Sofia, this sum to be divided among seventy notables, according to a list prepared by the Macedonians (I was down for 50,000 levas). What were we to do? We consulted and, taking into consideration the situation in the country (see my letter of 28 November), decided not to respond with a formal refusal but to negotiate a large reduction in the contribution. The commission of three negotiated and came back with this response: if we turned in 5 million levas within ten to fifteen days, the leaders of the ORM might declare themselves satisfied. A commission of ten members, named by the Macedonians, was charged with getting together

34. The Internal Macedonian Revolutionary Organization (ORIM/VMORO) was founded in 1893 in Salonika, reorganized after the Treaty of Neuilly (27 November 1919), and financed by Mussolini. The ORIM became notorious for its participation in the bloody reprisals of September 1923, for its assassination attempts, and for the reign of terror its members instigated at the borders of Bulgaria. It was dissolved in 1934.

that sum. It was able to raise only 1,200,000 levas, which were turned in, the lists were returned, and for two months there was no more talk of the matter.

At the end of December or beginning of January, three Macedonians presented themselves to the community and asked to speak to the communal council. They notified us that the ORM had been very dissatisfied with the lack of zeal shown by the Jews in satisfying its demands and that now, not 20 million, but 63 million were required from the Jews, in accordance with a new list of four to five hundred persons.

Those on the list began to be called in individually at the seat of the ORM, the Berlin Hotel, in the center of the city. They were shown the sum to be handed in and were given three days to come up with it. Through pleas and mediation, the victims succeeded in paying only a part of the contribution, generally a quarter or a third, and in obtaining delays for the rest. Each was given a printed receipt, duly signed by the ringleader Todor Alexandrof, of whom *Le Journal* and *The Times* have recently spoken at length.

Our consternation was profound and the impression all the more painful since one recalcitrant man, M. X., who had refused the 300,000 levas demanded of him, was beaten bloody in one of the rooms of the Berlin Hotel, after which the 300,000 levas had to be paid. A new assembly of notables took place and a second commission of fourteen members was named, to which full powers to negotiate with the Macedonians were given. The commission succeeded in bringing the sum of 63 million down to 20 million, but its members had to answer with their heads for the handing in of this sum. It immediately set to work. We were called in one by one before the commission, and the president said to each of us: "We are charged by the ORM with collecting the sum you are charged, according to a list remitted to us. We hope to be able to pay only half, perhaps less, but must for any eventuality ask you for half of what has been fixed for you by the Macedonians."

In saying this, the president remitted a strip of paper on which, for my part, I read "80,000."

"Do you wish to pay?" continued the president. "You are free not to do so. In that case, the slip will be returned to the ORM and you will settle with them."

No one refused.

Then they presented us with a blank note to sign for half the sum. I thus signed for 40,000 levas and was given a letter that contained these words: "You are invited to make the first payment on behalf of the commitment you have made, 10,000 levas, on 12 January." I read this letter, was asked to sign it, and it was taken from me.

On 12 January, I handed over 10,000 levas, was given my note for 40,000 levas, and signed another for 30,000.

On 25 February, I received another letter inviting me to make the second payment of 10,000 levas on 29 January. On that second date, I paid, signed a note for 20,000 levas, and was given back the earlier one for 30,000.

Of course, the formalities were the same for everyone: some were forced to pay as much as 600,000 levas, with payments proportionate to the total required.

But the scandal was becoming too great: the whole city, the whole country, all the authorities, all the foreign legations were aware of these acts of outrageous highway robbery, committed in broad daylight in the center of the capital. A sitting minister to whom I spoke one day gave me this stupefying response: "Well, if you cannot pay the entire sum, pay half." On that day, I understood we were no longer being governed, and at the insistence of my family, I paid. The minister of Italy told one of his constituents who complained about these exactions: "Arrange to pay as little as possible." It appears that M. Georges Picot proved more energetic and remitted a note to the government, accompanied by a receipt from the ORM.

We were at that phase of being systematically robbed when the communication I told you about at the beginning of this letter was made to me, and no doubt to others as well. What is the reason for this about-face in the attitude of the authorities? Without a doubt it is the signing of the Italian-Yugoslav treaty. I cannot tell you what I know on the matter, but the thawing of relations will bring something new to the Balkans. May our brothers, already so sorely tried, be spared in the coming storm!

This letter is strictly personal: retain its content, then tear it up. In this country peopled by assassins, where a man's life counts for nothing, any indiscretion on your part, or on the part of a member of the Alliance, would be fatal for me. I hope your response will bring me the assurance that you have deferred to my wishes. . . .

Archives of the AIU, Bulgarie V.B.118.

3 May 1924

. . . The synagogue committee of Sofia, like certain committees in the provinces, has just created a new tax. Each taxpayer is required to pay the Kéren Hayessod[35] a fee equal to twice what he pays to maintain the community.

---

35. The Keren Hayesod ("collection for Palestine," Hebrew) was founded in 1920 at the Zionist Congress held in London. This organization appealed to Zionists and non-Zionists for funds to be used for emigration to Palestine and for its colonization and also encouraged the investment of private capital. Contributions were made in the form of a voluntary annual tax with a fixed minimal fee.

Sofia will thus give more than 1,000,000 levas to the Kéren Hayessod this year.

This week, I received the visit of a commission charged with remitting to me—in exchange for a receipt—the communication from the synagogue committee in my regard and with collecting the total tax imposed upon me (2,000 levas).

I refused even to receive the communication and have just written the synagogue committee that I do not recognize its right as an official institution to concern itself with the Kéren Hayessod, and even less to impose a tax for that project, however deserving it might be. I added that I would like to know the consequences that will result from my refusal, in particular, whether the customary sanctions imposed on those who do not pay their communal taxes will be applied to me.

These sanctions are the prohibition of access to the synagogues and the refusal of religious weddings and burials for all members of the family. I am awaiting the response, which I do not doubt will be affirmative.

Thus, the Jews of this country who refuse to contribute to the Kéren Hayessod fund would face excommunication.

Most of the notables of Sofia refuse to accept Zionist tyranny, which is worse than that of the rabbis during the Middle Ages, who at least did not excommunicate except for questions of religious dogma and who had the excuse of a profound faith.

I intend to respond.

It is not the 2,000 levas, of course: we have submitted to far higher exactions from the party you know. The question is whether Zionism is going to become a credo apart from which it will not be permitted to remain Jewish, whether to remain a part of Judaism, we have to renounce our freedom of thought, or whether to preserve that freedom, it is preferable to leave Judaism.

I do not even wish to envision that eventuality.

I wish to defend my freedom of thought in relation to Zionism.

After mature reflection, I have decided to address myself in the first instance to the central committee of the Kéren Hayessod. Would you be kind enough to communicate its address to me and, if possible, the names and addresses of the members that compose it. I will set the question to that committee and ask it to give the committee in Bulgaria the necessary orders to put an end to this inopportune zeal.

If the Central Committee of the Kéren Hayessod refuses to carry out my request, I shall take up the question with the large Jewish organizations of Europe and America and will ask them to give the committee in Bulgaria the necessary orders to put an end to this inopportune zeal.

If the Central Committee of the Kéren Hayessod refuses to carry out my request, I shall take up the question with the large Jewish organizations of Europe and America and will ask them for protection against the internal persecution on the part of the Zionists of which we are the victims.

If that measure as well remains without result, we will turn to the authorities and, if need be, will pursue legislative measures to protect us from the excesses of a few Zionist agitators. And if the autonomy of our communities is called into question or succumbs, so much the worse.

I authorize you, if you judge it wise, to communicate this letter to the Central Committee of the Alliance and to the societies with which the Alliance has relations. . . .

Archives of the AIU, Bulgarie V.B.118.

Bibliography

ARCHIVES OF THE ALLIANCE ISRAÉLITE UNIVERSELLE

Bulgarie, I.C.9; I.C.22; I.C.27A; I.C.28; I.C.30; V.B.116; V.B.118; V.B.119; V.B.121; XII.E.153a; XIII.E.153b.
France, IX.F.16; XVI.F.27; XVII.F.28; XVIII.F.29.
Suisse, A.
Turquie, XXXVI.E; LXXIV.E; LXXV.E; LXXVI.E; LXXVII.E.

MANUSCRIPTS

[Arié, Nahim J., and] Tchelebi Moshé Abraham Arié II. "Biography of the Arié Family" (in Judeo-Spanish). 4 vols. Completed in 1914.
Genealogical trees by Eliyahu Nissim Arié, 1893; Gabriel Arié, 1929; Joseph Abraham Arié, 1963.

PUBLICATIONS OF THE ALLIANCE ISRAÉLITE UNIVERSELLE
(in chronological order)

Bulletins Semestriels de l'Alliance Israélite Universelle. 1860/65–1913.
L'Oeuvre des Ecoles. Paris, 1865.
Bulletins Mensuels de l'Alliance Israélite Universelle. 1873–1913.
Bigart, Jacques. *L'Alliance Israélite: Son action éducatrice.* Paris, 1900.
Revue des Ecoles de l'Alliance Israélite Universelle. 1901–4.
Instructions générales pour les professeurs. Paris, 1903.
Bulletin des Ecoles de l'Alliance Israélite Universelle. 1910–13.
Bigart, Jacques. *L'action de l'Alliance Israélite in Turquie.* Paris, 1913.
Paix et Droit. 1920–39.

PERIODICALS
(in chronological order)

El Amigo de Puevlo. Sofia, 1888–1902.
El Dia. Philippopolis, 1897–1914.
La Buena Esperanza. Smyrna, 1900–1909.
Ha-Shofar. Philippopolis, 1901–13.
Bolitino del Konsistorio sentral de Bulgaria. Sofia, 1920–39.
Annual—Godishnik. Sofia, 1966–87.

BOOKS AND ARTICLES

Abitbol, Michel. *Les deux Terres promises: Les Juifs de France et le sionisme, 1897–1945*. Paris, 1989.
Adler, Laure. *Secrets d'alcôve: Histoire du couple de 1830 à 1930*. Paris, 1983.
Ahmad, Feroz. *The Young Turks: The Committee of Union and Progress in Turkish Politics, 1908–1914*. Oxford, 1969.
———. "Unionist Relations with the Greek, Armenian, and Jewish Communities of the Ottoman Empire." In Benjamin Braude and Bernard Lewis, eds., *Christians and Jews in the Ottoman Empire*, 1:401–34. New York and London, 1983.
Alexandris, Alexis. *The Greek Minority of Istanbul and Greek Turkish Relations, 1918–1974*. Athens, 1983.
Anderson, Michael. *Approaches to the History of the Western Family, 1500–1914*. London, 1980.
Anderson, R. D. *Education in France, 1848–1870*. Oxford, 1975.
Andrew, Christopher, M., and A. S. Kanya-Forstner. *France Overseas*. London, 1981.
Arditi, Benyamin. *Well-Known Jews of Bulgaria* (in Bulgarian). 3 vols. Tel Aviv, 1969–71.
Arié, Gabriel. *Histoire juive depuis les origines jusqu'à nos jours*. Paris, 1923; 2d rev. ed., Paris, 1926.
Ariès, Philippe. *L'homme devant la mort*. Paris, 1977.
Ariès, Philippe, and Georges Duby, eds. *Histoire de la vie privée*. Vols. 4 and 5. Paris 1987.
Aron, Jean-Pierre, ed. *Misérable et glorieuse: La femme du XIXᵉ siècle*. Paris, 1980.
Barker, Elizabeth. *Macedonia: Its Place in Balkan Power Politics*. London, 1950.
Barnai, Yaakov. "The Jews in the Ottoman Empire." In Shmuel Ettinger, ed., *History of the Jews in the Land of Islam: The Modern Era to the Middle of the Nineteenth Century* (in Hebrew), 1:73–118. Jerusalem, 1981.
———. "The Jews in the Ottoman Empire." In Shmuel Ettinger, ed., *History of the*

Jews in the Land of Islam: From the Middle of the Nineteenth to the Middle of the Twentieth Century (in Hebrew), 2:183–297. Jerusalem, 1986.

Baron, Salo Wittmayer. *A Social and Religious History of the Jews.* Vol. 18, *The Ottoman Empire: Persia, Ethiopia, India, and China.* New York and Philadelphia, 1983.

Bat Ye'or. *Le Dhimmi: Profil de l'opprimé en Orient et en Afrique du Nord depuis la conquête arabe.* Paris, 1980.

Beaman, Ardern, and George Hulme. *M. Stambuloff.* London, 1895.

Bell, John Douglas. *Peasants in Power: Alexandur Stamboliski and the Bulgarian Agrarian National Union, 1899–1923.* Princeton, 1977.

Benbassa, Esther. "L'Alliance Israélite Universelle et l'élection de Haim Nahum au grand rabbinat de l'Empire ottoman (1908–1909)." In World Union of Jewish Studies, ed., *Proceedings of the Ninth World Congress of Jewish Studies,* 3:83–90. Jerusalem, 1986.

———. "Presse d'Istanbul et de Salonique au service du sionisme (1908–1914)." *Revue Historique* 276/2, 560 (Oct.–Dec. 1986): 337–65.

———. "Haim Nahum Effendi, dernier grand rabbin de l'Empire ottoman (1908–1920): Son rôle politique et diplomatique." 2 vols. Thèse de doctorat d'état, Université de Paris III, 1987.

———. "Israël face à lui-même: Judaïsme occidental et judaïsme ottoman (XIXe–XXe siècles)." *Pardès* 7 (1988): 105–29.

———. *Un grand rabbin sépharade en politique, 1892–1923.* Paris, 1990.

———. "Zionism in the Ottoman Empire at the End of the Nineteenth and the Beginning of the Twentieth Century." *Studies in Zionism* 11/2 (fall 1990): 127–40.

———. "Le procès des sonneurs de tocsin: Une accusation calomnieuse de meurtre rituel à Izmir en 1901." In Abraham Haim, ed., *Society and Community,* [35]–[53]. Jerusalem, 1991.

———. "La modernisation en terre sépharde." In Shmuel Trigano, ed., *La société juive à travers l'histoire,* 1:565–605. Paris, 1992.

———. "Zionism and the Politics of Coalitions in the Jewish Communities in the Early Twentieth Century." In Aron Rodrigue, ed., *Ottoman and Turkish Jewry: Community and Leadership,* 225–51. Bloomington, 1992. (Hebrew ed., Jerusalem, 1995.)

———. *Une diaspora sépharade en transition: Istanbul, XIXe–XXe siècles.* Paris, 1993. (Hebrew ed., Jerusalem, 1995.)

———. "Education for Jewish Girls in the East: A Portrait of the Galata School in Istanbul, 1872–1912." *Studies in Contemporary Jewry* 9 (1993): 163–73.

———. "Associational Strategies in Ottoman Jewish Society in the Nineteenth and Twentieth Centuries." In Avigdor Levy, ed., *The Jews of the Ottoman Empire,* 457–84. Princeton, 1995.

———. *Haim Nahum: A Sephardic Chief Rabbi.* Tuscaloosa, 1995.

———. "The Process of Modernization of Eastern Sephardi Communities." In Harvey Goldberg, ed., *Sephardi and Middle Eastern Jewries*, 89–98. Bloomington, 1996.

———. *Histoire des Juifs de France.* Paris, 1997.

———, ed. *Mémoires Juives d'Espagne et du Portugal.* Paris, 1996.

———, ed. *Transmission et passages en monde juif.* Paris, 1997.

Benbassa, Esther, and Aron Rodrigue. "L'artisanat juif en Turquie à la fin du XIXe siècle: L'Alliance Israélite Universelle et ses oeuvres d'apprentissage." *Turcica* 17 (1985): 113–26.

———. *The Jews of the Balkans: The Judeo-Spanish Community, 15th to 20th Centuries.* Oxford, 1995.

Benveniste, Annie. "Le rôle des institutrices de l'Alliance Israélite à Salonique." *Combat pour la Diaspora* 8 (1982): 13–26.

ben Yosef, Aharon. *Aharon ben Yosef, the Man and His Actions: Letters and Documents, Essays on Bulgarian Jewry* (in Hebrew). Tel Aviv, 1953.

Berkes, Niyazi. *The Development of Secularism in Turkey.* Montreal, 1964.

Berkovitz, Jay. *The Shaping of Jewish Identity in Nineteenth Century France.* Detroit, 1989.

Berov, Liuben. *Bulgaria's Economic Development through the Ages.* Sofia, 1980.

Black, C. E. *The Establishment of Constitutional Government in Bulgaria.* Princeton, 1943.

Bokov, Georgi. *Modern Bulgaria: History, Policy, Economy, Culture.* Sofia, 1981.

Brailsford, H. N. *Macedonia, Its Races and Their Future.* London, 1906.

Braude, Benjamin, and Bernard Lewis, eds. *Christians and Jews in the Ottoman Empire.* 2 vols. New York and London, 1982.

Burguière, André, et al., eds. *Histoire de la famille.* 2 vols. Paris, 1986.

Capdevielle, Jacques. *Le fétichisme du patrimoine: Essai sur un fondement de la classe moyenne.* Paris, 1986.

Casey, James. *The History of the Family.* Oxford and New York, 1989.

Castellan, Georges. *Histoire des Balkans, XIVe–XXe siècles.* Paris, 1991.

Chary, Frederick, B. *The Bulgarian Jews and the Final Solution, 1940–1944.* Pittsburgh, 1972.

Chouraqui, André. *Cent ans d'histoire: L'Alliance Israélite Universelle et la renaissance juive contemporaine (1860–1960).* Paris, 1965.

Cohen, Eliyahou. "L'influence intellectuelle et sociale des écoles de l'Alliance Israélite Universelle sur les Israélites du Proche-Orient." Doctoral thesis, Paris, 1962.

Cohen Albert, Phyllis. *The Modernization of French Jewry: Consistory and Community in the Nineteenth Century.* Hanover, N.H., 1977.

———. "Ethnicité et solidarité chez les Juifs de France au XIXe siècle." *Pardès* 3 (1986): 29–53.

Covo, Mercado J. "Contribution à l'histoire des institutions scolaires de la communauté israélite de Salonique jusqu'à la fondation de l'école des garçons de l'Alliance Israélite Universelle." *Almanach National au Profit de l'Hôpital de Hirsch* 8 (1916): 97–103.

Crampton, R. J. *Bulgaria, 1878–1918: A History.* Boulder and New York, 1983.

———. *A Short History of Modern Bulgaria.* Cambridge, 1987.

Crubellier, Maurice. *L'enfance et la jeunesse dans la société française (1800–1950).* Paris, 1979.

Daumard, Adeline. *Les bourgeois et la bourgeoisie en France depuis 1815.* Paris, 1991.

Davison, Roderich H. "Turkish Attitudes concerning Christian Muslim Equality in the Nineteenth Century." *American Historical Review* 59 (1954): 844–64.

———. *Reform in the Ottoman Empire.* Princeton, 1963.

Delhez-Sarlet, Claudette, and Maurizio Catani, eds. *Individualisme et autobiographie en Occident.* Colloque de Cerisy, 1979. Brussels, 1983.

Didier, Béatrice. *Le journal intime.* Paris, 1976.

Dumont, Paul. "Jewish Communities in Turkey during the Last Decades of the Nineteenth Century in the Light of the Archives of the Alliance Israélite Universelle." In Benjamin Braude and Bernard Lewis, eds., *Christians and Jews in the Ottoman Empire,* 1:209–42.

Eisenstadt, S. N., ed. *Patterns of Modernity.* 2 vols. London, 1987.

Encyclopedia Judaica. New English ed. 17 vols. Jerusalem, 1972.

Epstein, Mark Alan. *The Ottoman Jewish Communities and Their Role in the Fifteenth and Sixteenth Centuries.* Fribourg, 1980.

Fattal, Antoine. *Le statut légal des non-musulmans en pays d'Islam.* Beirut, 1958.

Franco, Moïse. *Essai sur l'histoire des Israélites de l'Empire ottoman.* Paris, 1897.

Galanté, Abraham. *Documents officiels turcs concernant les Juifs de Turquie.* Istanbul, 1931.

———. *Turcs et Juifs.* Istanbul, 1932.

———. *Histoire des Juifs d'Anatolie.* 2 vols. Istanbul, 1937–39.

———. *Histoire des Juifs d'Istanbul.* 2 vols. Istanbul, 1941–42.

Gaon, Moshe David. *The Press in Ladino: A Bibliography* (in Hebrew). Jerusalem, 1965.

Genchev, Nikolai. *The Bulgarian National Revival Period.* Sofia, 1977.

Genov, G. P. *Bulgaria and the Treaty of Neuilly.* Sofia, 1935.

Girard, Alain. *La réussite sociale en France, ses caractéristiques, ses lois, ses effets.* Paris, 1961.

———. *Le journal intime.* Paris, 1963.

Girard, Patrick. *Les Juifs de France de 1789 à 1860: De l'émancipation à l'égalité.* Paris, 1976.

Goffman, Erving. *Relations in Public: Microstudies of the Public Order.* New York, 1971.

————. *The Presentation of Self in Everyday Life.* New York, 1990.

Goldberg, Harvey, ed. *Sephardi and Middle Eastern Jewries: History and Culture in the Modern Era.* Bloomington, 1996.

Goody, Jack. *The Development of the Family and Marriage in Europe.* New York, 1983.

Graetz, Heinrich. *Histoire des Juifs.* 5 vols. Trans. from the German by M. Wogue and M. Bloch. Paris, 1882–97.

Graetz, Michael. *The Jews in Nineteenth-Century France: From the French Revolution to the Alliance Israélite Universelle.* Trans. Jane Marie Todd. Stanford, 1996.

Grellet, Isabelle, and Caroline Kruse. *Histoire de la tuberculose: Les fièvres de l'âme, 1800–1940.* Paris, 1983.

Grunwald, Kurt. *Türkenhirsch: A Study of Baron Maurice de Hirsch, Entrepreneur and Philanthropist.* Jerusalem, 1966.

Guillaume, Pierre. *Individus, familles, nations: Essai d'histoire démographique, XIXe– XXe siècle.* Paris, 1985.

————. *Du désespoir au salut: Les tuberculeux aux XIXe et XXe siècles.* Paris, 1986.

————. "Tuberculose et montagne: Naissance d'un mythe." *Vingtième Siècle: Revue d'Histoire* 30 (April-June 1991): 36–37.

Haramati, Shlomo. *Three Who Preceded Ben Yehudah* (in Hebrew). Jerusalem, 1978.

Helmreich, E. C. *The Diplomacy of Balkan Wars.* Cambridge, Mass., 1983.

Hirschman, Albert Otto. *Shifting Involvements: Private Interest and Public Action.* Princeton, 1982.

Ilieva, Nikolina, and Vera Oshavkova. "Changes in the Bulgarian Family-Cycle from the End of the 19th Century to the Present Day." In Jean Cusenier, ed., *Cycle de la vie familiale dans les sociétés européenees.* Paris, 1977.

Inalcik, Halil. "Jews in the Ottoman Economy and Finances." In C. E. Bosworth, Charles Issawi, et al., eds., *Essays in Honor of Bernard Lewis: The Islamic World,* 531–50. Princeton, 1989.

Israël, Gérard. *L'Alliance Israélite Universelle, 1860–1960: Cent ans d'efforts pour la libération et la promotion de l'homme par l'homme.* Paris, 1960.

Issawi, Charles. *The Economic History of Turkey, 1800–1914.* Chicago, 1980.

Jelavich, Charles. *Russian Policy in Bulgaria and Serbia, 1881–1897.* Berkeley, 1950.

————. *Tsarist Russia and Balkan Nationalism: Russian Influence in the Internal Affairs of Bulgaria and Serbia, 1876–1886.* Berkeley, 1958.

Karpat, Kemal H. *An Inquiry into the Social Foundations of Nationalism in the Ottoman State.* Princeton, 1973.

————. *Ottoman Population, 1830–1914: Demographic and Social Characteristics.* Madison, 1985.

Kasev, Dimitar, et al. *Précis d'histoire de Bulgarie.* Sofia, 1963.

Kaspi, André. "La fondation de l'Alliance Israélite Universelle." Mémoire de maîtrise, Faculté des Lettres, Paris, 1950.

Katz, Jacob. *Tradition and Crisis: Jewish Society at the End of the Middle Ages.* New York, 1961.

———. *Out of the Ghetto: The Social Background of Jewish Emancipation.* Cambridge, Mass., 1973.

———, ed. *Toward Modernity.* New Brunswick, 1987.

Kazamias, Andreas M. *Education and the Quest for Modernity in Turkey.* London, 1966.

Kedourie, Elie. "The Alliance Israélite Universelle, 1860–1960." *Jewish Journal of Sociology* 9 (June 1967): 92–99.

Keshales, Hayim. *History of the Jews of Bulgaria* (in Hebrew). 5 vols. Tel Aviv, 1969–73.

Keyder, Çaglar. *State and Class in Turkey: A Study in Capitalist Development.* London, 1987.

Kristov, Khristo Angelov. *Bulgaria—1,300 years.* Sofia, 1980.

Lampe, John R. *The Bulgarian Economy in the Twentieth Century.* London, 1986.

Lampe, John R., and Marvin R. Jackson. *Balkan Economic History, 1550–1950: From Imperial Borderlands to Developing Nations.* Bloomington and Indianapolis, 1982.

Laqueur, Walter. *A History of Zionism.* New York, 1972.

Laskier, Michael M. "Aspects of the Activities of the Alliance Israélite Universelle in the Jewish Communities of the Middle East and North Africa: 1860–1918." *Modern Judaism* 3 (May 1983): 147–72.

———. "Abraham Albert Antébi: Aspects of His Actions in the Years 1879–1914" (in Hebrew). *Peamim* 21 (1984): 50–82.

Launay, L., de. *La Bulgarie d'hier et de demain.* Paris, 1907.

Le Goff, Jacques. *Histoire et mémoire.* Paris, 1988.

Leibovici, Sarah. *Si tu fais le bien.* Paris, 1983.

Lejeune, Philippe. *L'autobiographie en France.* Paris, 1971.

———. *Le pacte autobiographique.* Paris, 1975.

Leven, Narcisse. *Cinquante ans d'histoire: L'Alliance Israélite Universelle, 1860–1910.* 2 vols. Paris, 1911–20.

Levy, Avigdor, ed. *The Jews of the Ottoman Empire.* Princeton, 1995.

Lévy, Marie-Françoise. *De mères en filles: L'éducation des françaises, 1850–1880.* Paris, 1984.

Lewis, Bernard. *The Emergence of Modern Turkey.* London and New York, 1961.

———. *The Jews of Islam.* Princeton, 1984.

Macdermott, Mercia. *A History of Bulgaria, 1393–1885.* London, 1962.

Mantran, Robert, ed. *Histoire de l'Empire ottoman.* Paris, 1989.

Markovski, Dimitur. *A History of Bulgaria.* Sofia, 1985.

Marrus, Michael. *The Politics of Assimilation: A Study of the French Jewish Community at the Time of the Dreyfus Affair.* Oxford, 1971.

McCarthy, Justin. *The Arab World, Turkey, and the Balkans (1878–1914): A Handbook of Historical Statistics.* Boston, 1982.

Meininger, Thomas A. *The Formation of a Nationalist Bulgarian Intelligentsia, 1835–1878.* New York, 1987.

Métral, Marie-Odile. *Mariage: Les hésitations de l'Occident.* Paris, 1977.

Mezan, Saül. *Les Juifs espagnols en Bulgarie.* Sofia, 1925.

Milano, Attilio. *Storia degli ebrei Italiani nel Levante.* Florence, 1949.

Mitterauer, Michael. *The European Family: Patriarchy to Partnership from the Middle Ages to the Present.* Trans. Karla Oosterveen and Manfred Horzinger. Chicago, 1982.

Modiano, Léon. *Le Judaïsme et l'Alliance Israélite Universelle.* Salonica, 1909.

Navon, A. H. "Contribution à l'histoire de la fondation des écoles de l'Alliance Israélite Universelle." *Le Judaïsme Sephardi* 1 (July 1932): 8–9.

———. "Contribution à l'histoire de la fondation des écoles de l'Alliance Israélite Universelle." *Le Judaïsme Sephardi* 4 (Nov. 1932): 64–66.

———. *Les 70 ans de l'Ecole Normale Israélite Orientale.* Paris, 1935.

Néhama, Joseph. *Histoire des Israélites de Salonique.* Vols. 6–7. Thessalonica, 1978.

Nicault-Lévigne, Catherine. *La France et le sionisme, 1897–1948: Une rencontre manquée?* Paris, 1992.

Nikolov, Georgy. *History of the Bulgarian Daily Press (1877–1932)* (in Bulgarian). Sofia, 1932.

Oren, Nissan. *Revolution Administered: Agrarianism and Communism in Bulgaria.* Baltimore and London, 1973.

Pitrou, Agnès. *La famille dans la vie de tous les jours.* Toulouse, 1972.

Polk, William R., and Richard L. Chambers, eds. *The Beginnings of Modernization in the Middle East.* Chicago, 1968.

Prost, Antoine. *Histoire de l'enseignement en France, 1800–1967.* Paris, 1968.

Pundeff, Marin. *Bulgaria: A Bibliographical Guide.* Washington, D.C., 1965.

Quale, G. Robina. *A History of Marriage Systems.* New York, 1988.

Rabb, Theodore K., and Robert L. Rotberg, eds. *The Family in History: Interdisciplinary Essays.* New York, 1973.

Ramsaur, E. E. *The Young Turks: Prelude to the Revolution of 1908.* Princeton, 1957.

Richarz, Monika, ed. *Jewish Life in Germany: Memoirs from Three Centuries.* Trans. from the German by Stella P. Rosenfeld and Sidney Rosenfeld. Bloomington and Indianapolis, 1991.

Rodrigue, Aron. "Jewish Society and Schooling in a Thracian Town: The Alliance Israélite Universelle in Demotica, 1897–1924." *Jewish Social Studies* 45 (summer/fall, 1983): 263–86.

———. "The Alliance Israélite Universelle and the Attempt to Reform Rabbinical and Religious Instruction in Turkey." In Simon Schwarzfuchs, ed., *L' "Alliance" dans les communautés du Bassin méditerranéen à la fin du XIXe siècle et son influ-ence sur la situation sociale et culturelle,* liii–lxx. Jerusalem, 1987.

———. *De l'instruction à l'émancipation: Les enseignants de l'Alliance Israélite Uni-verselle et les Juifs d'Orient, 1860–1939.* Paris, 1989.

———. "Abraham de Camondo of Istanbul: The Transformation of Jewish Philan-thropy." In Francis Malino and David Sorkin, eds., *From East to West: Jews in a Changing Europe, 1750–1870,* 46–56. Oxford, 1990.

———. "L'exportation du paradigme révolutionnaire: Son influence sur le jud-aïsme sépharade et orientale." In Pierre Birnbaum, ed., *Histoire politique des Juifs de France: Entre universalisme et particularisme,* 182–95. Paris, 1990.

———. *French Jews, Turkish Jews: The Alliance Israélite Universelle and the Politics of Jewish Schooling in Turkey, 1860–1925.* Bloomington, 1990.

———. *Guide to Ladino Materials in the Harvard College Library.* Cambridge, Mass., 1992.

———. "The Sephardim in the Ottoman Empire." In Elie Kedourie, ed., *Spain and the Jews: The Sephardi Experience 1492 and After,* 162–88. London, 1992.

———. *Images of Sephardi and Eastern Jewries in Transition: The Teachers of the Alliance Israélite Universelle, 1860–1939.* Seattle, 1993.

———. "The Beginnings of Westernization and Communal Reform among Istan-bul Jewry, 1854–1865." In Avigdor Levy, ed., *The Jews of the Ottoman Empire,* 439–56. Princeton, 1995.

———. " 'Difference' and Tolerance in the Ottoman Empire: Interview by Nancy Reynolds." *Stanford Humanities Review* 5/1 (1995): 81–90.

———. "From *Millet* to Minority: Turkish Jewry in the Nineteenth and Twentieth Centuries." In Pierre Birnbaum and Ira Katznelson, eds., *Paths of Emancipation: Jews within States and Capitalism,* 238–61. Princeton, 1995.

———. "Eastern Sephardi Jewry and New Nation-States in the Balkans in the Nine-teenth and Twentieth Centuries." In Harvey Goldberg, ed., *Sephardi and Middle Eastern Jewries: History and Culture in the Modern Era,* 81–88. Bloomington, 1996.

———, ed. *Ottoman and Turkish Jewry: Community and Leadership.* Bloomington, 1992.

Romano, A., Y. Ben, and N. Levi, eds. *Encyclopedia of the Diaspora: Bulgarian Jewry* (in Hebrew). Vol. 10. Jerusalem, 1967.

Rozanes, Salomon. *History of the Jews in Turkey and in the East* (in Hebrew). Tel Aviv and Sofia, 1930–48.

Said, Edward W. *Orientalism.* New York, 1978.

Segalen, Martine. *Sociologie de la famille.* Paris, 1981.

Shaw, Stanford J. *The Jews of the Ottoman Empire and the Turkish Republic.* New York, 1991.

Shaw, Stanford J., and Ezel Kural Shaw. *History of the Ottoman Empire and Modern Turkey.* 2 vols. New York, 1977.

Shipman, M. D. *Education and Modernisation*. London, 1971.

Shmuelevitz, Aryeh. *The Jews of the Ottoman Empire in the Late 15th and 16th Centuries*. Leiden, 1984.

Shorrock, William I. *French Imperialism in the Middle East*. Madison, 1976.

Shorter, Edward. *The Making of the Modern Family*. New York, 1975.

Silberman, Paul. "An Investigation of the Schools Operated by the Alliance Israélite Universelle from 1862 to 1940." Ph.D. diss., New York University, 1973.

Sokolow, Nahum. *History of Zionism, 1600–1918*. 2 vols. London, 1919.

Stoianovich, Traian. "The Conquering Balkan Orthodox Merchant." *Journal of Economic History* 20 (1960): 234–313.

Szajkowski, Zosa. "Jewish Diplomacy: Notes on the Occasion of the Centenary of the Alliance Israélite Universelle." *Jewish Social Studies* 22 (July 1960): 131–58.

———. "The Schools of the Alliance Israélite Universelle." *Historica Judaica* 22 (1960): 3–22.

———. *Jews and the French Revolutions of 1789, 1830, and 1848*. New York, 1970.

Tager, Abraham. *Notas istorikas sovre los Judios de Bulgaria en la komunitad de Sofia* (in Judeo-Spanish). Sofia, 1932.

Tamir, Vicki. *Bulgaria and Her Jews: A History of a Dubious Symbiosis*. New York, 1979.

Thobie, Jacques. *Intérêts et impérialisme français dans l'Empire ottoman*. Paris, 1977.

Thuillier, Guy. *Pour une histoire du quotidien*. Paris, 1977.

———. *L'imaginaire quotidien au XIXᵉ siècle*. Preface by Yves Pélicier. Paris, 1985.

Todd, Olivier. *La troisième planète: Structures familiales et systèmes idéologiques*. Paris, 1983.

Todorov, Nikolaï. *Précis d'histoire de la Bulgarie*. Trans. from the Bulgarian by Ivan Obbor. Sofia, 1975.

———. *The Balkan Town, 15th–19th Centuries*. Seattle, 1983.

Topencharov, Vladimir. *Bulgarian Journalism (1885–1903)* (in Bulgarian). Sofia, 1963.

Tritton, A. S. *The Caliphs and Their Non-Muslim Subjects*. London, 1930.

Valensi, Lucette. "La Tour de Babel: Groupes et relations ethniques au Moyen-Orient et en Afrique du Nord." *Annales, E.S.C.* 4 (July–Aug. 1986): 817–35.

Van den Staen de Jehan, F. *De la situation légale des sujets ottomans non musulmans*. Brussels, 1906.

Vital, David. *The Origin of Zionism*. Oxford, 1980.

———. *Zionism: The Formative Years*. Oxford, 1982.

———. *Zionism: The Crucial Phase*. Oxford, 1987.

Weiker, Walter. *Ottomans, Turks, and the Jewish Polity: A History of the Jews of Turkey*. Lanham, 1992.

Weill, Georges. "Charles Netter ou les oranges de Jaffa." *Nouveaux Cahiers* 21 (summer 1970): 2–36.

————. "Emancipation et humanisme: Le discours idéologique de l'Alliance Israélite Universelle au XIXe siècle." *Nouveaux Cahiers* 25 (spring 1978): 1–20.

————. "The Alliance Israélite Universelle and the Emancipation of the Jewish
Communities of the Mediterranean." *Jewish Journal of Sociology* 24 (1982):
117–34.

————. "Les oliviers de Djedeïda." Lecture given to the "Maghreb-Mashrek" collo-
quium, Jerusalem, spring 1984.

————. "L'Alliance Israélite Universelle et la condition sociale des communautés
méditerranéennes à la fin du XIXe siècle (1860–1914)." In Simon Schwarzfuchs,
ed., *L' "Alliance" dans les communautés du Bassin méditerranéen à la fin du XIXe
siècle et son influence sur la situation sociale et culturelle,* vii–lii. Jerusalem, 1987.

Wolff, Robert Lee. *The Balkans in Our Time.* Cambridge, Mass., 1974.

Yuhas, Esther, ed. *The Sephardi Jews in the Ottoman Empire* (in Hebrew). Jerusalem,
1989

Index of Personal Names

Index of Place Names

313